A popular history of the United States of America ( ) from the discovery of the American continent to the present time

Mary Howitt

Alpha Editions

This edition published in 2024

ISBN 9789361476242

Design and Setting By

Alpha Editions

www.alphaedis.com

Email - info@alphaedis.com

Contents

CHAPTER I.
COMMENCEMENT OF THE GREAT WARS.

In 1744, the disputed Austrian succession threw the whole of Europe into arms, and France and England were of course once more at war. In expectation of this event, when an invasion from Canada might be feared, New York fortified Albany and Oswego, and the friendship of the Six Nations was secured. This precaution was additionally necessary, as they had taken offence, owing to a collision which some of their people had come into with the backwoodsmen of Virginia. At a convention held at Lancaster, to which Virginia, Pennsylvania, and Maryland were parties, the Six Nations, with due oratory and ceremonial, relinquished all title to the valley of the Blue Ridge, the central chain of the Alleganies. The western frontiers thus secured, New England proposed a combination of the five northern colonies for their mutual defence, which New York declined, trusting to enjoy her former neutrality.

The war broke out. Fort Canso, in Nova Scotia, was taken by the French; Annapolis was besieged by a united force of Canadians and Indians; privateers issued from Louisburg, and the eastern Indians again attacked the frontiers of Maine. The northern provinces were routed, and Governor Shirley of Massachusetts resolved to attack Louisburg. Louisburg, the capital of Cape Breton, was called, from the strength of its fortifications, the Dunkirk of America. Its position was one of great importance, commanding the navigation of the St. Lawrence and the fisheries of the adjoining seas.

The scheme was a bold one, and Shirley applied to the British ministry for naval assistance, in the meantime laying open his views to the general assembly, after having first sworn all the members to secrecy. Six days were taken to deliberate upon it, and then the scheme was negatived as too hazardous and expensive. And so it might have ended, had not one of the members, during his evening devotions, been heard to pray for the success of the undertaking. The scheme got wind, and the populace approved; the plan was therefore again proposed in the council, and carried by one vote.

Troops were immediately raised by New England. Connecticut sent 500 men; Rhode Island and New Hampshire each 300; but those of Rhode Island did not arrive until Louisburg was taken. Pennsylvania, refusing troops, furnished provisions; and New York, £3,000, a quantity of provisions, and ten eighteen-pounders. The great burden of the war, of course, fell upon Massachusetts, who furnished an army of 3,250 men, with ten armed vessels,—all the fishermen, whose trade the war had interrupted, entering the service as volunteers. The command in chief was given to William Pepperell, a rich merchant in Maine, who was celebrated for his universal good fortune; and Whitfield, then preaching in New Hampshire, suggested as the motto of their flag, "Never despair with Christ for the captain;" and one of the army chaplains, a disciple of Whitfield, carried with him a hatchet, to hew down the images in the French chapels.[1]

An express sent to Commodore Warren, in the West Indies, requesting the co-operation of such ships as he could spare, returned with a negative answer just before the expedition was leaving Boston. Nothing daunted, however, they set sail, and approaching Cape Breton, were prevented from entering its harbours by the great quantity of floating ice. Returning then to Casco, they lay there for several days under a bright sky and in clear weather, and here were agreeably surprised by the arrival of a squadron from Commodore Warren, who had received subsequent orders to render all possible assistance. The next day, nine vessels from Connecticut joined them also, with the troops from that colony. On the 30th of April, the fleet, consisting of 100 vessels, entering Cape Breton, came in sight of Louisburg. This commanding fortress, the walls of which were forty feet thick at the base and from twenty to thirty feet high, was surrounded by a ditch eighty feet wide, and was furnished with 101 cannon, seventy-six swivels, and six mortars; its garrison numbered 1,600 men, and the harbour was defended by an island battery of thirty twenty-two pounders, and by the royal battery on the shore, having thirty large cannon, a moat, and bastions, all so perfect that it was supposed 200 men could defend it against 5,000. The assailants, on the contrary, had only eighteen cannon and three mortars. Reaching the shore, however, they effected a landing almost without opposition, and the following day Colonel Vaughan of New Hampshire led a detachment through the woods, past the city, which they greeted with three cheers. The French, at their approach, having spiked their guns, fled from the royal battery in the night, and the next morning Vaughan and thirteen of his men, having gained possession, defended it against the boats which were sent from Louisburg to retake it. Seth Pomroy, a gunsmith, and a major in one of the Massachusetts regiments, was now employed in the oversight of twenty smiths, who were employed in drilling the cannon; and in the meantime, and for fourteen nights in succession, the hardy besiegers were engaged in dragging their artillery over some miles of boggy morass impassable to wheels, and for the carriage of which a New Hampshire colonel, a carpenter, constructed sledges, which the men, with straps over their shoulders and midleg-deep in mud, drew safely over. Five unsuccessful attempts were made on a battery which defended the town, and the troops, insufficiently provided with tents and other comforts, suffered severely in that cold and foggy climate. But nothing could daunt their ardour. Seth Pomroy, the gunsmith-major, wrote to his wife: "Louisburg is an exceedingly strong place, and seems impregnable. It looks as if our campaign would last long; but I am willing to stay till God's time comes to deliver the city into our hands." And his wife replied in the same resolute spirit: "Suffer no anxious thoughts to rest in your mind about me. The whole town is much engaged with concern for the expedition, how Providence will order the affair, for which religious meetings every week are maintained. I leave you in the hand of God."

At length it was resolved that the fleet should enter the harbour and bombard the city, whilst the land forces attempted to scale the walls. Whilst this was under meditation, a French ship of sixty-four guns, laden with supplies, was taken, after an active engagement, within sight of the town. Fortunately for the besiegers, disaffection prevailed within the walls, and the governor, dispirited by this success of the enemy, sent out a flag of truce and offers of capitulation. On the forty-ninth day of the siege, Louisburg surrendered, together with the island of Cape Breton. When the conquerors entered the city and beheld the strength of the works, their very hearts sunk within them at the greatness of their undertaking; "God has gone out of the way of his common providence," said they, "to incline the hearts of the French to give up this strong city into our hands."

The loss of Louisburg exasperated the French nation, and a powerful armament was fitted out to ravage, in return, the whole coast of North America; but Providence again interfered in their behalf; the fleet, under the Duke d'Anville, was scattered and destroyed by storms and wreck, and, to complete its misfortunes, the commander died suddenly, and his successor, in a fit of delirium, committed suicide. The following year, a second fleet, sent out for the same purpose, was taken by Anson and Warren.

The capture of Louisburg was not less a cause of rejoicing in England than in the colonies. Pepperell was made a baronet, and commissioned as a colonel in the British army, and Warren promoted to the rank of rear-admiral. The report of Warren, however, as regarded the New England people, only confirmed the suspicions which were entertained of them at home. "They have," said he, "the highest notions of the rights and liberties of Englishmen, and, indeed, are almost levellers."

The Canadian French retaliated immediately for their loss, by attacking the English frontiers and taking several outposts, but no great damage was done. This success revived the favourite scheme of the conquest of Canada, and England, as well as the colonies, began active preparations for carrying it out. In Pennsylvania, where hitherto peace principles had been very carefully maintained, an active military spirit, excited by Benjamin Franklin, who now, after twenty years of industry, had acquired a handsome property, prevailed. "He was the originator," says Logan, "of two lotteries, that raised above £6,000 to pay for the charge of the batteries on the river, and he found out a way to put the country on raising above 120 companies of militia, of which Philadelphia raised ten, or about 100 men each. The women, too, were so zealous that they furnished ten pair of silk colours, wrought with various mottoes." Logan, himself a Quaker, though not a strict one, was highly satisfied, as he says, with "Benjamin Franklin for contriving the militia," and he adds, that, "Franklin, when elected to the command of a regiment, declined the distinction, and carried a musket among the common soldiers."

The peace of Aix-la-Chapelle, however, put an end to all these ambitious schemes of conquest, and the mutual restoration of all places taken during the war being one of its conditions, Cape Breton and Louisburg, to the grief and mortification of the northern colonies, were returned to France. The only thing which consoled Massachusetts for this loss was, that the British indemnified her for the expenses of this last enterprise, to the amount of £183,000, a very welcome boon, when her finances were suffering the most serious embarrassment, owing to her extensive issues of paper money and the depreciation of the currency. It was proposed by Thomas Hutchinson, grandson of the celebrated Anne Hutchinson, and now a wealthy merchant of Boston, and speaker of the House of Representatives, that the money thus granted should be imported in silver, and applied to redeem, at its current value, all the outstanding paper. This was done, and for a quarter of a century, says Hildreth, Massachusetts enjoyed the blessing of a sound currency.

It was just at this time when a great inroad was attempted on the rigidity of the Puritan manners, by the attempt of some young Englishmen at Boston to introduce theatrical entertainments. The play first announced was Otway's Orphan, but it proceeded no further than announcement, such exhibitions being at once prohibited, "as tending to discourage industry and frugality, and greatly to the increase of impiety and contempt for religion." Connecticut immediately followed the example; neither would she suffer such Babylonish pursuits. Two years afterwards, a London company of actors came over, and acted the Beau's Stratagem and Merchant of Venice, at Annapolis and Williamsburg in Virginia. Connecticut and Massachusetts being closed against them, they confined their labours to Annapolis, Williamsburg, Philadelphia, Perth-Amboy, New York and Newport.

The peace of Aix-la-Chapelle left the great causes of difference, the undefined limits of the French and English claims in America, still unsettled. The French, by virtue of the discoveries of La Salle, Marquette, Champlain and others, claimed all the lands occupied by the waters flowing into the St. Lawrence, the Mississippi and the Lakes, and all watered by the Mississippi and its branches. In fact, they claimed the whole of America, except that portion which lies east of the Allegany chain, the rivers of which flow into the Atlantic, and even of this they claimed the basin of the Kennebec and all Maine to the east of that valley. The British on the contrary, asserted a right to the entire country, on account of the discovery of Cabot, extending their claims under the old patents with more than equal extravagance, from the Atlantic to the Pacific Ocean. To strengthen this title, they had lately purchased from the chiefs of the confederated Six Nations, acknowledged by the treaties of Utrecht and Aix-la-Chapelle as being under British protection, their claim to the country of the Mississippi, which, it was stated, had at some former period been conquered by them.

The French, as we have already said, had in part carried out their plan of a chain of forts, to connect their more recent settlements on the Mississippi with their earlier ones on the St. Lawrence, when in 1750 a number of gentlemen of Virginia, among whom was Lawrence Washington, the grandfather of the celebrated George, applied to the British parliament for an act for incorporating "the Ohio Company," and granting them 600,000 acres of land on the Ohio river. This was done; the tract was surveyed, and trade commenced with the Indians. The jealousy of the French was roused; and the Marquis du Quesne, governor of Canada, complained to the authorities of New York and Pennsylvania, threatening to seize their traders if they did not quit this territory. The trade went on as before, and the French carried out their threat, burning the village of an Indian tribe which refused submission, and seizing the English traders and their merchandise; and the following year the number and importance of the French forts was increased.

Robert Dinwiddie, at that time royal governor of Virginia, alarmed at those violent proceedings, purchased permission of the Indians on the Monongahala to build a fort on the junction of that river with the Allegany, and determined to send a trusty messenger to the French commandant at Venango, to require explanation and the release of the captured traders. It was late in the season, and the embassy demanded both courage and wisdom. A young man of two-and-twenty, a major in the militia, and by profession a land-surveyor, and who when only sixteen had been employed as such by Lord Fairfax on his property in the Northern Neck, was selected for this service. This young man was GEORGE WASHINGTON.

The journey, about 400 miles through the untracked forest, and at the commencement of winter, though full of peril and wild adventure, was performed successfully. Washington was well received by the commandant, St. Pierre, who promised, after two days' deliberation, to transmit his message to his superiors in Canada; and all unconscious of the present or future importance of their guest, who was making accurate observations as to the strength of the fort, the French officers revealed to him, over their wine, the intentions of France to occupy the whole country.

The reply of St. Pierre, the contents of which were not known till opened at Williamsburg, leaving no doubt of the hostile intentions of the French, Dinwiddie began immediately to prepare for resistance, promising to the officers and soldiers of the Virginian army 200,000 acres of land to be divided amongst them, as an encouragement to enlist. A regiment of 600 men, of which Washington was appointed lieutenant-colonel, marched in the month of April, 1754, into the disputed territory, and, encamping at the Great Meadows, were met by alarming intelligence; the French had driven the Virginians from a fort which, owing to his own recommendation, they were building at "the Fork," the place where Pittsburg now stands, between the junction of the Monongahala and the Allegany, the importance of which position he had become aware of on his journey to Venango. This fort the French had now finished, and had called Du Quesne, in honour of the governor-general; besides which, a detachment sent against him were encamped at a few miles distance. Washington proceeded, surprised the enemy, and killed the commander, Jumonville—the first blood shed in this war.

On his return to the Great Meadows, Washington was joined by the troops from New York and South Carolina, and here erected a fort, which he called Fort Necessity. Frye, the colonel, being now dead, the chief command devolved upon Washington, who very shortly set out towards Du Quesne, when he was compelled to return and entrench himself within Fort Necessity, owing to the approach of a very superior force under De Villier, the brother of Jumonville. After a day of hard fighting, the fort itself was surrendered, on condition of the garrison being permitted to retire unmolested. A singular circumstance occurred in this capitulation: Washington, who did not understand French, employed a Dutchman as his interpreter, and he, either from ignorance or treachery, rendered the terms of the capitulation incorrectly; thus Washington signed an acknowledgment of having "assassinated" Jumonville, and engaged not again to appear in arms against the French within twelve months.

Hitherto, the intercolonial wars had originated in European quarrels; now, the causes of dispute existed in the colonies themselves, and were derivable from the growing importance of these American possessions to the mother-countries; the approaching war, in consequence, assumed an interest to the colonies which no former war had possessed. It was now, therefore, proposed by the British cabinet that a union should be formed among the colonies for their mutual protection and support, and that the friendship of the Six Nations should be immediately secured. Accordingly a congress was convened at Albany, in June, 1754, at which delegates appeared from New York, Pennsylvania, Maryland, Massachusetts, New Hampshire, Rhode Island and Connecticut; Delaney, governor of New York, being the president. A treaty of peace was signed with the Six Nations, and the convention entered upon the subject of the great union, a plan for which had been drawn up by Benjamin Franklin, the delegate from Pennsylvania, and which was carefully discussed, clause by clause, in the assembly. Both William Penn, in 1697, and Coxe in his "Carolana," had proposed a similar annual congress of all the colonies for the regulation of trade, and these were the bases of Franklin's plan of union.

This plan proposed the establishment of a general government in the colonies, the administration of which should be placed in the hands of a governor-general appointed by the crown, and a council of forty-eight members, representatives of the several provinces, "having the power to levy troops, declare war, raise money, make peace, regulate the Indian trade and concert all other measures necessary for the general safety; the governor-general being allowed a negative on the proceedings of the council, and all laws to be ratified by the king." This plan was signed by all the delegates excepting the one from Connecticut, who objected to a negative being allowed to the governor-general, on the 4th of July, the day on which Fort Necessity was surrendered, and the very day twenty-two years before the signing of the Declaration of Independence.

This scheme of union was, however, rejected by all the colonial assemblies, on the plea of giving too much power to the crown; and, strange to say, was rejected likewise by the crown, because it gave too much power to the people. The colonial union, therefore, being at an end for the present, it was proposed by the British ministry that money should be furnished for the carrying on of the war by England, to be reimbursed by a tax on the colonies. This scheme, however, the colonies strongly opposed, being averse, argued Massachusetts, to everything that shall have the remotest tendency to raise a revenue in America for any public use or purpose of government. It was, therefore, finally agreed to carry on the war with British troops, aided by such auxiliaries as the colonial assemblies would voluntarily furnish. These pending territorial disputes led to the publication of more complete maps, whereby the position and danger of the British colonies were more clearly understood. The British colonies occupied about a thousand miles of the Atlantic coast, but their extent inland was limited; the population amounted to about 1,500,000. New France, on the contrary, contained a population not exceeding 100,000, scattered over a vast expanse of territory from Cape Breton to the mouth of the Mississippi, though principally collected on the St. Lawrence. The very remoteness of the French settlements, separated from the English by unexplored forests and mountains, placed them in comparative security, while the whole western frontier of the English, from Maine to Georgia, was exposed to attacks of the Indians, disgusted by constant encroachments and ever ready for war.[2]

While negotiations were being carried on with France for the adjustment of the territorial quarrel, the establishment of French posts on the Ohio and the attack on Washington being regarded as the commencement of hostilities, General Braddock was selected as the American major-general, under the Duke of Cumberland, commander-in-chief of the British army. Braddock was a man of despotic temper, intrepid in action, and severe as a disciplinarian; and as the duke had no confidence in any but regular troops, it was ordered that the general and field officers of the colonial forces should be of subordinate rank when serving with the commissioned officers of the king. Washington, on his return from the Great Meadows, found Dinwiddie re-organising the Virginia militia, and that, according to the late orders, he himself was lowered to the rank of captain, on which he indignantly retired from the service.

In February, 1755, Braddock, with two British regiments, arrived in Chesapeake Bay, the colonies having levied forces in preparation, and a tax being already imposed on wine and spirituous liquors, spite of the general opposition to such imposts, and which excited a very general discontent, each family being required on oath to state the quantity consumed by themselves each year, and thus either to perjure or to tax themselves. This unpopular tax gave rise to several newspapers, the first newspaper of Connecticut dating from this time.

Braddock having arrived, a convention of colonial governors met at Alexandria, in Virginia, to concert the plan of action, when four expeditions were determined upon. Lawrence, the lieutenant-governor of Nova Scotia, was to reduce that province; General Johnson, from his long acquaintance with the Six Nations, was selected to enrol the Mohawk warriors in British pay, and conduct an army of Indians and provincial militia against Crown Point; Governor Shirley was to do the same against Niagara; while Braddock was to attack Fort Du Quesne, and thus recover the Ohio Valley and take possession of the North West.

Soon after Braddock sailed, the French sent out a fleet with a large body of troops under the veteran Baron Dieskau, to reinforce the army in Canada. Although England at this time had avowed only the design of resisting encroachment on her territory, Boscawen was sent out to cruise on the banks of Newfoundland, where he took two of the French ships; of the remainder, some aided by fog, and others by altering their course, arrived safely at Quebec and Louisburg; at the same time, De Vaudreuil, a

Canadian by birth, and formerly governor of Louisiana, arrived and superseded Du Quesne as governor of Canada.

Three thousand men sailed from Boston under Lieutenant-colonel Winslow, on the 29th of May, for the expedition against Nova Scotia. This Winslow was the great-grandson of the Plymouth patriarch, and grandson of the commander of the New England forces in King Philip's war; he was a major-general in the Massachusetts militia, and now, under the British commander-in-chief, was reduced to the rank of lieutenant-colonel. At Chignecto, in the Bay of Fundy, he was joined by Colonel Monckton with 300 British regulars, and advancing against the French forts at Beau Sejour and Gaspereau, took possession of them in five days, after slight resistance; and no sooner did the English fleet appear in the St. John's, than the French, setting fire to their fort at the mouth of that river, evacuated the country. The English thus, with the loss of about twenty men, found themselves in possession of the whole of Nova Scotia: when great difficulty arose, what was to be done with the people?

Acadia was the oldest French colony in America, having been settled by Bretons sixteen years before the landing of the pilgrim fathers. Thirty years before the commencement of the present war, the treaty of Utrecht had ceded Acadia to Great Britain, yet the settlement remained French in spirit, character, and religion. By the terms granted to them when the British took possession, they were excused from bearing arms against France, and were thence known as "French Neutrals." From the time of the Peace of Utrecht, they appear, however, almost to have been forgotten, until the present war brought them, to their great misfortune, back to remembrance. Their life had been one of Arcadian peace and simplicity; neither tax-gatherer nor magistrate was seen among them; their parish priests, sent over from Canada, were their supreme head. By unwearied labour they had secured the rich alluvial marshes from the rivers and sea, and their wealth consisted in flocks and herds. Their houses, gathered in hamlets, were full of the comforts and simple luxuries of their position; their clothing was warm, abundant, and home-made, spun and wove from the flax of their fields and the fleeces of their flocks. Thus were the Acadians prosperous and happy as one great family of love. Their population, which had doubled within the last thirty years, amounted at this time to about 2,000.

Unfortunately, these good Acadians had not strictly adhered to their character of neutrals; 300 of their young men had been taken in arms at Beau Sejour, and one of their priests was detected as an active French agent. It was resolved, therefore, to remove them from their present position, in which they had every opportunity of aiding the French. Lawrence, lieutenant-governor of Nova Scotia, Boscawen, and Mostyn, commanders of the British fleet, consulted with Belcher, chief-justice of the province, and the result was a scheme of kidnapping and conveying them to the various British provinces, although at the capitulation of Beau Sejour it had been strictly provided that the neighbouring inhabitants should not be disturbed. But no matter; they must be got rid of, for there was no secure possession for the English while they, bound by all the ties of language, affection, and religion to France, remained there. A sadder incident of wholesale outrage hardly occurs in history than this. The design was kept strictly secret, lest the people, excited by despair, should rise *en masse* against their oppressors. Obeying the command, therefore, to assemble at their parish churches, they were surrounded by soldiers, taken prisoners and marched off, without ceremony, to the ships, for transportation. At Grand Pré, for example, says Bancroft, 418 unarmed men came together, when Winslow, the American commander, addressed them, as follows: "Your lands and tenements, cattle of all kinds, and live stock of all sorts, are forfeited to the crown, and you yourselves are to be removed from this province. I am, through, his Majesty's goodness, directed to allow you to carry off your money, and your household goods, as many as you can without discommoding the vessels you go in." They were the king's prisoners; their wives and families shared their lot; their sons, 527 in number; their daughters, 576; the whole, including women and babes, old men and children, amounting to about 2,000 souls. They had left home in the morning; they were never to return. Wonderful it seems, that Heaven left such an outrage on humanity unavenged on the spot!

The 10th of September was the day of transportation. They were marched down to the vessels six abreast; the young men first, driven forward by the bayonet, but not a weapon was allowed to them. It was a scene of heart-breaking misery, and in the confusion of embarkation, wives were separated from their husbands, parents from their children, never to meet again! It was two months before the last of the unhappy people were conveyed away, and in the meantime many fled to the woods; but even this availed nothing, the pitiless conquerors had already destroyed the harvests, to compel their surrender, and burnt their former homes to the ground.

A quota of these poor, unhappy people were sent to every British North American colony, where, broken-hearted and disconsolate, they became burdens on the public charity, and failed not to excite pity by their misery, spite of the hatred to them as Catholics and the exasperation produced by the protracted war. Some few made their way to France; others to Canada, St. Domingo, and Louisiana; and to those who reached the latter country, lands were assigned above New Orleans, still known as the Acadian coast. A number of those sent to Georgia constructed rude boats, and endeavoured to return to their beloved homes in the Bay of Fundy. Generally speaking, they died in exile, the victims of dejection and despair.

It will be remembered by our readers, doubtless, that one of the finest poems which America has produced, "Evangeline," by Longfellow, is founded on this cruel and unjustifiable outrage on humanity.

The English, in the meantime, as if their arms were not to be blessed, had met with a severe repulse in their attempt to drive the French from the Ohio. Braddock's troops landed at Alexandria, a small town at the mouth of the Potomac, early in June; and Colonel Washington, being permitted to retain his rank in consequence of the reputation he had already attained, joined the expedition soon after. Braddock made very light of the whole campaign; being stopped at the commencement of his march, for want of horses and wagons, he told Benjamin Franklin, that after having taken Fort Du Quesne, whither he was hastening, he should proceed to Niagara, and having taken that, to Frontenac. "Du Quesne," said he, "will not detain me above three or four days, and then I see nothing which can obstruct my march to Niagara." Franklin calmly replied, that the Indians were dexterous in laying and executing ambuscades. "The savages," replied Braddock, "may he formidable to your raw American militia; upon the king's regulars it is impossible that they should make any impression."

Among the wagoners, whom the energy of Franklin obtained, was Daniel Morgan, famous as a village wrestler, who had emigrated as a day-labourer from New Jersey to Virginia, and who, having saved his wages, was now the owner of a team, all unconscious of his future greatness.[3] By the advice of Washington, owing to the difficulty of obtaining horses and wagons, the heavy baggage was left under the care of Colonel Dunbar, with an escort of 600 men; and Braddock, at the head of 1,300 picked men, proceeded forward more rapidly. Fort Du Quesne, in the meantime, was receiving reinforcements.

Braddock was by no means deficient in courage or military skill, but he was wholly ignorant of the mode of conducting warfare amid American woods and morasses; and to make this deficiency the greater, he undervalued the American troops, nor would profit by the opinions and experience of American officers. Washington urged the expediency of employing the Indians, who, under the well-known chief Half-king, had already offered their services as scouts and advance parties; but Braddock rejected both the advice and this offered aid, and that so rudely that Half-king himself and his Indians were seriously offended.

It was now the 9th of July, and the governor of Du Quesne almost gave up his fort as lost; for Braddock and his army were that morning only twelve miles distant. Washington, about noon riding a little a-head, looked back from the height above the right bank of the Monongahala, and beheld the advanced guard of regulars, headed by Lieutenant-colonel Gage, advancing, with all the glitter of their brilliant uniform, into an open wood. At that moment the Indian war-whoop sounded, and they were fired upon from all quarters by an invisible foe. The assailants, about 200 French and 600 Indians, hidden in some ravines on each side of the road and amid the long grass, poured in a deadly fire: the British troops, seized with sudden panic, were thrown into hopeless confusion, and would have fled, but that Braddock rallied them and exerted himself to the utmost to restore order. Succeeding in part, and preserving something like the order of battle, the horrors of the moment were increased; for his men, "penned like sheep in a fold," were the better mark for the invisible enemy, who themselves, expecting merely to harass, never hoping to defeat, were astonished at their own success. The Indians, singling out the officers, shot down every one; of eighty-six officers, twenty-six were killed and thirty-seven wounded; of the men one-half were killed or wounded. Washington alone seemed to be preserved as by an especial Providence. In vain the Indian singled him out also as a mark for his rifle; no bullet took his life, though two horses were shot under him, and four bullets, after the battle, were found lodged in his coat. Well might the savage exclaim, "Some powerful Manitou guards his life!" This singular preservation of the young Washington, in the midst of death, attracted the attention of all. "I cannot but hope," said a learned divine, a month afterwards, "that Providence has preserved that heroic youth, Colonel Washington, in so especial a manner for some important service to his country." And in England Lord Halifax inquired, "Who is this Mr. Washington? I know nothing of him; but they say that he behaved in Braddock's action as bravely as if he loved the whistling of bullets."

Braddock remained undismayed amid the shower of bullets; five horses were shot under him, and at length a ball entering his right side, he fell mortally wounded. With difficulty he was borne off the field; for many hours he remained silent; towards evening he said, "Who would have thought it?" On the 12th, Braddock being conveyed to Dunbar's camp, the remaining artillery was destroyed, the public stores and heavy baggage burnt, to the value of £100,000, Dunbar assigning as the reason, the dying general's commands. The next day they retreated, and the same night Braddock died; his last words being, "We shall know better how to deal with them another time." His grave may still be seen near the public road, about a mile west of Fort Necessity.[4]

Philadelphia was preparing for the triumph of victory, when the news of this shameful defeat reached the city, in the arrival of Dunbar, on whom the command had now devolved. The whole frontier of Virginia was thus left open to the depredations of the French and Indians. The French at Fort Du Quesne endeavoured to withdraw the Cherokees from their fidelity to the English, and news of this reaching the ears of Glen, governor of South Carolina, a council of Cherokee chiefs was called, the covenant of peace was renewed, and the cession of a large tract of land in South Carolina was obtained.

The expedition against Niagara was entrusted to Governor Shirley, who now, by the death of Braddock, was commander-in-chief of the British forces. It was intended that the troops destined for this service should assemble at Oswego, whence they were to proceed by water to the mouth of the Niagara. The march, however, was one of extreme difficulty, the troops being disabled by sickness and disheartened by the news of Braddock's defeat; and when after six weeks it was accomplished, various adverse circumstances, violent winds and rains, and the desertion of their Indian allies, rendered it unadvisable for them to proceed. Two strong forts were, however, erected, and vessels built in preparation for their embarkation.

The troops destined for the expedition against Crown Point, consisting principally of the militia of Connecticut and Massachusetts, were entrusted to General (afterwards Sir William) Johnson. In June and July, about 6,000 New England men, having Phineas Lyman as their major-general, reached the portage between Hudson River and Lake George, where they constructed a fort called Fort Lyman, afterwards Fort Edward. Here they were joined by General Johnson, with about 3,400 irregulars and Indians, towards the end of August, when he assumed command and advanced towards Lake George. Dieskau, in the meantime, having ascended Lake Champlain with 2,000 men from Montreal, was now pushing on to Fort Lyman, when, altering his route, probably at the request of his Indian allies, who dreaded the English artillery, he suddenly attacked the camp of Johnson. Already informed of his intended attack on Fort Edward, Johnson had sent out 1,000 Massachusetts men, under Ephraim Williams, and a body of Mohawk warriors, under a famous chief called Hendricks, for the purpose of intercepting their return. Unfortunately, however, this detachment fell in with the whole force of Dieskau's army in a narrow defile, and were driven back with great slaughter, Williams and Hendricks being soon slain. It was this Williams who, when passing through Albany, made his will, leaving his property, in case of his death, to found a Free School for Western Massachusetts, which is now the Williams College; a better monument, as Hildreth justly observes, than any victory would have been. The loss of the enemy was also considerable.

The firing being heard in the camp of Johnson, the repulse of Williams was suspected. A breast-work of felled trees was therefore hastily constructed, and a few cannon mounted, which had just been brought up from Fort Edward; and scarcely had the fugitives reached the camp, when the enemy appeared, who met with so warm a reception from the newly-planted cannon, that the Canadian troops and the Indians soon fled, greatly to the chagrin of Dieskau. Johnson, being early wounded, retired from the fight, and the New Englanders, under their own officers, fought bravely for five hours. It was a terrible day for the French; nearly all their regulars perished, and Dieskau was mortally wounded, though he still refused to retire. Two Canadians, who wished to carry him from the field, were shot dead at his side, and he himself soon after, being found seated on the stump of a tree, was wantonly shot by a renegade Frenchman. A small remnant fled, only to be pursued by a detachment from Fort Edward. Instead of pursuing his advantage, Johnson spent the autumn in erecting a fort on the site of his encampment, called Fort William Henry; and the season being late, dispersed his army to their respective provinces. In the meantime the French were strengthening their position at Crown Point, and fortifying Ticonderoga. These actions are known as the battle of Lake George.

Benjamin Franklin having about this time published an account of the rapid increase of population in the United States, the attention of England was turned to the immensely growing power of her colonies. Let us hear the reasoning of the two parties on this subject. "I have found," said the royal governor, Shirley, who had been appealed to, "that the calculations are right. The number of the inhabitants is doubled every twenty years." He admitted that the demand for British manufactures and the employment of shipping increased in an equal ratio; also that the sagacity which had been displayed in the plan of union proposed at the late congress at Albany, might justly excite the fear of England, lest the colonists should throw off their dependence on the mother-country and set up a government of their own. But, added he, let it be considered how various are the present constitutions of their respective governments; how much their interests clash, and how opposed their tempers are, and any coalition among them will be found to be impossible. "At all events," said he, "they could not maintain such an independency without a strong naval force, which it must ever be in the power of Great Britain to prevent. Besides, the 7,000 troops which his Majesty has in America, and the Indians at command, provided the provincial governors do their duty and are maintained independent of the assemblies, may easily prevent any such step being taken."

The royal governor of Virginia, Dinwiddie, urged upon parliament his plan of a general land and poll tax, begging, however, that the plan might come entirely as from them; he urged also the subversion of charter-governments, arguing that all would remain in a distracted condition until his majesty took the proprietary government into his own hands. Another advised that Duke William of Cumberland should be sent out as sovereign of the united provinces of British America, on the plea that in a few years the colonies of America would be independent of Britain.

These fears were prophetic of the future, and indeed were but an echo of the popular sentiment. Franklin was thinking, and acting, and scattering abroad words, which were winged seeds of liberty; Washington was already doing great deeds; and John Adams, then the young teacher of a New England free school, was giving words to ideas which thousands besides himself were prepared to turn into deeds. "All creation," said he, "is liable to change; mighty states are not exempted. Soon after the Reformation, a few people came out here for conscience sake. This apparently trivial incident may transfer the great seat of empire into America. If we can remove these turbulent Gallics, our people, according to the exactest calculation, will in another century become more numerous than England itself. All Europe will not be able to subdue us. The only way to keep us from setting up for ourselves, is to disunite us." They had learnt already that union was strength.

CHAPTER II.
PROGRESS OF THE WAR—THE CONQUEST OF CANADA.

The plan of the campaign for 1756, arranged by a convention of provincial governors at New York, was similar to that of the preceding year: the reduction of Crown Point, Niagara and Fort Du Quesne. The enrolling of volunteer militia went on; Benjamin Franklin being active for this purpose in Pennsylvania, and he himself now assuming military command as a colonel on the frontier from the Delaware to the Maryland line. The frontiers of Virginia continued to suffer severely, though Washington, with 1,500 volunteers, did his utmost for their protection. It was difficult to obtain a larger volunteer force, on account, said Dinwiddie, writing to the Board of Trade on this subject, "of our not daring to part with any of our white men to a distance, as we must have a watch over our negro-slaves."

The war had now continued two years without any formal declaration of hostilities between Great Britain and France. In May, however, of this year it was made.

In June, General Abercrombie, who superseded Shirley, arrived with two regiments from England, and proceeded to Albany, where the provincial troops and the remains of Braddock's army were already assembled—short of provisions, however, and suffering from small-pox. Abercrombie, deeming his forces insufficient for the proposed campaign, determined to wait for the arrival of Lord Loudon, now appointed commander-in-chief. This occasioned a delay until the end of July. In the meantime, the French, under the Marquis of Montcalm, successor to the Baron Dieskau, taking advantage of the tardiness of the English, had made an attack on Fort Oswego, which it had been intended to reinforce with a regiment of regulars under General Webb; but it was then too late; the Forts Oswego and Ontario were taken, and Webb retired precipitately to Albany. Upwards of 1,000 men, 135 pieces of artillery, a great amount of stores, and a fleet of boats and small vessels built the year before for the Niagara expedition, fell into the hands of Montcalm.

To gratify the Six Nations, and induce them to assume a position of neutrality, Montcalm destroyed the forts, after which he returned to Canada. These disasters were as discouraging as the defeat of Braddock had been in the former year. The march to Ticonderoga was abandoned, and Forts Edward and William Henry were ordered to be strengthened.

Feebleness and incapacity characterised the campaign. The Indians, incited by the French, renewed their border depredations; and the Quakers incurred no inconsiderable ignominy by persisting to advocate the cause of the Indians, holding conferences with them and forming treaties of peace. But though these measures were against the spirit of the time, they persevered, and succeeded in thus defending the frontiers of Pennsylvania as well as some of the other colonies by force of arms.

On July 9, 1757, Loudon sailed with 6,000 regulars against Louisburg, the important stronghold of the North, as Fort Du Quesne was of the West, and on the 13th reached Halifax, where he was reinforced by eleven sail of the line, under Admiral Holbourn, with 6,000 additional troops. Nothing, however, was done; for on learning that Louisburg was garrisoned by 6,000 men, and that a large French fleet lay in her harbour, the expedition was abandoned, and Loudon returned to New York. In the meantime, Montcalm, combining his forces from Ticonderoga and Crown Point, amounting to 9,000, with 2,000 Indians, ascended Lake George, and laid siege to Fort William Henry, which was at that time commanded by Colonel Munro, with upwards of 2,000 men, while Colonel Webb was stationed at Fort Edward, only fifteen miles distant, with 5,000. For six days the garrison made a brave resistance, until the ammunition being exhausted, and no relief coming from Fort Edward, Munro capitulated; honourable terms being granted, "on account," said the capitulation, "of their honourable defence." But the terms were not kept. The Indians attached to Montcalm's army fell upon the retiring British, plundering their baggage and murdering them in cold blood. Munro and a part of his men retreated for protection to the French camp; great numbers fled to the woods, where they suffered extremely; many were never more heard of.

In the civil history of the colonies there is very little to chronicle during this period. In Pennsylvania a dispute arose respecting the rights of the proprietaries to exempt their own lands from taxes raised for the defence of those lands. Benjamin Franklin visited England in consequence, and the question was decided by the proprietaries yielding on certain conditions. In Georgia, also, arose a dispute in which the Creek Indians took a lively interest, as it grew out of the claims of that Mary Musgrove, the Indian interpreter, who had materially aided Oglethorpe on his arrival in that country. Mary had now married, for her third husband, Thomas Bosomworth, Oglethorpe's former agent for Indian affairs, but who, having taken orders in England, had returned as successor of Wesley and Whitfield, and claimed the islands on the coast and a tract of land above Savannah, which the Creeks had made over to her, as well as twelve years' arrears of salary as Indian interpreter. The dispute, after having continued twelve years, was settled at this time to the entire satisfaction of Mary and her nation. The island of St. Catherine was secured to her and her husband, and £2,000 paid in liquidation of her other demands. Georgia was also, about the same time, divided into parishes, and the Church of England established by law.

The unfortunate results of the campaigns of 1756–7 were extremely humiliating to England, and so strong was the feeling against the ministry and their measures, that a change was necessary. A new administration was formed, at the head of which was William Pitt, afterwards Lord Chatham; Lord Loudon was recalled; additional forces were raised in America, and a large naval armament and 12,000 additional troops were promised. After this great expenditure of money and of blood on the part of the English, the French still held all the disputed territory. The English were still in possession of the Bay of Fundy, it is true; but Louisburg, commanding the entrance of the St. Lawrence, Crown Point and Ticonderoga on Lake Champlain, Frontenac and Niagara on Lake Ontario, Presque Island on Lake Erie, and the chain of posts thence to the Ohio, were still in the hands of the French. They had driven the English from Fort Oswego and Lake George, and had compelled the Six Nations to neutrality. A devastating war was raging along the whole north-western frontier; scalping parties advanced to the very centre of Massachusetts; to within a short distance of Philadelphia, and kept Maryland and Virginia in perpetual alarm.[5]

The campaign of 1758 began in earnest. Pitt addressed a circular to the colonies, demanding at least 20,000 men; the crown undertook to provide arms, ammunition, tents and provisions; the colonies were to raise, clothe and pay the levies, but were to be reimbursed by parliament. This energetic impulse was cheerfully responded to. Massachusetts voted 7,000 men, besides such as were needed for frontier defence. The advances of Massachusetts during the year amounted to about £250,000. Individual Boston merchants paid taxes to the amount of £500. The tax on real estate amounted to 13s. 4d. in the pound. Connecticut voted 5,000 men; New Hampshire and Rhode Island a regiment of 500 men each; New Jersey 1,000; Pennsylvania appropriated £100,000 for bringing 2,700 men into the field; Virginia raised 2,000. To co-operate with these colonial levies, the Royal Americans were recalled from Canada, and large reinforcements were sent from England. Abercrombie, the new commander-in-chief, found 50,000 men at his disposal—a greater number than the whole male population of New France. The total number of Canadians able to bear arms was 20,000; the regular troops amounted to about 5,000; besides which, the constant occupation of war had caused agriculture to be neglected. Canada was at this time almost in a state of famine.[6] "I shudder," wrote Montcalm to the French government, in February 1758, "when I think of provisions. The famine is very great; New France needs peace, or sooner or later it must fall; so great is the number of the English; so great our difficulty in obtaining supplies." The French army, and the whole of Canada, were put on restricted allowance of food.

The campaign, as we have said, began in earnest; there was no trifling, no delay. Three simultaneous expeditions were decided upon; against Louisburg, Ticonderoga, and Fort Du Quesne. The possession of Louisburg was deemed very important, as opening the Gulf of St. Lawrence, and thus admitting the English at once to the capital of Canada. In June, Boscawen appeared before Louisburg with thirty-eight ships of war, convoying an army of 14,000 men, chiefly regulars, under General Amherst, but including a considerable body of New England troops. The siege commenced. It was here that General Wolfe first distinguished himself in America; his amiable disposition and calm, clear judgment early won the esteem and admiration of the colonists. Here, also, served Isaac Barre, raised by Wolfe from a subaltern position to the rank of major of brigade. The siege was conducted with great skill and energy, and on the 27th of July, this celebrated fortress was in the hands of the English, and with it the islands of Cape Breton, Prince Edward's Island and their dependencies. The garrison became prisoners of war; the inhabitants were shipped off to France. Such was the end of the French power on the Gulf of St. Lawrence.

While the siege of Louisburg was going forward, General Abercrombie, with 16,000 men and a great force of artillery, advanced against Ticonderoga and Crown Point. On the 16th of July, having embarked at Fort William Henry, he advanced down Lake George, and landing near the northern extremity of the lake, the march commenced through a thick wood towards the fort, which Montcalm held with about 4,000 men. Unfortunately, the vanguard—headed by the young and gallant Lord Howe, who, like Wolfe, had already gained the enthusiastic affection of the Americans—ignorant of the ground, lost their way and fell in with a French scouting party, when a skirmish took place, and though the enemy was driven back, Lord Howe fell. The grief of the provincial troops, and, indeed, of the whole northern colonies, was very great for the loss of this brave young man, to whose memory Massachusetts afterwards erected a monument in Westminster Abbey.[7]

The death of Lord Howe is said to have considerably abated the ardour of the troops; nevertheless, Abercrombie, without waiting for the coming up of his artillery, hastened on the attack of Ticonderoga, having been assured that the works were unfinished, and that it might easily be taken. The result, however, proved the contrary. The breast-work was of great strength, and defended by felled trees, their branches sharpened, and pointing outwards like spears. The utmost intrepidity, however, was shown in the attack; but, with the loss of about 2,000 killed and wounded, Abercrombie was repulsed, and the next day made a disorderly retreat to Fort William Henry.

Colonel Bradstreet, being about to march at the head of the provincials of New York and New England against Fort Frontenac, obtained from Abercrombie, after this defeat, a detachment of 3,000 men, and with these, having marched to Oswego, he crossed Lake Ontario, and on the 25th of August attacked Fort Frontenac, which in two days' time surrendered. Three armed vessels were taken, and the fort, which contained military stores intended for the Indians, and provisions for the south-western troops, was destroyed. On their return, the troops assisted in erecting Fort Stanwix, midway between Oswego and Albany. Among the officers who served with Bradstreet were Woodhull and Van Schaick, afterwards distinguished in the revolutionary war.

The expedition against Fort Du Quesne was entrusted to General Forbes, who early in July commenced his march with 7,000 men, including the Pennsylvanian and Virginian levies, the royal Americans recalled from South Carolina, and a body of Cherokee Indians. Washington, who headed the Virginian troops, and was then at Cumberland ready to join the main army, advised that the military road cut by Braddock's army should be made use of; instead of which, Forbes, induced by some Pennsylvanian land-speculators, commenced making a new road from Ray's Town, where the Pennsylvanian forces were stationed, to the Ohio. Whilst a needless delay was thus caused, Major Grant, who, with 800 men, had been sent forward to reconnoitre, was repulsed with the loss of 300 men, and himself taken prisoner. This misfortune, and the loss of time caused by making the road, which drove them into the cold season, together with considerable desertion and sickness, so dispirited the troops, that a council of officers determined to abandon the enterprise for the present. Just at that moment, however, a number of French prisoners accidentally brought in, revealed the feeble state of the garrison, and the news of the taking of Fort Frontenac reaching them at the same time, it was resolved to push forward immediately; and though they were then fifty miles from Du Quesne, and had, at the commencement of winter, to traverse untracked forests, they succeeded in arriving at the fort on the 25th of November, when it was found to be a pile of ruins, the garrison having set fire to it the day before, and retired down the Ohio.

The possession of this post caused great joy. New works were erected on the site of Du Quesne, the name of which was now changed to Fort Pitt, afterwards Pittsburg, now the Birmingham of America.

The consequence of this success was immediately seen, by the disposition which the Indians showed for peace. The frontiers of Virginia and Maryland were relieved from their incursions; and at a grand council held at Easton, in Pennsylvania, not only deputies of the Six Nations, but from their dependent tribes, the Delawares and others, met Sir William Johnson and the governors of New York and New Jersey, and solemn treaties of peace were entered into. In order to check the north-eastern Indians, who still remained hostile, and to prevent their intercourse with Canada, Fort Pownall was erected; the first permanent English settlement in that district.

The great object of the campaign of 1759 was the so-long-desired conquest of Canada. The intention of the British minister was communicated to the various colonial assemblies under an oath of secrecy; and this, together with the faithful reimbursement of their last year's expenses, induced such a general activity and zeal, that early in the spring 20,000 colonial troops were ready to take the field.

In consequence of his disaster at Ticonderoga, Abercrombie was superseded, and General Amherst became commander-in-chief. The plan for the campaign was as follows: Wolfe, who after the taking of Louisburg had gone to England, and was now returning with a powerful fleet, was to make a direct attack on Quebec; Amherst was directed to take Ticonderoga and Crown Point, and so proceed northerly; while General Prideaux, who commanded the provincial troops and Indians, was to descend the St. Lawrence after taking Fort Niagara, and join Amherst in an attack on Montreal. Such was the proposed plan. The three divisions were intended to enter Canada by three different routes of conquest, all to merge finally in the conquest of Quebec, the great heart of the French power and dominion in America.

According to arrangement, Amherst arrived before Ticonderoga in July, with 11,000 men, when the garrison of the fort having been weakened by the withdrawal of forces for the defence of Quebec, both this and Crown Point surrendered without difficulty; the want of vessels, however, prevented him for some time either proceeding to join Wolfe at Quebec or attacking Montreal.

General Prideaux proceeded in the expedition against Niagara with his provincials and a body of warriors of the Six Nations, who, in spite of their treaty of neutrality, had been induced to join in this enterprise. Prideaux advanced by way of Schenectady and Oswego, and on the 6th of July effected a landing near Fort Niagara without opposition. The bursting of a gun, however, killed General Prideaux, when the command devolved on Sir William Johnson. Twelve hundred French, and an equal number of Indian auxiliaries, advancing to the relief of the garrison, gave battle to the English, and were routed with great loss, leaving a considerable number prisoners; on which the dispirited garrison capitulated. The surrender of this post cut off all communication between Canada and the south-west.

Sir William Johnson having so far accomplished his object, should, according to pre-arrangement, have descended Lake Ontario, to co-operate with Wolfe on the St. Lawrence; but again the want of shipping, shortness of provisions and the incumbrance of his French prisoners, prevented his doing so.

Thus disappointed in receiving these important reinforcements, Wolfe was compelled to commence the siege of Quebec alone. The presence of Wolfe had already inspired the most unbounded confidence. His army consisted of 8,000 men; his fleet, commanded by Admirals Saunders and Holmes, consisted of twenty-two ships of the line, and the same number of frigates and armed vessels. On board of one ship was Jervis, afterwards Earl St. Vincent; another had for master, James Cooke, the afterwards celebrated navigator. The brigades were commanded by Robert Moncton, afterwards governor of New York, and the conqueror of Martinique. Wolfe selected as his adjutant-general Isaac Barre, his old associate at Louisburg, an Irishman of humble birth, but brave, eloquent, and ambitious.

On the 27th of June, the whole armament disembarked on the island of Orleans, just below the city. We will give a rapid account of the events of this important siege from Mrs. Willard's excellent history.

"From the island of Orleans, Wolfe reconnoitred the position of his enemy, and saw the full magnitude of the difficulties which surrounded him. The city of Quebec rose before him upon the north side of the St. Lawrence; its upper town and strong fortifications situated on a rock whose bold and steep front continued far westward, parallel with the river, its base near to the shore, thus presenting a wall which appeared inaccessible. From the north-west came down the St. Charles, entering the St. Lawrence just below the town, its banks steep and uneven and cut into deep ravines, while armed vessels were borne upon its waters, and floating batteries obstructed its entrance. A few miles below, the Montmorenci leapt down its cataract into the St. Lawrence; and strongly posted along the sloping bank of that river and between these two tributaries, the French army, commanded by Montcalm, displayed its formidable lines.

"The first measure of Wolfe was to obtain possession of Point Levi, opposite Quebec. Here he erected and opened heavy batteries, which swept from the lower town the buildings along the margin of the river; but the fortifications, resting on the huge table of rock above, remained uninjured. Perceiving this, Wolfe next sought to draw the enemy from his entrenchments, and bring on an engagement. For this purpose he landed his army below the Montmorenci; but the wary Montcalm eluded every artifice to draw him out. Wolfe next crossed that stream with a portion of his army, and attacked him in his camp. The troops which were to commence the assault fell into disorder, having, with impetuous ardour, disobeyed the commands of the general. Perceiving their confusion, he drew them off, with the loss of 400 men, and re-crossed the Montmorenci. Here he was informed that his expected succours were likely to fail him. Amherst had possession of Ticonderoga and Crown Point, but was preparing to attack the forces withdrawn from these places at the Isle aux Noix. Prideaux had lost his life, and Sir William Johnson had succeeded him in the command; but the enemy were in force at Montreal, and from neither division of the British army could the commander at Quebec hope for assistance."

The bodily fatigues which Wolfe had undergone, and his anxiety and disappointment, threw him into a fever, which for a time disabled him from action; nevertheless he devised desperate means of attack, which, on proposing to his officers, were decided to be impracticable. Finally, it was determined to convey by night four or five thousand men to the level plain above the town, called the Heights of Abraham, and draw Montcalm "from his impregnable situation into open action."[8]

"Montcalm," continues Mrs. Willard, "perceiving that something was about to be attempted, despatched M. de Bourgainville with 1,500 men higher up the St. Lawrence, to watch the movements of the English. Wolfe, pursuant to his plan, broke up his camp at Montmorenci and returned to Orleans. Then embarking with his army, he directed Admiral Holmes, who commanded the fleet in which himself and the army had embarked, to sail up the river several miles higher than the intended point of debarkation. This movement deceived De Bourgainville, and gave Wolfe the advantage of the current and the tide to float his boats silently down to the destined spot.

This was done about one hour before daybreak. Wolfe and the troops with him leapt on shore; the light infantry whom the force of the current was hurrying along clambered up the steep shore, staying themselves by the roots and branches of the trees. French sentinels were on the shore; one of these hailed in French and was answered by an officer in that language. Escaping the dangers of the water's edge, they proceeded, though with the utmost difficulty, to scale the precipice. The first party which reached the heights secured a small battery which crowned them, and thus the remainder of the army ascended in safety. In the light of morning the British army were discovered by the French, drawn up on this lofty plain in the most advantageous position.

Montcalm, learning with surprise and consternation the advantage gained by the enemy, left his strong position, and displaying his lines for battle, intrepidly led on the attack. Being on the left of the French, he was opposed to Wolfe, who was on the right of the British. In the heat of the engagement both commanders were mortally wounded. This was the third wound which Wolfe had received, and Isaac Barre, who fought near him, received a ball in the head, which ultimately deprived him of sight. "Support me," said Wolfe to an officer near him; "do not let my brave fellows see me fall!" He was removed to the rear, and water was brought to quench his thirst. Just then a cry was heard, "They run! they run!" "Who runs?" exclaimed Wolfe, faintly raising himself. "The enemy!" was the reply. "Then," said he, "I die content;" and expired. Not less heroic was the death of Montcalm. He rejoiced when told that his wound was mortal, "For then," said he, "I shall not live to see the surrender of Quebec!"

After the battle, General Townsend conducted the English affairs with great discretion. The French on their part appear to have yielded at once to the suggestion of their fears. The capitulation of Quebec was signed five days after the battle. Favourable terms were granted to the garrison.

General Townsend returning to England, General Murray was left in command, with a garrison of 5,000 men. The French army retired to Montreal, and M. de Levi, who had succeeded Montcalm, being reinforced by Canadians and Indians, returned the following spring, 1760, with 6,000 men to Quebec. General Murray left the fortress, and a second still more bloody battle was fought on the Heights of Abraham. Each army lost about 1,000 men, but the French maintained their ground, and the English took refuge within the fortress. Here they were closely invested, until having received reinforcements, M. de Levi abandoned all hope of regaining possession of Quebec, and returned to Montreal, where Vaudreuil, the governor, assembled all the force of Canada.

DEATH OF GENERAL WOLFE.

Desirous of completing this great conquest, the northern colonies joyfully contributed their aid, and towards the close of the summer, three armies were on their way to Montreal; Amherst at the head of 10,000 men together with 1,000 Indians of the Six Nations, headed by Sir William Johnson; Murray with 4,000 men from Quebec; and Haviland at the head of 3,500 men, by way of Lake Champlain. The force which was thus brought against Montreal was irresistible; but it was not needed; Vaudreuil, the governor, surrendered without a struggle. The British flag floated on the city; and not alone was possession given of Montreal, but of Presque Isle, Detroit, Mackinaw and all the other posts of Western Canada. About 4,000 regular troops were to be sent to France, and to the Canadians were guaranteed their property and liberty of worship.

Great was the joy of New York and the New England states in the conquest of Canada, as their frontiers were now finally delivered from the terrible scourge of Indian warfare. But while they rejoiced from this cause, the Carolinian frontiers were suffering from incursions of the Cherokees, who had been instigated to these measures by the French, who, retiring from Fort Du Quesne, had passed through their country on their way to Louisiana. General Amherst, therefore, despatched Colonel Montgomery against them, who aided by the Carolinian troops, marched into their country, burned their villages, and was on his way to the interior, when they in their turn besieged Fort Loudon, which, after great suffering, the garrison were compelled to surrender, under promise of a safe conduct to the British settlements. This promise, however, was broken; great numbers were killed on the way and others taken prisoners; and again the war raged on the frontier. The next year Colonel Grant marched with increased force into their country; a terrible battle was fought, in which the Cherokees were defeated, their villages burned, and their crops destroyed. Finally they were driven to the mountains, and now subdued and humbled, besought for peace.

The war between England and France, though at an end on the continent of America, was still continued among the West India Islands, France in this case also being the loser. Martinique, Grenada, St. Lucia, St. Vincent's—every island, in fact, which France possessed among the Caribbees—passed into the hands of the English. Besides which, being at the same time at war with Spain, England took possession of Havanna, the key to the whole trade of the Gulf of Mexico.

In November, 1763, a treaty of peace was signed at Paris, which led to further changes, all being favourable to Britain; whilst Martinique, Guadalope and St. Lucia were restored to France, England took possession of St. Vincent's, Dominica and Tobago islands, which had hitherto been considered neutral. By the same treaty all the vast territory east of the Mississippi, from its source to the Gulf of Mexico, with the exception of the island of New Orleans, was yielded up to the British; and Spain, in return for Havanna, ceded her possession of Florida. Thus, says Hildreth, was vested in the British crown, as far as the consent of rival European claimants could give it, the sovereignty of the whole eastern half of North America, from the Gulf of Mexico to Hudson's Bay and the Polar Ocean. By the same treaty the navigation of the Mississippi was free to both nations. France at the same time gave to Spain, as a compensation for her losses in the war, all Louisiana west of the Mississippi, which contained at that time about 10,000 inhabitants, to whom this transfer was very unsatisfactory.

Three new British provinces were now erected in America; Quebec and East and West Florida. East Florida included all the country embraced by the present Florida, bounded on the north by the St. Mary's. West Florida extended from the Apalachicola River to the Mississippi; from the 31st degree of latitude on the north, to the Gulf of Mexico on the south, thus including portions of the present states of Alabama and Mississippi. The boundary of Quebec corresponded with the claims of New York and Massachusetts, being a line from the southern end of Lake Nipissing, striking the St. Lawrence at the 45th degree of latitude, and following that parallel across the foot of Lake Champlain to the sources of the Connecticut, and thence along the highlands which separate the waters flowing into the St. Lawrence from those which fall into the sea.[9]

All, however, was not yet peace in the northern provinces. The English might possess themselves of French territory, but they could not win the hearts of the Indian, whom the devoted missionaries and the kind and politic French traders had attached to their nation. When, therefore, the English, who treated the Indians with cold contempt, were about to take possession, Pontiac, the brave and intellectual chief of the Ottawas, who cherished the hope of restoring his nation to independence, endeavoured to excite the Red men against their new lords. "If," reasoned he, addressing his people, "the English have expelled the French, what should hinder, but that the Indian should destroy them before they have established their power, and thus the Red man once more be lord of the forest?" Pontiac, by his eloquence and energy, gained the co-operation of the whole north-western tribes, and the plan of a simultaneous attack on all the British posts on the lakes was formed without any suspicion being excited. The day fixed was the 7th of July, and on that day nine forts—all, indeed, excepting those of Niagara, Detroit and Fort Pitt—were surprised and taken. Nor was the outbreak confined to the forts; the whole frontier of Pennsylvania and Virginia, especially the former, was attacked, and the scattered traders and settlers plundered and cruelly murdered. The back settlers of Pennsylvania—principally Scotch and Irish Presbyterians, men of a character very different to that of the mild Quakers, and who, in the spirit of the older Puritans, regarded the Indians as the Canaanites of the Old Testament—rose up in vengeance, and the leaders of this movement coming principally from a place called Paxton, the body assumed the name of "the Paxton Boys," and pursued their victims with a bloodthirsty spirit, which aimed at nothing less than extermination. In vain Benjamin Franklin interfered to save such friendly Indians as had fled for refuge to Philadelphia and other towns; the avengers knew no mercy, and for these unhappy remnants of a once powerful race there appeared no place of refuge but the grave. Such of the Christianised Indians as escaped this cold-blooded massacre established themselves on a distant branch of the Susquehanna; though their peace there was but of short duration, being again compelled, within a few years, to emigrate to the country north-west of the Ohio, where they and their missionaries, the Moravians, settled in three villages on the Muskinghum.

The conquest of Canada and the subjection of the eastern Indians giving security to the colonists of Maine, that province began to expand and flourish. The counties of Cumberland and Lincoln were added to the former single county of York, and settlers began to occupy the lower Kennebec, and to extend themselves along the coast towards the Penobscot. Nor was this northern expansion confined alone to Maine; settlers began to occupy both sides of the upper Connecticut, and to advance into new regions beyond the Green Mountains, towards Lake

Champlain, a beautiful and fertile country which had first become known to the colonists in the late war. Homes were growing up in Vermont. In the same manner population extended westward beyond the Alleganies, as soon as the Indian disturbances were allayed in that direction. The go-a-head principle was ever active in British America. The population of Georgia was beginning to increase greatly, and in 1763 the first newspaper of that colony was published, called the "Georgia Gazette." A vital principle was operating also in the new province of East Florida, now that she ranked among the British possessions. In ten years, more was done for the colony than had been done through the whole period of the Spanish occupation. A colony of Greeks settled about this time on the inlet still known as New Smyrna; and a body of settlers from the banks of the Roanoke planted themselves in West Florida, near Baton Rouge.[10]

Nor was this increase confined to the newer provinces; the older ones progressed in the same degree. Hildreth calls this the golden age of Virginia, Maryland, and South Carolina, which were increasing in population and productions at a rate unknown before or since. In the north, leisure was found for the cultivation of literature, art, and social refinement. The six colonial colleges were crowded with students; a medical college was established in Pennsylvania, the first in the colonies; and West and Copley, both born in the same year—the one in New York, the other in Boston—proved that genius was native to the New World, though the Old afforded richer patronage. Besides all this, the late wars and the growing difficulties with the mother-country had called forth and trained able commanders for the field, and sagacious intellects for the control of the great events which were at hand.

CHAPTER III.
CAUSES OF THE REVOLUTIONARY WAR.

A vast amount of debt, as is always the case with war, was the result of the late contests in America. With peace, the costs of the struggle began to be reckoned. The colonies had lost, by disease or the sword, above 30,000 men; and their debt amounted to about £4,000,000, Massachusetts alone having been reimbursed by parliament. The popular power had, however, grown in various ways; the colonial assemblies had resisted the claims of the royal and proprietary governors to the management and irresponsible expenditure of the large sums which were raised for the war, and thus the executive influence became transferred in considerable degree from the governors to the colonial assemblies. Another, and still more dangerous result, was the martial spirit which had sprung up, and the discovery of the powerful means which the colonists held in their hands for settling any disputed points of authority and right with the mother-country. The colonies had of late been a military college to her citizens, in which, though they had performed the hardest service and had been extremely offended and annoyed by the superiority assumed by the British officers and their own subordination, yet they had been well trained, and had learned their own power and resources. The conquest of New France, in great measure, cost England her colonies.

England, at the close of the war—at the close, in fact, of four wars within seventy years—found herself burdened with a debt of £140,000,000; and as it was necessary now to keep a standing army in her colonies, to defend and maintain her late conquests, the scheme of colonial taxation to provide a regular and certain revenue began again to be agitated. Already England feared the growing power and independence of her colonies, and even at one moment hesitated as to whether it were not wiser to restore Canada to France, in order that the proximity of a powerful rival might keep them in check and secure their dependence on the mother-country. As far as the colonists themselves were concerned, we are assured by their earlier historians that the majority had no idea of or wish to separate themselves from England, and that the utmost which they contemplated by the conquest of Canada, was the freedom from French and Indian wars, and that state of tranquil prosperity which would leave them at liberty to cultivate and avail themselves of the productions and resources of an affluent land. The true causes which slowly alienated the colonies from the parent state may be traced back to the early encroachments on their civil rights and the restrictive enactments against their commerce.

The Americans were a bold and independent people from the beginning. They came to the shores of the New World, the greater and better part of them, republicans in feeling and principle. "They were men who scoffed at the right of kings, and looked upon rulers as public servants bound to exercise their authority for the benefit of the governed, and ever maintained that it is the inalienable right of the subject freely to give his money to the crown or to withhold it at his discretion." Such were the Americans in principle, yet were they bound to the mother-country by old ties of affection, and by no means wishful to rush into rebellion. It was precisely the case of the son grown to years of discretion, whom an unreasonable parent seeks still to coerce, until the hitherto dutiful, though clear-headed and resolute son, violently breaks the bonds of parental authority and asserts the independence of his manhood. The human being would have been less worthy in submission; the colonies would have belied the strong race which planted them, had they done otherwise.

England believed that she had a right to dictate and change the government of the colonies at her pleasure, and to regulate and restrict their commerce; and for some time this was, if not patiently submitted to, at least allowed. The navigation acts declared that, for the benefit of British shipping, no merchandise from the English colonies should be imported into England excepting by English vessels; and, for the benefit of English manufacturers, prohibited exportation from the colonies, nor allowed articles of domestic manufacture to be carried from one colony to another; she forbade hats, at one time, to be made in the colony, where beaver abounded; at another, that any hatter should have above two apprentices at one time; she subjected sugar, rum and molasses to exorbitant duties on importation; she forbade the erection of iron-works and the preparation of steel; or the felling of pitch and white pine-trees unless in enclosed lands. To some of these laws, though felt to be an encroachment on their rights, the colonies submitted patiently; others, as for instance, the duties on sugar and molasses, they evaded and opposed in every possible way, and the British authorities, from the year 1733, when these duties were first imposed, to 1761, made but little resistance to this opposition. At this latter date, however, George III. having then ascended the throne, and being, as Charles Townshend described him, "a very obstinate young man," it was determined to enforce this law, and "writs of assistance," in other words, search-warrants, were issued, by means of which the royal custom-house officers were authorised to search for goods which had been imported without the payment of duty. The people of Boston opposed and resented these measures; and their two most eminent lawyers, Oxenbridge Thatcher and James Otis, expressed the public sentiment in the strongest language. Spite of search-warrants and official vigilance, the payment of these duties was still evaded, and smuggling increased to a great extent, while the colonial trade with the West Indies was nearly destroyed.

In 1764 the sugar-duties were somewhat reduced, as a boon to the colonies, but new duties were imposed on articles which had hitherto been imported free; at the same time, Lord Grenville proposed a new impost in the form of a stamp-tax. All pamphlets, almanacs, newspapers; all bonds, notes, leases, policies of insurance, together with all papers used for legal purposes, in order to be valid, were to be drawn on stamped paper, to be purchased only from the king's officers appointed for that purpose. This plan met with the entire approbation of the British parliament, but its enactment was deferred until the following year, in order that the colonies might have an opportunity of expressing their feelings on the subject. Though deference was thus apparently paid to their wishes, the intention of the British government was no longer concealed. The preamble of the bill openly avowed the intention of raising a revenue from "His Majesty's dominions in America;" the same act gave increased power to the admiralty-courts, and provided more stringent means for enforcing the payment of duties and punishing their evasion.

The colonies received the news of these proposed measures with strong indignation. Massachusetts instructed her agent in London to deny the right of parliament to impose duties and taxes on a people who were not represented in the House of Commons. "If we are not represented," said they, "we are slaves." A combination of all the colonies for the defence of their common interests was suggested.

Otis, who had published a pamphlet on Colonial Rights, seeing the tide of public indignation rising very high, inculcated "obedience" and "the duty of submission," but this was not a doctrine which the Americans were then in a state of mind to listen to. Better suited to their feeling was Thatcher's pamphlet against all parliamentary taxation. Rhode Island expressed the same; so did Maryland, by their secretary of the province; so did Virginia, by a leading member of her House of Burgesses.[11] Strong as the expression of resentment was in the colonies, addresses in a much milder strain were prepared to the king and parliament from most of them, New York alone expressing boldly and decidedly the true nature of her feelings, the same tone being maintained by Rhode Island.

STAMP ACT RIOTS.

But the minds of the British monarch and his ministers were not to be influenced either by the remonstrances and pleadings of the colonies or their agents in London, or of their few friends in parliament. Grenville, the minister, according to pre-arrangement, brought in his bill for collecting a stamp-tax in America, and it passed the House of Commons five to one, and in the House of Lords there was neither division on the subject nor the slightest opposition. This act was to come into operation on the 1st day of November of the same year. It was on the occasion of its discussion in the House of Commons, that Colonel Barre, who had fought with Wolfe at Louisburg and Quebec, electrified the house with his burst of eloquence in reply to one of the ministers who spoke of the colonists as "children planted by our care, nourished by our indulgence, and protected by our arms." "They planted by your care!" retorted Barre. "No; your oppression planted them in America. They nourished by your indulgence! They grew up by your neglect of them. They protected by your arms! Those sons of liberty have nobly taken up arms in your defence. I claim to know more of America than most of you, having been conversant in that country. The people, I believe, are as truly loyal subjects as the king has, but a people jealous of their liberties, and who will vindicate them should they ever be violated."

The day after the Stamp Act had passed the house, Benjamin Franklin, then in London as agent for Philadelphia, wrote the news to his friend,

Charles Thompson. "The sun of liberty," said he, "is set; you must light up the candles of industry and economy." "We shall light up torches of quite another kind," was the reply.

Anticipating opposition to this unpopular measure, a new clause was introduced in the Mutiny Act, authorising the sending of any number of troops into the colonies, which, by an especial enactment, were to be found with "quarters, fire-wood, bedding, drink, soap and candles," by the colonists.

The news of the passage of the Stamp Act called forth a universal burst of indignation. At Boston and Philadelphia the bells were muffled, and rung a funeral peal; at New York the act was carried through the streets with a death's head affixed to it, and labelled, "The folly of England and the ruin of America."[12]

The House of Assembly was sitting when the news reached Virginia, and the leading aristocratic members hesitated to express an opinion. Several days passed, and nothing was said; but the popular sentiment found an utterance from the lips of Patrick Henry, a young lawyer and member of the Assembly, who introduced a series of resolutions, which were, in fact, the key-note to all that followed. The first four resolutions asserted the rights and privileges of the colonists; the last denied the authority of any power whatsoever, excepting their own provincial Assembly, to impose taxes upon them, and denounced any person as an enemy to the colonies, who should by writing or speaking maintain the contrary. These strong resolutions led to a hot debate, during which Henry, carried away by the fervour of his patriotism, styled the king of England a tyrant. "Cæsar," said he, "had his Brutus; Charles I. his Cromwell; and George III.——" the cry of "Treason! Treason!" interrupted him—"and George III.," continued the corrected orator, "may profit by their example. If that be treason, make the most of it!" Spite of strong opposition, the resolutions passed; the last and most emphatic, by only the majority of one vote. The next day, in the absence of Henry, it was rescinded. But the whole had already gone to Philadelphia in manuscript, and soon circulating through the colonies, met with a warm response, and gave an impetus to the popular feeling.

Before the proceedings in Virginia were known in Massachusetts, the General Court had met, and a convention or congress of deputies from the various colonial houses of representatives was called "to meet at New York on the first Tuesday in October, to consult on the difficulties in which the colonies were and must be placed by the late acts of parliament levying duties and taxes upon them;" and further, "to consider of a general and humble address to his majesty and the parliament, to implore relief."

In the meantime the popular feeling grew in intensity, and public meetings were held throughout the colonies—a new feature in colonial history,—and inflammatory speeches made, and associations formed, and resolutions agreed upon, to resist to the utmost this detested measure, which was stated to be "unconstitutional and subversive of their dearest rights." Nor were they contented with talking merely. Associations, under the name of "Sons of Liberty," a phrase taken from Colonel Barre's famous speech, were formed in Connecticut, New York, Massachusetts, Pennsylvania and New Jersey, who proceeded to express the popular sentiment in a very forcible manner. The stamp-officers in all these provinces were either compelled or persuaded to renounce their appointments; the stamps were seized and burned, and in Boston scenes even of disgraceful violence occurred. Public meetings were held under a large elm-tree, in an open space in the city, which hence took the name of the "Liberty Tree;" the effigies of such as were considered friends of the British government were hanged in its branches, beneath which inflammatory speeches were made. The house of Oliver, appointed stamp-distributor of Massachusetts, was attacked, the windows broken, and the furniture destroyed, and he compelled to resign. A violent sermon was preached against the Stamp Act, and this excited the mob still further; many houses of the public officers were attacked and destroyed, together with private papers and public records, as was particularly the case at the house of Hutchinson, the lieutenant-governor, whose furniture was piled into bonfires, the flames of which were fed with invaluable manuscripts, the carefully collected historical records of thirty years. These acts of violence were of course committed by such ignorant mobs as are the product of all periods of popular excitement. The respectable inhabitants of Boston expressed their "abhorrence," and a civic guard was organised to prevent their recurrence; nevertheless the offenders passed unpunished, whence it may be inferred that "the respectability" of Boston did not quarrel with the spirit of their proceedings.

And now, on October 7th, the first Colonial Congress met at New York; twenty-eight delegates being present from nine colonies; among these were Timothy Ruggles, president, Otis, of Massachusetts, William Johnson, of Connecticut, Philip Livingstone, of New York, John Dickinson, of Pennsylvania, John M'Kean, of Delaware, Christopher Gadsden and John Rutledge, of South Carolina—all names afterwards distinguished in the revolution. After mature deliberation, "a Declaration of the Rights and Grievances of the Colonies" was drawn up, in which all the rights and privileges of Englishmen were claimed as the birthright of the colonists; one of the most important of which was an exemption from all taxation, except such as was imposed by their own consent and by their own representatives. A petition to the king and parliament was also prepared, in which the cause of the colonies was eloquently pleaded.

These proceedings were sanctioned by all the representatives, excepting Ruggles, the president, and Ogden, of New Jersey, both of whom refused to sign, on the plea of the approbation of their several assemblies being first required. The petition and memorials, signed by the other delegates, were transmitted to England, and all the other colonies gave in their approval immediately afterwards.

On the important 1st of November, the day on which the Stamp Act came into operation, scarcely a sheet of all the many bales of stamped paper which had been sent out to the colonies was to be found. They had either been destroyed or shipped back to England. The day was observed as one of public mourning; shops were closed, vessels displayed their flags half-mast high, processions paraded the streets, and every means was used to show the public disapprobation. The very terms of the act caused, in the present state of the popular mind, a suspension of the whole machinery of the social state. Business for the time was at an end; the courts of law were closed; marriages could not take place, nor could the affairs of the dead be legally settled. This was a state, however, which could not continue, and by degrees things fell into their usual course, without any regard to the act of parliament at all.

On the 6th of November, a public meeting of the more influential inhabitants of Boston formed a combination of retaliation on Great Britain. The purport of this was, that no goods should be imported from England nor used by the colonies. The women entered into the scheme with the utmost enthusiasm. All British manufactures were foresworn, and every kind of domestic manufacture was to be encouraged. In order to promote the home manufacture of woollen cloths, it was determined for the present to eat neither mutton nor lamb, that the American flocks might thus be allowed to increase. By these means it was intended that the trade with Great Britain should be destroyed.

England received the news with mingled alarm and displeasure. Nevertheless, a change having taken place in the ministry, Lord Grenville being succeeded by the Marquis of Rockingham, a party more favourable to America was in power; and it was now, therefore, evident to all that one of two measures must be immediately taken—either the odious Stamp Act must be repealed, or the colonies must be compelled to obedience by force of arms. The former was the wiser course, and a strong party now existed to advocate it. Angry debates began in the British senate on the subject. Lord Grenville's party opposed repeal, which Pitt in the House of Commons, and Lord Camden in the House of Lords, as warmly advocated.

"You have no right," said Pitt, addressing the house, "to tax America. We are told that America is obstinate—is almost in open rebellion. I rejoice that America has resisted. Three millions of people, so dead to all the feelings of liberty as to voluntarily submit to be slaves, would have been fit instruments to make slaves of all the rest. The Americans have been wronged. They have been driven to madness by injustice. Let this country be the first to resume its prudence and temper. I will pledge my word for the colonies, that on their part animosity and resentment will cease!"

Franklin, summoned to the bar of the house as a witness, declared that the act could never be enforced; and the bill for the repeal was carried in the Commons. In the House of Lords it met with great opposition. Lord Camden advocated the cause of the colonies with great eloquence. "My position is this," said he—"I repeat it, I will maintain it to my last hour—taxation and representation are inseparable. This position is founded on the law of nature. It is more—it is itself an eternal law of nature; for whatever is a man's own is absolutely his own; no man has a right to take it from him without his consent. Whoever attempts to do it attempts an injury; whoever does it commits a robbery."

The bill for repeal passed, but it was accompanied by another, called "the Declaratory Act," which was intended to save the national honour by avowing the principle "that parliament had a right to bind the colonies in all cases whatever."

The repeal of the Stamp Act caused great joy in London to the merchants, manufacturers, and friends of America. In America it was received by a general outburst of loyalty and gratitude. A general thanksgiving was appointed; statues to Pitt and even to the king were voted, and erected in various places. Pitt became more than ever the idol of the colonies; and thanks were voted to him by most of the colonial assemblies.

The rejoicing, however, was only of short duration. The Declaratory Act made known the principle of action which it was intended to pursue towards the colonies, and accordingly the following year its operation commenced. Again the ministry was changed; and though Pitt, now Earl of Chatham, was at the head of affairs, and Lord Camden had a seat in the cabinet, advantage was taken of Chatham's illness, and Charles Townshend, now Chancellor of the Exchequer and a former member of Grenville's ministry, brought in a bill for taxing all tea, glass, paper and painters' colours, imported into the colonies. This bill being supposed less objectionable than the Stamp Act, passed the two houses with but little opposition. Nor was this all; a standing army was to be maintained in the colonies, and permanent salaries provided for the governors and judges, so as to make them independent of the colonial assemblies; while a third act empowered the naval officers to act as custom-house officers, armed with authority to enforce the trade and navigation acts. Punishment was also inflicted on New York and Georgia for their disregard of the late Quartering Act; the legislative assembly of New York was suspended until his majesty's troops were provided with supplies at the expense of the colony, and the troops were withdrawn from Georgia for the same cause, leaving her exposed to the incursions of Indians and the insurrection of negroes, which soon brought her to submission.

The passing of these bills in such quick succession left the Americans no longer in doubt of the line of policy which it was intended by England to adopt towards them, and the excitement and indignation which they occasioned equalled that produced by the Stamp Act. The colonial assemblies met, and the strongest dissatisfaction was expressed. Pamphlets circulated briskly, and the newspapers, now about five-and-twenty in number, entered boldly on the subject of colonial rights. The "Letters of a Pennsylvanian Farmer to the Inhabitants of the British Colonies," written by John Dickinson, flew from one end of the colonies to the other. Franklin caused an edition to be published even in London. The object of Dickinson's letters was to show how dangerous was the precedent of allowing parliamentary taxation in any form or to any extent whatever.

Again meetings were held and associations formed for the support and encouragement of home manufactures, and against the use and importation of British goods. This movement, which commenced in Boston, extended throughout the province, and the example was followed in Providence, New York and Philadelphia. In New Hampshire the non-importation agreement was not so warmly seconded, owing to the influence of the governor, Wentworth, while in Connecticut, under William Pitkin, the governor and an ardent patriot, it met with universal acceptation.

The assembly of Massachusetts invited by circular the co-operation of the other provinces for the maintenance of colonial rights; the prime movers in this measure being Thomas Cushing, the speaker of the House of Assembly, James Otis, Samuel Adams, John Hancock, and Joseph Hawley, all men of character and great influence. Otis was a lawyer; Cushing, descended from an old Puritan line in the colony; Adams, a stern Puritan likewise, educated for the ministry, but forced by circumstances to become a merchant—he had, however, been unsuccessful as such, and after various reverses and changes was now an active politician and patriot, a man though poor, and whose wife by her industry supported the family, yet who exercised an extraordinary influence upon the fate of his country. Hancock, the youngest of this patriot band, was a wealthy merchant, descended from a line of merchants, "young, gay, of winning manners, with a strong love of popular approbation." "Hancock," says Hildreth, "acted very much under the guidance of Adams, who saw the policy of putting him forward as a leader." Hawley was a member of Northampton County, a lawyer by profession, a man of sound judgment, religious feeling, and unimpeachable character. The leader in the House of Representatives at this time was James Bowdoin, the grandson of a French Huguenot, whose father from the smallest beginnings had become the most opulent man in Boston, his immense wealth being inherited by his son and only child at one-and-twenty; he, too, acted under the direction of Adams.

The revenue officers no sooner began to enforce the collection of duties, than, as might be expected in the existing state of public feeling, they found themselves violently opposed by the merchants. Before long, also, the sloop Liberty, belonging to Hancock, being seized on the charge of having smuggled goods on board, the smothered fires burst into open flame. The populace rose, and the terrified revenue officers fled for their lives to the barracks on Castle Island, at the mouth of the harbour.

About the same time orders were received from England that "the Circular," issued by the last court, and which had given great offence, should be rescinded, and great disapprobation was expressed in his majesty's name of "that rash and hasty proceeding." But the circular had already gone forth, and by a vote of ninety-two to seventeen the House of Assembly refused to rescind. Orders had also been received by all the other colonies, desiring them to pay no attention to this offensive circular; but Connecticut, New Jersey, Virginia, and Georgia, had already committed themselves to it; and Maryland and New York, instead of obedience, now put forth remonstrances of their own.

Still was New York in contention with the governor on the subject of the quartering of the troops, when General Gage, commander-in-chief of the British forces in America, at the request of Bernard, the governor, who had complained to England of the tumultuous and refractory character of the people of Boston, was ordered to establish a military force in the city, to keep the inhabitants in order, as well as to aid the revenue officers in performing their duties. Two additional regiments were in consequence sent over from England. Late in September they arrived, and with muskets charged, and fixed bayonets, marched in as to a conquered town. The people, however, remained refractory; nor, though ships of war were in their harbour, and 1,000 armed men in their streets, would they submit to find them quarters. At length the discomfited governor was compelled to yield; one regiment encamped on Boston common, and the State-house was thrown open for the accommodation of the rest. It was Sunday when all this happened, and as the State-house stood opposite the great church, the inhabitants were disagreeably disturbed in their worship by the beating of drums and the marching of the troops, only to find themselves challenged by sentinels stationed in the street on their way home. These were not circumstances calculated to mollify the popular resentment; the most irritating language passed between the soldiers and the citizens, and the public excitement increased daily.

The news of this reception given to the troops, which was transmitted to England both by Gage and Governor Bernard, caused an equally violent excitement in England. Parliament declared the conduct of Massachusetts to be "illegal, unconstitutional, and derogatory to the rights of the crown and of parliament, and urged upon the king, that the governor should be ordered to obtain all information regarding this treason, and to send suspected persons over to England for trial, under an old statute of Henry VIII., for the punishment of treasons committed out of the kingdom." And a bill to the same effect, spite of the opposition of Barre, Burke, and Pownall, was immediately passed.

Every new step now taken, either by the colonies or the mother-country, increased the distance between them. The news of these instructions called forth immediately the most decisive expression of opinion from the colonial assemblies. The Virginian Assembly, in which Thomas Jefferson now first distinguished himself, and which was sitting when these tidings reached, passed a resolution denying boldly the king's right, either to tax the colonies without their consent, or to remove an offender out of the country for trial. As soon as Lord Boutetout, the governor, heard of this, he dissolved the assembly, but the members, instead of submitting, resumed their sittings in a private house, and choosing Peyton Randolph as their speaker, passed resolutions, drawn up by Colonel Washington, against the use of British goods. Their example was followed, and the "non-importation agreement" of Boston, Salem and New York, now became general. In North Carolina the assembly was also dissolved, as well as in Massachusetts. In Massachusetts, indeed, the military still occupying the town of Boston and the State-house, the rupture became so violent, that when Sir Francis Bernard communicated to the assembly his intention of going to England, to represent to parliament the disaffected state of the province, the assembly drew up a petition praying that he might be removed for ever from the government of the province, and denouncing, in the strongest terms, the fact of a standing army being maintained among them in a time of peace, and against their express desire. Leaving the administration in the hands of Lieutenant-governor Hutchinson, Bernard departed.

In the following year, 1770, an event occurred at Boston, which caused great excitement throughout America. An affray having taken place between some citizens and soldiers, the populace became greatly exasperated, and on the 5th of March, a crowd insulted the city guard under

Captain Preston, and dared them to fire. The soldiers fired, three of the people were killed, and others seriously wounded. At once the whole city was roused, and thousands appeared in arms. After great difficulty, and by promise that justice should be done them on the morrow, the lieutenant-governor succeeded in appeasing the tumult. Captain Preston and his company were tried for murder; two of the most distinguished American lawyers and patriots, John Adams and Josiah Quincy, very nobly volunteering their services in their defence. Two of the soldiers were convicted of manslaughter, the rest were acquitted; but this circumstance only tended to increase the ill-feeling between the citizens and the soldiers.[13]

On the very day of the outrage at Boston, Lord North, who was now at the head of the British administration, brought in a bill for the repeal of the detestable Quartering Act, and the removal of all the late offensive duties, excepting those on tea. It was time, in fact, to do something, as during the last year the amount produced by these very taxes had been swallowed up in their collection; British trade with the colonies was nearly at an end, and the military expenses amounted within the same period to £170,000. But even this conciliatory measure could do little. The Americans would accept nothing which still recognised the principle that parliament had a right to tax the provinces, and *tea* became now an article especially marked out by the non-importation agreements.

The concessions of government were not, however, without their effect in America; two parties began now to exist; those who inclined to moderation and adherence to the mother-country, called *Tories*, and the opponents, *Whigs*. In New York the party of Tories was strong, being composed of wealthy merchants, and members of the Church of England. These having power in the assembly, which now, after a suspension of two years, was allowed to meet again, submitted to the "Quartering Act," and provided for the soldiers, to the extreme disgust of the patriots and sons of Liberty, at whose head was a wealthy merchant, Alexander M'Dougall, a man who had raised himself by his own energy from poverty, and who was afterwards a major-general in the revolutionary army. This man having expressed his views very strongly, was imprisoned by the assembly, thus glad to show their zeal and loyalty, and M'Dougall became at once a popular hero and martyr, and his prison the gathering-place of patriots.

The non-importation and non-consumption agreements led to results of a beneficial character in social life which had not been contemplated. The senseless pomp of mourning and funeral expenses in which the colonists had indulged was discontinued; American manufactures were stimulated, "home-made was the fashion; and in 1770, the graduating students at Cambridge took their degrees in home-spun suits."

As we have before said, every successive act of Britain only served to alienate still more the hearts of her colonies. In 1772, parliament provided for the maintenance of the governor and judges of Massachusetts out of the royal revenues of the province, independent of the colonial assembly, and this was resented as an intended bribe to the governor and an infraction of their rights. Public meetings were again held throughout Massachusetts, and corresponding committees were formed, whose business was to discuss and consider the rights of the colonists and to communicate and publish the result. In the following year these committees commenced operation in New Hampshire, Rhode Island, Connecticut, Pennsylvania and Maryland, as well as in Massachusetts. These, "the nurseries of independence," gave again great offence in England.

During June of the same year, the Gaspe, an armed revenue schooner, which had been a great cause of annoyance in Narrangansett Bay, was purposely enticed into shoal-water by a vessel to which she gave chase, boarded and burnt by a party from Providence. This daring outrage called forth the indignation of parliament, and an act was passed for sending to England for trial all persons concerned in destroying his majesty's ships, etc. A reward of £600 was offered for the discovery of the persons concerned in the destruction of this vessel, and powerful machinery of examination was put in action; but though the perpetrators were well known, so strong was public feeling in their favour, that no legal evidence could be obtained against them.

"While ardent discussions," says Hildreth, "on the subject of colonial and national rights were going on in Massachusetts, some reflecting persons were struck with the inconsistency of contending for their own liberty and depriving other people of theirs. Hence arose a controversy as to the justice and legality of negro slavery. This controversy led to trials at law, in which the question was freely canvassed, and it was proved by legal decisions 'that the colonists, black or white, born there, were free-born British subjects, and entitled to all the essential rights of such.' These were the first steps towards the abolition of slavery in Massachusetts."

Whilst disputes were maturing themselves into the great national contest between the mother-country and the colonies, the colonies were not altogether at peace among themselves; the question of boundary being fruitful in controversy. Pennsylvania and Connecticut quarrelled violently about the possession of the Wyoming Valley, on the Upper Susquehanna, and blood was even shed. Virginia quarrelled with Pennsylvania, also, about her western frontier, laying claim to Pittsburg and the whole district west of the Laurel Mountains. The boundary dispute which had long agitated New York and New Jersey was happily adjusted about this time, as was also that between New York and Massachusetts. Violent were the disputes, however, between New York and the settlers in the infant Vermont, the territory lying west of the Connecticut, "the Green Mountain Boys," as they were called, and the leaders of whom were Ethan Allen and Seth Warner, emigrants from Connecticut to the Green Mountains. But, spite of disputes both at home and abroad, settlers extended themselves farther and still farther, to the north and to the west. The formidable Six Nations had now disposed of all their vast territory south of the Ohio, as far as the Cherokee or Tennessee River, to the British Crown, for the sum of £10,460. Settlers were already occupying the banks of the Kenhawa River, flowing north into the Ohio, beyond the great Allegany Range. In consequence of this immense cession of territory, land companies started up in England for the establishment of new colonies, but the growing troubles with the mother-country prevented their plans being carried out.

The first settlements in the present state of Tennessee were made by emigrants from North Carolina, who established themselves on the Wataga, one of the head streams of the Tennessee, in the land of the Cherokees. Like the early settlers of New England, these emigrants organised themselves into a body politic, and drew up a code of laws to which every individual assented by signature. About the same time that settlers extended themselves to the Tennessee, an Indian trader, returning to North Carolina from one of his far journeys west, induced Daniel Boone and four other settlers on the Yadkin, in Maryland, by his glowing accounts of the wonderfully beautiful regions which he had discovered, to return with him for their exploration. They set out, reached the head waters of the Kentucky, and as hunters traversed the fertile plains and magnificent forests in pursuit of the buffalo and other game. They had encounters with Indians, and Boone was taken prisoner, but managed to escape, and was soon after joined by his brother, who had come out in search of him. Boone was a second Nimrod, a mighty hunter; and as such, explored the beautiful region between the Upper Kentucky and the Tennessee. The country pleased him greatly, and hastening back to the Yadkin, he sold his farm, and with his wife and children and five other families, returned to this "New Western Paradise," being joined by volunteer settlers to the number of forty as he journeyed along. All, however, did not go smoothly with them; they were met by hostile Indians and some of their number killed; and war having broken out between the backwoodsmen of Virginia and the Indians on the Ohio, they were detained a year and a half by the way. While the west was thus opened to the colonists, Georgia also acquired a large increase of territory by the purchase of land from the Creeks and Cherokees.

About this time Whitfield died in America, and Wesley sent over disciples to establish the Wesleyan Church in that country; soon after which, Mother Ann Lee also arrived, the foundress of the Shakers, whose singular communities exist to this day, here and there, throughout the country. About the same time, also, the sect of the Universalists began to attract attention, under the preaching of John Murray; and though at first few dared to avow this so-called heresy, it gained great acceptation, and tended considerably to soften the stern, rugged heart of puritan New England.

We now return to the great contest which cast all minor subjects into the shade.

The British ministry intended by cunning policy to effect what open measures had failed to do. The East India company were allowed by act of parliament to export tea to the American colonies free from English duties, liable only to threepence per pound, to be paid by the colonists, and which would thus give them tea cheaper than that purchased by the English. Tea was shipped in great quantities to America, which the colonists, who objected as strongly as ever to the principle involved in the measure, determined should never be permitted to land.

The pilots, therefore, in Philadelphia harbour were ordered not to conduct the ships into the river, and their cargoes were consequently returned to England; at New York, the governor commanded the tea to be landed under protection of soldiers, but the people gained possession, and prohibited its sale. At Charleston, also, its sale was forbidden and it was stored up in damp cellars to render it unfit for use. At Boston, the tea being consigned to the governor and his friends, it was feared that it would be landed spite of the public, to prevent which a number of men, disguised as Indians, boarded the vessels at night, and threw their cargoes overboard. Three hundred and thirty-two chests of tea were thus broken open and destroyed.

The news of this determined and offensive procedure caused the utmost astonishment and indignation in England, and it was resolved in parliament "to make such provisions as should secure the just dependence of the colonies and due obedience to the laws throughout the British dominions and as an especial punishment of the contumacious Bostonians, a bill passed the house in March, 1774, to oblige them to repay the value of the destroyed article, and also interdicting all commercial intercourse with the port of Boston, and prohibiting the landing and shipping of any goods at that place;" and by the same act the custom-house and its dependencies were removed from Boston to Salem, which it was intended to raise on the ruins of its neighbour city and port.

THROWING THE TAXED TEA INTO BOSTON HARBOR.

General Gage superseded Hutchinson as governor of Massachusetts, in consequence of the unpopularity of the latter. A number of manuscript letters, written by him to various members of parliament, had fallen into the hands of Benjamin Franklin, now agent in London for Massachusetts, New Jersey, Georgia and Pennsylvania, and having been sent by him to Boston, and circulated extensively though privately, caused his removal from office.

When, in May, the news of the Boston Port Bill reached that city, together with instructions to the new governor, to send to another colony or to England, for trial, any persons indicted for murder, or any other capital offence committed in aid of the magistrates in the fulfilment of their duty, an astonishment of grief and anger fell upon the citizens, and a meeting of the inhabitants declared that "the impolicy, injustice and inhumanity of the act exceeded their powers of expression."

The General Assembly met, but was adjourned by the governor to Salem, and it was then resolved that a colonial congress should be convened to take into serious consideration the present difficult state of affairs. James Bowdoin, Thomas Cushing, Samuel Adams, John Adams and Robert Treat Paine, were therefore at once appointed as their representatives to such a congress, and the speaker of the house was ordered to inform the other colonies of this measure. The governor, hearing of these proceedings, ordered the assembly to dissolve, but in vain;

his officer was not admitted, and in defiance of orders, the assembly finished its business.

The colonies sympathised warmly with Massachusetts, and Massachusetts was true to herself. The behaviour of the inhabitants of Salem, whom it was intended to benefit at the expense of Boston, was very noble. They replied to the governor's proclamation, "That nature, in forming their harbour, had prevented their becoming rivals to Boston in trade; and that, even if it were otherwise, they should regard themselves as lost to every idea of justice and all feelings of humanity, if they could indulge a thought of seizing upon the wealth of their neighbours, or raising their fortunes upon the ruins of their countrymen." More than this; the inhabitants of Marblehead and Salem offered to the suffering merchants of Boston the use of their harbour, wharfs and warehouses, free of all charge; and in Virginia, where Lord Dunmore, now governor, found it impossible to manage the "the refractory people," "a day of fast, humiliation, and prayer," was appointed for the 1st of June, the day on which the Boston Port Act came into effect, "that they might beseech of God to avert the evils which threatened them, and to give them one heart and one mind firmly to oppose, by all just and proper means, every injury to the American rights."

In September, the great congress proposed by Massachusetts met at Philadelphia, composed of delegates from eleven of the colonies—the most important assembly which had yet come together in America, and for the result of whose deliberations all parties waited with extreme interest and anxiety.

By unanimous consent, Peyton Randolph, of Virginia, was chosen president; to each province was given one vote; they proceeded in their deliberations with closed doors; and a committee, composed of two persons from each province, was appointed to state the rights of the colonies in general, together with every known instance in which these rights had been infringed by the mother-country, and the proposed means of redress. The conduct of Massachusetts, in her "conflict with wicked ministers," was approved, and a continuance of supplies for her relief was voted. A letter of remonstrance was addressed to the governor, General Gage, who was erecting fortifications on Boston Neck, begging him to "desist from military operations, lest a difference altogether irreconcilable should arise between the colonies and the parent state."

The committee appointed for that purpose drew up a document setting forth, in a string of resolutions, the rights of the colonies, which, being approved, was published as the well-known "Bill of Rights." A suspension of all commercial intercourse with Great Britain was resolved upon, until the grievances of the colonies were redressed; an address to the king was voted, together with others to the people of Great Britain and British America. The non-importation agreement bound them, "under the sacred ties of virtue, honour, and love of liberty," not to import or use any British goods after the 1st of December, 1774, particularly the articles, tea and molasses. Agriculture, the arts and manufactures, were to be promoted in America by all possible means; committees were appointed to see this agreement entered into, and all who violated it were to be regarded as enemies to their country. To the honour of this assembly it must be stated, that they bound themselves also not to be in any way concerned in the slave-trade.

The proceedings of this congress awoke, as might be expected, a still stronger spirit of animosity in England. In vain the congress deplored to the king "the apprehension of his colonists being degraded into a state of servitude from the pre-eminent rank of English freemen;" in vain they besought that "the royal indignation might fall on those designing and dangerous men, who, by their misrepresentations of his American subjects, had compelled them by the force of accumulated injuries to disturb his majesty's repose;" in vain they prayed for "peace, liberty, and safety; wishing not the diminution of the royal prerogative, nor soliciting the grant of any new right in their favour;" in vain they concluded their petition by earnestly beseeching the king, "as the father of his whole people, not to permit the ties of blood, of law, and loyalty, to be broken." In vain did Lord Chatham stand before the British senate as the eloquent advocate of America, declaring that the way must be immediately opened for reconciliation, or it would be soon too late. "His majesty," argued he, "may indeed wear his crown, but the American jewel out of it, it will not be worth wearing. I say," continued he, taking up the argument of American wrongs, "you have no right to tax the colonies without their consent. They say truly, representation and taxation must go together; they are inseparable. This wise people speak out. They do not hold the language of slaves; they tell you what they mean. They do not ask you to repeal your laws, as a favour; they claim it as a right—they demand it; and the acts must be repealed. Bare repeal, however, will not satisfy this enlightened and spirited people. You must go through with the work; you must declare that you have no right to tax them; thus they may trust you—thus they will have some confidence in you."

In vain did the merchants of London and other commercial towns petition in favour of America. Dr. Franklin and other colonial agents were refused a hearing before the house. America was condemned. The two houses of parliament, by a large majority, assured the king that "the Americans had long wished to become independent, and only waited for ability and opportunity to accomplish their design. To prevent this, therefore, and to crush the monster in its birth, was the duty of every Englishman; and this must be done, at any price and at every hazard." Such was the temper of parliament.

In the meantime, the colonies were not indifferent to the increasing difficulties of the times. Massachusetts already assumed a military aspect. The congress, which, spite of the opposition of the governor, continued to hold its sittings, seeing that the military stores were already seized by the governor, proceeded themselves to take measures for the defence of the province. £20,000 were voted for this purpose, and the collectors of taxes received orders no longer to forward their moneys to the government treasurer, but to a new one of their own appointment. Further, it was ordained that a number of the inhabitants should be enrolled as a militia of 12,000 men, ready to march at a minute's notice; officers were chosen, and committees of supplies and safety held their regular sittings. Gage denounced their proceedings, but no notice was taken of his denunciations; "he had no support except in his own troops and a few trembling officials, while the zealous co-operation of an intelligent, firm, energetic, and overwhelming majority of the people, gave to the provincial congress all the strength of an established government."[14]

In November, at the very time when the king and the British parliament were resolving to keep terms no longer with the colonies, Massachusetts sent agents to New Hampshire, Rhode Island and Connecticut, to inform them of her measures, and to solicit their co-operation in raising an army of 20,000 men, ready to act in case of need.

In the midst of all these growing internal excitements, and while the colonists were deeply occupied in the maintenance of their rights, the frontiers of Pennsylvania and Virginia were again visited by the miseries of Indian warfare. It was at this time that the family of the famous chief Logan, an old and faithful friend of the whites, was murdered in cold blood; and this and other atrocities committed by the explorers of Ohio and Kentucky, led to the sorrows of the present Indian war. Daniel Boone, the hunter of the Kentucky plains, was placed in command of a frontier fort by Lord Dunmore, governor of Virginia, and a war of extermination was carried on against the Indians. At length, negotiations of peace were entered into, and it was on this occasion that Logan made his celebrated speech: "I appeal to any white man," spoke the eloquent chief of the forest, "if he ever entered the cabin of Logan hungry, and he gave him not meat; if he ever came cold and naked, and he clothed him not. During the last long and bloody war, Logan remained idle in his cabin; and such was his love for the whites, that his countrymen pointed as they passed, and said, 'Logan is the friend of the white men!' I even thought to live with you, but for the injuries of one man. Colonel Cresop, last spring, in cold blood, and unprovoked, murdered all the relatives of Logan, not sparing women and children. There runs not a drop of my blood in the veins of any living creature! This called on me for revenge! I have fully glutted my vengeance! For my people, I rejoice at the beams of peace; but mine is not the joy of fear—Logan never felt fear. Who is there to mourn for Logan? Not one!"

At the commencement of 1775, America very generally stood in a position of hostility to the mother-country. The congress of Massachusetts had held its third sitting; volunteers were in arms throughout the province, and every town had its committees of safety, correspondence and inspection. John Thomas, of Plymouth, and William Heath, a Roxbury farmer, were appointed generals of the Massachusetts army.

In Rhode Island, in consequence of the royal prohibition of the exportation of military stores to America, and the removal of armed ships from Narrangansett Bay, the people of Providence conveyed forty-four pieces of cannon thither from Newport; and when called upon by the British naval commander for an explanation, Governor Wanton, a stout patriot, bluntly replied, that they were removed to prevent their falling into his hands, and were intended to be used against any force which might molest the colony. In New Hampshire, John Sullivan a lawyer, and John Langdon, a merchant of Portsmouth, headed a party who entered the fort at that place, and possessed themselves of 100 barrels of powder, cannon and small arms. The convention of Maryland ordered the enrolment of militia, and voted £10,000 for the purchase of arms. In Pennsylvania, the public spirit was less unanimous. The provincial convention of that province expressed themselves less decidedly than suited the temper of the ardent patriots, one of the leaders of whom was Thomas Mifflin, a young Quaker, possessed of much energy of character, and remarkable powers of popular eloquence. Mifflin, however, was an exception to the general body of Quakers, who, whatever their original opposition to established forms, have ever been loyal and obedient to the powers that be; and now, in their yearly meeting held in Philadelphia at the commencement of 1775, they put forth their "testimony of abhorrence to every measure and writing tending to break off the happy connexion of the colonies with the mother-country, or to interrupt their just subordination to the king." Very different was the spirit of the sects and their ministers in New England. Everywhere it evinced opposition to the king and the mother-country, whose attempts to force an established episcopal church, with a bishop at its head, upon the colonies, had only tended still more to increase that very spirit of resistance which had first sent their forefathers to these shores. The Presbyterians of every New England state were all staunch Whigs. The episcopal clergy and their congregations, wherever found, were Tories; so also were the landed proprietors and merchants, especially the more recent settlers. The Episcopalian and Tory party was more numerous in New York than in any other of the northern provinces. In Georgia they were also considerable, and the influence of Governor Wright prevented this province from joining the American Association; and in the southern provinces, the law of primogeniture, which still considerably prevailed, together with the institution of slavery, had given rise to a local aristocratic class, totally opposed in sentiment to the democracy of the north.

These were the elements upon which England depended to establish her power in the coming contest;—nor were these all; she depended, not only on the loyalty and attachment of the Episcopalians everywhere, but on the peace-loving principles of the Quakers, who were an influential portion of New Jersey, Pennsylvania, Delaware and North Carolina; she expected if not aid, at least no opposition from the numerous German settlers, who, established in large colonies, had not yet acquired the English language nor amalgamated with the British colonists; and at the same time she depended for aid upon the Scotch Highlanders, who abounded in New York and North Carolina, and who were at the same time ignorant and loyal.

It being determined therefore to show no concession to the rebellious spirit of the colonies, a bill was brought in in February, 1775, for cutting off the trade of Massachusetts, Connecticut, Rhode Island and New Hampshire, excepting with Great Britain and her West India possessions, and to prohibit also their fishing on the banks of Newfoundland, which was then a great branch of their trade and industry. While this bill was under discussion, news reached England of the adhesion which was given by the other colonies to the measures of the American Congress; and all the colonies, excepting New York, North Carolina and Georgia, were included in the bill of restriction. At the very time that this New England Restraining Bill was agitating all parties, Lord North proposed what he called a conciliatory plan, which was, in fact, that Great Britain should forbear any scheme of colonial taxation, on condition that the assembly of each province should raise a suitable amount of money, which should be disposable by parliament. This plan, though vehemently opposed in England, as conceding too much to the colonies, was utterly rejected by the colonies, as compelling them to yield that over which they claimed to have a right. In the midst of all these attempts at coercion and conciliation, an endeavour at negotiation also failed between Benjamin Franklin and some members of the cabinet who were friendly to America.

The West India merchants petitioned against the restraining bill, as interfering fatally with their commercial relationships, and foretelling famine and ruin to the West India islands in consequence. The assembly of Jamaica petitioned parliament on behalf of "the claim of rights set up by the North American provinces," and protested against the "plan almost carried into execution for reducing the colonies into the most abject state of slavery." Petitions for conciliation were presented from the British Quakers and the British settlers in Quebec, and Wilkes, as lord mayor of London, presented a remonstrance to the king from the city authorities, expressing "abhorrence of the measures in progress for the oppression of their fellow subjects in the colonies." But all was of no avail. Nothing was to be done; and Franklin, seeing the hopeless state of affairs, set sail for America, and almost at the same moment the battle of Lexington was fought.

CHAPTER IV.
THE REVOLUTIONARY WAR.

When, in February, 1775, the provincial congress met again at Cambridge, the committee of supplies took the most active measures for the raising and drilling of the militia, and for the procuring of ammunition and military stores of all kinds. A day of fasting and prayer, according to puritan custom on solemn and important occasions, was also appointed; New England was preparing temporally and spiritually for the great time of trial.

The British forces under the command of General Gage, at Boston, amounted to about 3,000. Gage, aware of what was going forward around him, resolved to disable the insurgent colonists by gaining possession of the stores and ammunition which had been collected by them, and stored at Salem and Concord. At Salem the search was unsuccessful, the troops being driven back from a bridge, the passage of which was disputed on the Sunday. The attempt at Concord was of a much more serious character, military stores being collected there to a great extent. Eight hundred men were sent out on this expedition, with orders of despatch and secrecy, under the command of Colonel Smith and Major Pitcairn, on the night of April 18th, and arrived at Lexington, within five miles of Concord, just before sunrise. But the alarm had been already given, and it being supposed that the intention was to seize John Hancock and Samuel Adams, who were then there, the minute-men of the place were drawn up to resist them. Pitcairn, at the head of his regulars, advanced within musket-shot, and exclaimed, "Disperse, rebels! Throw down your arms, and disperse!" No notice being taken of these words, a volley was then fired, which killed eight of the minute-men and wounded several others. The British, however, declared that the minute-men fired first; but be that as it may, they then fled, and the firing was continued, the regulars marching on to Concord, where they destroyed and took possession of the stores, while the minute-men being reinforced by different bodies which had hurried there at the sound of the firing, a skirmish ensued. A considerable number of the regulars were killed, and the rest forced to retreat, the colonial militia pursuing them hotly all the way back to Lexington, where, fortunately for themselves, they found Lord Percy with a reinforcement of 900 men. But for this timely aid, it is doubtful if any of their number would have reached Boston; the Americans, having the advantage of the knowledge of the ground, and availing themselves of the Indian mode of warfare, took fatal aim from behind bushes, stone walls, barns, or whatever offered a means of concealment. At sunset the exhausted regulars reached Bunker's Hill, near Boston, having lost in killed and wounded about 300 men, while the loss of the provincials amounted to eighty-five.

The news of this battle, of this first shedding of blood, flew like wild-fire through the colonies. Couriers were despatched at full speed from place to place, bearing tidings which called all to arms. "The war has begun!" was shouted in the market-place; at the ferry on the river; in the crowded meeting-house on the Sabbath; and all rushed to arms. It was twenty days, however, with their utmost speed, before the news reached Charleston in South Carolina; yet, long before that time, volunteers had marched from all parts of the New England colonies.

From Rhode Island, a body of volunteers hastened to Boston, under the command of a young Quaker, Nathaniel Greene, who was disowned by his brethren for this violation of their principles. Nor could the admonitions and threats of discipline of the elder Friends of Philadelphia keep the martial spirit of their young men under control. Mifflin's example and influence was stronger than all the advice they could give, and Quaker-Philadelphia sent out a company of brave volunteers. Delaware, Maryland, and North Carolina, all were moved by the same spirit; while Patrick Henry, the young patriot lawyer of Virginia, marched with a troop of volunteer riflemen to Williamsburgh, the capital of the Old Dominion, and compelled the royal treasurer to refund the value of ammunition which Lord Dunmore, the governor, had lately seized. Dunmore, incensed, issued a proclamation declaring them rebels, and fortified his residence. Soon after, letters of his, addressed to the English government, and which were considered false to the colony, being intercepted, the public indignation waxed hot against him; whereupon, fearing for his life, he fled to a man-of-war lying at Yorktown, and abandoned his government. Governor Martin, of North Carolina, about the same time, fled also in terror on board a ship of war, at the mouth of Cape Fear River; and in South Carolina, Lord William Campbell, the governor, being suspected of secret negotiations with the Cherokees, was likewise obliged to retire. Georgia, the hitherto "defective link in the American chain," soon became soldered by the kindling flame of liberty. In vain Sir James Wright, the governor, did his utmost to maintain the loyalty and allegiance of the province. The powder was removed from the magazine at Savannah; and the cargo of a powder-ship, which lay at the mouth of the river, forwarded to the camp at Boston.

Georgia sent five delegates to the provincial congress about to assemble at Philadelphia; and henceforth the style of the "Thirteen United Colonies" was assumed.

The battle of Lexington was soon followed by other events. The Massachusetts committee of safety had already contemplated gaining possession of Ticonderoga and Crown Point, on which depended the control of Lakes George and Champlain, when, without waiting for higher commands than those of patriotism, the bold Ethan Allen and Seth Warner, at the head of their "Green Mountain Boys," set out on the enterprise. Without being aware of this movement, Benedict Arnold, a New Haven trader, then in camp before Boston with a company of volunteers, received a commission from the committee of safety, to raise a body of troops in Vermont and proceed on this enterprise. Arnold was well pleased, for it was a favourite scheme of his own, but presently found, to his surprise, that others were before him. Taking command, therefore, under Allen, they marched together to Ticonderoga, which they reached on the 9th of May, and on the 10th, by break of day, entered the fort unperceived, with eighty men, and surprising De la Place, the commandant, in his bed, ordered him to surrender, "in the name of the Great Jehovah and the Continental Congress." No resistance was attempted; and Crown Point was taken with equal ease. The garrison of both forts did not amount to more than sixty men, but above 200 pieces of artillery and a valuable quantity of powder, of which there was great want in the provincial camp, fell into the hands of the captors. After this, Arnold manned a small schooner, and proceeding down the lake, surprised the Fort of St. John and seized a sloop-of-war laden with stores; the pass of Skeensborough, now Whitehall, was likewise secured. Three important posts which commanded the lakes, together with much needed cannon and munitions of war, being thus secured in rapid succession and without bloodshed, raised the hopes of the Americans and inspired them with confidence.

While these events were going forward, Lord North's conciliatory proposition was laid before the various colonial assemblies and rejected. On May 10th the colonial congress met at Philadelphia. Its meeting was momentous. Thomas Jefferson was chosen president, and Thomas Hancock secretary. Bills of credit were issued for defraying the expenses of the war. It was resolved, that hostilities had been commenced by Great Britain; allegiance was still avowed, and an anxious desire expressed for peace; nevertheless it was voted that the colonies ought to put themselves in a posture of defence against the parliamentary schemes of compulsory taxation. After much opposition, another petition to the king was agreed upon. The New England states entertained and freely acknowledged the desire for independence; the middle and the southern states still hesitated, though all had sent delegates to the congress. Addresses were also prepared to the people of Great Britain and Ireland, as well as an appeal made to the "oppressed inhabitants of Canada," as through Canada it was expected that England would make an attack on the colonies.

In order to prevent General Gage from penetrating into the country, which was his intention, congress recommended to the council of war completely to blockade him in Boston; for which purpose, Colonel Prescott, with a detachment of 1,000 men, including a company of artillery and two field-pieces, was ordered to march at nightfall of June 16th, and take possession of Bunker's-hill, an elevation just within the peninsula of Charlestown, and commanding the northern approach to Boston, which city it overlooked. By some mistake, however, they proceeded to Breed's Hill, a lower height and still nearer to Boston. With the utmost silence and despatch they laboured all night, and before morning had thrown up a considerable redoubt, capable of defending themselves from the fire of the enemy. Great was the astonishment of the British the next morning, and a fire was immediately opened upon them from the ships in the river. The work, however, went on uninterruptedly, when, about noon, 3,000 picked men, under command of Generals Howe and Pigot, embarked in boats and landed at the foot of Breed's Hill, and advanced slowly in two columns; the artillery in the meantime being directed against the works. At this critical moment no system prevailed in the American army; the same troops who had been at work all night were still in the intrenchments; neither General Warren nor Israel Putnam, though on the ground, had troops under their command; forces which had been ordered thither had not arrived and the stock of ammunition was very small.

It was a splendid summer's afternoon, when the British advanced up the hill. Clinton and Burgoyne were stationed on a height in Boston to watch the action; and all the surrounding eminences, spires of churches, and roofs of houses, were crowded with spectators, awaiting anxiously, though with opposing interests, the result of the approaching conflict. Slowly and uninterruptedly advanced the British, until within about ten rods of the redoubt, when such a deadly fire assailed them that their ranks were mown down, the whole line broken, and they fell back in disorder. Again they were rallied and brought back to the charge by their officers, but again were repulsed with loss. Infuriated by defeat, and in consequence also, it is said, of shots being fired from a house on the left, Gage ordered Charlestown to be set on fire; the wooden buildings burned rapidly and the tall spire of the meeting-house was wrapt in flame; 2,000 people at least being thus rendered houseless. Amid the terrors of the burning village, the British regulars made a second and yet a third attack, and this time with better success. The ammunition of the provincials began to fail, and the British artillery, now brought up to the breast-work, swept it from end to end, while three simultaneous attacks carried it at the point of the bayonet. Courage now could avail nothing, and the provincials under Colonel Prescott made good their retreat across Charlestown Neck, exposed to an incessant fire from the shipping, and entrenched themselves on another height still commanding the entrance to Boston. The British took possession of Bunker's Hill. This defeat the Americans esteemed as a victory; in England the victory was considered little less than a defeat, and General Gage was in consequence superseded by Sir William Howe, brother of Lord Howe, who perished before Ticonderoga. Of 3,000 British engaged in this conflict above 1,000 fell. The loss of the Americans was in about the same proportion; out of 1,500, 450 were killed and wounded, but among the former was General Warren, whose loss caused the deepest regret to his country.

This second encounter, in which undisciplined troops had so bravely withstood the flower of the British army, raised still higher the hopes and confidence of the Americans. The English discovered also that they had no insignificant enemy to deal with.

The day before the battle of Bunker's Hill, the Provincial congress at Philadelphia, having voted to raise an army of 20,000 men, proceeded to elect George Washington, then present as delegate from Virginia, to the rank of commander-in-chief. The northern colonies had resolved, in order to secure the adherence of the South, to choose a southern commander, and the superior wisdom of Providence guided them in the selection. God provides the man for the work, and Washington was the appointed agent of a great people's emancipation. Divine wisdom, and not that of man, guided the choice. Washington, with great modesty and dignity, accepted the appointment, declining all compensation for his services beyond the defrayment of expenses. At the same time that Washington received the command in chief, Artemas Ward, of Massachusetts, Colonel Lee, formerly a British officer, Philip Schuyler, of New York, and Israel Putnam, of Connecticut, then with the camp before Boston, were appointed major-generals, and Horatio Gates adjutant-general.

Washington, accompanied by a number of ardent young men from the South, soon appeared in the camp and assumed command. He found excellent *materiel* for an army, but great want of arms and ammunition as well as deficiency of discipline. The troops, now amounting to 14,000 men, were arranged in three divisions; the right wing under General Ward, at Roxbury; the left, under Lee, on Prospect Hill; and the centre at Cambridge, where were Washington's head-quarters. The post of quarter-master-general was given by Washington to Mifflin, the young Quaker of Philadelphia, who had accompanied him as aide-de-camp; and Robert Harrison, a lawyer of Maryland, was chosen by him for the important office of his secretary, the duties of which he faithfully performed for several years. Among the new companies which now joined the camp was one from Virginia, led by that same village wrestler, Daniel Morgan, who was hired by Benjamin Franklin to aid in the removal of stores for Braddock's army, and in whose defeat he was wounded. The British, thus hemmed in at Boston, suffered greatly from want of provisions.

While Washington was occupied in organising his army and endeavouring to introduce order and discipline among troops unaccustomed to subordination, congress was employed in providing the necessary means for the support of the war. A declaration of war was also issued, in which the causes and necessity for taking up arms were set forth. This document, which was ordered to be read from every pulpit in the colonies, asserted that their cause was just, their union perfect. "Our internal resources are great," said the declaration, "and if necessary, foreign aid is undoubtedly attainable." "Nevertheless," it went on to say, "we have not raised armies with the ambitious design of separating from Great Britain. We have taken up arms in defence of the freedom which is our birthright. We shall lay them down when hostilities shall cease on the part of the aggressors, and all danger of their renewal shall be removed."

The importance of keeping on good terms with the Indians at this critical juncture was not overlooked; and three boards were established for the management of Indian affairs. An armed body of Stockbridge Indians, the last remains of the New England tribes, was already with the camp at Boston; and overtures were made to the Six Nations. Louis, the chief of the French Mohawks, a half-blood Indian, received a commission as colonel, and at the head of an Indian troop faithfully served the American cause.

The first complete line of postal communication was established at this time by congress, amid its multifarious concerns, and Benjamin Franklin was appointed post-master-general, with power to appoint deputies for the conveyance of the mail from Falmouth in Maine to Savannah in Georgia.

While the British army was blockaded at Boston, and the highway to Canada opened for the Americans by their possession of Ticonderoga and Crown Point, it was resolved by congress to invade and possess themselves of that province, and thus counteract the movements of Sir Guy Carleton, the governor, who was evidently under orders from England to attack the colonies from the north-west. Two expeditions were therefore sent out— the one under Generals Schuyler and Montgomery, by way of Lake Champlain; the other by the Kennebec, under General Benedict Arnold; the whole of these forces amounting to about 3,000 men.

On the 10th of September, Schuyler and Montgomery appeared before St. John's, the most southern British fort in Canada, but finding it too strong for attack, retired to the Isle aux Noix, 115 miles from Ticonderoga, which they fortified, and where Schuyler issued circulars to the Canadians, inviting them to join the Americans and assert their liberty. But soon after hastening to Ticonderoga for reinforcements, he fell sick, and the whole command devolved upon Montgomery.

Having received reinforcements, though in want of artillery and ammunition, and having engaged the Indians in a treaty of neutrality, Montgomery returned to St. John's, which he besieged with but little success, though he took Fort Chambly, at a few miles distance, where he was fortunate enough to obtain several pieces of cannon and a considerable quantity of powder. Colonel Ethan Allen, the hero of Ticonderoga, being sent out, during the siege of St. John's, with a detachment of about eighty men, to secure a party of hostile Indians, met on his return with another officer as rash and daring as himself, and they, without orders, madly determined to attempt the surprise of Montreal. Montreal did not yield so easily as Ticonderago fort had done; Allen was taken prisoner, treated with great severity, and sent to England in irons. Montgomery, however, having renewed the siege of St. John's, that fort surrendered on the 3rd of November, after which he advanced rapidly to Montreal, which Carleton had abandoned, making his escape down the river to Quebec. The following day, Montgomery, having engaged to leave the inhabitants undisturbed in the free exercise of their laws and religion, took possession of the town, where his troops found a very welcome supply of woollen goods, with which they were enabled to clothe themselves—a necessary circumstance at the commencement of a rigorous Canadian winter. Although the kindness of Montgomery's disposition and conduct induced many Canadians to enlist under his arms, he suffered greatly from the insubordination and desertions of his own troops; while others, the time of their service being expired, returned to their own homes. Nevertheless, with the remnant of his army, amounting merely to about 300 men, he proceeded rapidly towards Quebec, expecting to meet there General Arnold, with his detachment of 1,000 men, who was to advance thither by the Kennebec.

The hardships which Arnold and his men had in the meantime endured, in the trackless and desolate forests of Maine, at the commencement of winter, were almost incredible; nevertheless, on the 9th of November, he arrived at Point Levi, opposite Quebec. Could he have immediately crossed the St. Lawrence, the city, which was indifferently defended and which was alarmed at his approach, might easily have been taken; but, for want of boats, it was not until the 13th that he was able to cross, and by that time Carleton, who had escaped from Montreal, had gained the city and put it in a state of defence. On the night of the 13th, therefore, Arnold crossed with his army, now reduced to 700 men, and ascending the cliffs to the Heights of Abraham, as Wolfe had done before, hoped to take the city by surprise. Finding, however, the garrison prepared for his reception, and not being strong enough to hazard an assault, he retired twenty miles down the river, there to await the arrival of Montgomery.

Montgomery joined Arnold on the 1st of December, all his Connecticut men having by this time returned home, so that the united forces of the two generals did not amount to 1,000. On the 5th, a message to surrender being sent to Carleton, the messenger was fired upon. It was then resolved to batter the town, but their artillery was found insufficient for the purpose, and after a siege of three weeks, during which the assailants suffered incredibly from the severity of the season, an assault was resolved upon as the only chance in their desperate circumstances. On the last night of the year, therefore, in the midst of a violent snow-storm, and with the ground several feet deep in snow, the American troops set forth in four divisions, commanded by Montgomery, Arnold, Brown and Livingston; and whilst the two latter were to make a feigned attack on the Upper Town, the two former, each at the head of their respective forces, were to assault the Lower Town at two opposite quarters. Montgomery had already passed the first barrier, the enemy flying before him, when the discharge of a piece of artillery deprived this brave man and two other officers of life. Disheartened by the death of their leader, the next in command ordered a retreat. Arnold, in the meantime, was boldly pushing his way forward into the town, when a ball, while cheering his men onward, shattered his leg. He was unwillingly borne from the combat, while Daniel Morgan, at the head of his Virginian riflemen, pushed forward and made himself master of the second battery. For several hours he and the fragments of the companies who now met, sustained their ground, but at length, overcome by superior numbers, they were obliged to surrender as prisoners of war. Not less than 400 men perished in this unfortunate attempt, and 300 more were made prisoners. Wounded as he was, Arnold retired with the small remains of his army to a distance of three miles, where, covering his camp with ramparts of frozen snow, he kept Quebec in a state of blockade through the winter.

Carleton treated his prisoners with great kindness; they were well fed and clothed, and afterwards allowed a safe return home. This humane policy greatly strengthened the British interests in Canada. Reinforcements arrived early in the spring for Arnold, but small-pox had already broken out among the troops, of which frightful disease General Thomas, who was sent out to supersede Arnold, died. The Americans retreated; and one by one, before midsummer, nearly all the posts which had been taken by them fell into the hands of the British.

In the midst of the anxieties and disturbances of the preceding year, the new province, which is now Kentucky, received still further accession of settlers through the means of Richard Henderson, a North Carolina lawyer, a man of great enterprise and energy, who had purchased a large tract of country from the Cherokees for a few wagon-loads of goods. Henderson, now associated with Boone, the bold hunter and settler of the wilderness, who had already established himself at Boonesburgh, and with other early settlers, especially an adventurous backwoodsman named Harrod, the founder of Harrodsburg, proceeded to organise themselves as the province of Transylvania. Courts and a militia were established, and laws enacted; and soon after a delegate sent thence to the continental congress at Philadelphia. Unfortunately for the new colony, Virginia laid claim to the territory as lying within her charter, and the Transylvanian delegate could not be recognised. About the same time that this early settlement of Kentucky was going forward, 400 families from Connecticut left their old homes to seek new ones under General Lyman, in the province of West Florida.

While the Americans were wasting their strength in unsuccessful attempts in Canada, the seaports of New England were kept in continual alarm by British cruisers, who not only landed to obtain supplies of which the royal forces were in great need, but also sailed under orders to lay waste and destroy in case of resistance. Hence Falmouth, now Portland, a rising town of 500 houses, was burned by Lieutenant Mowatt, which caused an increase of exasperation in the minds of the colonists, and led them also to attempt maritime warfare. Congress authorised the fitting out of thirteen war-frigates, and the raising of two battalions of marines. Privateering was established, and courts of admiralty formed for the adjudication of prizes. All ships of war employed in harassing the colonies, and all vessels bringing supplies to the British forces, were declared lawful prizes.

Great anxiety existed in the mind of the commander-in-chief, owing to the extreme scarcity of ammunition and military stores in his army. The utmost efforts were used to discover lead mines in the country, and to establish the manufacture of saltpetre; a secret committee was also formed for the importation of powder and lead from the West Indies. Another cause of anxiety, and still the greater, existed in the insubordination of the army itself. At the close of 1775, the term of enlistment having in many cases expired, thousands had marched away to their homes, disgusted with the hardships and discomforts of military life. The enthusiasm of patriotism had died out in many breasts; whilst jealousies among the officers, selfishness and faithlessness, gave reason for an anxious looking forward to the future.

In the meantime, the petition of congress to the king, or "the Olive Branch," as it was called, and which had been intrusted to the care of Richard Penn, grandson of the proprietary, and long time resident in America, had been presented. This was the last hope of the colonists for reconciliation, and the tidings regarding it were anxiously waited for. The news came. His majesty deigned no reply; and in his opening speech to parliament accused the Americans of hostility and rebellion, and declared the object of their taking up arms to be the establishment of their own independence. In vain did the friends of America in the House of Commons earnestly advocate their cause; in vain did the merchants of London again remonstrate against coercive measures; a bill was passed declaring them rebels, prohibiting all trade with the thirteen colonies, and making their ships and goods and all persons trafficing with them, lawful prize. The same act authorised the impressment of the crews of all captured vessels for service in the royal navy. Commissioners of the crown were, however, empowered to pardon and remit from penalty all such colonies or individuals as by ready submission merited such favour. Furthermore, treaties were entered into by the British government with the Landgrave of Hesse Cassel and other German princes, for 17,000 men to be employed against the Americans. Twenty-five thousand additional English troops and a large fleet, abundantly supplied with provisions and military stores, were ordered to America.

These tidings convinced America that she had no longer anything to hope from the mother-country; sorrow, indignation and anxiety filled all hearts. These measures gave, however, by no means unqualified satisfaction, even in England. It is worth recording, as an instance of noble sacrifice to principle, that Lord Effingham, and the eldest son of the Earl of Chatham, threw up their commissions rather than act in this American war, which they considered so unjust. The office of commander-in-chief having been offered likewise to General Oglethorpe, the founder of Georgia, was declined by him naturally enough, and that rank was now held by General Howe.

Howe and his army spent their winter in Boston as best they could, suffering greatly from want of supplies. Fuel was obtained by pulling down houses, and the poorer class of inhabitants were sent out of the city, in order to decrease the consumption of food. Three companies, however, of "Loyal American Associators" were formed; and, spite of puritanism, balls and a theatre were got up by the British officers, and the largest of their meeting-houses was turned into a riding-school.

The growth of the British interests in the colonies was not, however, confined by any means to Boston. New York had long been suspected of a growing partisanship; and the government newspaper, "Rivington's Gazette," now became so offensive to the "Sons of Liberty," that some members of this distinguished body, to the number of seventy-five, rode at noonday to the suspected Tory newspaper-office, broke the presses, and carried off the type; a proceeding which was very satisfactory to the Whig portion of the public, both there and elsewhere. At Albany, too, on the

Hudson, at the extreme frontier of New York, the party of loyalists was becoming very formidable, under Sir John and Guy Johnson; the one the head of a colony of Scotch Highlanders, the other the Indian agent there. General Schuyler had already compelled these men to give their word of honour not to take up arms against America; nevertheless, Guy Johnson had withdrawn into Canada with a large body of Mohawks, under the celebrated chief Brandt, who had long served on the British side. Sir John Johnson also fled to Canada, where he too became a powerful adversary, at the head of his "Royal Greens"—two battalions raised from his tenants and dependants.

Nor was Lord Dunmore inactive in the South. Having carried off in his turn a printing-press, he printed and dispersed a proclamation declaring martial law, calling upon all who could bear arms to join him in the king's name, and offering freedom to all slaves and indented servants of rebels who would join his standard. By this means he gained a great number of adherents, amongst whom were many fugitive slaves, after which he took up his position near the town of Norfolk, where he was defeated by the colonial militia, and again driven to his ships, accompanied by great numbers of royalists. Norfolk was bombarded by him and finally burnt, which was a cause of great indignation in Virginia, this being one of the richest and largest of her towns. Great was the damage which for the next several months Dunmore effected on the coast, burning towns and houses, plundering plantations and carrying off slaves. Finally pursued, harassed, and suffering from want of provisions, he and his adherents were compelled to retire to St. Augustine in the West Indies.

CHAPTER V.
THE REVOLUTIONARY WAR (continued).— EXPULSION OF THE BRITISH FROM BOSTON.—DECLARATION OF INDEPENDENCE.—LOSS OF NEW YORK, ETC.

At the commencement of 1776, the American army under Washington was reduced to little more than 9,000 men. By the united strenuous efforts, however, of congress and the commander-in-chief, it was raised in February, to 14,000, and was moreover brought into a state of more perfect organisation.

His anxieties with regard to the army being now so far removed, Washington resolved to expel the enemy from Boston, which they had occupied so long. A portion of the British troops still being encamped on Bunker's Hill, where they had lain all the winter and suffered severely, Washington sent a strong detachment on the night of the 4th of March, when there was no moon, to take possession of Dorchester Heights, on the opposite side of the city, and which commanded it entirely. Carrying the necessary tools with them, the Americans silently ascended the heights, and before daylight had thrown up a strong redoubt. The sight of these works astonished General Howe the next morning, and he immediately made preparations for dislodging the Americans, plainly perceiving that unless this were done he must evacuate the city. A violent storm, however, rendered the embarkation of the troops impossible, and the Americans had thus time afforded for the completion of their works.

Before, however, an attack on either side was made, Washington received a proposal that he should allow the British troops to pass out unmolested, on condition that Howe left the town uninjured. Accordingly, on the 17th, the whole British force, amounting to 7,000, with about 2,000 marines, and accompanied by about 1,500 loyalists, quietly left the city and embarked for Halifax. Of the loyalists it must be remarked, that many of them were persons of large property, who thus sacrificed all for the maintenance of principle. Their conduct was admirable, though it met with no reward but misery and ruin. The embarkation occupied eleven days, and as the rear-guard was passing on board, Washington and his troops entered the city, with colours flying and drums beating, while the inhabitants knew not how to give sufficient evidence of their joy. Many fugitive families also now returned to their homes, and all Massachusetts rejoiced exceedingly. A medal was struck, by order of congress, to celebrate this event.

The British fleet sailed for Halifax, Washington being convinced that its ultimate destination would be New York, which, from its central situation and the great number and influential character of the British partisans there, would be an easy and important acquisition. No sooner, therefore, had he placed Boston in a suitable state of defence, than, leaving five regiments there, under the command of General Ward, the main body of the army was put in motion towards New York, which was intended to form his head-quarters. Washington arrived there in April.

The plans of the British for 1776 embraced the recovery of Canada, the reduction of the southern colonies, and the possession of New York. Canada, as we have said, was soon regained; and about the time when the first detachment of Washington's army reached New York, Sir Henry Clinton appeared off Sandy Hook, with a fleet from England. Finding, however, that any attempts were at this time impracticable, Clinton sailed to the south, and at Cape Fear River was joined by Sir Peter Parker, who had sailed from England with seven regiments on board.

A packet of intercepted letters to Governor Eden and others had given to congress information of the enemy's intended movements, and General Lee was appointed to the command in the southern provinces. All was in readiness, therefore, at Charleston, the point of attack. The most vigorous means had been used for this purpose throughout the Carolinas. Charleston was fortified, and a fort on Sullivan's Island at the entrance of Charleston harbour, built of palmetto wood, was garrisoned with about 400 men, and placed under command of Colonel Moultrie.

On the 4th of June, the British fleet appeared off the harbour, and after considerable delay, a strong force having landed under General Clinton, on Long Island, east of Sullivan's Island, the palmetto fort was subjected to a heavy bombardment; but the balls took little effect, sinking into the soft wood as into a bed of earth, and at the same time three ships, attempting to gain a position between Sullivan's Island and the shore, were stranded; two of them being afterwards got off with damage, and the third abandoned and burnt. Moultrie and his brave 400 Carolinians defended the fort with such cool and resolute courage, that after an engagement of eight hours, from eleven in the morning to seven in the evening, the British vessels retired with considerable damage and loss, the admiral himself being wounded, and the ex-governor, Lord Campbell, who fought on the flag-ship, mortally so. The loss of the garrison was only ten killed and twenty-two wounded. This fort has borne the name of Moultrie ever since.

One little incident of this attack may be related, as it proves the cool courage of the garrison. At one moment, after a heavy cannonade, the anxious Americans, who were watching the fight from the shore, beheld the American flag suddenly disappear from the ramparts. They now feared that it was all over, and expected to see the British ascend the parapets in triumph. But no! a moment afterwards and again the republican banner was floating on the walls. The fact was, that the flag-staff was shot away and the banner fell outside the fort, when, without a moment's hesitation, a sergeant of the name of Jasper leaped over the walls, and amid a shower of English bullets returned with the flag and hoisted it once more. Within a few days after this repulse, the British set sail, with all their troops on board, for the neighbourhood of New York.

Thirty-five thousand men, well supplied with provisions and all the necessary munitions of war, were now in array against the Americans. It was evident that Britain would remit none of her demands, and now aimed at nothing but the entire subjection of the colonies. For a long time, and even after they appeared in arms, had the colonies sincerely wished to preserve their allegiance to the monarch and attachment to the mother-country. Now, however, a change was rapidly taking place in their feelings; the sentiment of loyalty was giving way before republican principles and the desire for independence.

Early in this year, Thomas Paine, a recent emigrant to America and editor of the "Pennsylvania Magazine," published a pamphlet, called "Common Sense," which spoke out at once the secret sentiment of the people. It went direct to the point, showing in the simplest but strongest language the folly of keeping up the British connexion, and the absolute necessity which existed for separation. The cause of independence took, as it were, a definite form from this moment.

Early in May, in accordance with the growing sentiment of the public, congress, on the motion of John Adams, recommended to the colonies no longer to consider themselves as holding authority under Great Britain. "The exercise of all powers of government," said congress, soon after, "must be under authority from the people of the colonies, for the maintenance of internal peace, the defence of their lives, liberties and properties, against the hostile invasions and cruel depredations of their enemies."

Virginia had already acted on these principles, and other colonies soon followed the example. On June the 7th, Richard Henry Lee, of Virginia, at the request of his colleagues, formally introduced into congress a motion declaring that, "The United Colonies are, and ought to be, free and independent states; that they are absolved from all allegiance to the British crown; and that their political connexion with Great Britain is, and ought to be, totally dissolved." This important resolution, like all other proceedings of congress, was debated with closed doors, and finally was carried; though it encountered great opposition from some even of the warmest friends of American independence, but who now considered it premature. It was carried by a bare majority, and then left for final deliberation on the 1st of July.

In the meantime, a committee, consisting of Thomas Jefferson, Benjamin Franklin, John Adams, Roger Sherman, and R. R. Livingstone, had been appointed to draw up a declaration in accordance with the purport of the resolution. Each, it was agreed by the committee, should prepare such a statement as his own judgment might dictate; all should then be compared, and the most complete selected; or one be finally drawn up from all. The one prepared by Thomas Jefferson was at once, it is said, declared by his brother committeemen to be so superior to the rest that it was unanimously adopted, with but little alteration.

The Declaration of Independence was read in congress on the day appointed. Delegates for nine out of the thirteen colonies adopted it at once. New York declined to vote for want of instructions; Delaware was divided; the delegates of Pennsylvania were three for and four against it; of South Carolina one for and three against. On the 4th of July it received the votes of all, with the exception of New York, which, however, was formally given a few days afterwards.

Miss Bremer tells us, in her recent work on America, that everything in the hall where the Declaration of Independence was signed, is preserved as it was then to the present day. The green table still stands, around which the members of the government sat, and upon which this important document was signed. She relates also an amusing expression of Benjamin Franklin's on this occasion. Some of those present appeared doubtful and uncertain as to whether it were wise to sign, and were half-inclined to draw back. "Nay, gentlemen," said some one, wishing to insure their adherence, "let us not be divided, let us all hang together." "Yes," said Franklin, in his quiet way, "or else we shall all have to hang separately!" All laughed and all signed.

The Declaration of Independence for the whole Thirteen United States went abroad, and was received by demonstrations of joy. Public rejoicings were made, and the ensigns of royalty everywhere destroyed; leaden statues of the monarch being, wherever found, melted down for bullets. The legal position of the Tory party now became very serious. Many of these, being persons of high principle as well as of education and wealth, were exposed to the violence of political mobs, whose practices of tarring, feathering and carting, were disgraceful to the cause of liberty, of which they called themselves the supporters. As party-feeling in the course of the war grew more violent, the sufferings of the royalist party became extreme. The new state governments enforced obedience to their authority by severe penalties, confiscation of property, imprisonment, banishment, and finally death. As yet, however, they contented themselves with admonitions, fines, recognisances to keep the peace and prohibitions to go beyond certain bounds.[15]

Besides all these important measures in congress, it must be borne in mind that money had to be raised for the carrying on of the war. The United States congress had already an enormous debt, and again about £1,000,000 was issued in paper money.

Whilst the Declaration of Independence was occupying congress, General Howe arrived on June 25th from Halifax before Sandy Hook, just by New York, and on the 2nd of July took possession of Staten Island. On July 12th, Admiral, brother of General Howe, arrived from England with large reinforcements, and soon after, Sir Henry Clinton, with his fleet from the south. General Howe thus found himself at the head of 24,000 of the finest troops in Europe, well-appointed and supplied; while further reinforcements were expected daily, which would swell his numbers to 55,000.

As Washington had supposed, the intention of the British was to gain possession of New York, and having command of the Hudson river, open communication with Canada, and thus separate the eastern from the middle states and be able to carry the war into the interior; while Long Island, adjacent to New York, which abounded in grain and cattle, would afford subsistence to the army. By the middle of summer, as we have already seen, the American forces were driven out of Canada, and the northern frontier exposed to attack.

One of Washington's first measures, on taking up his quarters in New York, where the British party was strong, was to prevent any communication with the enemy's ships, or between the ex-governor Tryon, who had been for some time on board the Asia in the harbour, and his friends in the town. Nor were these precautions needless; among other plots discovered was one for seizing Washington, and conveying him on board a British ship, some of Washington's own soldiers having been corrupted for that purpose, one of whom was tried by court-martial and shot in consequence. The mayor also of the city was imprisoned for carrying on a correspondence with Tryon.

Although the force under Washington at this time amounted to 27,000 men, yet great numbers were again undisciplined militia, many invalids, and all very indifferently provided with arms. The really effective force amounted, perhaps, to 17,000. Among other distinguished men who now entered the American service was Thadeus Kosciusko, afterwards so distinguished in Poland, and who served during the whole war as an engineer.

Soon after the landing of the British army, the admiral, Lord Howe, who had brought with him from England authority to the royal governors "to grant pardon and exception from penalty of all such colonies or individuals as might by speedy submission merit that favour," sent a letter containing a statement of this authority, and an offer of pardon to all who would submit. This letter was directed to George Washington, Esq. Washington, however, declined receiving in his private capacity any communication from the enemies of his country; the style of the address was then changed to that of George Washington, etc., etc., etc., and it was requested that the offer of pardon contained in the letter might be made known as widely as possible. Congress ordered it to be published in every newspaper throughout the Union, "that everybody might see how Great Britain was insidiously endeavouring to amuse and disarm them;" and replied, that "not considering that their opposition to British tyranny was a crime, they therefore could not solicit pardon."

Nothing being gained by this attempt at conciliation, the British now proceeded to the prosecution of the war, which they were prepared to carry on with the utmost vigour. Washington, aware that the enemy would advance to New York by way of Long Island, had entrenched a portion of the American army, 9,000 strong, at Brooklyn, opposite New York, under General Greene. Greene, unfortunately, being taken dangerously ill, the command was transferred to Israel Putnam, who, being a stranger to the ground and unacquainted with the works, was not qualified for the command of so important a position.

On August 22nd, the English landed on the southern shore of Long Island, and advanced to within four miles of the American camp, between themselves and which stretched a range of wooded hills, through which ran two roads, while a third followed the shore at the western base of the hills. On the 27th, dividing their forces into three divisions, under Grant, Heisler and Clinton, the British silently advanced at night by these three several roads towards the American army. Early in the morning, Clinton, proceeding by the eastern road, having seized an important defile, which through carelessness had been left unguarded, descended with the morning light into the plain, and within sight of the American camp. In the meantime General Sullivan, who, on the first alarm of the British approach, had hastened out to meet them with a considerable force, had fallen in with Generals Grant and Heisler; whilst Clinton, who by this time was safe on the plain, hastened forward and threw himself between Sullivan's corps and the American camp. The moment Clinton's approach had been perceived, the Americans attempted a retreat, but it was too late. The English drove back upon Heisler's Hessians, and thus locked in between two hostile armies, some few managed to escape, but the greater number were killed or taken prisoners. It was a disastrous day. The true number of the Americans killed was never ascertained; about 1,000 were taken prisoners. The English lost only about 400. The victors, 15,000 strong, encamped directly opposite the American lines. Among the prisoners were Generals Sullivan, Stirling and Woodhull, late president of the provincial congress. This latter was taken the day after the battle, being surprised with a small party driving off cattle. He was wounded and treated with such cruel neglect that his wounds mortified and he died. The Tories of Long Island, who had been treated with severity, now retorted the same on the adverse party.[16]

This defeat was more disastrous even than the loss of so much life, in the effect which it produced on the American mind. The utmost doubt and depression prevailed, and again regiments which were enlisted only on a short term, quitted the service the moment it had expired, and even in some cases deserted before that was the case.

The British not following up their advantage immediately, Washington, aware that his position could not be maintained, withdrew silently to New York on the night of the 29th, greatly to the surprise and vexation of the enemy; who, however, had now the entire and undisputed possession of Long Island. A descent upon New York was the next object of the British commanders; but before this was attempted, another endeavour was made for compromise and accommodation. Howe sent over his prisoner, General Sullivan, to desire a conference for this purpose, offering an exchange of Generals Sullivan and Stirling for Generals Prescott and M'Donald, which took place; and a deputation, consisting of Benjamin Franklin, John Adams and Edward Rutledge, met the British commissioners on Staten Island; but no favourable result followed, the American deputies insisting that "the Associated Colonies should not accede to any peace or alliance but as free and independent states."

This attempt having again failed, the next movement was to enlist a loyalist force. Oliver Delaney, brother of a former governor of New York, and Courtlandt Skinner, late attorney-general of New Jersey, were commissioned to raise four battalions each; while Tryon, still claiming to be governor of New York, was appointed major-general. Landing a considerable force in the city of New York, Washington, on the 12th of September, removed his head-quarters to the heights of Harlem, seven miles above the city. The British fleet appeared in the Sound and sailed up each side of Manhattan, or New York Island, on which New York stands; a battery was erected, and while the attention of the Americans was diverted by the fire from Howe's ships stationed in the East River and the Hudson, he landed his troops at Bloomingdale, about five miles above the city and only two from the American camp. Troops had been stationed to guard this landing; but seeing now the advantage gained by the alacrity of the English, they fled panic-stricken, without even firing a gun, as did also two New England brigades, in company with Washington, who had come down to view the ground. Washington, thus left undefended, except by his immediate attendants, within eighty paces of the enemy, was so distressed and excited by their dastardly conduct, that he exclaimed, "Are these the men with whom I am to defend America?" His attendants turned his horse's head, and hurried him from the field.[17] The next day, a skirmish taking place, the Americans retrieved their character in some degree, though it was with the loss of two able officers.

The loyalists of New York received the British army with the utmost joy. A few nights after, a fire breaking out, which destroyed the largest church and about one-third of the city, this disaster was attributed to "the Sons of Liberty," some of whom, seized on suspicion by the British soldiers, were thrown into the flames. The fire, however, is supposed to have originated in accident.

The utmost depression prevailed in the American camp at Harlem. The favour of Heaven, it was feared, had deserted their cause. Anxiety, despondency and dread filled all hearts; and sickness, the necessary concomitant of such a state of mind, prevailed greatly. There were no proper hospitals; the sick lay in barns and sheds, and even in the open air under walls and fences. The army was wasting away by the expiration of service and desertion; few would enlist. It seemed as if ere long America must yield from the mere inability to sustain her army. Washington did his utmost to revive hope and courage, and also appealed to congress for aid, without which success was impossible. A bounty of twenty dollars was offered therefore on enlistment, and grants of land promised to the soldiers and officers. So far good; in the meantime, Washington was unwilling to risk a general engagement, and Howe also on his side not venturing to attack the American camp, satisfied himself by making a movement to gain Washington's rear, in order to cut off his connexion with the eastern states and thus prevent his receiving supplies from that quarter. For this purpose a portion of the royal troops was withdrawn from New York to Westchester, while three frigates were sent up the Hudson, to prevent any intercourse with New Jersey. Reinforcements were received by the British army.

Washington, to avoid being thus enclosed on all sides, crossed over with his army from New York Island, and took up his position along the western bank of the Bronx River, which separated him from the English, and so extending towards White Plains. On the 28th of October, a skirmish took place, in which the Americans were driven from their ground with considerable loss; immediately after which, Washington took up a much stronger position on the heights of North Castle, about five miles further northward.

Discontinuing the pursuit of Washington, Howe now turned his attention to the American posts on the Hudson, with the design of entering New Jersey. Aware of this intention, Washington crossed the Hudson with his army, and joined General Greene at Fort Lee, on the western bank of the Hudson, at the town of Hackensack in New Jersey, three miles only to the south-west of Fort Washington, where was a garrison of 3,000 men, and ten miles only from New York city. Scarcely, however, were these arrangements made, when Fort Washington was assaulted by a strong British force. The commander, Colonel Magaw, made a brave defence and the assailants lost 400 men in gaining the outworks; but no sooner were the British within the fort, than the garrison, to the number of 2,000, overcome with terror, refused to offer any resistance, and all, together with a great quantity of artillery, fell into the hands of the British.[18] Two days afterwards Lord Cornwallis crossed the Hudson with 6,000 men, against Fort Lee, which also surrendered with the loss of baggage and military stores.

Misfortune was the order of the day. Alarm and distrust increased; Washington and his daily diminishing army fled from point to point. The New York convention moved its sittings from one place to another, the members often sitting with arms in their hands to prevent surprise; when just at this disastrous crises, new alarm arose from the proposed rising of the Tories in aid of the British. Many suspected Tories, therefore, were seized, their property confiscated and themselves sent into Connecticut for safety. The gaols were full; so also were the churches, now employed as prisons, while numbers were kept on parole. These resolute measures effected their purpose; the Tory party yielded to a force which they were not yet strong enough to control, and deferred active co-operation with the British to a yet more favourable time.

On the last day of November, the American army amounted but to 3,000 men, and was then retreating into an open country at the commencement of winter, without tents, blankets, or intrenching tools, and but imperfectly clad. The prospect was hopeless in the extreme. The towns of Newark, New Brunswick, Princetown, and Trenton, all in New Jersey, were taken possession of by the British. Finally, Washington, on the 8th of December, crossed the Delaware, which was now the only barrier between the English and Philadelphia. The first state legislature of New Jersey, of which William Livingston was governor, like that of New York, had been driven, during these commotions, from one place to another; nor had their most urgent endeavours to call out a militia been availing, so depressed was the public mind.

Nor was the prospect more cheering in Pennsylvania. The hearts of many began to fail them; and saving for the energy of Mifflin and a few others, the American party in Philadelphia might have gradually melted away. But Israel Putnam had command of the city, and Mifflin put forth all his eloquence, and patriotism and courage still survived. In the meantime the disasters of the Americans were not ended. General Lee, an ambitious and conceited man, who ranked his own military experience as superior to that of the commander-in-chief, instead of hastening across the Hudson to join the main army, as Washington had earnestly requested him to do without loss of time, determined on a brilliant and independent achievement which should at once startle both English and Americans, and give him a great reputation. Lingering, therefore, among the hills of New Jersey while he decided what his great exploit should be, he lodged one night with a small guard at a house some little distance from his army, when he was surprised by a body of British cavalry sent there for the purpose, and carried prisoner to New York. The command of his troops falling on General Sullivan, the latter conducted them without further delay to join Washington, whose forces were thus increased to 7,000 men.

On the very day also on which Washington crossed the Delaware, a British squadron from New York, under command of Sir Peter Parker, took possession of Newport in Rhode Island, the second city in New England, the few troops stationed there abandoning the place without a blow for its defence. The American squadron, under Commodore Hopkins, was thus blocked up in Providence River, where it lay for a long time useless.

Having gained this important hold on the colonies both by land and sea, the Howes issued, as royal commissioners, a proclamation "commanding all insurgents to disband, and all political bodies to relinquish their assumed authority, granting sixty days within which to make this submission." On this, great numbers of wealthy persons, many of whom had already been active in the revolutionary movements, to the amount even of from two to three hundred a day, came in to make the required submission. The cause of American independence appeared hopeless, and would have been so had all the people been cowards and time-servers. But there were thousands of true hearts left within her yet. Congress, sitting at that time at Philadelphia, adjourned to Baltimore in Maryland, and Washington was invested for six months with unlimited powers. Authority was given him to raise sixteen battalions of infantry, in addition to those already voted, and to appoint officers; the bounty on enlistment was increased, as were also grants of land for service. He was also empowered to raise and equip 3,000 light horse, three regiments of artillery, and a corps of engineers; to call out the militia of the different states; to displace and appoint all officers under the rank of brigadier-general, and to fill up all vacancies. He was further authorised to take whatever he might require for the use of the army at his own price, and to arrest and confine all such as should refuse the continental money, a new trouble which had arisen, owing to the vast issue of paper money. The entire power was thus placed in the hands of Washington, and he was worthy of the confidence.

Christmas was now at hand, and gloom and despondency pervaded the American mind. The sixty days were passing on, and the timid and vacillating were giving in their adherence to the British, when Washington, as it were, rose up and girded his loins for action. Aware that the festivities of the season would be fully enjoyed in the British camp, he resolved to avail himself of the time for an unexpected attack, and selected the Hessians stationed at Trenton as its object. On Christmas-eve, therefore, he set out with 2,500 picked men and six pieces of artillery, intending to cross the Delaware nine miles below Trenton, while two other forces, under Generals Cadwallader and Irving, were to cross at other points at the same time. The river was full of floating masses of ice, and it was only after great difficulty and danger that the landing was effected by four o'clock in the morning, when, amid a heavy snow-storm, Washington's force advanced towards Trenton; the other bodies under Cadwallader and Irving not having been able to effect a landing at all.

It was eight o'clock when Washington reached Trenton, where, as he expected, the Hessians, fast asleep after a night's debauch, were easily surprised. Their commander was slain, and their artillery taken, together with a thousand prisoners. Of the Americans two only were killed, two frozen to death, and a few wounded, among whom was Lieutenant Monroe, afterwards president of the United States. Without waiting for any movement on the part of the British, whose forces so far outnumbered the Americans, Washington immediately re-crossed the Delaware, and entered Philadelphia in a sort of triumph with his prisoners.

This unexpected and brilliant achievement created an immediate reaction. Several regiments, whose term of enlistment was about expiring, agreed to serve six weeks longer, and militia from the adjoining provinces marched in. Nor was the effect on the British less striking. General Howe, astounded by this sudden movement in the depth of winter, in an enemy whom he considered already crushed, detained Lord Cornwallis, then just setting out for England, and despatched him with additional forces to New Jersey, to regain the ground which had been lost. Washington, in the meantime, knowing the importance of maintaining the advantage he had gained, re-crossed the Delaware, and established himself at Trenton, where reinforcements were ordered immediately to join him. On January 2nd, 1777, Lord Cornwallis, with the van of the British army, approached. On this, Washington withdrew to some high ground on the eastern bank of a small river which divides the town, and commenced to entrench himself. The British attempting to cross, a sharp cannonade ensued, which produced little effect on either side, when Cornwallis, thinking it most prudent to wait for reinforcements which he expected the next day, encamped for the night.

Washington knew that his position was a very hazardous one. It was a great risk to wait for a battle, with his 5,000 men, most of them militia, new to the camp, and that against a greatly superior and well-disciplined force. To re-cross the Delaware, then still more obstructed with floating ice, was equally dangerous, with the enemy behind him. With great sagacity and courage, therefore, he decided on a bold scheme, which fortunately was executed with equal courage and skill. This was no other than to attack the enemy's rear at Princetown, and, if possible, gain possession of his artillery and baggage.

Replenishing, therefore, his camp fires, and silently sending his own heavy baggage to Burlington, and leaving parties still busied at their entrenchments within hearing of the enemy, Washington marched with his army, about midnight, towards Princetown, where three British regiments had passed the night, two of which, marching out to join Cornwallis, were met and attacked about sunrise by the Americans. A sharp conflict took place, and the Americans were giving way, General Mercer, an officer of great promise, being mortally wounded, when Washington and his select corps came up, and the battle was renewed. One division of the British fled to New Brunswick, the rest rallied and continued their march to Trenton. About 400 of the British were killed and wounded; the American loss was somewhat less.

At dawn, Lord Cornwallis beheld the deserted camp of the Americans and heard the roar of the cannonade at Princetown, on which, discovering Washington's artifice, and fearful lest his military stores and baggage at New Brunswick should fall into his hands, he immediately put his army in motion, and reached Princetown when the Americans were about to leave it. Again was Washington in great danger. "His troops," says Hildreth, "were exhausted; all had been one night without sleep, and some of them longer; many had no blankets; others were barefoot; all were very thinly clad." Under these circumstances the attack on New Brunswick was abandoned, and Washington retired to strong winter-quarters at Morristown. There he remained till spring, having, in fact, repossessed himself, in the most masterly manner, of New Jersey. General Putnam was stationed at Princetown, and other officers at various places, and skirmishes went on continually, in which the Americans were mostly successful, being eagerly joined by the inhabitants, who had many wrongs and ravages to complain of. The British, in fact, suffered greatly through the winter, from want of forage and fresh provisions.

The effect of Washington's rapid successes in the Jerseys was like a succession of electric shocks through the states; and even to this day it is said, when any unexpected and exciting intelligence is about to be given, the phrase "Great news from the Jerseys!" is made use of.

"The recovery of the Jerseys," to use again the words of the able historian Hildreth, "by the fragments of a defeated army, which had seemed just before on the point of dissolution, gained Washington a high reputation, not only at home, but in Europe, where the progress of the campaign had been watched with great interest, and where the disastrous loss of New York and the retreat through the Jerseys had given the impression that America would not be able to maintain her independence. The recovery of the Jerseys created a reaction. The American general was extolled as a Fabius, whose prudence availed his country no less than his valour. At home, also, these successes had the best effect. The recruiting service, which before had been almost at a stand, began to revive, and considerable progress was again made in organising the new army."

The powers with which congress had invested the commander-in-chief enabled him to make many important changes and provisions for the well-being of his troops. For instance, the whole hospital department, which had been very inefficiently filled, was now reorganised; and in order to prevent the visitation of small-pox, which had proved hitherto a fatal scourge in the army, every recruit was properly inoculated before entering the service. An exchange of prisoners took place also at this time, though the British at first refused, on the plea that the Americans were rebels. The number of prisoners amounted to about 5,000 in the hands of the British, and 3,000 in those of the Americans. Great indignation was excited in consequence of the condition to which, it was discovered, the Americans taken at Long Island and Fort Washington were reduced by the hardships of their confinement. They were placed in the custody of the New York Tory party, by whom they had been so cruelly treated that many had died, and the rest were so emaciated and feeble that Washington refused to return an equal number of well-conditioned Hessians and British.

Congress, in the meantime, was again sitting at Philadelphia, and wiser heads or braver hearts never met for a country's need. The business which occupied them was of the most momentous character.

Though Hopkins and his squadron were blocked up at Providence, privateering had been carried on, principally by New England frigates, to a great extent. The homeward-bound British ships from the West Indies offered rich prizes, and in the year just concluded no less than 350 British ships had been captured. A new foreign trade had also been opened with France, Spain and Holland, principally by way of the West Indies; and though great risk attended it, still it was the successful commencement of the great American trade; and the national flag of thirteen stars and stripes, as appointed by congress, was now first hoisted in this maritime service.

By no European nation was the progress of the war of independence in America watched with more interest than by France, who still was smarting under the loss of her American possessions; hence the American privateer found ever a ready sale for his prizes in the French ports; and armed French vessels, sailing under American commissions, were secretly fitted out. Early in the struggle with the mother-country, the colonies had avowed their reliance on foreign aid, if necessary; and at the commencement of the preceding year, Silas Deane, member of congress for Connecticut, had gone to Paris, ostensibly as a private merchant, but, in fact, to negotiate with France for the supply of arms and ammunition.

After the Declaration of Independence, however, Benjamin Franklin was openly sent to Paris, and other persons to different European courts, for the same purpose. "The distinguished talents, high reputation, and great personal popularity of Dr. Franklin," says Willson, "were highly successful in increasing the general enthusiasm which began to be felt in behalf of the Americans." His efforts were in the end successful; and although France delayed for a while the recognition of American independence, yet she began to act with less reserve, and by lending assistance in various ways— by loans, gifts, supplies of arms, provisions and clothing—she materially aided the Americans. The tardy action, however, of the French court was outdone by the general zeal of the nation. Numerous volunteers, the most eminent of whom was the young Marquis de Lafayette, offered to risk their fortunes and bear arms in the cause of American liberty. Lafayette fitted out a vessel at his own expense, and in the spring of 1777 arrived in America. He at first enlisted as a volunteer in Washington's army, declining all pay for his services; but congress soon after bestowed upon him the appointment of major-general.

While all these important affairs were going on in the north, the western frontier of the Carolinas and Georgia was again visited by Indian warfare, which was only concluded by the Cherokees ceding a large portion of territory. About the same time, the newly-attempted colony of Transylvania quietly gave up its plans of independent existence and became a portion of

Virginia, the new county of Kentucky including the whole of the present state of that name.

CHAPTER VI.
THE REVOLUTIONARY WAR (continued), 1777.

The fear of the invasion of Canada by the British, had, as we have already seen, led the Americans to make a disastrous attempt at the conquest of that province. The so-much-feared invasion was now at hand. In the meantime, as the spring of 1777 advanced, although as yet the main armies were inactive, various little attacks and reprisals were made. An armament sent up the Hudson by Howe for that purpose destroyed the military stores of the Americans at Peekskill, and General Lincoln, stationed at Boundbrook in New Jersey, was surprised by Lord Cornwallis, and escaped only with the loss of a considerable portion of his baggage and about sixty lives. A few days afterwards, Tryon, late governor of New York, at the head of 2,000 men, landed in Connecticut and advanced to Danbury, an inland town, where a large quantity of provisions was collected; having destroyed these, set fire to the town, and committed various acts of atrocity, he departed as rapidly as he had come. Arnold and Wooster, however, pursued him at the head of militia, hastily collected for that purpose, and three several attacks were made, in which the veteran and greatly respected Wooster was killed and Arnold had two horses shot under him. Tryon made good his escape with a loss in killed, wounded, and prisoners, of about 300; and congress, in acknowledgment of Arnold's bravery, presented him with a horse fully caparisoned, and raised him to the rank of major-general. In return, a small party of Americans under Colonel Meigs landed on Long Island, destroyed twelve vessels, and took a large quantity of provisions and forage collected at Sag Harbour, and carried off ninety prisoners, without himself losing a single man. Another little triumph of the Americans is worth recording. General Prescott, who had been taken prisoner at Montreal, two years before, when Governor Carleton made his escape, now being stationed at Newport in Rhode Island, irritated the Americans no little by offering a reward for the capture of Arnold; on which Arnold, in return, offered half the amount for the capture of Prescott. Accordingly, it being presently ascertained that Prescott frequented without precaution a country-house near the town, a party of forty men under one Colonel Barton set out with the intention of carrying him off, landed at night on the island, entered the house, and taking the general from his bed, hurried away with their prize. Until now the Americans had not been able to ransom their General Lee, who had been taken much in the same manner, and the two officers were shortly exchanged.

In the meantime Washington remained with his army at Morristown, waiting with great anxiety the development of the enemy's plans of operation, and increasing his own strength by the arrival of recruits, who still came in only slowly. The plans of the British general appeared for a long time uncertain, whether to march directly upon Philadelphia or to co-operate with Burgoyne, who had now assumed the command in Canada. In the north, the American army was so very feeble, that it was feared lest Ticonderoga, almost the sole remains of the American conquests in that quarter, might be seized by a sudden movement from Canada over the ice. The service in the north was indeed so unpopular, that a species of conscription was obliged to be resorted to in order to fill up the regiments. Indeed the reluctance to serve was felt so generally throughout the northern provinces, that the prohibition against the enlistment of negro-slaves was removed, and now recruits of any colour were joyfully received, and many negro-slaves gained their freedom in this manner. In the south, also, indented servants enlisting were declared to be freemen.

As spring came on, General Burgoyne, who had served in Canada under Governor Carleton, and who had gone to England for the purpose of urging upon parliament the reduction of America by a powerful descent upon the colonies by the way of Lake Champlain and the Hudson, returned with a large army and military stores for that purpose.

GENERAL BURGOYNE AND THE INDIANS.

On the 16th of June, Burgoyne, at the head of an army of nearly 10,000 men, British and German, with a great number of Canadians and Indians, set forth on his expedition. His first encampment was on the western shore of Lake Champlain, near Crown Point, where he met the Six Nations in council, and was joined by about 400 of those powerful warriors. Burgoyne, however, so little understood the character of the red men, that he addressed them in a very pompous speech, endeavouring to induce them to alter their irregular mode of warfare. To just as little purpose was the proclamation which he issued at the same time, in an equally pompous manner, in which, after demonstrating his own power and that of the British, he threatened the colonists with extermination, before the fury of the savage Indian, if they persisted in resisting his arms.

Burgoyne's plan of operation was, after taking Ticonderoga, to advance upon Albany on the Hudson, where he would be met by Colonel St. Leger, who, with 2,000 men, chiefly Canadians and Indians, was to proceed by way of Oswego, against Fort Schuyler or Stanwix, and so gain the same point, after which both armies were to join General Clinton at New York.

Two days after Burgoyne had published his formidable proclamation, he appeared before Ticonderoga, then garrisoned by General St. Clair with about 3,000 men. Spite of all the labour and expense which had been bestowed on this fort, one important circumstance had been most singularly overlooked. The fort was commanded by a neighbouring height, called Mount Defiance, which being considered inaccessible, had been left undefended. Burgoyne, however, at once perceiving the advantage to be obtained by the possession of this height, lost no time in preparing to gain it, and three days after he had made his appearance, his artillery was placed on the summit. St. Clair seeing that no chance remained for himself and his troops, resolved upon immediate evacuation. The baggage and stores, under the convoy of the last remains of the American flotilla, were secretly despatched down to Skeensborough, and the troops also in two divisions, the one under St. Clair, the other, which left two hours later, under Colonel Francis, commenced their retreat at the dead of night, but were discovered by the enemy owing to the accidental burning of a building on an adjoining height. The next morning, therefore, the rear division was overtaken by General Fraser at the head of a British troop, near Hubbardton, where an engagement took place, in which the Americans were routed, and flying before the enemy, spread throughout the adjoining country the terror of the British arms. One thousand Americans were killed, wounded and taken prisoners on this disastrous day, among the former of whom was Colonel Francis. Nor was this all; General Reidesel with a corps of Germans pursued and overtook the American stores and baggage, which fell into his hands; and the garrison of Skeensborough, on learning this melancholy intelligence and of the approach of Burgoyne, set fire to the works, and fled to Fort Anne, half-way between them and the Hudson. Pursuit followed; a skirmish took place, and in the infectious terror of the time, having set fire to the works of Fort Anne, they fled to Fort Edward, the head-quarters of General Schuyler. At this same point, also, arrived St. Clair, who with his division had been wandering about for seven days. Thus, after defeat and flight, were assembled the whole force of the American northern army, amounting only to 5,000 men, many of whom were only hastily-summoned militia, wholly unorganised, while of ammunition there was great scarcity.

Again despondency and gloom overspread the American mind. The successes of Burgoyne came, says Hildreth, like a thunderclap on congress. "We shall never be able to defend a fort," wrote John Adams, "till we shoot a general." Disasters, the inevitable result of weakness, were attributed to the incapacity or cowardice of the officers. The New England prejudice against Schuyler revived, and all the northern generals in fact were recalled; and but for the interference of Washington, the northern army must have been disbanded for want of officers. Schuyler, in the meantime, was doing the best that he could under existing circumstances. Before leaving the various positions, he took every means to annoy and impede the movements of the enemy, obstructing navigation, breaking up roads and bridges, and closing up every passable defile by felling trees on either side, which, interlacing their branches in the fall, formed an almost insuperable barrier. Schuyler, in whom, however, Washington never lost confidence, was superseded, and Gates was appointed by congress to take his place. Reinforcements also were sent up; Daniel Morgan with his rifle corps, the impetuous and bold Arnold and Lincoln, who was a great favourite with the Massachusetts men. Kosciusko was also in the army as its principal engineer.

Burgoyne, making himself sure of speedily establishing the royal power in the north, called a convention by proclamation for concerting measures for this purpose. A circumstance connected with the history of Vermont, as an infant state, gave him additional hopes of the popular adhesion in this quarter. Vermont having organised herself into an independent state, had solicited admission into the union as such, and been refused, through the influence of New York, who claimed that country as a portion of her territory. Burgoyne was, however, disappointed in his hopes; Vermont entertained no feelings of animosity; and Schuyler, in return, published his counter-proclamation, threatening the punishment of traitors to all who foreswore their allegiance to American independence.

Burgoyne, not without great difficulty, at length reached the Hudson, to the great joy of the British army; and Schuyler, unable to face him, retreated to Saratoga, where the tidings of new disasters soon reached him. Burgoyne had several weeks before despatched Colonel St. Leger, with Sir John Johnson and his Royal Greens, together with a body of Canadian rangers, and the formidable Brandt and his savages, to harass the western frontier of New York. Fort Schuyler, commanded by Colonels Gansevoost and Willett, was attacked, and General Herkimer, hastening to his relief with militia, which he had raised for that purpose, fell into an ambush near the fort and was mortally wounded, besides losing 400 men, amongst whom were many of the leading patriots of that part of the country. This was sad news for Schuyler, and as the north-west abounded in Tories, it was necessary, if possible, to relieve Fort Schuyler, so as to prevent its falling into the hands of the enemy, which would cause, it was apprehended, a general disaffection. Arnold volunteered to undertake this perilous service, and Schuyler, having despatched him with three regiments, withdrew from Saratoga to the islands at the confluence of the Mohawk and Hudson rivers.

Although success had followed the British, and Burgoyne was in possession of so many strong posts, and had command of Lakes Champlain and George, and great amount of stores and provisions lay at Fort George for his use, yet the means of transport were so difficult, that the army was reduced to the greatest straits. To obtain immediate supplies, therefore, he despatched Colonel Baum, a German officer of rank, with 500 men, together with a body of Canadians and Indians, to seize a quantity of provisions which the Americans had stored at Bennington. There was at this time at Bennington, under the command of Colonel Stark, a corps of New Hampshire militia, raised by a merchant of Portsmouth, named Langdon, on the news of the loss of Ticonderoga. As soon as Stark heard of the attack which was to be made on the stores, he sent off for Seth Warner's Green Mountain Boys, his own force having also been strengthened by volunteers and fugitives from the defeat at Hubbardton. Baum, seeing Stark prepared for him, entrenched himself about six miles from Bennington, intending to make an attack the following day. But violent rain came on, and both Stark and Baum deferred any movement, both hoping for reinforcements, Baum from Colonel Breyman, who was marching to his assistance, and Stark from the Green Mountain Boys, who were hourly expected. But the violence of the weather kept both back, and the next morning, Stark, at the head of his New Hampshire men, marched out to meet the enemy. The address of Stark to his men is worthy of being remembered. "There they are;" said he, pointing to the British; "there they are! We must beat them, my boys, or Molly Stark will be a widow this night!"

The assault was vigorous, and after a desperate fight of about two hours the intrenchments were carried, Baum was killed, and the Germans were mostly slain or taken prisoners, and the Indians and Canadians fled to the woods. Hardly, however, was the victory gained, when Breyman and his reinforcements appeared, and the fight was renewed, Seth Warner and his brave Boys having fortunately appeared at the same moment on the other side. The battle lasted till dark, and then Breyman fled, leaving his baggage and artillery behind him. The British lost about 600, the greater number however being taken prisoners, besides 1,000 stand of arms and four pieces of artillery. The American loss was merely fourteen killed and forty-two wounded.

This defeat was the turning point in the career of the British; the tidings dispirited and embarrassed them, and for the first time showed their grand plan of dividing the northern from the southern provinces to be doubtful. The effect on the Americans was still greater; hope and confidence woke anew, and the worthy Schuyler might soon have regained his character, had not Gates appeared a few days afterwards to assume the command. Schuyler, however, like a true patriot, who is able to sink self-interest in the well-being of his country, removed merely to Albany, where he continued to render every possible assistance to the carrying on of the campaign. Gates was also immediately joined by Daniel Morgan and his riflemen, and by a New Hampshire regiment.

The tide had now completely turned. Not only had Stark's victory revived the hopes of the Americans, but the cruelties and treacheries of Burgoyne's Indian allies had roused the popular indignation, and the tragical fate of a young woman, while it called forth universal sympathy, completed the measure of hatred which was given to the British. Jenny M'Crea, a young lady of Fort Edward, the daughter of a loyalist family, and betrothed to a loyalist officer, was murdered in the woods by the Indian guard whom her lover had appointed to conduct her to a place of safety, and whose fidelity he believed secured by a promised reward. On the road, however, it appeared that the Indians quarrelled respecting this reward, and the poor girl was murdered in the dispute, her bloody scalp with its long tresses being the Indian signal to the lover of the cruel fate of his mistress. Such was Burgoyne's version of this tragedy; but besides the daughter, the whole family was murdered, they being carried off to the woods, murdered and scalped in a most barbarous manner. These cruel individual instances, which every man and woman would take home to themselves, roused the whole northern provinces. The death of Jenny M'Crea sent out hundreds of volunteers.

The Indians, also, now began to desert the camp of the British in great numbers; and Arnold, on his way to the relief of Fort Schuyler, having spread everywhere exaggerated accounts of his numbers, St. Leger fled from his newly-acquired possession, leaving his tents standing and his stores and baggage behind him.

The American army now amounted to upwards of 5,000, and Gates left his camp on the Islands, and took up his position on Behmus Heights at Stillwater, on the west bank of the Hudson, close to the river. With great labour and difficulty Burgoyne had brought down from the depôt on Lake St. George thirty days' provisions for his troops, and now, therefore, he crossed the Hudson by a bridge of boats, and encamped on the 14th of September at Saratoga. On the 19th, skirmishing began between the advanced parties; reinforcements were sent in by the two armies as the fortunes of the combat seemed to vary, till at length the battle became general. The fighting continued furiously and without intermission, till night at length made it impossible to distinguish friend from foe. Victory had changed sides many times during the fight; but the British retired, and left the Americans masters of the field. Both claimed the victory, but the loss of the British was the greater.

Two days before the battle of Stillwater, a considerable advantage had also been gained by a party of Lincoln's militia, who surprised the posts at the outlet of Lake George, took a considerable number of prisoners and armed vessels; after which, in concert with another party, they advanced to Ticonderoga. Burgoyne's position thus became perilous and difficult in the extreme. His provisions and forage were diminishing; his allies were daily deserting; and if he retreated, the Americans, flushed with what was vaunted as a great victory, were in his rear. In the midst of this anxiety one hope remained, which was communicated by a letter in cypher, that troops would be sent by Clinton from New York to make a diversion on the Hudson, and thus the alarming position of Burgoyne be relieved. The present time must, however, be cared for. The two camps were within a short distance of each other, and skirmishes were of daily occurrence; and at length, on October 7th, a battle took place—the famous battle of Saratoga. Morgan and his riflemen distinguished themselves early in the combat. "Gates," says Hildreth, "did not appear on the field; but Arnold, though without any regular command, took, as usual, a leading part. He seemed under the impulse of some extraordinary excitement, riding at full speed, issuing orders and cheering on the men." The battle was fought with the utmost bravery on both sides, until night again put an end to the fighting. The Americans slept on their arms, intending to renew the combat with the morning; their advantages so far were decisive. Of the British, 400 men were killed, wounded, or taken prisoners; tents, ammunition and artillery, fell into the hands of the Americans. Next morning the British commander was found to have quietly retired during the night, and to be drawn up in order of battle on some high ground near.

Gates was too wary to venture another battle with the enemy posted to so much advantage, and made preparations, therefore, for enclosing him as he lay, which Burgoyne perceiving, prepared for retreat. In the meantime skirmishing went on; General Lincoln was severely wounded on the American side, and General Fraser, a British officer of high rank, was killed, and buried on the hill which bears his name. The Baroness de Reidesel, who, with her young children, followed the camp, and whose quarters were turned into a sort of hospital for the wounded officers, has left a pathetic account of the horrors of that day, and the retreat which followed.[19]

Burgoyne fell back upon Saratoga, abandoning his sick and wounded amid drenching rain; the bridges were broken down, the rivers were swollen, and though the distance was but six miles, this retreat consumed the whole day. His situation was now lamentable in the extreme. He heard nothing from New York of the expected aid; he was in the midst of a hostile country hemmed in by an enemy whose forces, now amounting to 12,000 men, were daily increasing, while his had melted away to less than one-half of that number, nor could even these be depended upon. His boats laden with provisions were taken, and there remained now but a three days' supply. In this terrible and unlooked-for emergency, a council of war was called, to which every officer was summoned, and a treaty of capitulation was agreed upon.

Gates demanded unconditional surrender, but Burgoyne would not consent to this. And it being feared that the long-expected diversion from New York should be made, and thus change again the fortunes of the day, Gates did not hesitate long as to terms. On the 27th of October, Burgoyne surrendered his army as prisoners of war, it being agreed that on laying down their arms they should be conducted to Boston, thence to embark for England under condition of not again serving against the United States. The prisoners included in this capitulation amounted to 5,642, the previous losses being upwards of 4,000. There fell also into the hands of the Americans thirty-five brass field-pieces and 5,000 muskets, besides baggage and camp equipage. The colours of the German regiments were preserved by being cut from their staves, rolled up, and stowed away in the baggage of Madame Reidesel.

The British troops thus subjected to humiliation were, however, treated with great delicacy by the Americans; their officers, and Burgoyne in particular, receiving many kind attentions. Burgoyne was entertained with distinguished hospitality by General Schuyler, although his country-house and much of his property had been destroyed by order of the British commander.

As soon as the surrender of Burgoyne was known, the British garrison at Ticonderoga destroyed the works and retired to Canada. Clinton, with Tryon and his Tory forces, on the same intelligence, dismantled the forts on the Hudson, and having burnt every house within their reach, and done all the damage in their power, returned to New York. Thus ended an enterprise from which the British had hoped and the Americans feared so much, and its results were in the highest degree advantageous to the cause of the republicans. The enemy was not only weakened and humiliated, a large and welcome supply of arms and stores obtained, but the Americans rose greatly in the estimation of foreign nations, who watched the contest with anxious and eager attention.

The joy of the Americans, especially those of the Northern States, was almost beyond bounds, and, as might be expected, the military reputation of Gates stood very high—nay, even for the time, outshone that of Washington, whose loss of Philadelphia, of which we have yet to speak, was placed unfavourably beside the surrender of a whole British army. The good General Schuyler, who had been superseded by the prosperous Gates, was acquitted with the highest honour after strict investigation of his military conduct. He resigned his commission in the army, but still continued to serve his country no less zealously as a member of congress.

We must now return to Washington at Philadelphia, whom we left in anxious uncertainty as to the intentions of the British general, whether he would march upon Philadelphia according to former plans, or seize upon the passes of the Hudson, and carrying up his large forces to the north, co-operate with Burgoyne in that quarter. In order, however, to be prepared for either of these movements, a large camp was formed under General Arnold on the western bank of the Delaware; and towards the end of May, Washington, with about 8,000 men, moved to Middlebrook, ten miles from Princetown, where he might have a better opportunity of watching and interrupting the movements of the enemy.

Howe, whose real intention was to bring on a general engagement with Washington, in which case he calculated on certain victory, marched out from New Brunswick, where he had concentrated his army, after leaving his winter-quarters at New York. Finding, however, the position of Washington too strong, he fell back to Amboy, threw a bridge across to Staten Island, and sent over his heavy baggage and some of his troops. Washington, deceived by this manœuvre, ordered his troops out in pursuit, and himself moved to Quibbleton. This was what Howe had in view, and now suddenly turning round, he attempted to gain the strong ground which the American commander had left; but Washington, perceiving the drift of the enemy, made a hasty retreat to his old position, not, however, without some loss both of men and artillery. Finding his plans unsuccessful, Howe finally on the 30th of June withdrew with all his troops to Staten Island, leaving Washington in undisturbed possession of New Jersey.

Again Washington knew not the intentions of the British either by land or water. A fleet of transports, he knew, was fitting out in New York harbour, but its destination was unknown. At length, on the 23rd of July, the fleet, under command of Admiral Howe, set sail northward with troops to the amount of 18,000 on board, and Washington, suspecting that its operations would be in that quarter, marched also in the same direction. By the end of July, however, it was heard of as approaching Cape May, and Washington then returned to the Delaware. After still continued uncertainty as to its object, the fleet at length sailed up the Chesapeake, and on the 25th of August the troops landed near the head of Elk River in Maryland, fifty miles south-west of Philadelphia. While the unascertained intentions of the British left Washington unemployed, other minor objects engaged his attention. An expedition was made against the loyalists of Staten Island, who were a great annoyance to the inhabitants of New Jersey, against whom they made armed incursions, plundering their dwellings and driving off their cattle. The non-combatant Quakers also of Pennsylvania and New Jersey became a cause of anxiety, and were subjected to punishment. It happened that the papers and advices of the two several yearly meetings of this body came in possession of the leaders of the expedition against Staten Island. These being examined by the Council of Philadelphia, were found to contain matter of a treasonable character, and eleven wealthy and leading Quakers of Philadelphia, among whom was the father of the president of the council, were arrested. So great indeed was the suspicion excited by the Quaker loyalty, that it was deemed necessary not only to send these eleven but various other leading men, John Penn, the late governor, and Benjamin Chud, the late chief justice, being of the number, prisoners to Fredricksburg in Virginia. So alarming indeed was this detected treason considered to be, that congress recommended every state to arrest all persons, Quakers or others, who had in any way evinced a disposition inimical to the cause of America, also to seize the papers of the Quaker yearly meetings, and transmit the political portion of their contents to congress.

Howe, on landing in Maryland, published as usual his offer of pardon to all who would submit at once to the British sway, and security to such as remained peaceably at home; after which he commenced his march towards Philadelphia. Washington awaited his approach at Wilmington, under circumstances, as the historian[20] remarks, much less favourable than those which enabled the northern army so successfully to repel the contemporaneous advance of Burgoyne. There was no New England here to pour in her militia; no bold forces of New Hampshire and the young

Vermont to come down like a mountain torrent; Pennsylvania was impelled by no general zeal either of patriotism or liberty; the greater part of the Quakers, a wealthy and influential body, were, if not strongly tinged by British loyalty, at all events neutral. The militia of Pennsylvania, even at this moment, when the enemy was advancing on the capital, amounted barely to 3,000. Washington's force was greatly inferior to that of the enemy, not much exceeding 11,000 men. The militia of Maryland and Virginia it is true, had been called out to his aid, but as yet had not arrived. Nevertheless, he now resolved upon a battle, and after considerable manœuvring and skirmishing, on Sept. 10th he crossed the Brandywine River, a shallow stream, on the opposite side of which the enemy was encamped, and awaited the event of the next day.

Early on the morning of the 11th, the British force crossed the Brandywine in two columns. The Hessians, under General Kniphausen, having commenced a spirited attack, the intention being to deceive the Americans by the idea that no other attack was intended, whilst Lord Cornwallis, with a still larger force, having made a circuitous march, crossed the Brandywine at another point, with the design of falling on the American rear. Aware of this movement only too late, and confused by contradictory statements, General Sullivan, who had been despatched by Washington to interrupt it, was soon driven back and the fortunes of the day terminated wholly in favour of the British. The Americans retreated during the night, and the next day reached Philadelphia, their loss in the battle being above 1,000 in killed, wounded and prisoners, while the loss of the British was not above half that number. Among the officers who suffered and distinguished themselves on the American side were three foreigners—La Fayette who was wounded in the leg while attempting to rally the retreating troops; the Baron St. Ovary was taken prisoner; and Count Pulaski, a Pole, who had entered the army as a volunteer, displayed so much courage and conduct that he was rewarded by congress a few days afterwards with the rank of brigadier-general and command of the horse.

The day after the battle, a party of the enemy entered Wilmington and took prisoner the governor of Delaware, and seized beside a considerable amount of property, both public and private.

After a few days' rest, Washington resolved to hazard another battle, and accordingly, on the 16th, re-crossed the Schuylkill, and marched against the British at Goshen, twenty miles from Philadelphia; but violent rain coming on after the action had commenced and the powder in the defective cartridge-boxes of the Americans becoming wet and unfit for use, he was obliged to recall his men and retire. In another instance also, were they unfortunate on the same day. Washington had left Colonel Wayne, with a detachment of 1,500 men, concealed in a wood to annoy the rear of the

British, tidings of whom being carried to the British commander by some of the numerous disaffected in the neighbourhood, they were surprised by a strong detachment sent out for that purpose, and compelled to fly with the loss of 300 men; the British lost but seven.

On the 22nd, Howe crossed the Schuylkill, lower down than Washington had done, and thus, to the infinite annoyance of the American commander, placed himself between him and Philadelphia. Nothing, says Hildreth, could now save the city but a battle and victory. Washington's troops, inferior in number, had been fatigued and harassed by their recent marches. They were sadly deficient in shoes and clothing; their arms were bad; while the irregular supplies consequent on recent changes in the commissary department, and the increasing financial embarrassments of congress, had sometimes even deprived them of food. Under these circumstances it seemed almost too hazardous to risk a battle. The necessity of abandoning Philadelphia had already been foreseen; the hospitals, magazines and public stores had been removed; congress had adjourned to Lancaster, having first invested Washington with the same unlimited powers which had been given to him on a former occasion. Washington entrusted to the young Hamilton, one of his aides-de-camp, the important office of obtaining a supply of shoes, blankets, and clothing for his army from Philadelphia, before the city passed into the hands of the enemy, which was accordingly done.

On the 25th of September, Howe entered Philadelphia, where he was received with a warm welcome by many; Duche, the late chaplain of congress, writing to Washington and advising him "to give up the ungodly cause in which he was engaged." Four regiments were quartered in the city, and the main army encamped at Germantown, ten miles distant.

Washington in the meantime passed down the Schuylkill, and encamped with his army at Shippack Creek, eleven miles from Germantown, where he was at length joined by the Maryland militia, though diminished to half its promised amount by desertion. Having learnt that a part of the British army had been sent to the Delaware, Washington resolved on attacking the remainder at Germantown, and accordingly, on the evening of the 3rd of October, set out for that purpose, and succeeded in surprising the British early the next morning. For some time everything went well for the Americans, when a heavy fog coming on, and the British availing themselves of the cover of a stone house, the fortune of the day turned. The darkness was such that friend could not be distinguished from foe; the Americans fell into confusion; the ammunition of some corps was expended, and others, seized with a panic, fled. That which had promised to be a victory was changed into defeat. The American loss was about

1,000, 400 of whom were taken prisoners; among the killed was General Nash, of North Carolina. The British lost about half that number.

Washington retired about twenty miles inland, where he received reinforcements from the north with the welcome news of Burgoyne's surrender, and additional militia from Maryland and Virginia, after which he returned to his old quarters at Shippack Creek. Howe also removed from Germantown to Philadelphia. Instead of pursuing Washington, shortness of provisions rendered it necessary for Howe to open the navigation of the Delaware, the command of which was held by Forts Mifflin and Mercer, still in the hands of the Americans, and which prevented any communication between the British army and their fleet then lying in Delaware Bay. This measure indeed was absolutely necessary, as but little subsistence could be obtained from the adjacent country, for although considerable defection prevailed throughout Pennsylvania, still the presence of the American army formed a great check; and the late edict of congress, which Washington was there to enforce, and which rendered liable to the punishment of death any person daring to afford supplies to the British, rendered help from the country impossible. "The British commander," said Dr. Franklin, wittily, "now discovered that instead of taking Philadelphia, Philadelphia had taken him."

Forts Mifflin and Mercer were therefore attacked on the 22nd of October. Fort Mercer, which was garrisoned by somewhat less than 500 men, under the quaker commander Nathaniel Greene, was assailed by General Count Donop, at the head of 2,000 Hessian grenadiers, who, after having succeeded in taking the outworks were repulsed with great loss, Donop himself being mortally wounded. The attack on Fort Mifflin, which was made by shipping, was at first equally unsuccessful, two of the enemy's ships being destroyed in the attempt. Every effort was now made to strengthen the defences of both forts, but in proportion as the efforts on the one hand increased, so did those on the other; and finally, after the utmost bravery had been displayed, Fort Mifflin, which was almost battered to pieces by the fire of the enemy, was abandoned in the night by its garrison who withdrew to Fort Mercer, which was also evacuated on the 16th of November, before the accumulated force of the British. With the loss of those forts, the American shipping was reduced to great danger. Some few, under the cover of night, succeeded in ascending the river above Philadelphia; and seventeen were burnt by their crews that they might not fall into the hands of the enemy. The navigation of the Delaware was now opened and the British commander could freely communicate with the fleet.

Soon after these events, Washington, wishing to confine the enemy within as close quarters as possible, established his winter-quarters at Valley

Forge, a high and strong position on the south side of the Schuylkill, and about twenty miles from Philadelphia. Contrary to the wishes of some of his more ardent officers, Washington refused to attack Philadelphia, nor would he be drawn out to battle by any of the repeated attempts which Howe made for that purpose. A season of sorrow and of hard trial was at hand for Washington. As we have said, the brilliant success of Gates in the north had eclipsed the reputation of the commander-in-chief, and a plot was formed at this time to supplant him by his more successful rival. But patience as well as achievement is the virtue of heroes; and Washington, calm in the midst of enemies, abated not one jot of patriotic endeavour, nor allowed himself to be turned either by friend or foe from the path which, though yet dark, he knew to be that of duty; and ere long events justified him before the world.

A gloomy winter was at hand. We will give Hildreth's picture of the state of the camp at Valley Forge. "Such was the destitution of shoes, that all the late marches had been tracked in blood, an evil which Washington had endeavoured to mitigate by offering a premium for the best pattern of a shoe made of untanned hides. For want of blankets, many of the men were obliged to sit up all night before the camp fires. More than a quarter of the troops were reported unfit for duty, because they were 'barefoot and otherwise naked.' Even provisions failed; and on more than one occasion there was famine in the camp.[21] Diseases ensued as a matter of course; the temporary buildings used as hospitals were crowded and unfit for the purpose. Great numbers died from hospital fever alone. There was no change of linen; nor were even medicines to be obtained. The hospitals, it is said, resembled rather receptacles for the dying than places of refuge for the sick."

Such was the American camp at Valley Forge.

Other national events besides those of war took place in the past year, to which we must now for a moment revert, and which we will give in the condensed form of Marcius Willson.

"After the colonies had thrown off their allegiance to the British crown, and had established separate governments in the states, there arose the further necessity for some common bond of union which should better enable them to act in concert as one nation. In the summer of 1775, Benjamin Franklin had proposed to the American congress articles of confederation and union among the colonies; but the majority in congress not being prepared for so decisive a step, the subject was for the time dropped, but was resumed again shortly before the declaration of independence in the following year.

"On the 11th of June, congress appointed a committee to prepare a plan of confederation. And the plan, reported by the committee in the following July, was, after various changes, finally adopted by congress on the 15th of November, 1777. Various causes, the principal of which was a difference of opinion respecting the disposition of the vacant western lands, prevented the immediate ratification of these articles by all the states; but at length those states which claimed the western lands having ceded them to the Union for the common benefit of the whole, the articles of confederation were ratified by Maryland, the last remaining state, on the 1st of March, 1781, at which time they became the constitution of the country.

"The confederation, however, amounted to little more than a mere league of friendship between the states; for although it invested congress with many of the powers of sovereignty, it was defective as a permanent government, owing to the want of means to enforce its decrees. While the states were bound together by a sense of common danger, the evils of the plan were little noticed; but after the close of the war they became so prominent as to make a revision of the system necessary."

CHAPTER VII.
REVOLUTIONARY WAR (continued), 1778.

Let us now see the effect of the war so far, both in the mother-country and America. The surrender of Burgoyne's army caused a great sensation in England, and efforts were immediately made in several of the large Scotch and English towns to send out troops to supply the loss; in London also, where the progress of the war had raised an anti-American spirit, £20,000 was raised by subscription for that purpose. On the other hand, subscriptions were also raised to relieve the American prisoners, who, from the cupidity and heartlessness of those in whose hands they were placed, were suffering from the want of the very necessaries of life.

When parliament met in January of this year, the American war was the first and most important topic of discussion, and Burke and the Duke of Richmond, Lord North, and the whole of the Rockingham party, entered more or less into the advocacy of the colonies. As to the war itself, the loss of life it had occasioned, the enormous expenses which it had entailed, and the hopelessness of its results, formed a strong argument in the mouths of all reasonable men. Still the war-party was strong, and Burgoyne could neither obtain an audience from the king nor get a hearing in parliament. To increase the inveteracy of feeling also, congress appeared ready to evade the terms of the convention of Saratoga. On some plea of suspicion regarding the intentions of the British officers who objected to the troops embarking at Boston, and had ordered the transports for their conveyance to Rhode Island instead, they were detained in the country as prisoners of war.

Nevertheless, plans of conciliation were proposed, for which purpose two bills were introduced into the house; the one renouncing all intention of levying taxes in America—conceding, in effect, the whole subject of dispute; the other authorising the appointment of three commissioners, who in conjunction with the naval and military commanders, should be empowered to treat for the re-establishment of the royal authority. "Great Britain," in fact, as the American historian justly says, "had reason to be weary of a war which had cost her already more than 20,000 men and five millions sterling in expenditure. Five hundred and fifty British vessels, besides those which had been recaptured, had been taken by the American cruisers. These cruisers so infested even the British seas, that convoys had become necessary from one British port to another. To this must be added the loss of the American trade, a large mass of American debts held in suspense by the war, the exile of the American loyalists, and the confiscation of their property. The British West Indies suffered for want of their accustomed supplies of provisions and timber from the North American colonies; and the British merchant complained that the slave-trade was reduced by the war to one-fifth of its former amount. And to all these was now added the fear of French intervention and French war."

An address also was moved to his majesty, which spoke freely the sentiments of this party, expressing "strong indignation at the conduct of his ministers, who had brought about the present unhappy state of his dominions, who had abused his confidence, and by their unfortunate counsels dismembered his empire, disgraced his arms, and weakened his naval power; whilst, by delaying to reconcile the difference which they had excited amongst his people, they had taken no means of counteracting a fatal alliance with the ancient rival of Great Britain."

It was in the great debate which followed on this plain-speaking address that Earl Chatham, when protesting vehemently against any measures which might tend to the dismemberment of the empire, was seized with that fainting-fit in the midst of the Lords which was the prelude of his death eleven days afterwards.

In vain was the eloquence of the Duke of Richmond and other members of the opposition—the motion for the address was lost; nevertheless, so earnest was the feeling on the subject, that a noble protest, signed by twenty peers, was entered; "because," said they, "we think that the rejection of the address at this time may appear to indicate in this house a desire of continuing that plan of ignorance, concealment, deceit and delusion, by which the sovereign and his people have already been brought into so many and so great calamities; and because we hold it absolutely necessary that both sovereign and people should be undeceived, and that they should distinctly and authentically be made acquainted with the state of their affairs, which is faithfully represented in this proposed address."

The Americans had still greater reason even than the British to deplore the war, from which their sufferings were so great in every way. The Newfoundland fisheries and the trade to the West Indies, both so vitally important to the New England colonies, were at an end. Nine hundred vessels had fallen into the hands of the enemy. The coasting trade had been destroyed, and Boston and the other New England seaports, cut off from their usual supplies, experienced great scarcity of food, enhanced by internal embargoes which now began to be laid on by the different states. Add to which, great public debts rapidly accumulating, and a constantly depreciating currency. The war had been carried on at great expense; the frequent draughts of militia, besides the interruption to agriculture, had proved a most costly and wasteful expedient. Besides all this, there had been great want of system and accountability in every department; and peculation, a customary incident of all wars, had not failed to improve so convenient an opportunity. Already the liabilities contracted by congress amounted to upwards of eight millions sterling; nor indeed was this the whole amount; the private debt of Massachusetts alone amounted to about one million, besides her share of the general liabilities. The loss of life too, had been enormous; vast quantities had died of sickness, of suffering from insufficiency of food and needful comforts and clothing. A sadder or more disastrous war could hardly have been conceived.

Nevertheless, spite of all these unlooked-for calamities and this unimagined expenditure, the war-spirit at the commencement of 1778 was far more extensively spread than had ever before been the case. The very calamities of the war, which had now entered, as it were, into every individual home, had estranged the national heart from the mother-country. Any conciliation, any termination of the struggle, short of entire separation from England, would not be listened to. Besides, when the Americans looked at the position of affairs after a three years' war, spite of all their losses and sufferings, they saw no cause for despair—as indeed, there was none. The British after all, retained possession but of Long Island and Staten Island, of the insular cities of Newport in Rhode Island and New York, and of Philadelphia on the mainland. As yet they had no interior hold on the country, and though a strong loyalist party existed in various states, and loyalist troops had been raised in Pennsylvania, New York and among the Catholics of Maryland, still the whole number did not amount to above 3,600 men, and their influence tended rather to increase the bitterness of hatred against Britain, who had thus caused civil war in the land, than in reality to weaken or endanger their cause.

While the British parliament was debating the subject of conciliation, the colonies were preparing to carry on the war with renewed vigour. The cabal against Washington had ended in the disgrace of its originators, and that great man now stood higher than he had hitherto done in the regard and confidence of the nation. Advantageous changes were made in all the war departments, in accordance with Washington's wishes, and to the displacement of his enemies. Nathaniel Greene, a favourite officer of Washington's, was appointed quarter-master-general; Colonel Jeremiah Wadsworth accepted the office of commissary-general, in the place of Mifflin, one of the cabal; while General Conway, its head, and a man of weak character, was displaced as army inspector by Baron Steuben, a Prussian officer, who had lately offered his services to congress, and who soon introduced a complete system of exercise and tactics into the American army. By the new organisation the colonial force would have amounted to 60,000 men, but not being fully carried out, to about only half that number; no troops were demanded from Georgia and South Carolina, in consequence of their great slave population. Two independent corps were also raised; the one under Pulaski, the Pole; the other under Armand, a French officer; a third entirely composed of cavalry, was raised by Henry Lee, of Virginia, already distinguished in the war. The fortifications of the Highlands were vigorously prosecuted under the direction of Kosciusko.

Again large issues of paper money were made, which, causing still further depreciation, led to the greatest perplexity and embarrassment. The reduced pay of the officers, insufficient for their simplest needs, must have compelled many able and long-tried officers to throw up their commissions, had not Washington induced congress to promise half-pay for seven years to all officers who served to the end of the war, and a gratuity to the common soldiers.

About the middle of April, at the very moment when all was in active operation to carry on the war with renewed vigour, the first tidings of the conciliatory bills reached New York, and ex-governor Tryon and the Tory party used their utmost endeavours to diffuse them throughout the colonies. To counteract the influence of these measures, congress ordered them to be immediately published in every newspaper of the States, accompanied by the printed resolutions of their body on the subject. "There was a time," said Governor Turnbull, "when this step from our acknowledged parent would have been accepted with joy and gratitude, but that time is irrevocably past. No peace can be concluded now with Great Britain on any other terms than the most absolute, perfect independence. Nevertheless," concluded he, "the union by a lasting and honourable peace is the ardent wish of every American. The British nation will then find us as affectionate and valuable friends as we now are determined and fatal enemies, and will derive from that friendship more solid and real advantage than the most sanguine can expect from conquest."

On the 22nd of April, congress officially declared, that any man or body of men, who should presume to make any separate or partial agreement with the commission under the crown of Great Britain, should be considered as enemies of the United States; that the United States would enter into no treaty with Great Britain until her fleets and armies were withdrawn, or the independence of America acknowledged.

Scarcely were these resolutions published, than, as if to give them value with the public, Simon Deane arrived at Yorktown, where congress was then sitting, in a royal frigate from Paris bringing with him for ratification two treaties of alliance and commerce between France and the United States; the last of which was signed the 30th of January, and the former on the 6th of February. On the 4th of May, they were ratified by congress, and the utmost joy and exultation prevailed throughout the United States. There was an end now to the hatred of France in America; her independence was acknowledged by that nation, and congress extolled "the extraordinary equity, generosity and unparalleled honour of the French monarch."

By the treaty of alliance it was stipulated that in case of war occurring between France and England, the two parties should aid each other with counsel and with arms, and that neither should conclude truce nor peace with Great Britain without consent of the other. This treaty being considered equivalent to a declaration of war between France and Great Britain, the English ambassador was recalled from Paris, and active preparations for war were made by both nations.

On May 8th, Sir William Howe having at his own request resigned the command of the American army, Sir Henry Clinton arrived at Philadelphia to take his place, and early in June the three commissioners appointed under Lord North's Conciliatory Bill—the Earl of Carlisle, William Eden, brother of the late governor of Maryland, afterwards Lord Auckland, and Governor Johnson—arrived at the same city a few days before the British troops evacuated. The day after their arrival, a passport being refused by Washington to Dr. Ferguson, the secretary of the commission, a letter was despatched by them, together with the late acts of parliament and other papers, directed to congress. A suspension of hostilities was proposed, and as the basis of a final adjustment of the contest, an extension of the privileges of trade hitherto allowed to the colonies was promised; no military force was to be kept up in any colony without the consent of its assembly; the continental bills of credit were to be taken up and ultimately discharged; the colonies were to be represented in parliament, and the British government in the colonial assemblies;—almost everything was to be conceded excepting the acknowledgment of independence.

These concessions came too late. Two years before they would have been accepted with gratitude. They were now rejected; it could not have been otherwise. Congress gave a very summary reply in the words of the resolution already stated, and firmly refused to treat in any way with Great Britain, unless she withdrew her troops or acknowledged the independence of the States. The commissioners returned a long and argumentative reply, to which congress made no answer.

In the meantime a French fleet, under the command of Count D'Estaing, being despatched to America with the design of blockading the British fleet in the Delaware, and Philadelphia being no longer safe quarters for the British army, active preparations were made for its evacuation. On the 18th of June, accordingly, Sir Henry Clinton marched out of Philadelphia with about 12,000 men, while the baggage and a great amount of stores and a considerable number of non-combatants were sent to New York by water, whither also the army was bound by land. Washington, already aware of this intended evacuation, broke up his camp at Valley Forge, and while with his main army, the number of which considerably exceeded that of the British, he cautiously followed the enemy, he despatched General Maxwell with a brigade to co-operate with the New Jersey militia in harassing them, and throwing every possible impediment in their way, so that time might be given him to bring up his full force and to profit by any opportunity which offered. The wish of the commander-in-chief was to bring on a general engagement, but in this wish he was overruled by a council of officers.

The progress of the British was very slow, and many were the difficulties which they encountered; the weather was rainy and the heat intense, and they were encumbered with so enormous a quantity of baggage, that their line of march through the narrow roads of the country occupied twelve miles. The cause of this quantity of baggage, as far as provisions were concerned, was a matter of prudence with General Clinton, who knew that no subsistence was to be obtained for his troops in the hostile country through which they had to march. On the 25th of June the two armies were so near each other, that Washington despatched General Lee, now but recently exchanged, with two brigades to press upon Clinton's left, and prevent him from occupying the strong position of the Nevisink Hills, near Middletown, which he was then approaching. On the 28th, Clinton encamped at Monmouth, now Freehold, twelve miles from Middletown, and Lee, who was six miles in advance of Washington, received orders from his commander to attack the enemy, himself promising to bring up the main army to support it. Washington, accordingly advancing for this purpose, was astonished to meet Lee retreating; according to his own account, having merely ordered his men to retreat for the purpose of gaining a more favourable position. Washington, however, incensed at perceiving what appeared to him flight rather than any other movement, severely reprimanded the general, and ordered the line of battle to be immediately formed. This was done; the battle was renewed till the darkness of night closed the combat. The Americans lay on their arms, fully determined to attack the British in the morning; but availing themselves of the cover of night, the British retired with profound silence to the high grounds of Nevisink, which it had been Washington's object to prevent them gaining, and where they were now safe from attack. The number of killed and wounded on both sides has been very differently stated; but in both armies many died without a single wound, from fatigue and the excessive heat of the weather, which on that day was unusually extreme; fifty-nine English soldiers are said to have died from this cause. Several officers of great ability were killed also on both sides.

As regarded General Lee, the day after the battle he wrote a very angry letter to Washington, on the subject of the reprimand which he had received, and again, in answer to Washington's reply, wrote a second of a similar character. The consequence was the arrest of Lee, and his trial by court-martial, on the charges of disobedience to orders, misbehaviour before the enemy, and disrespect to the commander-in-chief. Of a portion of these charges he was found guilty, and suspended from command for twelve months. He, however, never re-entered the American army, and died at Philadelphia shortly before the conclusion of the war.

Immediately after the battle of Freehold, Clinton proceeded from his position on Nevisink Hills to Sandy Hook, where, fortunately for him, the fleet of Lord Howe, which had been detained in the Delaware by contrary winds, had arrived only the evening before. By these means he was enabled to reach New York in safety, totally unconscious of a new danger from which he was so opportunely removed.

A new enemy was now approaching the scene of action. Two days after the British fleet had sailed, news arrived that Count D'Estaing was off the Delaware, with a French fleet of twelve ships of the line and four frigates, with 11,000 French troops on board. Had he been only eight-and-forty hours earlier he might have met the British transports, heavily laden as they were, totally unconscious of this new danger, and convoyed only by two ships of the line, and their destruction would have been inevitable; while the English army, unable to proceed to New York, would have been enclosed by the Americans on the one hand, and on the other, cut off from supplies by the French fleet, and a second surrender must have been the consequence. Two days made all the difference.

The arrival of the French fleet was, however, a cause of great exultation to the Americans. With it also came out M. Gerard, late secretary to the king's council, as ambassador to the United States, and soon after Benjamin Franklin, still in France, was appointed to the same office in that country.

D'Estaing, having failed to surprise the British fleet in the Delaware, proceeded without loss of time to Sandy Hook, and came to anchor off New York Harbour, on July 11th. A joint attack on the British by land and sea was now decided upon, and for this purpose Washington crossed the Hudson with his army, and encamped at White Plains. The utmost alarm prevailed among the British and the loyalists of New York. The British fleet was not in the best condition for this formidable encounter. Most of the ships of the line, having been long on service, were out of condition and badly manned; they had, however, the advantage of position, being within the harbour which is formed by Sandy Hook, and the entrance to which is covered by a bar. The French fleet was in excellent condition, and among its ships of the line were several of great force and weight of gun. These heavy ships were the salvation of the British fleet, and the ruin of the French enterprise. The New York pilots would not venture to take them across the bar, and after having lain outside the harbour for about eleven days, the British fleet locked up within it and looking out anxiously every hour for the arrival of an expected squadron from England, under Admiral Byron, D'Estaing was seen to sail away with a favourable wind, and in a few hours was out of sight. The expected British reinforcements arrived very shortly after D'Estaing was gone.

This projected attack of the British fleet being necessarily abandoned, Washington recommended D'Estaing to proceed against Newport in Rhode Island, which was still held by the British, under General Pigot, with 6,000 men. For the purpose of co-operation in this expedition, which Washington had anticipated, General Sullivan had been already sent with a detachment to Providence, where he was joined by 5,000 militia of Massachusetts and Connecticut, and shortly after by two brigades under Generals Greene and La Fayette. The utmost enthusiasm prevailed everywhere, and perfect success was calculated upon. The plan of the expedition was simple. D'Estaing was to enter the harbour of Newport, while the army advanced from the other side, and thus place the British once more between two fires.

The French fleet already occupied Narrangansett Bay, and was in communication with the American army; nay, even having advanced into Newport harbour, had compelled the British to burn or sink six of their frigates, to prevent their falling into the hands of the enemy.

On the 10th of August, the American army, 10,000 strong, landed on the north end of Rhode Island proper, on which Newport stands, expecting to be joined by 4,000 French troops from the fleet, as had been arranged with D'Estaing, when all unexpectedly the British fleet under Lord Howe appeared in sight. This fleet, as soon as released from its blockade in New York harbour and strengthened by its reinforcements, set sail for the relief of Newport, where it arrived at this critical moment. No sooner was this perceived by the French admiral, who knew that his force was superior to that of the British, than he sailed out to give them battle, carrying the troops with him. Astonished and disappointed by this unexpected movement, the American army continued their march towards Newport and encamped within two miles of the enemy's works. Meanwhile, the two admirals striving each to secure the weather-gage, two days were spent in this contest of seamanship, when a violent storm arose and separated the two fleets at the very moment when about to engage. For two days more the tempest raged fearfully, and scattered and damaged the ships greatly. Five days later the French admiral reappeared off Newport with two of his ships, one of which was his own, dismasted, and others seriously injured. The British squadron had also suffered equally. On the 22nd of August, two days later, D'Estaing, contrary to the earnest entreaties of the American generals, insisted on giving up the attempt against Newport, and sailed away to Boston to refit.

The American army in Rhode Island and the people of the northern colonies in general were indignant at this desertion, and the old hatred of the French was in such danger of reviving, and indeed did express itself by a riot in Boston, that it required all Washington's influence to allay it; while congress, in order to pacify D'Estaing, who was becoming angry on his part, passed a resolution approving of his conduct. In the meantime, General Sullivan, now placed in the most difficult circumstances in Rhode Island, and deserted by great numbers of his own troops, commenced a retreat. On the 29th of August, having already sent off his artillery and baggage, he put his troops in motion, and though vigorously pursued and attacked on every possible quarter by the British forces, he had yet taken all his measures so well, that he arrived without any considerable loss at his old post on the north of the island, and the next day passed his army over to the mainland in safety. Nor was his fortunate retreat made too soon, as Sir Henry Clinton arrived from New York with a strong force immediately afterwards.

The same day that Sullivan abandoned Rhode Island, Lord Howe entered the Bay of Boston in pursuit of D'Estaing, whom he however found so securely defended by the batteries and other measures of defence taken both by the Americans and the French, that any attack upon him was impossible.

Late in the autumn, the English fleet, which had been sent out under Admiral Byron to counteract D'Estaing, arrived at New York, having encountered and been detained by severe tempests. Byron sailed to Boston, as Howe had done before, to look after and attack the French admiral; but again a violent storm arose, the fleet was dispersed, and one of the English ships was wrecked on Cape Cod; after which, D'Estaing, having now refitted, sailed for the West Indies, the principal seat of war between France and England, and whither had sailed also 5,000 British troops from New York, under Commodore Hotham, escorted by a strong squadron.

The three commissioners who had come over for the purpose of conciliation having, as we said, produced no effect on congress, afterwards attempted to corrupt the minds of private individuals, or at least this charge was proved upon Governor Johnstone. Under this suspicion congress ordered all the letters written by that gentleman to his American friends— among whom were General Reed, Francis Dana and Robert Morris,—to be laid before them. These letters, as regarded General Reed, proved that a Mrs. Ferguson, a lady of Philadelphia, had been employed to offer him £10,000 and any office which he might desire in the colonies, if he would aid in bringing about the proposed reconciliation. His reply was worthy of an American patriot: "I am not worth purchasing," said he; "but such as I am, the king of England is too poor to buy me."[22] These discoveries called forth a declaration from congress that Johnstone was guilty of an attempt at bribery, and such being the case, it was incompatible with the honour of that body to hold any intercourse with him. This led to a violent reply from Johnstone, accompanied by a document from his fellow-commissioners, by no means calculated to decrease the difference between the two parties. Congress vouchsafed no reply, making use only of the public press to utter their sentiments.

Besides the attempt at conciliation, the commissioners endeavoured to use their influence, with equally little success, in obtaining the discharge of Burgoyne's troops, who were still detained in the country, contrary to capitulation. Whatever the reasoning of congress might be on this subject, nothing but the quibbles of lawyers could be produced in support of it; and the unfortunate troops, contrary to all honour, after having suffered greatly in the north, were marched off to Charlottesville in Virginia, where they could be more easily guarded and more cheaply fed. There they were quartered in log-huts, gardens were allotted to them, and their encampment formed a village. Some of the officers were afterwards exchanged, but the greater number remained prisoners to the end of the war.[23]

The last act of the commissioners was the publication of a violent manifesto, addressed not only to congress and the assemblies, but to the people at large, intended to separate them from their rulers, by charging upon them all the miseries and the consequences of the war, declaring that the contest changed its nature when America estranged herself from the mother-country and mortgaged herself and her resources to the enemies of Great Britain; the clergy were reminded that the French were papists, and the lovers of peace were appealed to against ambitious men who were subjecting their country to unnecessary warfare. Forty days were allowed for submission, after which, if the offer were rejected, the country was threatened with desolation as the future object of the war. The circulation of this manifesto under flags of truce was prohibited by congress, but it was published in all the newspapers with a counter-manifesto and with comments from the pens of some of their most able men.

As the commissioners had disparaged France in this document, the Marquis La Fayette, as the representative of his country, sent a challenge to the Earl of Carlisle, which that nobleman declined to accept, on the plea that he was responsible only to his sovereign for his public acts. Shortly after this time the Marquis La Fayette returned to France, in which country he believed that he could serve the rising interest of America more effectually than in her armies.

At the end of the forty days, having flung their firebrand into the country, the commissioners departed, much to the relief of congress, but not before their threatened warfare of desolation had commenced its work.

Sir Henry Clinton, finding all quiet at Newport, returned to New York, whence he despatched Major-General Grey on an expedition against the southern shores of Massachusetts and the adjacent islands. In Buzzard's Bay, a great resort of American privateers, he destroyed about 100 vessels with all the stores in the neighbourhood, burnt the towns of New Bedford and Fairhaven, and carried off from the inhabitants of the fertile island of Martha's Vineyard a vast quantity of sheep and oxen. But this was little in comparison with his next achievements. He surprised, in the dead of the night, a sleeping American regiment of light horse, near Tappan, killed a number of them in cold blood, wounded many others and took the rest prisoners. The town of Egg-harbour in New Jersey was burnt, and all the houses and mills and property belonging to the Whig party in that neighbourhood destroyed; while a detachment under one Captain Ferguson, guided by deserters, surprised and cut to pieces the greater portion of Pulaski's legion. Such was the spirit of ferocity which existed at this moment in the British soldiery; but horrible as were these instances of merciless warfare, they were trivial in comparison with what was going forward in remoter regions, where the Indian savage became the bloody tool of the American loyalist. All our readers know the tragedy of Wyoming. It was enacted at this time. We have already mentioned the settlement of this beautiful valley of the Susquehannah by a number of the quiet people of Connecticut. It had greatly flourished and become very populous, although from the first it had been a cause of dispute between Connecticut and Pennsylvania, both of which states claimed it as belonging to their territory. A few years before the present time, some Scotch and Dutch settlers from New York had come to the valley, thirty of whom having been lately seized on suspicion of being Tories, were sent to Connecticut for trial. Nothing being proved against them, they were discharged, and immediately, as if in confirmation of the accusation, they enlisted in the partisan corps of Butler and the half-blood Indian Brandt, then stationed in the Mohawk valley, eager for the moment of revenge, which was not far off.

Although Wyoming had been only settled since the last war, it numbered about 4,000 inhabitants, one-third of whom it had sent out to the American army, thus leaving itself undefended. This weak state was well known to the offended party, who induced Butler and Brandt to lead to Wyoming a body of 1,500 men, partly Indians, and partly loyalists disguised as such, for the purpose of extermination. On the first rumour of the probability of such an invasion, a body of men was raised to garrison the valley; but they were hardly organised when, at the commencement of July, Butler and his terrible army appeared and commenced their bloody work by waylaying and murdering some of the inhabitants. There were four forts in the valley; the upper fort, being held by a disaffected party, surrendered at once; the few soldiers hastily mustered marched out to meet the enemy, but being a mere handful, were surrounded, many were killed on the spot, and others who were taken prisoners were put to death with every Indian ingenuity of torture. Such as escaped fled to Fort Wyoming, which was then besieged. Under pretence of a parley, the principal officer was drawn out with a number of his men, when the fort was attacked and the greater part slain. The remnant which remained, on desiring to know what terms might be expected, received for reply the emphatic words, "The hatchet." At last compelled to surrender, the men were put to the sword, and the women and children shut up in the houses and the barracks, which were consumed in one general conflagration. The last fort offered no resistance, and surrendered on the promise of security to life and property; but the promise was not kept, the unhappy people suffered the fate of the others. Butler, it is said, marched away with his Tories at the surrender of the fort, but could not induce the Indians to follow his example; and frenzied with the rage of blood, they remained behind, burning the houses, ravaging the fields, killing and maiming the very cattle with horrible tortures, murdering the men who resisted, and driving such women and children as escaped with life into the forests and mountains. According to some historians there were loyalists among these Indians, who excelled even them in barbarity.

The fate of Wyoming awoke the liveliest indignation; and an expedition of retaliation was very soon undertaken against the Indians of the Upper Susquehannah; and though the Indians, aware of their approach, fled, yet were their harvests destroyed and their fields laid waste. Another expedition was undertaken against the Canadian settlers, most of whom were loyalists, west of the Alleganies. These incursions served only to call forth reprisals; and in November, the flourishing settlement of Cherry Valley, in New York, was surprised by a party of Indians and loyalist regulars. The fort, which was garrisoned by about 200 soldiers, was not taken; but its colonel, who lodged in the town, was killed, the lieutenant-colonel taken prisoner, and the inhabitants suffered the cruel fate of those of Wyoming.

We have already mentioned that Commodore Hyde Parker had been sent in November with a detachment of 3,500 men, under Colonel Campbell, against Georgia; at the same time instructions had been forwarded to Major-General Prevost, who commanded the troops in East

Florida, to make all necessary preparations for the defence of Fort St. Augustine, and to co-operate in the views of the present expedition by entering the province of Georgia from that side, and advancing, if possible, so far as to assist Colonel Campbell in the intended attack on Savannah.

The scene of events is now about to be in great measure removed from the North to the South. While the northern provinces had been so long harassed, and had suffered from the calamities of war, the southern had enjoyed such comparative tranquillity that they had duly cultivated their affluent lands and gathered in their abundant harvests, and had carried on their export trade with most of the European markets without impediment, except from British cruisers in the ocean. There had, it is true, been a continuance of petty hostilities between Georgia and East Florida, which had kept up a rumour of war in the south; and in West Florida the British settlements had quietly submitted to the Americans; but as yet all had been comparative peace.

The shortness of provisions in the north, from which the British suffered, rendered it additionally important for them to gain possession of Georgia, the feeblest of the southern provinces. As regards, indeed, the want of provisions, it was felt by the Americans equally with the British; and it is stated that D'Estaing would have found it impracticable to have victualled his ships at Boston but for the opportune seizing, by the New England cruisers, of so large a number of English provision-ships on their way to New York, that there was not only abundance for the French fleet, but the general price of food was lowered thereby in Boston market. This event, which was a great triumph to the Americans, was a serious cause of increased anxiety and suffering to the British army.

But the possession of Georgia was not only important to the British, as furnishing an abundant supply of its staple commodity, rice, and its other numerous products, but as enabling East Florida to join her forces, and thus to form an aggregate establishment in the south, which might greatly influence the ultimate fortunes of the war; besides which, a door would thus be opened into South Carolina.

The commander of the American forces in the southern department was at this time Major-General Robert Howe, who, however, not having given satisfaction to congress, was about to be superseded by General Lincoln, when, on the 23rd of December, the British fleet arrived at the island of Tybee, near the mouth of the river Savannah. The Americans were wholly unprepared for the removal of the scene of war from the north to the south, and no measures of defence had been taken to secure Savannah. Though Howe was there with the whole regular force of the southern department, consisting of six South Carolina and the one Georgia regiments, the whole force did not amount to 800 men; while the batteries which had been constructed for the defence of the river had been suffered to fall into decay.

The capture of Savannah was very easy. On the 28th, the enemy landed just below the town, Major-General Howe having drawn up his forces about half a mile to the east, his left resting on the river, and his right and rear covered by rice-swamps, across which he believed there was but one road. "Fortune, however," says the British report of this enterprise, "whose favours no prudent officer will ever deny, threw a negro into the hands of the commander, whose intelligence turned to the happiest account." This man led a British detachment, by a private road known to himself, to the back of Howe's force, and the Americans, thus at once attacked in front and rear, were completely routed. The British loss was less than thirty; of the Americans 450, while several commissioned officers were taken prisoners; and Savannah, with its artillery, shipping and stores, fell into the hands of the British. The remains of Howe's army fled into South Carolina.

This was the greatest acquisition made by the British in the present year. Washington had gone into winter-quarters at Middlebrook. The two hostile armies of the north were now, at the close of 1778, after two years' struggles and manœuvres, in very nearly the same relative position as at the close of 1776. The British, driven from the mainland, were now again entrenched on New York Island; and Washington, speaking of the present state of affairs, nobly remarked: "The hand of Providence had been so conspicuous in all this, that he who lacked faith must have been worse than an infidel, and he more than wicked who had no gratitude to acknowledge his obligations."

CHAPTER VIII.
REVOLUTIONARY WAR (continued), 1779.

While the war was being carried forward on the eastern borders of the States, and the people suffered grievously from the natural consequences of the prolonged struggle, the spirit of enterprise was no less alive in the remoter provinces, and adventurers were advancing towards that Great West which has ever been so attractive to the American mind. As had been so often the case before, the restlessness of the Western Indians led now to the conquest of their territory. It was reported to congress that the Indians of the Ohio had been stimulated to hostility by Hamilton, the British commandant at Detroit, and in consequence it was determined to send an expedition against that post; but before this was done, one still more important was accomplished by George Rogers Clarke, a young backwoodsman of Kentucky. Clarke was a man of great sagacity; and having come to the conclusion that the best way of putting an end to Indian hostilities was to destroy the sources whence they derived encouragement and support, and having correctly ascertained that these border Indians were not merely the tools of the British, but that great numbers amongst them were well-inclined towards the Americans, he proposed in December, 1779, to the executive council of Virginia, a plan for the reduction of the British posts of Detroit, Vincennes and Kaskaskia, all founded, as we may remember, by the French in the days of their American prosperity. The governor and council approving of Clarke's plan, afforded him such facilities as he required for its accomplishment. Early the following year he enlisted 200 men for three months, and, accompanied by thirteen emigrant families, descended the Ohio to the Falls, where the emigrants parted company and settled themselves in Corn Island, the little band of warriors thus dropping, as it were, by the way the seeds of civilisation and domestic life. Again Clarke embarked on the river, and advanced to within sixty miles of its mouth, where, hiding his boats, he marched by land to Kaskaskia, which he reached on the evening of July 5th. The march had been difficult, and having long been short of food, they were on the point of starvation, but the town and fort being taken by surprise yielded to the famished men without a struggle. M. Rocheblave, the British commandant, was taken in his bed, and not a drop of blood was shed. The inhabitants were mostly French, and the news of the French alliance with the Americans, and the respect shown by the conqueror to life, property and religion, disposed the inhabitants to be satisfied, if not pleased, with the change. The papers of the governor, among which it was suspected were orders from Hamilton to excite the Indians to hostility, were immediately either destroyed by his wife or concealed among her clothes, for "the conqueror, as a gallant son of Virginia, would not tarnish the fame of his state by an insult to a female;" therefore the papers remained undiscovered.

After a few days' rest and refreshment in Kaskaskia, Clarke and his men proceeded to Cahokia, a small but important post which possessing a great trade with the Indians, was the depôt of arms and ammunition; this and another neighbouring post also surrendered without bloodshed. Besides these conquests, the people of St. Vincent's, or Vincennes, on the Wabash, swore allegiance to Virginia, and friendly relations were established with the Spanish commander at St. Louis, on the other side of the Mississippi. A party was also sent by Clarke to build a stockade at the falls of Ohio, which was the first germ of the present city of Louisville.

Returning to Kaskaskia, Clarke convened the hitherto hostile Indian tribes, who filled with dread of this boldest of the "Big Knives," as they called the Virginians, were easily induced to transfer their allegiance from the British to the Americans. The territory thus acquired, embracing all the country north of the Ohio, was erected by the assembly of Virginia into the county of Illinois.

The army of Washington passed this winter more comfortably than the last. A supply of clothing had been received from France; and provisions were secured by congress having laid an embargo on all exports. In fact, the army was now better fed and supplied than at any former period. Great discouragement and distress, however, prevailed, owing to the depreciation of the bills of credit, which had reduced the pay of the army to a mere trifle, totally insufficient for their needs. The Tory party also caused many troubles and anxieties; and so dangerous an element was this in the state, that even after the evacuation of Philadelphia by the British, when congress had resumed its sittings in that capital, many wealthy and respectable citizens became amenable to the law; and two Quakers, John Roberts and Abraham Carlisle, were found guilty of treason, and spite of every effort being made to save them, were executed. These trials and executions greatly inflamed the hatred of the Tories, and party-spirit became still more bitter.

In the minds of the Americans this inveteracy was increased by the late conduct of the once popular General Arnold, who, in consequence of his wounds, had been appointed to the military command in Philadelphia, and to the astonishment and disgust of his friends, showed a great leaning towards the adverse party, and very soon married a young wife, the daughter of a Tory family.

Towards the close of the past year America obtained, through her commissioners in France, a loan from the French court of 3,000,000 of livres—a very insufficient sum to relieve their present difficulties, and the obtaining of which led to much quarrelling and party-spirit. Congress, occupied with disputes which originated in this loan, "was reduced," says Hildreth, "to a very low ebb. Many of the abler members left it; frequently there were not more than twenty-five in attendance. Washington passed five weeks at the commencement of the year in Philadelphia, and his letters at that time evince serious alarm at the state of affairs."

A scheme for the invasion of Canada by the aid of a French fleet was entertained at this time by congress, but discouraged by Washington, who had strong suspicion that if successful it would tend only to the advantage of France. It was resolved therefore, that all offensive operations should be confined to an attack on Detroit, and an expedition against the Six Nations.

The year 1779 commenced by a new issue of paper money, to the amount of ten millions, and additional bills to about the same amount, at various times before the month of June. Under this rapid issue, Hildreth tells us, increased depreciation took place, together with a spirit of speculation and fraud on the one side, and unfounded jealousies and suspicion on the other. Prices rose enormously, and while it was remarked that Tories and speculators grew rapidly rich, honest men and patriots were reduced to poverty.

But spring was now coming on, and it was necessary to organise the army for operation. Exclusive of the few troops in the south, the American army, at the commencement of the campaign of the year, amounted barely to 16,000. Three thousand of these were with Gates at Providence; 7,000 in the neighbourhood of Middlebrook, the winter-quarters of Washington; of the remaining 6,000, part were in the Highlands completing the defences of West Point, under M'Dougall, and the remainder under Israel Putnam, on the east side of the Hudson. As the British had 11,000 men at New York, and 5,000 at Newport, Washington did not deem it prudent to attack either of these places.

We now return to the South. When Colonel Campbell was despatched to Georgia, orders were sent to General Prevost in East Florida, to march his troops to his aid and to assume command. In this march along the uninhabited coast, which at that time lay between Florida and Georgia, his soldiers suffered greatly, having frequently no other provisions than oysters. Sunbury, a fort garrisoned by 200 provincials, Savannah being at that time in the hands of the British, surrendered with but little show of resistance. Arrived at Savannah, General Prevost assumed command, and then despatched Colonel Campbell against Augusta, which also surrendered, the garrison and the more patriotic inhabitants escaping across the river

Savannah into South Carolina. The whole of Georgia was thus in the hands of the British.

When the news of this easy conquest reached Charleston, the South Carolina militia were called out, but the call was reluctantly obeyed. The American forces under General Lincoln, principally consisting of North Carolina militia, amounted to about 1,400, and these were stationed to guard the passages of the Savannah river, which formed the boundary between Georgia and South Carolina. Although the troops of Prevost amounted to a much larger number, he hesitated to attack Charleston, but sent an expedition against Port Royal, which was so bravely defended by General Moultrie, that they were defeated with considerable loss.

The population of the three southern provinces, Georgia and the two Carolinas, was of a mixed character, without any bond of religion or interest, very different indeed to that of the north. The wealthy planters along the sea-coast were mostly Whigs, but the excess of slave population left the country without soldiers. The interior of the country was occupied by scattered settlements of Dutch, Germans, Quakers, Irish Presbyterians and Scotch Highlanders, who held little intercourse with each other. The Quakers, Dutch and Germans, meddling little with politics, inclined to submit to the British army for the sake of peace and quietness. The Irish Presbyterians were Whigs, the Scotch Highlanders Tories, as were the so-called Regulators of North Carolina, and the Scotch and British traders of the interior.[24]

The success of the British in Georgia encouraged the loyalists of these remote regions to rise. They were many of them men to whom excitement of any kind was welcome. Hardy and desperate in their lives, they are described by a writer of those days as having long been in the condition of outlaws, ready to attach themselves to the Indians or any others for incursions on the frontiers. The nature and remoteness of the country enabled them to keep up a free intercourse with their old friends, like-minded with themselves, who had however, for the sake of remaining quiet, submitted to the present government. From these circumstances, and the cast of mind acquired by their constant intercourse with the savages, they were ever ready to take up arms, and many of those who continued in the occupation of their farms and had the character of peaceable men, occasionally joined those parties which were openly in arms on the frontiers, and bore a share in all the devastation they committed.[25]

About 700 of these people therefore embodied themselves, and set out towards Augusta, intending there to join the royal troops, and committing great devastation and many cruelties by the way. They were, however, attacked by a body of South Carolina militia, under Colonel Pickens, when very near the end of their march; their leader, Colonel Boyd, was slain; 400 of their number killed or taken prisoners, seventy of whom, being put on trial for treason, were found guilty, but five only of the most influential executed; the remaining 300 reached Augusta.

The most terrible feature of the war in the south was the rancorous party-spirit which prevailed in it. Four battalions of Carolina loyalists had already joined the British army in Georgia, one of which was commanded by a Colonel Brown, originally a trader. This man who had formerly been tarred and feathered by the Whigs now pursued them with implacable hatred, and, following the example set at Augusta, hung all his Whig prisoners.

General Lincoln being reinforced by accessions of militia which had arrived for the protection of South Carolina, was stationed at Purysburg, on the north bank of the Savannah, about twenty miles above the city of that name, and now despatched General Ashe, with about 2,000 men of the Georgia and Carolina militia, to take up a position nearly opposite Augusta. On this movement General Prevost recalled the British force from that place, with orders to take up their post at Hudson's Ferry, lower down the river. On the retreat of the British, Lincoln, whose intention it was to retake Georgia and confine Prevost to the coast, ordered General Ashe to leave his baggage behind, to cross over into Georgia and take up his position at Briar Creek, a very strong situation. This was done; Briar Creek, which was too deep to be forded, covered his front, the river Savannah and a deep morass covered his left, and 200 horse guarded his right. No attack was suspected; General Prevost manœuvred on the banks of the river between Ebenezer and Savannah, and Lincoln kept himself on the alert, expecting that the danger lay in that quarter. In the meantime a detachment was proceeding by a circuitous march to attack Ashe's rear, while another detachment advanced as if to attack Lincoln in front, where he was unassailable, but in fact merely to divert his attention. The feint was entirely successful. The rear, totally unprepared for attack, was surprised in open daylight, and throwing down their arms without firing a shot, whole regiments of militia fled. The deep creek and the marsh, otherwise their security, became thus the means of their destruction. Stupified by terror, great numbers were drowned in the one and swallowed up in the other. A few officers and one North Carolina regiment endeavoured to retrieve the fortunes of the day by a brave but ineffectual defence; but the chances were all against them. About 400 were killed and made prisoners, among the latter of whom was Brigadier-General Elbert, a brave man and the second in command; the numbers who perished in the river and the swamp are unknown; 450 were all who rejoined Lincoln's army. Seven pieces of cannon, almost all their arms and ammunition, and such baggage as they had with them, fell into the hands of the British, whose loss only amounted to five killed and eleven wounded.

This disastrous and disgraceful defeat enabled the British to reoccupy Augusta, and gave them once more undisputed possession of Georgia. Such being the case, Prevost secured the co-operation of the loyalists, by proclaiming Sir James Wright governor and reestablishing a royal legislature, as it existed before 1775.

The present alarming state of affairs was useful in arousing the Carolinians. Every effort was now made to reinforce General Lincoln's army. John Rutledge, a popular man, in whom all had confidence, was appointed governor and vested with extraordinary powers; a stringent militia law was enforced, and by the middle of April, two months after the defeat at Briar Creek, Lincoln found himself at the head of 5,000 men. About the end of that month, therefore, leaving General Moultrie with 1,500 troops to garrison the lower passes of the river, at Purysburg and the Black Swamp, Lincoln, hoping to recover the upper parts of Georgia, as well as to protect the meeting of the assembly of that state, quitted his position, which had hitherto enabled him to protect Charleston, and proceeded towards Augusta. The movement was unfortunate. No sooner was he gone than General Prevost, whose force had received a considerable accession of loyalists from South Carolina as well as Georgia, resolved to cross the river and penetrate into Carolina, where he knew that the royal cause had many friends, and at the same time to obtain a good store of provisions, of which he was in want. Crossing the Savannah, therefore, at the end of April, with about 3,000 men, Prevost advanced forward with but little opposition from Moultrie, whose troops behaved no better than those of Ashe at Briar Creek, though defended like them by almost impassable swamps, and who now fled before him to Charleston. The ease with which every impediment was overcome by the British army, the assurance which the general received on all hands from the loyalist party that Charleston would surrender without resistance on his first appearance, furnished a new object to his enterprise.

Lincoln was on his way to Augusta, when news reached him of the British army having crossed the Savannah, and believing it only a foraging expedition, he contented himself with sending off a battalion to reinforce Moultrie. A few days later an express conveyed to him the more serious information that the British army was now several days on its march towards Charleston; the country was up, and hundreds flocking to the royal standard. Without a moment's delay the American army now re-crossed the river, and a detachment on horseback was sent forward for the greater despatch.

The British army was in the meantime advancing on the capital of South Carolina, almost without opposition. Moultrie's militia, which was retreating before him, was weakened at every turn; for as the effects and families of the militia lay on the very line of retreat, they deserted for considerations which were nearer to them than patriotism and honour. The British general himself, astonished at his undertaking, delayed and deliberated instead of availing himself of all the advantages which offered; which had he done, and marched at once upon Charleston, he might have taken the city at once. As it was, the townspeople had time to throw up fortifications, at which every master and slave laboured alike; and Charleston was saved for that time.

On the 11th of May the British army appeared before the city, and Moultrie, with the remains of his troops, the battalion despatched by Lincoln, and Rutledge with 500 militia, were then within its walls. Pulaski and his legion arrived at the same time as the enemy, while Lincoln with his army might be daily expected. There was no immediate fear, therefore, for the town, and Rutledge, when summoned to surrender under favourable conditions, proposed stipulations of neutrality for South Carolina during the war. The terms of each party were rejected by the other, and the townspeople and garrison prepared for a general assault, which was expected on the morrow. The British general now found himself in a difficult and dangerous position. The spirit friendly to the royal cause, which he had been led to expect in Charleston, did not meet him there; on the contrary, the town was prepared for vigorous resistance; he had neither battering artillery nor a naval force to co-operate with him, and Lincoln, with a force equal if not superior to his own, might hourly be looked for. Under these considerations it was better to provide for his own safety than to risk a doubtful contest. Leaving, therefore, a guard at the river Ashley, the British troops quietly retreated during the night, the garrison, who stood to their arms all night in fear of a sudden attack, not having the least suspicion of such a movement. The enemy had retreated to the islands of St. James and St. John, which lie to the southward of Charleston harbour— the commencement of a labyrinth of islands which continue to the sea. These islands, being well cultivated and fertile, afforded good quarters and excellent provision for his army, which retired in a few days, carrying off with them about 4,000 slaves as booty. Lincoln, in the meantime, having arrived, attacked the British at Stono River, where was a strong redoubt between the mainland and St. John's Island. The attack was made with great spirit, and so vigorously repelled, that the Americans were obliged to retire with considerable loss.

The hot season was now at hand, and both the British and American troops began to suffer severely from fever. In order, therefore, to have an eligible retreat for his army during the intense heats and the unhealthy season which was commencing, and at the same time to keep hold on South Carolina, General Prevost determined to secure possession of Beaufort, in Port Royal, by placing a garrison there under Colonel Maitland, after which he retired to Savannah with his main army.

While these events were occurring in South Carolina, Sir Henry Clinton despatched from New York a fleet under command of Commodore Collier, now appointed to the naval command in America, with 2,000 troops under Major-General Mathews, to make a descent upon Virginia, and by devastating the coast and plundering the country, to inflict as much misery and ruin on the colonies as possible. Entering the Chesapeake, the squadron which escorted the troops advanced up Elizabeth River, and took possession of the town and fort of Portsmouth, the garrison of which, knowing themselves incapable of defence, fled at the approach of the enemy. On the opposite side of the river stood the town of Norfolk, which having already been destroyed in the present war was just recovering from its ruin, and now also fell into the hands of the enemy. These two towns were the seats of the Virginian foreign export trade, which, spite of the war, was considerable; and higher up the river lay Gosport, where the state of Virginia had established a navy yard. A great number of ships lay at these different places, among the rest two large French merchantmen laden with tobacco, which the Americans burnt, together with several of their own ships, on the approach of the fleet, to prevent their falling into the hands of the enemy. In the meantime detachments having landed carried fire and sword inland. The town of Suffolk was attacked and plundered, as were the villages of Kempes', Shepherd's and Tanner's Creeks. "Within a fortnight," says the British chronicler of that day, "while the fleet and army continued on the coast, the loss of the Americans was prodigious." To say nothing of cruelty, outrage, and general devastation practised on defenceless people, above 130 ships and vessels of various kinds were destroyed. "Seventeen were brought away as prizes, all that were on the stocks were burnt, naval stores were carried off or destroyed, as well as everything relative to the building or fitting up of ships. Among other booty carried off were 3,000 hogsheads of tobacco. The damage done in this expedition was estimated at above half a million sterling."[26]

Spite of the flattering assurances of support which the naval and military commanders received from the loyalist inhabitants of Virginia, and which were eagerly reported by them to Sir Henry Clinton, and spite of the advantages which they urged would accrue to the royalist cause by converting Portsmouth into a place of arms, and thus destroying the trade of the Chesapeake, Sir Henry issued orders of recall; and the fleet and the army having fired the storehouses and dock-yard buildings of Gosport, set sail with their booty and prizes, and reached New York within a month of their setting sail.

The British troops were needed to assist in an attack on the American works, situated at Stony and Verplank's Points, two opposite projections on the Hudson, about forty miles north of New York, and highly important to the Americans, as commanding a ferry, the loss of which would oblige them to make a detour of ninety miles through the mountains, to communicate with the eastern and southern provinces. To prevent the completion of these works, therefore, Sir Henry Clinton undertook an expedition in person, which set out on the last day of May. His first object of attack was Stony Point on the west bank of the river, which being unfinished and incapable of defence was evacuated at his approach. Cannon placed on the heights of Stony Point unfortunately commanded Verplank's Point, on which a little fortress called La Fayette was just completed, and this being invested from the land side also was compelled, after a brave resistance, to surrender. These important works being secured, Clinton ordered them immediately to be completed, and on the 2nd of June encamped his army at Philipsburg, half-way between Verplank's Point and New York; and Washington, in order the better to cover the yet unfinished works of the Americans in the Highlands, which were endangered by the garrisons of these conquered posts, removed his army from Middlebrook to New Jersey.

While the campaign on land was confined to the surprise of posts and desultory expeditions, the Connecticut cruisers, with their whaleboats and other small craft, seriously inconvenienced and distressed the British army and the loyalist city of New York, by intercepting and taking almost every vessel that came upon their waters, and in preventing any intercourse with Long Island, whence the supplies of the army and city were principally sent. To put a stop to this annoyance, as well as to make a most severe retaliation, Sir Henry Clinton ordered ex-governor Tryon, now a general officer, to embark with about 2,600 men. On July 5th, the fleet reached New Haven, which was plundered and the fort with everything available for naval or military purposes destroyed; but the town was spared because the inhabitants made but small resistance. Fairfield and Norwalk, however, two other ports having a stronger military force, fared much worse; both towns, together with Greenfield, a village near Norwalk, were set on fire and everything of value destroyed. The loss which the Americans sustained in this predatory expedition was very great; besides houses and other property, shipping of all kinds with stores and merchandise were destroyed totally. After these devastations on the mainland, he was proceeding to Long Island, intending to make a descent on New London, when he was suddenly recalled. Whether he had exceeded the orders of Clinton in these outrages, or whether his forces were required in another direction, of which we shall speak anon, is not known; but probably the former cause had some influence, for Tryon deemed it necessary to excuse the fires and destruction which marked his career, by a letter to the general, in which he said that the Americans, or *usurpers*, as he called them, placed their hopes of securing the empire by avoiding decisive actions, and in the escape of their own property during the protraction of the war. Their power, he said, was supported by the dread of their tyranny and the arts which they practised to inspire the credulous public with confidence in the forbearance of the royal forces. It had been his wish, therefore, to detect this delusion, and that without injury to the loyalists. All that he regretted was that places of worship were burnt; but these, he said, being built of boards and standing among the houses, could not be preserved, it being impossible to fix limits to a conflagration.

The surprise of Verplank's and Stony Points had, as we have said, called Washington out of New Jersey, and he was now encamped on high and strong ground above those places, and on each side of North River. Sir Henry Clinton desired nothing more than to draw him down from these fastnesses into the flat country, and bring on a general engagement in such ground as would insure success to the British army. But Washington was too wary to be seduced into such an error. Nevertheless he was not inactive. While the two armies lay, as it were, watching each other, a bold enterprise was undertaken and executed with so much spirit and success as to be the most brilliant action of the whole campaign. This was no other than the surprise and retaking of Stony Point, the works of which had been now carefully completed and strongly garrisoned by the British.

Washington appointed General Wayne to this arduous task. On the 15th of July this detachment set out, having to march over mountains, across morasses, and through difficult defiles, where they were obliged to advance in single file the greater part of the way. By eight in the evening they were within a mile of the fort, when they halted and formed into two columns as they came up; after which Wayne and his officers silently reconnoitred the works. About midnight the two columns marched to the attack from different points; and here it is worth observing that the van, consisting of 150 picked men, advanced with unloaded muskets and bayonets fixed—the bayonet, which had been so often fatal to the Americans, being the only weapon used in this attack. The most wonderful discipline prevailed in these troops; both columns were commanded not to fire a shot, and not a shot was fired. They advanced through the most difficult approaches, the ground being covered at that time with the tide, through a morass, removing as they went the formidable works in front and flank, and in the face of an incessant fire of musketry. On they went, their numbers thinned at every step, and at about one in the morning the two columns met at the same moment in the centre of the works. Wayne, though wounded in the head, refused to retire; his loss in killed and wounded was about 100; about fifty of the garrison were killed; the remainder, 450, were made prisoners.

As soon as Stony Point was taken, the artillery was turned against Verplank's; but before anything could be effected, the news of the former achievement had reached Sir Henry Clinton, and the whole British army marched out, whilst the navy advanced up the river to the scene of action. But Washington, who had already completed the object he had in view, which was no other than the destruction of the works and the carrying away the artillery and stores, abandoned the place before the arrival of the British either by land or water.

About the same time that Stony Point was recaptured by Wayne, Major Lee surprised the British garrison at Paulus Hook, New Jersey city, a point of land opposite New York; killed thirty and took 160 prisoners. These triumphs, however, were painfully counterbalanced by an unsuccessful attempt in the north. During the summer an expedition had been undertaken by the British to plant a strong post on the Penobscot, in the eastern and unsettled parts of Maine, which, causing serious alarm, led the state of Massachusetts to fit out an expedition to prevent its accomplishment. So urgent and important was the undertaking considered, that in order to secure armed vessels and transports, Massachusetts laid an embargo on its shipping for forty days. By this means a very considerable armament was fitted out with no loss of time, under the conduct of Commodore Saltonstall, a Connecticut sea-captain.

Fifteen hundred militia were embarked in this fleet, under General Lovel, a man greatly beloved and esteemed, though without military experience.[27] On the 25th July, the fleet, to the amount of thirty-seven sail, appeared in the Penobscot, the British colonel, Macleane, having in the meantime put the unfinished fort in as complete a state of defence as the time permitted. With great labour and the loss of about 100 men, the American general at length effected a landing, and on the third day opened a battery, in spite of which, and for many days afterwards, the internal works of the fort went on every day adding to its strength. For a whole fortnight this was continued, cannonading from without, and increasing strength within. At length a general attack both of the fort and the shipping was resolved upon; intelligence of which being carried to the commander by a deserter, he instantly threw up new works which covered the place. But this precaution was unnecessary; news of this expedition had already reached Sir Henry Clinton, and Sir George Collier was despatched with five ships of war to the Penobscot. The commander and the garrison were awaiting the expected attack on the 11th of August, the day intended for it, when, to their infinite astonishment, the Americans were gone; they had during the night re-embarked their forces and artillery, and were nowhere to be seen. At the first approach of the British they had fled up the river. The enemy pursued, three sloops of war which had been confined to the harbour now joining in the chase. Escape was impossible; five frigates and ten smaller vessels were run ashore and blown up; the remainder were taken. The soldiers and sailors escaped to the shore, but the whole region in which they found themselves was a desolate and uninhabited wilderness. The indignation of the land forces on this dastardly termination of their enterprise was so great, that they are said to have come to blows with the seamen in the dreary solitudes through which they had to travel before they could reach an inhabited country. Saltonstall was tried by court-martial and cashiered.

Besides the humiliation and shame of this flight, the loss to Boston in its shipping was almost ruinous. Nineteen vessels of which the squadron consisted were destroyed or taken—a force, it is said, little inferior to that of the royal navy of England at the accession of Elizabeth.

We must now for a moment return to the frontiers to see what is going on there, and taking Hildreth for our guide we shall receive a lucid summary of events. "George Rogers Clarke, still commanding in the newly-conquered Illinois, was giving fresh proofs of vigour and enterprise, and extending also the authority of Virginia. Hamilton, the British commandant of Detroit, descended the Wabash with eighty soldiers to watch Clarke, and organise an expedition against him, in which he expected to be greatly aided by the Indians. Informed of these facts by a French trader, Clarke mustered 170 men, and after sixteen days' march, five of which were spent in wading the drowned lands on the Wabash, suddenly appeared before Vincennes, which the British had recaptured, and where Hamilton then was. The fort surrendered in a few days, and Hamilton was sent prisoner to Virginia on the charge of having instigated the Indians to cruelty against the colonial settlers.

Security being thus given against the Indians north of the Ohio, the settlement of Kentucky began rapidly to increase, and in April of this year a log-erection formed the commencement of the present city of Lexington. By the Virginia land system, all who had settled west of the mountains before June of the preceding year were entitled to 400 acres, merely for the payment of the taxes on that quantity of land. The whole tract between the Green River and the Tennessee was reserved for military bounties.

While Clarke was extending the domains of Virginia, the first settlements took place in Western Tennessee, under the guidance of James Robinson, who eleven years before had been the patriarch and founder of Eastern

Tennessee. With a company of ten persons he followed the Oby to its junction with the Cumberland; some of his companions embarked there, while the rest pursued the riverbanks by land to the spot where now stands the city of Nashville. Here, planting a crop of corn, and leaving three persons to watch it, they returned for their families. Some travelled through the woods, driving their cattle before them; others embarked with the women and children on the head waters of the Tennessee, intending to descend that river to its mouth and then proceed up the Cumberland. But a severe winter delayed them by the way, and their destination was not reached till the following spring.

Thus sprung up the future states of the West, and the red man retired from before the white. In the meantime war, which the Indian rendered so much more formidable from his British alliance, was continued on the western frontiers of the eastern states. Again we will follow our former guide. "The Six Nations, with the exception of the Oneidas, carried on a border warfare. The Senecas, and the loyalist refugees among them, ravaged the frontiers of New York and Pennsylvania; and the Onondagas, though professing neutrality, shared in their hostilities.

"To check these depredations, a strong force under General Sullivan was sent against them. The troops assembled at Wyoming, where they were joined by a New York brigade, under James Clinton, who effected the junction of the troops in a singular manner; crossing from the Mohawk, where he had been stationed, to Lake Otsego, he dammed up the lake, and so raised up its level, and then, by breaking away the dam, produced an artificial flood, by which the boats were rapidly earned down the north-east branch of the Susquehannah. While this was being effected, the terrible Brandt surprised, plundered and burnt the village of Minisink, near the north-west corner of Jersey; and a detachment of militia sent in pursuit, falling into an ambush, were nearly all slain.

"Sullivan's army, amounting to 5,000 men, passed up the Chemung branch of the Susquehannah, in the month of August, and at Elmira encountered a strong body of combined Indians and loyalists, under Brandt, Butler and Johnson, which they completely defeated, and in pursuit crossed into the hitherto unexplored valley of the Genessee. In order that the want of food might compel the Indians and their allies to quit that part of the country, everything was ravaged. The ancient Indian orchards were cut down, vast quantities of corn were destroyed, and eighteen villages burnt to the ground. This expedition, through an unknown country, covered for the most part with thick forests, was extremely laborious, nor did it wholly accomplish its object; the Indians and loyalists, though dispersed for the moment, soon renewed their depredations, which were continued as long as the British war lasted, and to which the fury of revenge now added increased ferocity."

CHAPTER IX.
REVOLUTIONARY WAR (continued).

The struggle between Great Britain and her colonies was watched with great anxiety by Spain, who, having herself a colonial empire, dreaded the effect of example. Spain offered herself as mediator in the quarrel, and was accepted as such, though nothing was effected thereby; not even the terms of mediation being agreed upon. Various considerations, however, inclined her now to favour the cause of the Americans, although she did not acknowledge their independence. She was desirous of recovering Gibraltar, the loss of which had so deeply humiliated her national pride, besides Jamaica and the two Floridas, with a territory on the east bank of the Mississippi, which latter she hoped to obtain through the gratitude of America. She declared war, therefore, against Great Britain, and, in conjunction with France, a formidable armament appeared on the English coast—a second armada, to be dispersed like the former one by tempest, and desolated by disease as pitiless as war itself, upwards of 5,000 soldiers dying in their ships within a very few weeks.

While Spain was assuming the character of mediator between the two contending parties, there had been so little good faith on her part, that the Spanish governors and commanders in the West Indies and America were aware of the intended declaration of war before it was made known in Europe. The infant settlements of Louisiana were as yet attached to those of West Florida, and though, as we have already said, they had submitted to the Americans in the preceding year, the submission had been but temporary, and British troops had been since then stationed there to preserve their allegiance. The moment, therefore, that Don Bernando de Galvez, the Spanish governor of Louisiana, heard of the declaration of war with Great Britain, he proclaimed the independence of America by beat of drum, and having already assembled his forces, consisting of Spanish regulars, American volunteers and negroes, at New Orleans, set out on an expedition against the British settlements on the Mississippi. So well had he laid all his plans, that Major-General Campbell, who commanded at Pensacola, was not aware of danger even threatening the western part of that province, until the Spaniard was in possession of it. With the same address and expedition he succeeded in taking a royal sloop which was stationed on Lake Pontchartrain, as well as several vessels laden with provisions and necessaries for the British troops. In this manner were Baton Rouge and Fort Panmure, near Natchez, taken, and a few months later Mobile; and for the honour of the Spanish general it must be told that, in all his successes, his conduct was marked by good faith, humanity and kindness. By the end of the year 1779, Pensacola was the only post of West Florida remaining to the British.

In the meantime, events of some importance had been occurring in the West Indies. The island of Dominica had already been taken from the British by an expedition from Martinique, when the English and French fleets, which respectively sailed from Boston and New York on the same day, reached the West Indies. The British fleet first arriving, proceeded immediately against St. Lucie, which was taken, spite of D'Estaing's attempt to retain it. On its surrender, the French fleet retired to the harbour of Port Royal in Martinique. The fleets of the French and English were about equal, and the latter used every means in their power to bring about a naval engagement; but D'Estaing was not to be provoked to action. His imperturbability was unaccountable, excepting that he was in daily expectation of reinforcements. Reinforcements came, but not alone for the French—Admiral Rowley joined the British squadron about the same time, with several ships of war. The noxious climate of St. Lucie, however, having caused a terrible mortality in the British troops, Admiral Byron left the island to convoy a numerous fleet of merchantmen to England, and D'Estaing sent out a detachment against St. Vincent's, which was surrendered at once without a shot being fired. Large reinforcements again arrived from France, and D'Estaing, now willing enough for action, proceeded against the island of Granada, with a fleet of six-and-twenty ships of the line, with frigates, and 10,000 land forces. The whole defence of the island was less than 1,000 men, and its sole strength consisted in a fortified hill, which commanded the capital, St. George, its forts and harbour. The island had just surrendered after a bloody defence, when Byron returned, and hearing of the loss of St. Vincent's and the attack on Granada, proceeded at once to the latter place, though his fleet was now considerably weakened by the convoy he had sent to England. To his disappointment, the French flag was flying on the fort as he came within sight of the island. An engagement however took place, but of an indecisive character, and the English fleet, greatly damaged, retired to St. Christopher's to repair.

Soon after these events D'Estaing, leaving the West Indies, proceeded to the coast of Georgia with twenty-two ships of the line. The strong position which the British forces had so easily gained in Georgia and South Carolina, was not only distressing in its present effect, but alarming with regard to its probable consequences in the American struggle. The scene of action was almost out of the reach of the main army and the seat of council, while the British marine force afforded decided advantages to their troops in a country bordered by the sea, and chequered with inland navigation. To all appearances the subjugation of the Southern States was almost complete. The most serious apprehension prevailed, and it was determined to bring, if possible, the French fleet into useful operation. As yet America had derived no essential service from her French allies. The attempt on Rhode Island had been productive of expense, danger, and loss, without the slightest benefit. The mischief and inconvenience to the southern provinces had been permitted without the slightest interference. As regarded the whole conduct of the French commander, the Americans had the utmost cause for dissatisfaction; they had supplied and equipped his fleet at Boston, only to enable him to abandon their southern coasts at the moment of their greatest danger, and when the seizure of Savannah and Georgia opened the whole Carolinas to the British. Finally, the Americans complained that while the French were enriching themselves in the West Indies, they were left to bear all the burden of the war, contrary to the stipulations of the treaty. The Americans complained bitterly.

Immediately, therefore, after the action before Granada, and in consequence of this dissatisfaction, D'Estaing received orders from home to render some essential service to his allies. He was firstly commanded to free the southern colonies from their present danger, by the destruction of the small force under Prevost; and secondly, to co-operate with Washington in a simultaneous attack by land and water on New York.

At the end of August, D'Estaing stood for the coast of Georgia with twenty-two ships of the line, and news being sent to General Lincoln at Charleston of his approach, no time was lost in preparing for an attack on Savannah. As if in good augury of their success, the French fleet, by its sudden appearance on the coast, surprised and captured some British vessels, laden with provisions. Lincoln, in the meantime, reinforced by several North Carolina regiments, despatched by Washington to the south, and by the militia, which marched out in great numbers, hastened to Savannah, which, greatly to the surprise and displeasure of the American general, D'Estaing had summoned to surrender "to his most Christian Majesty of France."

Prevost, on the first rumour of the danger which awaited him, summoned to Savannah the greater part of the British forces from Port Royal and other places; and removing the shipping higher up the river, destroyed the batteries on the island of Tybee, and put the city in a rapid state of defence. In reply to D'Estaing's summons of surrender, Prevost, whose expected reinforcements had not yet arrived, requested a suspension of hostilities for four-and-twenty hours, to which D'Estaing agreed, who not having, as yet, formed a junction with the American forces under Lincoln, knew not the importance and necessity of an immediate attack. Within the four-and twenty hours the reinforcements arrived. Three cheers, which rung from one end of the town to the other, welcomed them, and Prevost notified D'Estaing the following day that he would defend the place.

Pulaski with his legion, and Lincoln with 3,000 men, proceeded to besiege the town, with regular approaches. On the 24th of September the siege commenced; D'Estaing grew impatient of these operations, and at midnight, between the 3rd and 4th of October, a heavy bombardment, which lasted for five days, was commenced. The effect of this fell mostly upon the town, where, besides the destruction of houses and people, women, children and negroes were the greatest sufferers. Prevost, touched by the sufferings of these defenceless people, whose distress and danger were increased by the number of burning houses, wrote a letter to D'Estaing, requesting permission to send them down the river in vessels intrusted to the care of the French, there to await the result of the siege, acquainting him that his own wife and family should be the first to profit by this permission. For three hours the discharge of cannon and shells was continued, and then a refusal, signed both by Lincoln and D'Estaing, was returned.

The siege promised to be tedious, and D'Estaing's patience was worn out. The obstructions in the narrow part of the channel prevented his fleet from approaching the shore; and he now became afraid that one of those hurricanes common to this season might drive it out to sea, or it might be attacked by the British while so many of his guns and troops were otherwise employed. Full of impatient fears, he insisted upon the town being carried by assault; and on the 9th of October, two columns, the picked men of both armies, were led to the assault by D'Estaing and Lincoln. It was a fatal step; by a strange mistake, the attack that was to be made at four in the morning was delayed till broad daylight; and the garrison directed their guns with fatal aim upon the advancing assailants. Some of the outer works were taken, but the most fearful carnage marked every step. At length, Pulaski, at the head of his legion, was mortally wounded, and the Americans fled; D'Estaing received two wounds, and the French were repulsed with great slaughter.

The loss of the French and the Americans was about 1,100, that of the British only fifty-five. On the 18th the siege was raised, and D'Estaing, as soon as he could re-embark his troops, set sail for the West Indies. Lincoln returned to Charleston, and the militia were disbanded. It was the most disastrous attempt which had been made during the war. This second failure at co-operation with the French caused still greater dissatisfaction.

Among others who fell at Savannah was that Sergeant Jasper who had distinguished himself so gallantly in the defence of Fort Moultrie, on

Sullivan's Island, in 1776. Moultrie's regiment had been presented with a stand of colours, by a Mrs. Elliot, embroidered by her own hands; and Jasper, as a reward of his own individual merit, had received a handsome sword from Governor Rutledge. During the assault of Savannah, two officers having been killed in endeavouring to plant these colours, and a third wounded, Jasper seized them and was in the act of planting them, when he too fell mortally wounded. Pulaski, severely wounded, was carried on board a vessel for Charleston, but he died on the way, and was buried beneath the waves. Funeral rites were performed at Charleston, and all America mourned for him who had been one of the truest and bravest supporters of her cause.

The appearance of D'Estaing on the southern coast suspended all active operations at New York, in the apprehension of a formidable concerted attack by sea and land, from the combined French and American forces. Washington also, on his part, expected this co-operation, and had prepared himself for it by calling out the militia of the northern provinces; it being supposed by all parties that Savannah would soon surrender, and D'Estaing then proceed northward. Clinton took active measures for the strengthening of New York, and so momentous was the crisis considered, that the troops were withdrawn from Newport, in Rhode Island, as well as from Verplank's and Stony Points, all of which were thus again suffered to fall into the hands of the Americans. When, however, it was clearly ascertained that D'Estaing was gone, Sir Henry Clinton, relieved from any apprehension regarding the north, set sail for Savannah with 7,000 troops, 2,000 of whom were American loyalists, while the same number remained behind under Kniphausen, who held New York with a powerful garrison. The militia of the northern provinces was disbanded; and Washington, anxious for the future, and disappointed and disgusted by the conduct of his allies, went into winter-quarters near Morristown.

Although the American efforts at naval warfare were now considerably diminished, owing to the increased vigilance of the British squadron, and to want of funds on the part of the colonies; still many armed vessels, both public and private, were on the seas, and a considerable amount of the French loan was employed in the fitting out of cruisers in the French ports.

It was in the autumn of this year that the renowned sea-fight took place, which made the name of Paul Jones one of terror in the British seas. Paul Jones was a native of Scotland, who emigrated to America, made money and in 1773 settled in Virginia. On the breaking out of the war, he was one of the first officers commissioned in the American navy. He cruised in the West Indies, picked up many prizes, and showed on all occasions great boldness and address. In 1777 he was sent to France, and there appointed to the command of a French ship under American colours. The next year, cruising on the coast of Great Britain, from the Land's End to Solway Frith, where as yet the American flag had never ventured, he made a descent on the Scotch coast near Kirkcudbright, and plundered the house of the Earl of Selkirk, where, tradition says, he had once lived as servant, and a second by night on the Cumberland coast, at Whitehaven, where he spiked the guns in the fort, and burned one or two vessels. For a whole summer he kept the north-western coast of England and the southern coast of Scotland in a continual state of alarm, and made his name one of terror. The next year he returned to cruise on the eastern coast, no longer with a single ship, but a squadron, manned by French and Americans. This squadron consisted of the Bonhomme Richard, of forty guns, which he himself commanded, the Alliance of thirty-six, the Pallas, a frigate of thirty-two, and two other smaller vessels. Cruising with these ships, he fell in with a British merchant-fleet, on its return from the Baltic, under convoy of Captain Pearson, with the Serapis, of forty-four guns, and a smaller frigate; and one of the most desperate naval engagements on record took place off Flamborough Head. About seven o'clock in the evening, Paul Jones in the Bonhomme Richard, engaged Captain Pearson in the Serapis, the ships advancing nearer and nearer, until at length they dropped alongside of each other, head and stern, and so close that the muzzles of the guns grated. In this close contact the action continued with the greatest fury till half-past ten, during which time, Jones, who had the greater number of men, vainly attempted to board, and the Serapis was set on fire ten or twelve times. Every time the fire was extinguished, till at length, a cartridge of powder taking fire, a great number of officers and men were killed. After a desperate and last attempt to board Paul Jones, Captain Pearson hauled down his colours, two-thirds of his men being killed or wounded, and his main-mast gone by the board. The Bonhomme Richard was in little better condition, for, to add to her misfortunes, the Alliance coming up in the darkness and confusion of the night, and mistaking her for the enemy, had fired a broadside into her, not discovering his error till the glare of the burning Serapis had revealed it. The next day, Paul Jones was obliged to quit his ship, and she sank at sea almost immediately, with, it is said, great numbers of the wounded on board. Of the 375 men whom she carried, 300 were killed or wounded. The Pallas captured the Countess of Scarborough, and Jones, on the 6th of October, succeeded in carrying his shattered vessels into the waters of the Texel.[28]

The gloom which overspread the public mind at the close of this year had its origin in many causes, not the least of which was the disappointment arising from the French alliance. Not alone had the French been useless to the republican cause, as far as their own efforts went, but this alliance with a powerful nation, from which such great advantages were expected, had disposed a considerable portion of the American public to sink into an apathetic state, waiting, as it were, for others to do the work; and now that the others had not done it, they were depressed and almost hopeless of the cause itself. This despondency and apathy alarmed the earnest patriots, and Washington and the other leaders called upon the nation in the most earnest and solemn manner to rouse from their lethargy, and trust neither to chance nor to strangers, but to their own exertions for the establishment of their rights. There was but little response to the appeal; the very army itself seemed affected by the lethargic torpor of the public mind.[29]

Another cause of anxiety and distress we have already alluded to. This was the depreciation of the paper currency. At the close of this year a dollar in specie could scarcely be obtained for forty in bills. But the very paper was fluctuating in value. Hence a set of men arose, who, speculating on this currency, amassed immense wealth, while honest men and the nation itself were reduced to beggary. One cause of the depreciation of the American paper at this time, was the disgraceful fact that England herself turned forger, and sent over immense quantities of spurious bills, so well imitated as scarcely to be distinguished from the true, and which her emissaries distributed through the country, causing the utmost distress and confusion, and the recall of several issues of American paper.

Very different was the state of things in England. Spite of her having to carry on war at this time both with France and Spain, and though several of the European nations joined in an "armed neutrality" against her, renewed exertions were made at the close of this year for prosecuting the war with the colonies. Eighty-five thousand marines, and 35,000 troops, in addition to those already engaged, were voted by parliament for the following year, together with the enormous sum of five millions for carrying out this service.

Admiral Arbuthnot had been sent from England in the spring with reinforcements, but did not arrive at New York till August. In December, his fleet conveyed Sir Henry Clinton and his 7,000 troops to the south, and after a tempestuous voyage, landed them at Tybee Island in Savannah harbour, on the last day of January, 1780.

The winter of 1780 was extremely severe; the Hudson and the harbour of New York were frozen over. The garrison and the inhabitants, cut off from their usual supplies by water, suffered extremely from the great scarcity of fuel and fresh provisions. In the expectation that Washington might cross the ice for a general attack, the whole population was put under arms, and the so-called "Board of Associated Loyalists" formed for the defence of the city. But Washington was in no condition to undertake such an enterprise. His entire force did not exceed 10,000 men—a smaller number than composed the garrison of New York; many were militia, whose term of enlistment was expiring; and though congress had called upon the states to send in their quotas, so as to form an army of 35,000 men, this was not done. Recruits could only be obtained on increased bounties, which caused great dissatisfaction to the old soldiers enlisted for the war. Indeed, as regarded the whole state of the American army, nothing could be more discouraging. In a report sent to congress this spring, it was said, "the army was five months unpaid; it seldom had more than six days' provision in advance, and was on several occasions, for sundry successive days, without meat; it was destitute of forage; the medical department had neither sugar, tea, chocolate, wine, nor spirits; every department was without money or even the shadow of credit."[30]

Such was the gloomy prospect in the North; in the South it was even worse. As soon as the transports, which had suffered severely in the voyage, were refitted at Savannah, Sir Henry Clinton embarked, and proceeding to Charleston, landed his troops on St. John's island, and afterwards took possession of St. James's, the same islands, lying at the mouth of Charleston harbour, which we have already mentioned in General Prevost's expedition. The intention being to blockade the town, the British army gradually advanced through the islands to the mainland. Several weeks were spent in this occupation, and Lincoln employed the same time in strengthening and completing the fortifications. Governor Rutledge was invested with dictatorial powers, and slaves were impressed to labour at the works. The neighbouring militia was called upon, but the call was not obeyed, the plea being that no man dared to leave his home, fearing an insurrection of the negroes, and their desertion to the enemy. In this emergency it was earnestly recommended by some to raise 2,000 negro troops, to be purchased at a certain price from their owners, and emancipated when the war was over. But this plan was not agreed to, though it may be mentioned here that many negroes served in the war of the southern states, with great credit as soldiers, and received their freedom in consequence.

The British operations before Charleston were rapid and successful; the success both at Savannah and Charleston being attributed in great measure to the skill of the British engineer Moncrief. General Lincoln depended upon four American and two French frigates for the defence of the harbour; but in defiance of these, the English ships crossed the bar, and entered the harbour without loss or difficulty. To prevent the enemy from ascending Cooper's River, between which and the Ashley River Charleston stands, a number of merchant vessels now useless were sunk. Taking, however, advantage of wind and water, the British admiral having overcome these obstacles, passed with but trifling loss the heavy batteries of Fort Moultrie on Sullivan's Island, which had already become so celebrated for the obstinate and successful defence made against the attack of Sir Peter Parker. As yet the communication with the country north of Cooper's River was kept open by two regiments of horse, stationed about twenty miles above Charleston. These, however, were surprised, dispersed and partly cut to pieces by a detachment of British cavalry, led by the enterprising Colonel Tarleton, and supported by light infantry under Major Ferguson. By these means the passes of Cooper's River were in the hands of the British, and the only road for retreat was closed, and shortly afterwards, a large reinforcement arriving from New York, the collected remains of the cavalry were again attacked, and again defeated by Tarleton. The whole country north of Cooper's River was now occupied by the British, and the investment of the town was complete. Step by step the defences of Charleston had given way. On the very day that the cavalry were defeated, Fort Moultrie, threatened both by land and sea, surrendered. The inhabitants losing all hope and courage, proposed to abandon the town, but Lincoln would only consent to capitulation. On the 7th of May, therefore, he opened a correspondence with Sir Henry Clinton; but the terms which he proposed were rejected, as higher than a commander in his condition had a right to ask. Hostilities again commenced; the British pushed their operations vigorously; one outwork after another was gained; they had advanced to the very ditch of the town. A new negotiation was opened, and the town surrendered upon the terms which were then offered, and which were considered favourable, the British commanders declaring themselves wishful to conciliate by clemency. On May 12th, the garrison marched out with cased colours and silent drums, surrendering their arms as prisoners of war. The continental troops and seamen were allowed to keep their baggage but were to remain prisoners of war until exchanged; the militia were dismissed on parole, not to serve again in the war. The British report states that seven general officers, ten continental regiments and three battalions of artillery, became prisoners on this occasion. The whole number of men in arms who were taken, exclusive of 1,000 seamen, amounted to 5,611. More than 400 pieces of artillery were also lost to the Americans, besides four frigates.

The lieutenant-governor and five of the council were included in the capitulation, but Governor Rutledge and the three other councillors had left the city before the investment was completed.

A series of rapid successes followed. Three expeditions were immediately sent out—one towards the Savannah River; another seized an important post called Ninety-Six, 150 miles from Charleston; and a third scoured the country between the Cooper and the Santee Rivers. The object of this last expedition, under Lord Cornwallis, was to defeat a body of troops under Colonel Burford, on its march to Charleston. Burford, on receiving tidings of the surrender of the town, retreated rapidly up the north-east bank of the Santee, but Tarleton in pursuit moved more rapidly than he did. By a forced march of 105 miles in fifty-four hours, he came up with him at Waxhaws, on the frontier of North Carolina, took his troops by surprise, attacked and completely defeated them, granting no quarter; and "Tarleton's quarter," in memory of the merciless slaughter of this day, has become a Carolina proverb. Burford and a very few only escaped, while the British lost but eighteen. The celerity of British conquest, the rapid speed of the cruel Tarleton, who seemed to possess a terrible ubiquity, spread a panic fear through the South. The patriots fled, and the great mass of the inhabitants rushed to meet the royal troops and offer their allegiance to the British crown. The reduction of South Carolina seemed so complete, that Sir Henry Clinton wrote to England that there were few men in the province who were not prisoners to, or in arms with, the British forces. "South Carolina is English again," said he, in his exultation.

The conquest of South Carolina thus accomplished, and the hot weather coming on, Sir Henry Clinton began to make arrangements for his return to New York, leaving Lord Cornwallis with 4,000 troops to hold and extend his conquests. Before this was done, however, the royal government was established and a mode of settling the affairs of this province adopted which had long been recommended in England to the British commanders in America. This was by establishing such an internal force in each subjugated province as should in a great measure secure its defence and allegiance, and suppress every tendency to rebellion. Accordingly, proclamations were issued promising full pardon to all who would immediately return to their duty as British subjects. But no neutrals were to be allowed; every man who admitted himself to be a British subject must take up arms in support of the British government. All must be in readiness with their arms at a moment's notice; they who had families must form a militia for home defence; they who had none must serve in the royal forces any six months in the ensuing twelve. Thus were citizens armed against citizens, and the members of a family one against another. The worst miseries of civil war were introduced; and this was to be done, said the proclamation, "to drive out the rebel oppressors and all the miseries of war from the province."

This system of intercolonial subjugation was expected to work so efficiently, that Sir Henry Clinton returned to New York, fully believing that a few months would complete the subjection of the whole South, at least. So certain was the British commander of the success of his plans, that before leaving Charleston he sent to bid the loyalists of North Carolina to gather in their crops and keep quiet till autumn, when the British army would march to their assistance.

While these events had been occurring in the South, the American prospects in the North were by no means flattering. The Honourable Board of Associated Loyalists, as they called themselves, organised at New York, possessed at this time, among other means of annoyance to their countrymen, a considerable fleet of small privateers and cruisers, which did great damage. Their enterprises are described as being bold and successful, their intimate knowledge of the coasts, creeks and villages giving them great advantage in their predatory excursions. Many outrages and excesses were committed; party-spirit and private hatred finding here occasions of ample revenge, which was retorted whenever opportunity occurred. In this manner the adjoining coasts of the continent, especially the nearer parts of the Jerseys, became scenes of havoc and waste.[31]

A few days previous to the return of Sir Henry Clinton, Generals Kniphausen and Tryon, with 5,000 men, passed over by night from Staten Island to Elizabeth Town in New Jersey, being desirous of bringing Washington from his strong position at Morristown; and the next day marched through a fertile region, scattered parties of the country's militia firing upon them wherever cover of any kind enabled them to lie concealed. As a little incident of the march, it may be mentioned that they burned a pleasant, peaceful settlement called the Connecticut Farms, with its little Presbyterian meeting-house; and shot, through the window of her house, the wife of the minister, who sat there clustered with her children. This cold-blooded action, like the Indian murder of Jenny M'Crea, excited the utmost indignation, and greatly increased the hatred which was felt towards the British in those parts.

From Connecticut Farms the army advanced to Springfield, where the American general Maxwell, with the Jersey militia, was strongly posted, on finding which, after a little skirmishing and burning a few houses, the British retired towards Elizabeth Town, being vigorously pursued all the way. On the arrival of Sir Henry Clinton, with his troops from Charleston, the attack on Springfield was again determined upon, and such movements took place among the shipping and such preparations were made, as led Washington to suppose that the strong posts of the Highlands were about to be attacked. Accordingly he marched a considerable number of his troops in that direction, and again the British general hoped that Washington might be seduced from his impregnable camp. In the meantime General Greene, with Stark's and the Jersey militia, were stationed at Springfield, which lay at the foot of those very hills and defiles which constituted the strength of the country. A column of 6,000 men marched upon Springfield, and a sharp action took place, not less than a hundred were killed on either side, and the village was set on fire. The sight of the flames, it is said, kindled New Jersey. The old spirit of the early days of the revolution was once more awoke. The British were pursued with such vigour that, passing rapidly through Elizabeth Town, they were glad to take refuge in Staten Island.

CHAPTER X.
REVOLUTIONARY WAR (continued), 1780.

Sir Henry Clinton left the South, believing that the revolutionary spirit there was so nearly quelled that but little apprehension need be felt regarding it. And as if to strengthen this opinion, a decided victory was gained very soon by Lords Cornwallis and Rawdon (afterwards the Earl of Moira), over the combined American forces, under Baron de Kalb and General Gates, at Camden.

General Gates had been sent by Washington, with a strong force from the North, for the relief of the southern provinces. The season was unhealthy; they marched through a barren and disaffected country, were greatly in want of food, and eating unripe peaches and green corn which soon produced disease, their numbers were sadly weakened and thinned. In the meantime De Kalb, with the Delaware and Maryland regiments, marching south with the same object, suffered equally, collecting their own supplies on the march—lean cattle from the canebrakes and Indian corn, the only grain of those regions.[32]

The approach of Gates raised the hopes of the patriots of South Carolina, and Colonel Sumter, who had fled with his partisan-band to North Carolina, on the late triumphs of the British, returned with his fearless followers and made successful attacks on the British posts; while Marion, another bold leader, issuing from the swamps of the Lower Pedee with a number of only half-clad men, began to attack their outposts with equal success. These partisan-bands having joined Gates, he advanced from Clermont, about thirteen miles distant from Camden, on the 5th of August, with the intention of surprising the British camp; while Cornwallis, who had, on his junction with Rawdon, assumed the command, was advancing from Camden with the design of surprising the Americans. The next morning by break of day the two armies encountered each other. Although the Americans greatly outnumbered the British, Gates' militia, which were new to the field, on the first charge of the British bayonets threw down their arms and fled, General Gates and Governor Casswell being fairly carried off the field by the fugitives, whom they could not rally. In vain did the better disciplined and more experienced regiments of Maryland and Delaware sustain their ground with firmness, and even compel the enemy to retire; they too, being attacked in flank and De Kalb their leader mortally wounded, were broken and fled. The pursuit lasted for twenty-eight miles; every corps, says Hildreth, was scattered; men and officers, separated from each other, fled singly or in small parties through the woods. The road was strewn with killed and wounded. Arms, knapsacks, broken-down wagons and dead horses scattered the road for many miles. Of the Americans, 900 were killed, and about the same number taken prisoners, many of whom were wounded. The British lost only between 300 and 400 men.

A few days afterwards disastrous news reached Gates, and about 200 men, the collected fragments of his late considerable force, now assembled in the Valley of Wateree in North Carolina, about eighty miles from the scene of their terrible defeat. This was, that Sumter, having fled with his followers to the same district, had been pursued by the rapid and merciless Tarleton, in whose furious career more than half his cavalry had broken down. Coming with the remainder in hot speed upon the camp of the partisan leader, who, believing himself safe, had relaxed his guard, he had been surprised, his prisoners released, 300 of his own men captured, and 150 killed, while he himself narrowly escaped with his life.

The Carolinas might now be considered subdued, for no organised American forces remained within them. To make the subjection more complete, and to awe the spirit of insurrection which had shown itself on Gates' approach, Lord Cornwallis adopted measures of extreme severity. Orders were issued to hang every man now found in arms, who had formerly taken British protection, and several such persons having been discovered among Sumter's followers, they were accordingly hanged on the spot. The property of all such as had left the province to avoid the British rule, and of all that held commissions under congress, was declared to be sequestrated, and Gadsden and forty other of the principal inhabitants of Charleston, suspected of having corresponded with their friends in arms, were put under arrest and sent prisoners to St. Augustine.

These extreme measures, however, failed of their intended purpose. A reaction, as was sure to be the case, followed. The people, who had been awed into subjection, were now exasperated to revolt. Marion again had a ragged but formidable band under his control among the swamps of the Pedee, and Sumter presently collected a new force with which he harassed the north-western districts, and in which he was aided by volunteers from the mountains. Both were now commissioned as generals, and a guerilla warfare was kept up by them.[33]

Nor was the public reaction confined only to the men—it raised the women of South Carolina into heroism. They gloried in being called "rebel-ladies," refused their presence at the scenes of gaiety offered them by the conquerors of their cities, and occupied themselves instead, in visiting and relieving the sufferings and wants of the wounded soldiers, and encouraged their husbands, sons, or brothers, still to be "rebels," and die, if it must be so, rather than submit to the British. Nor was this noble patriotism confined only to the South. Mrs. Willard assures us, eloquently, that patriotism glowed in the hearts of women throughout all parts of the country, and that they displayed great activity in collecting materials and making clothes for the soldiers. In Philadelphia, a society for this purpose was formed, at the head of which was Martha Washington, the wife of the commander-in-chief. All this was as it should be, but not more than we have a right to expect from the daughters of a parentage so worthy as was that of many an American. The earth's best blood was in their veins. The daughters of those pilgrim-mothers who left their native land to establish purer and more Christian homes in the American wilderness, could not so belie their ancestry as to fail in the charities of womanhood.

But we now come to a dark passage, which forms a strong contrast to the patriotism of the above.

The utmost gloom hung over the American affairs in the North. France had once more, it is true, under the influence of La Fayette, who now returned to America, sent over a fleet and a considerable number of troops, to co-operate with the republicans; but nothing as yet had been done. So doubtful indeed did it appear, towards the autumn of 1780, whether the army could even be maintained for another campaign, that Washington was anxious, while he had yet any forces under his command, to strike some decisive blow, and he accordingly proposed to Count de Rochambeau, the French general, who lay with his troops at Newport, to make an attack on New York. In order to concert this proposed plan, Washington went to Hartford, and during his absence a scheme of treason, in the very bosom of the American camp, came to light, which fell like a thunderbolt on the country, and which has so much interesting detail connected with it, that we must be allowed to give it somewhat fully, and in doing so we will principally follow the excellent American historian Hildreth, and the Annual Register of 1781.

In September, a plot was laid for betraying the important fortress of West Point, and other posts of the Highlands, into the hands of the enemy, the traitor being no other than Arnold, the most brilliant officer and one of the most honoured in the American army. Arnold, however, with all his fine qualities as a soldier, was a man of an overbearing and reckless spirit; he had in many cases shown great want of integrity and disregard of the rights of others; nevertheless his valour and his many brilliant achievements had cast his faults into the shade and placed him in command at Philadelphia. There, however, as we have already mentioned, his conduct had given rise to much dissatisfaction. He occupied the best mansion in the city, and lived in so expensive a style as to become involved in debt, to free himself from which he entered into mercantile and privateering speculations. This mode of living and these speculations led to the interference of congress, and the sentence of a reprimand from the commander-in-chief. His debts and moneydifficulties caused him to request, but in vain, a loan from the French minister. The same causes had already led him to open a correspondence with Sir Henry Clinton, though how this was first commenced, and through whom carried on, is not known. When, however, he was satisfied that the treacherous purpose he had in view would be satisfactorily entered into, and in order to enable him to accomplish it most effectually, he solicited from Washington the command in the Highlands, and Washington, who, spite of Arnold's faults, had confidence in him, and who was glad to show this after the humiliation he had just laid upon him, placed that important trust in his hands.

The peculiar circumstances of these highland strongholds at this crisis must be borne in mind. The failure of the French fleet with regard to the attack on New York having overthrown all prospects of active operation on the side of the Americans for the present season, Washington stationed his army for the winter in these very posts, on each side of the North River, where, besides security, they had an opportunity of watching the motions of the British and repressing any incursions from New York. In this arrangement, the strong and very important post of West Point, with its neighbouring dependencies and one wing of the army, were intrusted to the custody and conduct of General Arnold.

In order to arrange the terms of the bargain, an interview was necessary with some confidential British agent, and Major André, with whom Arnold had already carried on a correspondence under the feigned names of Gustavus and Anderson, volunteered for this purpose. The outlines of the project were that Arnold should make such a disposition of the wing under his command, as should enable Sir Henry Clinton to surprise their strong posts and batteries, and throw the troops so entirely into his hands that they must inevitably either lay down their arms or be cut to pieces on the spot. Nor was this all; other consequences followed: the remainder of Washington's army would thus he laid open to the joint attack of the British forces both by land and water, so that nothing would remain for the American cause but slaughter, rout, dispersion and final ruin. Such a blow, it was deemed, would be irrevocable. Independent of the loss of artillery, magazines and stores, such a destruction of their disciplined troops and of their best officers must be immediately fatal.

If a presentiment of woe falls like a great cloud over the sensitive and occult spirit at the approach of evil, we may well understand why the mind of Washington at this moment was overcast by gloom and apprehension. A few hours after he had gone to Hartford, under great depression and anxiety, the necessary steps were taken for the accomplishment of this stratagem of evil. The British sloop-of-war Vulture, with Major André on board, having already ascended the Hudson, and lying now some few miles below King's Ferry, a boat was sent off by Arnold at nightfall, which brought André on shore and landed him on the west side of the river, just below the American lines, where Arnold was waiting for him. It was morning before the arrangements were completed, and then Arnold persuaded André to enter the American lines and remain secreted all day in the house of one Smith, the person who had brought him on shore. In the meantime the Vulture, having attracted the notice of the American gunners, had found it necessary to change her position, and probably from the dread of discovery, though the true cause has never been really known, Smith refused to take André back to the ship at night as he had engaged to do.

On the second day, therefore, towards sunset, laying aside his uniform, which he had till now worn under a plain surtout, assuming an ordinary dress, and being furnished with a pass from Arnold, in the name of John Anderson, he set out on horseback, with Smith for a guide, and having passed through a remote part of the camp, and all the guards and posts, in safety, they crossed King's Ferry and spent the night with an acquaintance of Smith's. The next morning, the guide having conducted him safely across Croton River, left him to pursue the rest of his journey alone. He had now to pass through a district some thirty miles above the Island of New York, known as "neutral ground," a populous and fertile region, infested by bands of plunderers, called "Cow-Boys and Skinners." The "Cow-Boys" lived within the British lines, and bought or stole cattle for the supply of the British army. The rendezvous of the "Skinners" was within the American lines. They professed to be great patriots, making it their ostensible business to plunder all who refused to take the oath of allegiance to the State of New York. But they were ready in fact to rob anybody, and the cattle thus obtained were often sold to the "Cow-boys," in exchange for dry goods brought from New York. By a state law, all cattle driven towards the city beyond a certain line were lawful plunder, and a general authority was given to arrest suspicious travellers.[34]

In passing through a place called Tarrytown, André was stopped by three young men, John Paulding, David Williams and Isaac van Wert, on the look-out for cattle or travellers. His passport at first seemed to satisfy them, and they allowed him to proceed. He had not, however, gone many yards, when one of them on recollection was so forcibly struck by some peculiarity in the stranger's manner or countenance, that he peremptorily insisted on returning with his companions, and examining more strictly. This second thought on his part was fatal to André. André, not used to, or not prepared for such an encounter—or, as he himself said in his letter to Washington, too little versed in deception to practise it with any degree of success—offered his captors a considerable purse of gold, a valuable watch, or anything which they might name, if they would suffer him to proceed to New York.

His offers were rejected; he was searched, suspicious papers were found in his boots, and he was carried before Colonel Jamison, the commanding officer on the lines. The papers found upon André, who still maintained the name of Anderson, a supposed inhabitant of New York, were found to contain precise accounts of the state of the forces, ordnance and defences of West Point and its dependences, with the artillery orders, critical remarks on the works, the amount of men on duty each day, together with interesting particulars, which had been laid before a council of war by the commander-in-chief. Although these papers were in the handwriting of Arnold, Jamison, unable to believe that his commanding officer was a traitor, forwarded them by express to Washington at Hartford, and sent the prisoner to Arnold, informing him of his assumed name, his passport, and that papers of a very suspicious character had been found upon him. Circumstances favoured Arnold in various ways. Major Talmadge, who had been absent, returning at this moment, retained André, though the letter went forward to Arnold, and the express, with the papers themselves, sent to Washington, missed him on the road, he being then on his return to Hartford. Washington's aides-de-camp, who preceded him, were breakfasting with Arnold when Jamison's letter arrived. Pretending that it was an immediate call to visit one of the forts on the other side of the river, Arnold rose from table, called his wife up stairs, told her sufficient to throw her into a fainting-fit, mounted a ready-saddled horse, rode to the river-side, threw himself into a barge, passed the forts, waving a handkerchief by way of flag, and ordered his boatmen to row for the Vulture. Safe on board, he wrote a letter to Washington, declaring that the love of his country had been the ruling principle of his life; but the main purpose of the letter was to ask protection for his wife, whom he declared innocent of what he had done.[35]

When André found that Arnold had escaped, and that no means of delivery remained for himself, he wrote a letter to Washington, avowing his name and character. The imputation of treachery and the dread of appearing in the base light of a spy, appeared worse to him than death. Strange, that a noble nature, such as André's unquestionably was, had not perceived from the first that the whole transaction was base, and that he was the tool of a second Judas. The burden and shame, however, of the consequences of his act bowed him down to the very dust, and he now besought of Washington that to whatever fate a rigorous policy might doom him, a decency of treatment might be observed which should testify that, though unfortunate, he was branded with nothing dishonourable, and that he was involuntarily an imposter. André was examined before a board of officers, and upon the very story which he himself told he was pronounced a spy, and as such was doomed to speedy death.

Sir Henry Clinton used the utmost efforts to save him, but the manly and frank behaviour of André, and the amiable character which he bore, pleaded for him more than all these, or than the letter which Arnold wrote to Washington on the same subject, threatening the severest retaliation if the life of André were taken. The public heart sympathised with him, but martial justice demanded his life, and his last prayer that he might be shot rather than hanged was denied. And it was right so far, that if it be justifiable to take human life, and this were a crime of which death was the penalty, the quality of the offender should make no difference; on the contrary, perhaps, even in proportion as his nature was pure and generous, so could there be the less excuse to him of a dull perception between a base and a noble action; and the intended treachery of Arnold was base in the extreme.

The day after the sentence was passed, Oct. 2nd, it was carried into execution, and the dignity and composure of the criminal is said to have excited the utmost admiration, while it melted all hearts. The sympathy which André excited in the American army, says the British chronicler of this event, is perhaps unexampled under any circumstances. It was said that the whole board of general officers shed tears at the drawing-up and signing the report, and that even Washington wept upon hearing the circumstances of his death. All those about him treated him with the most marked attention, with the greatest kindness and the most scrupulous delicacy.

There is a touching pathos in the whole sad history, and a calm dignity in the behaviour of all parties, the offender and the offended, which elevate humanity and are deeply affecting to contemplate. Nor as regarded Arnold, the willing Judas of American liberty, was this noble Christian dignity compromised. Washington sent Mrs. Arnold to her husband at New York, who was himself obliged to confess his obligation to the commander-in-chief for the kindness and protection which she had received from him, as well as the many obligations she was under to the gentlemen of his family. The clothes and baggage which he had sent for were likewise forwarded to him, but as regarded all other matters, his letters and himself were passed over without the smallest notice.[36] Somewhat later, however, when he had published an address to the inhabitants of America, calling upon them to "surrender to Great Britain, and to be no longer the tools and dupes of congress and France," his name was publicly placed by the executive power of Pennsylvania at the head of a list of ten traitors, who were summoned to surrender by a given day, or to be subjected to all the pains, penalties and forfeitures of high-treason. Beyond that, Arnold was dead to the country;

the magnitude of his offence placed him below her recognition. For himself he received £10,000, and was made a brigadier-general in the British army. He was also authorised to raise a corps of cavalry and infantry among the disaffected, who were to be clothed and fed like the other troops in the British service, and to whom a bounty of three guineas per man was given, besides payment at full value for horses, arms and accoutrements. All these being intended as strong baits in opposition to the distress, want of pay, hunger and nakedness of the republican army.

As regarded the treachery of Arnold, Washington took immediate measures to protect his camp and works from its consequences; but it did not appear that he had any party in the army; no defection followed, and the example tended probably rather as a warning than otherwise.

During these events in the north, the two hostile parties in the south had not been inactive. General Gates, who had not sustained in South Carolina the reputation which he gained by the surrender of Burgoyne, was superseded by General Greene. Both Lee and Steuben were ordered to the south, as well as Kosciusko, who acted as engineer.

In September, Cornwallis detached Colonel Ferguson to the frontiers of North Carolina, for the purpose of encouraging the loyalists to take arms. A large number of the most profligate and abandoned repaired to his standard, and under the conduct of their leader committed atrocious excesses. This roused the country; the militia were out; and a force of mounted backwoodsmen, armed with rifles and their provision at their backs, led by Shelby and Sevier, afterwards first governors of Kentucky and Tennessee, and joined by various partisan corps, marched against Ferguson, who was advancing towards the mountains. On the first tidings of this formidable force Ferguson fled, pursued by 1,000 of the best mounted and surest marksmen out of double that number; and so rapid was the flight and the pursuit, that in thirty-six hours the mountaineer-backwoodsmen dismounted but once. Ferguson, finding escape impossible, chose a strong position at King's Mountain, on the Catawbee River, the boundary line between North and South Carolina. The attack was furious and the defence exceedingly obstinate; but, at length, Ferguson being slain, and 300 of his followers killed or wounded, the survivors, to the number of 800, threw down their arms and surrendered. Ten of the most obnoxious of these were immediately hanged as traitors, an outrage which was soon richly retaliated. After this the backwoodsmen retired as rapidly to their homes, and their victory, when trumpeted abroad, raised the sinking spirit of the South.[37]

Again Marion and Sumter were in the field, and the ubiquitous Tarleton, with his rapid cavalry, was despatched first against one and then the other.

Marion was driven back to his swamps; and Sumter, having joined with other partisan corps in an attack on Fort Ninety-Six, defeated and took prisoner Major Wemyss, after which, having received intelligence through a deserter that Tarleton and his troop were out in pursuit, he took up a position on Blackstock Hill. Tarleton, after a severe loss, was obliged to retreat, leaving Sumter severely wounded, and in possession of the field. The close of the year was now approaching, and Sumter being conveyed to a place of safety, his followers dispersed.

On December 2nd, Greene joined the American army at Charlotte and assumed command. He found the troops without pay, and their clothing in tatters. There was scarcely a dollar in the military chest, and subsistence was obtained by impressment; nevertheless he entered at once on active operations; determining, however, rather to harass the British army than, in the present weak condition of his troops, to risk a general action. But it was not the army alone which was on the alert. All the scattered settlements of Whigs and Tories were in hostile array, and pursued each other with almost savage fury. The excitable temperament of the South gave to the struggle a more terrible character than it had in the North. Everywhere were small parties under arms, some on one side some on the other, desperately bent on plunder and blood.

At the close of this year England was satisfied with the progress which her arms had made in America; no ground of any consequence was lost in the North, while in the South, Georgia was entirely subdued and the royal government re-established. The possession of Charleston, Augusta, Ninety-Six and Camden, supported by an army in the field, secured entire control over the populous and wealthy parts of South Carolina. North Carolina was full of Tories, impatient to acknowledge the British crown on the arrival of Cornwallis. The three southern states were incapable of helping themselves, and the North, exhausted and penniless, was in no condition to help them. The colonies seemed almost sinking under the accumulated pressure of this long-protracted struggle. England, in the meantime, assailed by three European nations, and sustaining a war against two hemispheres, America and the East Indies, was putting forth energies and voting supplies on the most immense scale, as if the very demand increased her powers of exertion. The siege of Gibraltar, under its commander Elliot, was going on; great battles were fought on the West Indian and European seas; fleets and armies went to the East and to the West, and the new year commenced with preparations in all these various and remote scenes of action for new enterprise, for new effort.

As regarded America herself, France, in addition to the troops under Rochambeau, sent out a large fleet at the commencement of this year, under the Count de Grasse, which, after having performed certain service in the West Indies, was to co-operate with Rochambeau and Washington on the coast of America.

The state of affairs, however, was most anxious and critical, and calculated to create the most serious alarm. Although the efforts made during the past year, and the late successes in the South, had revived the public spirit, still no sufficient or permanent means had been provided for supplying the increasing wants of the army. The country seemed upon the brink of ruin. Nor can any situation be imagined more painful than that of the American congress at this moment. The enemy had advanced into the heart of the country; they had important militia operations to carry forward, but were wholly without money. Their bills of credit had so completely lost their value, that they had ceased to be a legal tender, and were not received even in payment of taxes. In this emergency their agents, as already had been done, were directed to borrow from France, Spain, and Holland. They resorted to the unpopular measure of taxation, the tax being apportioned among the several state governments, by whose authority it was collected; and in order as much as possible to introduce economy and to prevent disorder, waste, or peculation, they appointed Robert Morris of Philadelphia as their treasurer, a man whose pure morals, ardent patriotism, and great knowledge of financial concerns, eminently fitted him for this important station.

The zeal and genius of Morris soon produced the best results. A national bank was established, wealthy individuals were induced to deposit here their funds, and by borrowing in the name of government from this bank, and pledging in return the taxes not yet collected, he was enabled to anticipate them, and command a supply. He also made use of his own credit, which was good, and bills were in circulation at one time, bearing his signature, to the amount of £100,000. Franklin also obtained a loan of 4,000,000 of livres from the court of France, which likewise gave its guarantee to Holland for a loan of 10,000,000. Spain refused to lend money unless she received a monopoly of the navigation of the Mississippi, which was steadily refused.[38]

So far a better prospect dawned, but before the effects were perceived to any extent, an alarming revolt took place among both the Pennsylvanian and the New Jersey troops, the causes of which were the exact terms of their enlistment, and the want of necessaries. The Pennsylvanian troops, to the number of 1,300, abandoning their camp, commenced their march to Princetown, where congress was sitting, that they might lay their grievances before it. On their way they were met by emissaries from Sir Henry Clinton, who wished to entice them into the British service; but indignant at this attempt to corrupt their fidelity, they seized their tempters and gave them up to General Wayne to be punished as spies. At Princetown they were met by a committee from congress, which, fearing the effect of this revolt at this moment, relieved their necessities in part, and allowed such as claimed their discharge on a three years' service, to leave the ranks, which most of them did. To their credit, however, be it said, that when offered a reward for apprehending the British emissaries, they nobly refused it, saying, they wanted no reward for doing their duty to their country against her enemies. The revolters in New Jersey did not, however, come off so well. Washington, determined to put a stop to further insubordination, despatched at once a force on which he could rely, from West Point, under Colonel Howe, which suddenly surrounding the camp of the insurgents, compelled them to submission, and two of their leaders being tried by court-martial and shot, there was no more revolt in the army.

In October of this year, General Leslie sailed from New York, with 3,000 men, to reinforce Lord Cornwallis, and lay for some time at Portsmouth on the Chesapeake, to be in readiness against North Carolina. On the news, however, of Ferguson's defeat, he proceeded to Charleston, and shortly after—in fact, at the very commencement of 1781—Sir Henry Clinton despatched the traitor, now Brigadier-General Arnold, to occupy Portsmouth and to make a diversion in Virginia, not doubting but that the force of his name and character would attract great numbers to the British standard. The force under Arnold amounted to about 1,700, most of them loyalists, a small corps of 200 having been raised in New York by Arnold himself, together with a considerable number of armed vessels. Arriving in the Chesapeake, and leaving a sufficient force at Portsmouth, Arnold ascended the James River, and commenced a series of ravages on the unprotected settlements. Governor Jefferson called out the militia, but the white population were so scanty and scattered on their distant plantations, and were so much occupied in keeping their slaves in order, that the call was hardly obeyed, 200 only appearing for the defence of Richmond, the capital.

Arnold entered without opposition, and immediately commenced to destroy the public stores, as well as many public and private buildings, after which he retired to Portsmouth, which he fortified and made his head-quarters. A plan in the meantime was formed by Washington to capture him and his army. La Fayette was sent down into Virginia, and at the earnest request of Washington, the French fleet stationed at Rhode Island, with a number of French troops on board, sailed to co-operate with him. The British, however, being apprised of this project, Admiral Arbuthnot sailed from Gardiner's Bay in Long Island, where he had lain with his squadron all the winter, attacked the French fleet off the capes of Chesapeake, and compelled it to return to Rhode Island. The British squadron entered the Chesapeake, and shortly after, a reinforcement of

2,000 men being sent from New York to Portsmouth, Arnold, happily for himself, was delivered from the imminent peril which had threatened him of falling into the hands of his countrymen. The British frigates ascending the rivers of Virginia, levied contributions upon all the tide-water counties. One of these vessels entering the Potomac, reached Mount Vernon, the home and plantation of Washington, whose manager, to save the buildings from destruction, supplied a quantity of provisions, greatly to the displeasure of the American commander-in-chief when he heard of the fact.[39]

CHAPTER XI.
THE REVOLUTIONARY WAR (continued), 1781.

With the commencement of the year all parties in the South prepared for war. On the 1st of January, Lord Cornwallis left his camp at Winnsborough, intending to advance into North Carolina and interpose between Greene and Morgan, who were now actively on the alert, and against the latter of whom Tarleton had been despatched, with orders to "push him to the utmost." Greene, at the head of 1,000 men, was encamped at the confluence of Hick's Creek with the Peedee, while Morgan, with the same number, had been sent westward by him to guard the passes of the Pacolet river. On Tarleton's approach Morgan retreated; Tarleton crossed the river, and the pursuit began. The situation of Morgan was perilous, the enemy was behind him, the Broad River before him, to cross which was impossible. But Morgan, the stout quondam wrestler and teamsman, was not easily daunted; on his right lay a hilly district which might afford him protection; choosing, therefore, his ground hastily, he drew up his men in order of battle, at a place called the Cowpens, about three miles south of the boundary of South Carolina. The forces were about equal. Tarleton was confident of victory; Morgan also intended that the day should be his; about half of his troops, however, were South Carolina militia, under General Pickens, new to war, and therefore little to be relied upon. These he placed in the van, while the continentals, on whom he could depend, were posted in an open wood, and the cavalry on a slope in the rear. As he expected, the militia gave way immediately before the impetuous attack of Tarleton; the British troops shouted for victory, and rushed forward in pursuit, but then the real struggle of the fight commenced. The continentals, too, had retrograded for a moment before the rapid advance of the British, who, mistaking this for retreat, rushed forward in some confusion, and the next moment a deadly fire from the Americans, who had suddenly faced about, turned the British pursuit into flight; and while these rapid movements had been taking place, the American cavalry coming up decided the fortune of the day. The ground was in an instant, as it were, covered with killed and wounded. Tarleton's whole force was completely routed. The British lost 400 in killed and wounded, while 500 prisoners, with a large quantity of baggage, and 100 dragoon horses, fell into the hands of the Americans, whose loss was less than eighty men.

Immediately on the news of this unexpected disaster, Lord Cornwallis, then on the left bank of the Broad River, despatched a part of his army, disencumbered of baggage, in the hope of intercepting Morgan before he could pass that river, and recovering, at least, the prisoners; but Morgan, ever active, and aware of his probable danger, pushed on without loss of time for the fords of the river, which he was fortunately able to cross two hours before the van of the enemy appeared on the opposite bank, and by that time a sudden rise of the river had rendered it impassable.

Disappointed, therefore, in this design, and knowing that the loss of the light troops could only be remedied by the general activity of the whole army, Lord Cornwallis spent two days in burning all superfluous baggage and stores, himself setting the example by destroying every unnecessary article or luxury which belonged to himself. Upon this principle all the wagons, excepting those loaded with hospital stores, salt, or ammunition, and four empty ones reserved for the sick or wounded, were destroyed; all casks of spirituous liquors or wine were staved, and the only supply of flour they could depend upon was the pittance they might obtain and carry along with them.

The heavy rains which had been so serviceable to Morgan in preventing the further progress of the enemy continued for two days, and all the fords for forty miles were not only impassible from the accession of the waters, but vigilantly guarded by American detachments; and Greene himself, on receiving intelligence of the battle of the Cowpens, hastened forward from the Peedee, and assumed in person the command of Morgan's division, being now desirous of keeping the enemy on the other side of the river until the whole force arrived.

On the first falling of the water, Lord Cornwallis, who had in the meantime come up, detached a party of the army to attack a private ford which was held by 300 Americans, and of which they succeeded in forcing a passage. Again the American army retreated, and again the British were in pursuit, and a second time came very close upon their rear as they were about to cross the Yadkin, as the Peedee is called in its upper course. Again the American army crossed safely, and only a small portion of their baggage remained on the other side, when the British came in sight, and a smart skirmish took place between the advance and rear guards. But again the river rose, and the pursuers were unable to cross. The hand of Providence seemed extended as of old to open for his people a path through the waters, which he closed again to their enemies. So it appeared to the Americans safe on the other side, and so it was regarded throughout the country.

From the Yadkin, Greene proceeded to Guildford Court-house, having effected a junction with his main army, which, under General Huger, had advanced up the left bank of the river, and continued his flight, still vigorously pursued by Cornwallis, who was anxious to prevent his entering Virginia, whence alone supplies and recruits could be expected. It was now for the third time a trial of speed between the two armies, and for the third time also the British reached the banks of the river Dan, an upper branch of the Roanoke, just as the American rear were safely across. Here Cornwallis, mortified at such repeated disappointments after the extraordinary efforts which he had made, gave up the pursuit and turned slowly towards the South. It was well that he did so, for the American army needed repose; the march of the last day had been forty miles; the shoes were worn from the soldiers' feet, many were quite barefoot, and this long and hasty flight was tracked with their blood.[40]

The American army thus driven out of North Carolina, Lord Cornwallis, after giving his troops a day's rest, led them slowly back to Hillsborough, the seat of the state government, where he erected the royal standard, and issued a proclamation inviting all loyal subjects to repair to him and aid in restoring the constitutional government to the colony. We have mentioned the sufferings of the American army—those of the British were not much less. "The wants and distresses of the English troops," says the British chronicler of these events, "were only equalled by their toils and fatigues. They traversed a country which was alternately a wild and inhospitable forest, or inhabited by a people who were, at least, highly adverse, however they might venture or not to be hostile. When to these are added all the possible incommodities incident to bad roads, heavy rains, want of cover, and the continual wading through numberless deep creeks and rivers in the depth of winter, some idea may be formed of their sufferings."

While these events were going forward, and the state authorities having fled from Hillsborough to Newbern, a British detachment from Wilmington marched to that place, entered it without impediment, burned the shipping, and having destroyed all the salt, sugar, rum, and stores of every kind, returned to Wilmington.

In response to the proclamation of Lord Cornwallis, the Tories of North Carolina began to embody themselves, and on February 21st, Tarleton was despatched into the district between the Haw and Deep rivers to assist in their organisation. In the meantime, General Greene, reinforced by a body of Virginians, re-entered North Carolina, and hearing of this movement among the Tories, sent Colonel Lee, with a body of militia, to prevent it. On his way Lee encountered the newly-embodied loyalist troops, with whom Tarleton had not yet come up, and they mistaking these troops for those of their friends, eagerly made known their loyalty by shouts of "Long live the King!" when being at once surrounded by the Americans, the greater number were cut to pieces, and the remainder made prisoners.

Greene, though still receiving reinforcements, did not consider himself as yet strong enough to encounter an engagement; and in order to avoid surprise, took up a new position every night, never informing any person the day before where his next encampment would be. Indeed, the strict reserve which this commander maintained regarding his plans caused the utmost embarrassment to the British throughout the whole southern campaign. The prisoners taken on any occasion from the American army would give no account of the numbers and disposition of the troops, nor yet of the ground where they lay. Lord Cornwallis complains repeatedly, that "either from stupidity or design the country people would give him no information, or if they did, it was unintelligible or contradictory; the little reliance to be placed on any information which was obtained being among the distinguishing features of the war in this province."

Lord Cornwallis moved from point to point, anxious to cover the country and afford the loyalists encouragement and opportunity to join his army, and at the same time to keep open the communication of Cape Fear River, which the "grievous distresses" of his army rendered necessary. At length, towards the middle of March, Greene's forces, now amounting to about 4,500 men, and being at a great distance from his supplies, and in the midst of a country where his friends were few and wavering, he, too, sought a battle in his turn. For many days Cornwallis had been harassed by uncertain rumours as to the course of his enemy, when, on the 15th, he received the authentic intelligence that Greene had reached Guilford, twelve miles only from the British camp, and that a battle might be expected.

The country in which the two armies were to meet was a wilderness covered with tall wood, and a thick undergrowth of shrubs, with here and there a clearing. Greene, having left his baggage seventeen miles in the rear, posted his men on advantageous ground on a wooded hill with an open field in front, about two miles from Guilford Court-house. The North Carolina militia, many of them compelled to serve as a punishment for their suspected loyalty, were posted in the front. At the first charge these militia fled, throwing away their arms and knapsacks; the Virginian militia, however, stood firm and fought resolutely for a considerable time, when, being driven back, the action became general; but owing to the nature of the ground the order of battle was completely broken, and consisted rather of a series of irregular, hard-fought and bloody skirmishes. At length the Americans were driven back, and their artillery captured, when Greene ordered a retreat, which was made without confusion, and the same night he reached the Iron Works of Troublesome Creek, at eighteen miles' distance.

The loss on both sides was said to be between 400 and 500; and as the fighting had extended over a great space of ground, the wounded were scattered as widely. "There were neither houses nor tents to receive them," says Hildreth. "The night that followed the battle was dark and tempestuous; horrid shrieks resounded through the woods; many expired before the morning."

The Americans were routed, but the British were in no condition to follow them; the troops in the first instance were worn down by the excessive fatigues of a long march; their wounded, which lay so wide and so ill provided for, required attention; and besides, such was the desolate state of the country, that during the two days they remained here they had no bread, nor was forage to be obtained nearer than nine miles; and though the victory was gained in a part of the country which boasted of its loyalty, very little assistance was given, nor did any great number join the royal cause. Leaving, therefore, seventy of the worst wounded behind him, in a Quakers' meeting-house converted into a hospital, Lord Cornwallis retired by easy marches to Cross Creek, now Fayetteville, again issuing a proclamation, and using all means in his power to encourage and call forth the loyalists of the district, but with little effect. He was disappointed also in the store of provisions which he expected to have found here; the absolute scarcity compelled him still to advance; and after a toilsome circuitous march of 200 miles, the victors, who according to their own phrase, "had gained so much glory at Guilford," reached Wilmington worn out and famished, and thankful to find at length shelter and rest.

Though Greene did not fare much better as regarded the subsistence of his army, no sooner had Cornwallis retired towards Wilmington, than he determined to march into South Carolina, now held in subjection by Lord Rawdon and a small force. Early in April, therefore, Greene was advancing through that barren region in which Gates and his troops had suffered so much eleven months before, towards Camden, where Lord Rawdon lay with about 900 loyalists. Despatching Colonel Lee with his cavalry to join Marion and other partisan corps immediately on his entering South Carolina, Greene took up his position at Hobkirk's Mill, about two miles from Camden, and on April 25th a battle took place, the victory at first strongly inclining to the Americans. A Maryland regiment, however, falling into confusion, a rout ensued, but the loss was about equal on both sides; and in consequence of the American artillery having been run down a steep hill among some brushwood, it was overlooked by the British troops in their pursuit, and the American cavalry carried it safely away before their return. Greene retired the same night to Rugeley's Mills, about twelve miles off, where he encamped.

The news of Greene's bold advance into South Carolina reached Lord Cornwallis at Wilmington, too late for him to march to the succour of Lord Rawdon; he, therefore, imitating the American general's policy, marched at once into Virginia, to join the British force under Arnold and Philips, which was committing great ravages there.

Although the British had defeated the Americans in the last engagement, this victory no more than the former produced any favourable results to the British cause. Already before this battle was fought, Fort Watson, on the Santee River, and one of the lines of communication between Camden and Charleston, had surrendered to Lee and Marion; the whole country was in arms, and Colonel Watson on his way to reinforce Lord Rawdon, was in consequence obliged to pass and repass the Santee, going down almost to the very mouth of the river for the first, and up to the confluence of that river with the Congaree for the second, before he was able to reach Camden, where he had long been anxiously expected. But with his arrival came the intelligence that Fort Motte, situated at the junction of the Congaree and Santee, was invested by Lee and Marion. This being the case, Lord Rawdon, now reinforced, withdrew to Nelson's Ferry, sixty miles from Camden, having first made a vain attempt to draw General Greene into another engagement. On the 9th of May he abandoned Camden, having destroyed all the works, and leaving behind him such sick and wounded as were unable to bear the removal, and on the 13th arrived at Nelson's Ferry, the unwelcome news having reached him by the way of the surrender of Fort Motte. This was a heavy loss, for at this place were deposited all the provisions that were intended for the supply of Camden. More bad news followed: Sumter took another strong post at Orangeburg, and Fort Granby surrendered to Lee, who was then sent against Augusta. Scarcely had these tidings been received than Colonel Balfour, the commandant of Charleston, made his appearance, full of apprehensions regarding the state of affairs there, and the alarming turn which they had taken in so short a time. So little, indeed, had this been expected, that the whole fortifications of the town had been removed, and the new were not yet completed; and so strong was his belief in the general disaffection of the people, that if any misfortune happened to Lord Rawdon's forces, the loss of the province and capital might be anticipated. As a proof of the disaffection of the country, it is related by the English that for five days after Lord Rawdon had crossed the Santee, not a single person of any sort whatever came near his camp, nor could the spies and emissaries which he sent out in all directions procure for him any true intelligence as to the situation of the enemy. The enemy, however, was busy all this time, and as we have said, one strong post after another was taken. Alarmed at these ominous proceedings, Lord Rawdon, accompanied by a great number of Tory families, retreated from Nelson's Ferry to Monk's Corner, still nearer to Charleston, that he might protect the town and the fertile country which intervened.

The next tidings were that General Greene was investing Ninety-Six, the principal British stronghold in the upper country, which the garrison of American loyalists was very bravely defending. On this, being fortunately just then reinforced by three regiments from Ireland, Lord Rawdon hastened to its relief. It was then the middle of summer, and marching with as much speed as the excessive heat would allow, he had the mortification of learning by the way, that Augusta had surrendered, and that the forces employed in its reduction had now joined Greene.

The Americans were attempting an unsuccessful assault on Ninety-Six, when the unwelcome tidings reached them, that Lord Rawdon, strongly reinforced, was advancing to the relief of that fort. The utmost bravery had been displayed in the attack, the ditch was full of killed and wounded, when Greene determined to abandon the attempt, and not even to face the new foe. He had already, it appeared, anticipated such an event, by sending off all the heavy baggage across the Saluda, whither he now also followed. The British pursued for forty miles, as far as the fords of Ennoree, but finding then that the Americans had crossed safely two hours before, and the troops being spent with fatigue and the excessive heat, Lord Rawdon slowly returned to Ninety-Six, which was then abandoned, and the British army, again accompanied by great numbers of terrified loyalists, retired to Orangeburg, where leaving the greater part of his forces to aid the loyalists in embodying themselves, he marched with the remainder to Congaree, closely pursued by Greene, who hoped to be able to surround him while he waited for promised reinforcements. It happened, however, that Lord Rawdon arrived at Congaree two days sooner than was expected, and finding the enemy so near, and suspecting their intentions, he made a rapid move again towards Orangeburg, and Greene, now joined by Marion, having altered his intentions, retired as suddenly to the hills of the Santee, to refresh his troops and wait for reinforcements.

The summer in the South closed the campaign. The sufferings of the British in this climate were excessive. During renewed forced marches, under the rage of a burning sun, they were frequently, when sinking under the extremest fatigue, not only destitute of every comfort, but almost of every necessary. They were for the greater part destitute of bread, and the country afforded no vegetables as a substitute—salt too failed them, at length, and their only resource was water and the wild cattle found in the woods. About fifty men in this last expedition sunk under the rigour of their exertions and died of sheer fatigue. Nor did the Americans suffer less. Twice they had been defeated in two pitched battles; yet upon the whole the campaign terminated in their favour. The greater part of Georgia was recovered, as were also the two Carolinas; the British being now limited to the district between the Santee and the Lower Savannah.

Although operations between the main armies were suspended during the hot and unhealthy season, the partisan corps on both sides were actively employed. This it was which added such additional horrors to the war in the South. Houses were plundered and burned and their inhabitants murdered, women and children seldom being spared. One great object of plunder was slaves. Sumter paid his men in this manner. The number of slaves carried off during the war is estimated at 30,000. Lord Dunmore, at the commencement of the struggle, armed the slaves against their masters; and had the British persevered in this plan, and, treating the slaves as men and king's subjects, converted them into soldiers, the conquest of the Southern States would have been almost inevitable.[41]

Lord Rawdon soon after returned to England, in consequence of ill health, and the command devolved upon Colonel Stuart. Before his departure from Charleston, however, a tragical circumstance occurred there which greatly irritated the Carolinians and threw great odium upon the British. This was the execution of Colonel Isaac Hayne, a firm patriot, who, at the commencement of the war, had entered with ardour into the republican struggle and assisted in person at the defence of Charleston. On the surrender of the city, having been offered British protection or rigorous confinement, he was weak enough to choose the former, it being urged in his excuse, that his wife and children were ill of the small-pox, and this was his only alternative to avoid being separated from them. When the British were driven from his neighbourhood, he took up arms against them, and in this condition was taken prisoner and brought before Colonel Balfour, the commandant of the place, who condemned him to death. Every effort was used to save his life; General Greene avowed his determination to retaliate; the loyalists, with the governor at their head, and the most distinguished women of Charleston, begged for his life, as did his little children, dressed in deep mourning. But in vain; Lord Rawdon reluctantly gave his consent to the execution, which accordingly took place, causing a universal execration.

While these events had been occurring in the Carolinas, General Phillips and the traitor Arnold were carrying everything before them in Virginia, and successively defeated such bodies of militia as could be suddenly brought into the field, while their best troops were fighting the battles of others in the Carolinas[42]. After having fortified Portsmouth at the mouth of the James River, and thus secured a place of retreat, Phillips advanced up that river, which, with its numerous dependent branches and creeks, laid the whole central country on either hand open to him. On the Appomatox, a confluent of James River, he took Petersburg, where he destroyed 4,000 hogsheads of tobacco, collected there for shipment to France. Besides this, shipping and vessels of all kinds, on the stocks and in the river, public buildings and warehouses, with their contents of timber, provisions and all other stores, were destroyed; after which, Arnold advancing up the river where a considerable fleet of vessels had taken refuge, the greater number were burned or scuttled to prevent their falling into his hands. From Petersburg the enemy proceeded to Manchester, just opposite Richmond, where they destroyed nearly 2,000 hogsheads of tobacco; La Fayette, who had just arrived there with a detachment of New England troops, and to whose presence Richmond owed its temporary safety, having the mortification of witnessing the conflagration from the opposite shore. Havoc and devastation marked the career of these ruthless invaders, who, after collecting an immense booty in tobacco and slaves, and having destroyed ships, warehouses and mills, everything, in short, which came in their way and was of value to the inhabitants, returned to their shipping and fell down the river towards its mouth.

As regarded the force collected for the defence of Virginia, it was totally inadequate to the necessities of the province. The entire force of the Virginia line now under arms did not exceed 1,000 men, and were at this time absent serving under Greene; about 500 recruits, unarmed and unclothed, whom Steuben was vainly endeavouring to equip, were at Richmond. The only effective force were drafts of the New England regiments, under La Fayette, who, little inclined to serve in this unhealthy climate, were only kept together by his threats to shoot deserters, and by winning their fidelity through their gratitude, inasmuch as, on his own credit, he supplied them with hats, shoes and blankets, of which they were in grievous need.

We have already said that Lord Cornwallis, informed of the unfortunate turn which the British affairs had taken in South Carolina, resolved, although his own force was reduced, to hardly more than 1,000 effective men, to march to Virginia and effect a junction with General Phillips. Again the British commander complained bitterly of the sufferings and destitute condition of his troops. Neither cavalry nor infantry, he said, were fit to move, yet they must commence on the morrow a march of several hundred miles, through a country chiefly hostile, frequently desert, which did not afford one active or useful friend, where no intelligence was to be obtained, and where no communication could be established.[43]

The march, however, was made through all these difficulties and impediments; and on the 25th of April, about a month after he had set out, he reached Petersburg, where he found the troops of General Phillips, who himself had died only a few days previously, and shortly after was reinforced also by four regiments sent from New York. On the approach of Cornwallis, La Fayette, having removed the most valuable stores from Richmond, abandoned that town and retired towards the north-west, to form a junction with General Wayne, who was now on his march with 1,000 of the Pennsylvanian levies to join the southern army. The assembly of Virginia, on the abandonment of Richmond, adjourned to Charlottesville, and increased powers, suitable to the emergency, were conferred upon Governor Jefferson. The prisoners under Burgoyne's capitulation, who had been living for the last two years in this neighbourhood in great comfort, in their huts amid their gardens, were now also suddenly removed across the mountains to Winchester.

In this central province all the scattered operations of active hostility converged, as it were, to a point. Cornwallis pursued La Fayette for thirty miles, in hopes of preventing his union with General Wayne, but being disappointed in this object, overran the country for sixty miles on the borders of the James River, and destroyed a vast amount of both public and private property; among the former the Virginian laboratory and armoury, in which a large quantity of arms, ammunition, and other stores, greatly needed by the Virginian army, were consumed. Whilst this devastation was going on in one direction, Tarleton was sent to make a dash at the Virginian assembly at Charlottesville and to carry off Jefferson. On his way he met twelve wagons laden with clothing and stores for Greene's army, all of which he destroyed; he succeeded also in capturing seven members of assembly, but Jefferson, who had been warned of his danger, escaped.[44]

Lord Cornwallis, on the return of the detachments, having received orders from Sir Henry Clinton, who was apprehensive that Washington was about to attack New York with the aid of the French fleet, removed his army, towards the end of June, from Richmond to Williamsburg, considerably nearer the sea, and about midway between the great rivers James and York, destroying, as was customary, whatever property lay in his way. La Fayette having now joined Wayne, and being still further strengthened by Baron Steuben's troops, as well as by such militia as Virginia herself was able to raise, was in so powerful a condition as to render any movements of the British a matter of great caution; nevertheless Cornwallis was active, and his cavalry, mounted on the very horses which the planters had refused to Greene, and which the British had now seized, scoured the country, carrying terror into all quarters.

From Williamsburg, Cornwallis proceeded to Portsmouth, which it was strongly recommended, both in England and by Sir Henry Clinton, should be occupied as a permanent position convenient for naval operations, and for such warfare as, while it was defensive on their part, would be extremely distressing to Virginia. On his way thither, and when just about to cross James River, Cornwallis was attacked, in the afternoon of July 6th, by La Fayette, who erroneously supposed that a portion of the army had crossed the river. General Wayne, who led the advance, seeing on the contrary the whole British army drawn out against him, made an impetuous attack and then suddenly retreated, leaving his cannon behind. The darkness of evening coming on, and Cornwallis suspecting an ambuscade, no pursuit followed, and the British crossed the river in the night.

Arrived at Portsmouth, Cornwallis, on personal examination, not deeming it suitable for the intended purpose, and conceiving that nothing less than offensive war would be effectual in Virginia, selected, in preference, the two posts of York Town, on the river of that name, and Gloucester Point on the opposite side, which he immediately commenced fortifying, his force amounting in the whole to about 7,000.

"The Southern States were very anxious for the personal presence of Washington, but he believed that the South might be most effectually served by striking some decisive blow at New York. The means, however, for such a blow were not so obvious. The superiority of the British naval force still kept the French army idle in Rhode Island. The Southern States, invaded and overrun, were hardly able to defend themselves; while the Eastern States, hitherto so sturdy, seemed now almost exhausted. Recruits for the army came in very slowly. The New York regiments had been detached to defend that state from Tory and Indian invasion. The Pennsylvanian line, and even some drafts from the eastern regiments, had been sent to Virginia. Late in the spring the entire force under Washington's immediate command fell short of 7,000 men, not equal to the number of loyalists employed at that time in the British service. It was with the utmost difficulty that even this small force was fed. To obtain a supply of provisions, Washington was obliged to send Heath to the Eastern States with a circular-letter and pressing representations."[45]

Washington's letter obtained some supplies from New England, and Pennsylvania consented to furnish more, on the credit of taxes just imposed; but impressment, after all, continued to be the principal means for feeding the army, and the only money which could be obtained was by selling bills on Benjamin Franklin, which it was hoped the French court would enable him to meet.

About the same time that Cornwallis entered Virginia, Washington received the welcome intelligence from the French admiral, the Count de Grasse, in the West Indies, that he was about to proceed with a powerful fleet to the American coast, on which the French army, which, had lain idle for eleven months in Rhode Island, marched to join Washington; who, breaking up his camp in July, passed the North River to meet them. Their junction took place at the White Plains, on the New England side of the Hudson, and the combined armies encamped at Philipsburg, within twelve miles of King's Bridge, sufficiently near New York to excite great alarm. The apparent intention of these great movements was an attack on New York, which became confirmed by an intercepted letter from Washington to the French commander, Rochambeau, in which such an attack was spoken of in undisguised terms. But the intentions of Washington, whatever they might have been in the commencement, soon became very different; nevertheless, the object now was to confirm Sir Henry Clinton's suspicion, that time might be given to carry out the still more formidable plan, of which no idea appeared to exist in the mind of the British commander. It was under the apprehension of this combined attack that Sir Henry Clinton recalled a considerable part of the troops under Lord Cornwallis, from Virginia, immediately afterwards countermanding his recall, being himself reinforced by the arrival of 3,000 Hessians; the same apprehension also rendered it desirable to occupy some strong position in Virginia.

Now, therefore, in the month of July, New York was kept in a state of perpetual alarm. A body of 5,000 French and American troops, on one occasion, took up a position near King's Bridge, in the night, which they occupied for forty-eight hours, with every appearance of an intended attack. The two commanders, Washington and Rochambeau, attended by their principal officers and engineers, reconnoitered the island of New York; the report of the expected daily arrival of the Count de Grasse was sedulously propagated, and when the precise time of that admiral's arrival at the Chesapeake was ascertained, the French troops advanced to Sandy Hook and the coasts opposite Staten Island, as if with a view of seconding the operations of the fleet. So far, indeed, was this deception carried, that ovens were erected near the mouth of the Raritan, on Sandy Hook, as if for the supply of the army.

The intention was very different. The object was to strike a blow at Cornwallis in Virginia. Orders, therefore, were sent to La Fayette to take up such a position as would cut off the retreat of the British army into North Carolina, and on August 19th, Washington crossed the river and marched directly into the Jerseys, to Trenton upon the Delaware, this very movement being considered in the first instance merely to conceal his ultimate intentions. So carefully, indeed, had Washington concealed the object he had in view, that the New England troops were ignorant of their destination, and on arriving at Philadelphia and discovering that they had a long southern march before them, showed such signs of dissatisfaction that it appeared necessary to pacify them by a small payment in specie, which could only be done by borrowing from the French military chest. Fortunately, too, at that moment Laurens had arrived from France with a supply of clothing, arms, and ammunition; so that the troops proceeded in good humour, and better clad than usual.

While Washington was preparing for his operations in the South, Greene, whose ardour was ever unabated, having profited by his temporary retirement, during the unhealthy season, among the hills of the Santee, appeared at the beginning of September once more in the field. His former successes had revived the hopes of the North Carolina Whigs, and it was now determined to make one great effort for his support. Measures were accordingly taken for keeping 2,000 militia in the field; he received a number of horses for the use of his cavalry, together with a fresh supply of arms. Three hundred horses, imported by Jefferson to prevent their falling into the hands of the British, were also sent to him from Virginia.

Thus recruited and reinforced, Greene, being joined also by the partisan corps of Marion, at the commencement of the cool season, marched up the Wateree to Camden, in South Carolina, crossed first that river, then the Congaree, and thus approached the British army, commanded by Colonel Stuart, who had succeeded Lord Rawdon, which retired before him down the Santee to Eutaw Springs, whither Greene pursued them. It was the 8th of September when the two armies, about equal in force, engaged. The British were at first driven back in great confusion, victory strongly inclining to the American side, but rallying again in a favourable post, the British repulsed their assailants with heavy loss. The battle of Eutaw Springs is memorable as being one of the bloodiest and the most valiantly-contested fields of the war, and also for being the last of any consequence at the South. The loss of the British was about 500, with 250 prisoners, that of the Americans about the same.

Both sides, Hildreth tells us, claimed the victory, but all the advantage accrued to the Americans. The British immediately retired to Monk's Corner, and were thus restricted to the narrow tract between the rivers Ashley and Cooper. Congress, in acknowledgment of Greene's service in this battle, voted him their thanks and presented him with a conquered standard and a medal struck for the occasion. He, however, was too much exhausted to continue active operations. His troops were barefoot and half naked; he had no hospital stores, hardly even salt, and his ammunition was very low. He retired again to the hills of the Santee.

CHAPTER XII.
CLOSE OF THE REVOLUTIONARY WAR.

We now return to Washington, who at length received the long-wished-for intelligence, that De Grasse, with the French fleet, was approaching the Chesapeake. Admiral Rodney, who had been busy in the West Indies, whither De Grasse had also sailed, apprehending that a part of the French fleet would proceed to the American coast, had sent Hood, with fourteen ships of the line, to reinforce Admiral Graves, who commanded on the American station. Hood arrived off the Chesapeake, August 25th, and not finding Graves there as he expected, proceeded to New York, where he learned that Du Barras, who commanded the French squadron at Newport, in Rhode Island, had put to sea three days before, evidently with the design of a junction with the French West India fleet. In the hope of intercepting this junction, Graves sailed with the united English fleet; but had the mortification of discovering on his arrival, September 5th, off the entrance of the Chesapeake, that De Grasse had arrived six days before, and now, with four-and-twenty ships of the line, lay safely at anchor inside Cape Henry.

All the present operations of the combined American and French forces were evidently the result of a well-concerted plan, besides which an extraordinary coincidence occurred in their several movements by sea and land, which was beyond the reach of calculation. We have already seen that Du Barras sailed from Rhode Island on the 25th of August; on the 28th De Grasse arrived with his fleet at the Chesapeake. On the same day the French and American armies reached the Head of Elk, and an hour after their arrival received an express from De Grasse, with the welcome intelligence of his safe anchorage at Cape Henry. This is the more remarkable when we consider the distance of the parties from each other as well as the scene of action, and the difficulties and delays to which all were liable.[46] But the run of ill luck which had hitherto attended every combined attempt of the French and Americans appeared now to have changed. All went well with them, as in the rapid winding up of a long story, where the heroes are crowned with especial success as a compensation for past sorrows and sufferings.

Du Barras, however, did not arrive in the Chesapeake for near a fortnight after De Grasse, having put out to sea from fear of being intercepted by the British fleet, which was a very necessary caution, as he had under his charge the transports which conveyed from Rhode Island the heavy ordnance and other necessaries indispensable for the siege of York

Town, and upon which the success of the enterprise depended. De Grasse, in the meantime, sent four ships of the line and several frigates to block up James and York rivers, so as to cut off the retreat of Cornwallis, and landed also 3,000 French troops, under the Marquis St. Simon, who had joined La Fayette, then at Williamsburg.

The first intelligence which Admiral Graves received of the French fleet, was the discovery of it, early in the morning of September 5th, lying within the mouth of the Chesapeake. Each enemy was an unwelcome sight to the other, and the French ships immediately stood out to sea. For five days the two fleets manœuvred in sight of each other; a distant cannonade was kept up; but De Grasse had no intention of coming to a close action, his sole object was to keep possession of the Chesapeake, and to cover the arrival of Du Barras with his squadron and convoy from Rhode Island. All this was done so successfully that Du Barras entered the bay without the slightest impediment, on the 10th of September, which was in fact signing the doom of Lord Cornwallis; and the French fleet, no whit the worse, returned to their old anchorage in the Chesapeake; while Graves, who had suffered considerably, having lost two of his ships and been obliged to burn a third, sailed immediately to New York to refit. On the 17th of September, transports began to bring down a portion of the French and American armies from the Head of Elk, while Washington proceeded with the remainder to Annapolis, whence they too were conveyed by the same easy mode to Williamsburg, where all had arrived by the end of the month. Washington and the principal commanders having already had an interview, the plan of operations was agreed upon. Before, however, we proceed to this, we must return to Sir Henry Clinton.

Having at length discovered the true purpose of Washington's deeply-laid scheme, Sir Henry Clinton attempted to prevent its full accomplishment, by rendering it necessary for that commander to divide his forces. Arnold, therefore, having now returned from Virginia, was immediately despatched on a plundering expedition against Connecticut, of which state he was an unworthy native.

Landing his troops from the shore of Long Island, in the night of the 6th of September, at New London, a resort of privateers and the seat of the West India trade, Arnold advanced up the Thames, at the mouth of which New London is situated, and having taken Fort Trumball, about a mile below the town, New London was plundered and then burned, and a large amount of property destroyed. On the other side of the river was Fort Griswold, which, being strongly garrisoned, was resolutely defended by Colonel Ledyard. At length, however, it was carried by assault, with a loss to the British of 200 men, and the retaliation for this loss was as cowardly as it was bloody. Entering the fort, a British officer inquired who was the commander. "I was," replied Colonel Ledyard, presenting his sword, "but now you are." On these words the weapon so surrendered was plunged into the bosom of the late brave commander, and an almost general slaughter followed; forty out of 160 being all that escaped.

Washington, to Clinton's disappointment, took no notice of this movement, but proceeded calmly with his operations in the South; and these enormities having roused a spirit in Connecticut which Arnold did not dare to encounter, he retreated to New York. The loss which the Americans sustained, besides about a dozen ships which were burnt, was very great. The quantities of naval stores, of European manufactures, and of East and West India goods found here, was almost incredible. Everything on the town-side of the river was destroyed by fire. Nothing was carried off excepting such small articles of spoil as afforded no trouble in the conveyance.[47]

The British had taught the Americans much important war-craft during this long struggle; as for instance, in the general orders which Washington gave to his American troops, he charged them to use and depend upon the bayonet, as their best and most essential weapon, in case they should be encountered on the march from Williamsburg, assuring them that they would by that means effectually cure the vanity of the British troops, who attributed to themselves so decided a superiority in that sort of close and trying combat. Nor did he omit any opportunity of exciting that honourable emulation between the allied troops which appeared so conspicuously in the subsequent operations.[48]

The combined French and American armies having, by the help of the French transports, formed a junction with La Fayette at Williamsburg, proceeded on the last days of September to invest Lord Cornwallis in York Town. Their whole force amounted to 16,000, 7,000 of whom were French picked men, the very flower of the army. The British force, about 8,000 in number, were chiefly at York Town, which had been made as strong as possible, Cornwallis having abandoned his more distant posts, which had been intended to command the peninsula, as too much exposed to be maintained under present circumstances. These, therefore, were all immediately seized by the combined armies. The post at Gloucester Point, opposite to York Town, was occupied by the famous Tarleton, with both cavalry and infantry, amounting to about 600 men.

On the evening of the 9th of October the batteries were opened against the town, the works of which, even had they been completed, would have been incapable of sustaining such a weight of force; but, as it was, the British troops were as much employed in their construction, amid the fire of the enemy, as in their defence. In a few days most of their guns were dismounted and silenced; their defences in many places broken down. Shells and red-hot ball had reached even the British ships in the harbour, several of which were burned.

In the meantime, Sir Henry Clinton, who had learned the junction of the Rhode Island squadron with the French fleet, from Admiral Graves on his return to New York, and of the peril which threatened Lord Cornwallis, lost no time in refitting and equipping a fleet to aid in extricating him and his army. Accordingly, on the 19th of October, with upwards of 7,000 of his best forces, Sir Henry Clinton set sail on this important service, with twenty-five ships of the line and eight frigates. All felt the greatness of the enterprise; the spirit, it is said, which influenced both officers and common men was full of enthusiasm, all believing that whatever the result might he, they were about to be engaged in one of the most obstinate and bloody naval battles ever fought.

On the 5th of October, Lord Cornwallis received a letter from New York, informing him of the relief that would sail thence for him about that date. But it was a fortnight later before the fleet passed the bar of New York harbour; and in the meantime, while Lord Cornwallis was anxiously expecting relief which never came, events were proceeding rapidly.

The most interesting feature of the siege was the storming of two redoubts, which, standing forward, greatly impeded the progress of the besiegers. It was determined, therefore, to attack these as the darkness of night fell, on the 14th. The attack of the one was committed to the Americans, under Colonel Hamilton, Washington's aide-de-camp, and the other to the French, the one nation emulating the other in the honour and the duty of the enterprise. Both were successful; both redoubts were taken, when daylight appeared, but the loss of the French was the greater.

So important did Lord Cornwallis consider the taking of these redoubts, that, writing to Sir Henry Clinton the following day, he said that "he considered his situation desperate." Using, however, all means to procrastinate, he anxiously and impatiently waited for relief from New York; but in vain.

At length, when no relief came, and when, on the 16th, a hundred pieces of heavy ordnance had so ruined the works and overpowered the batteries that the besieged could not show a single gun, and their shells, their sole means of defence, were nearly exhausted, Lord Cornwallis determined, as a last resource before surrendering, to attempt an escape with the greater part of his troops. Accordingly boats were secretly prepared; and abandoning the baggage, the troops during the night were to pass over to Gloucester Point, to cut their way through a French detachment posted in the rear of that place, and by rapid marches to reach New York in safety. The first debarkation had been made towards midnight in safety, when the weather, which had hitherto been moderate, instantly changed, and a violent storm drove the boats down the river. It was impossible to bring back the landed troops; and thus weakened and discouraged, the danger of the army was still further increased.

Means of defence there were none; their hopes of succour were at an end; the troops were diminished and worn out by constant watching and unremitting fatigue.

To avoid, therefore, the useless shedding of blood by an assault, Cornwallis wrote to Washington on the 17th, proposing a suspension of hostilities for twenty-four hours, and that commissioners might be appointed to settle terms of capitulation.

On the 19th, the posts of York Town and Gloucester were surrendered, and the British troops, about 7,000 in number, became prisoners of war to Washington. The ships and naval stores, with 1,500 seamen, were given up to the French. The officers and soldiers retained their baggage, but all visible property was liable to be seized. Washington would not grant any expressly favourable conditions, as Lord Cornwallis wished, on behalf of the loyalists who were under British protection in the town, alleging that theirs were civil offences which did not come under the authority of a military commander. One favour, however, was granted—that Cornwallis should be allowed the use of a ship ostensibly to convey despatches to New York, and which should be allowed to pass unexamined. In this vessel many obnoxious persons escaped.

General Lincoln, who had surrendered his sword to Lord Cornwallis at Charleston, by a sort of poetical justice, was appointed to receive the sword of the British commander on this occasion; and not forgetting what the British had then demanded, the capitulating force was now required to march out of the town with their colours cased.

As regarded the general treatment both of officers and men, nothing, however, could have been nobler. Lord Cornwallis, in his public letter to England, testified to the "kindness and consideration of the enemy." The kindness and attention shown by the French officers in particular, he says, "have really gone far beyond what I can possibly describe, and will, I hope, make an impression on the breast of every British officer, whenever the fortune of war shall put any of them in our power."

It is mentioned as a singular circumstance in the events of this surrender that the American commissioner appointed to draw up the terms of capitulation was Colonel Laurens, son of Laurens, late president of congress, who was at that time prisoner in the Tower of London.

On the 24th of October, five days after the fall of York Town, Sir Henry Clinton and the British fleet arrived off the capes of Chesapeake, where they first learned that they had arrived too late, and that Cornwallis had surrendered, on which mortifying intelligence, and unwilling to encounter the superior French fleet, they hastily returned to New York.

Washington would gladly have finished this successful campaign by an attack on Charleston; but the Count de Grasse, fearing to remain on the American coast in the stormy season which was at hand, sailed shortly after for the West Indies. Count Rochambeau cantoned his troops during the winter at Williamsburg. Wayne, with 2,000 Pennsylvanian continentals, marched to reinforce Greene's army in South Carolina, while the main body of the American army returned to their old positions on the Hudson. The prisoners of Cornwallis's army were marched over the mountains to Winchester, whence a part of them were sent to Lancaster in Pennsylvania.[49]

The surrender of Cornwallis was in effect the end of the war. The British power was now reduced merely to defensive measures, and was confined principally to the cities of New York, Charleston and Savannah. Wilmington was very soon evacuated, thus putting an end to all the hopes of the loyalists of North Carolina; and early in January, Greene approaching Charleston, so distributed his troops as to confine the British to the Neck and the adjoining islands.

The news of the important victory of the allied armies in the South caused a general rejoicing throughout the Union. Nothing could equal the joy and satisfaction caused by the prospect which it afforded. Washington ordained a particular day for the performance of Divine service in the army, recommending that all the troops should engage in it with a serious deportment and that sensibility of heart which the surprising and particular interposition of Providence in their favour claimed.

Congress, on receiving the official intelligence, went in procession to the principal church in Philadelphia, to return thanks to Almighty God for the signal success of the American arms, and appointed the 13th day of December as a day of public thanksgiving and prayer.[50]

The official intelligence of the surrender of Lord Cornwallis reached the British cabinet on Sunday, Nov. 25th. The tidings were a blow to the minister, Lord North, who according to Lord George Germaine's account, received them as he would have done a cannon-ball. He paced up and down the apartment, exclaiming with the deepest emotions of consternation and distress, "Oh God, it is all over!" The king was more calm, perhaps because he was of a more stolid nature. Lord George Germaine communicated the "dismal intelligence" by letter. The king replied that he "particularly lamented the unfortunate result of the operations in Virginia, on account of the consequences connected with it, and the difficulties which it might produce in carrying on the public business, or in repairing the misfortune. It would not, however," he asserted, "make the slightest alterations in those principles of his conduct which had hitherto directed him, and which would always continue to direct him, in the prosecution of the present contest."[51]

Accordingly, the speech from the throne, on the re-opening of parliament, two days after this news had arrived, breathed the same warlike spirit as at the late close of the session. Nevertheless, a strong opposition existed in parliament; the war was extremely unpopular with the British nation at large; and from the 12th of December to the 4th of the following March, motion after motion was brought forward in the house, for the termination of the war, when, on this latter day, a resolution was moved by General Conway, "that all those should be considered as enemies to his majesty and the country who should advise, or by any means attempt, the further prosecution of the war in America."

On the 20th, the administration of Lord North terminated, and the advocates of peace and American independence immediately came into power, the Marquis of Rockingham being at the head of the ministry. Hopes of some possible accommodation were entertained, by Lord Shelburne and his party, according to Lord Chatham's ideas. Overtures were made to Adams at the Hague, and to Franklin at Paris, to ascertain whether the United States would agree to a separate peace, and to something short of the entire recognition of their independence. Sir Guy Carleton, who was appointed to supersede Sir Henry Clinton, was commissioned to treat for peace. He addressed, therefore, a pacific letter to Washington, and put a stop to the predatory incursions of the loyalist Indians, which had been long the scourge of the New York frontiers. Powers to treat were communicated to congress; but that body declined to negotiate except in conjunction with France, and at Paris. Franklin also had returned for answer, through Richard Oswald, a British merchant who had formerly large commercial dealings with America, and who had been sent to Paris for the purpose of sounding him, that nothing short of independence, satisfactory boundaries, and a participation in the fisheries, would be admitted as the foundation for a treaty.

On July 1st, Lord Rockingham died, and Lord Shelburne succeeded him. The views of the king were now strengthened by his minister's disinclination for the dismemberment of the empire. Rodney had captured nearly the whole fleet of De Grasse in the West Indies, and England was again triumphant in the western hemisphere. Nevertheless the king, in proroguing parliament on July 11th, spoke of his anxious wish for peace. In

August, an act of parliament was obtained, authorising a negotiation with America, and Oswald returned to France, to treat with the American agents and commissioners, Franklin, Adams and Jay.

Difficulties arose immediately. The commissioners were authorised to conclude a peace with the agents of certain Colonies. Jay objected, and refused to proceed until Oswald came empowered to treat with the agents of the "United States of America." This objection being overcome, others had arisen in the meantime. The French minister, Vergennes, from what motive does not exactly appear—perhaps from not being wholly favourable to the new republic—while he instigated the Americans to insist on their share of the Newfoundland fishery, urged the British government not to make the concession. The British agents, however, aware of the double dealing of Vergennes, exposed it, and satisfied the American commissioners that in this respect nothing was to be feared; and no time was lost in bringing the treaty to a conclusion. On the 30th of November, therefore, the preliminaries of the articles of peace were signed at a private meeting unknown to Vergennes, although this proceeding was contrary to their original treaty with France and the late orders of congress.

Vergennes complained of being duped, and felt, or pretended, great indignation at what he called American chicanery; nevertheless, so little did it affect him that, a few days afterwards, he agreed to advance a new loan of six million of livres, to enable America to meet the expenses of the coming year. But there was good reason for suspicion: Vergennes was soon afterwards discovered, in conjunction with Spain, labouring to limit the boundaries assigned to the United States, and earnestly advising the British not to yield too liberally.[52]

So anxious was the British minister to announce the coming peace, that eight days before the preliminaries were signed by the American agents, he addressed a letter to the lord mayor of London, to acquaint him with the speedy conclusion of the negotiations, and that parliament would be prorogued in consequence from the 26th of November to the 5th of December.

On the 5th of December parliament accordingly met, and the king announced that, in pursuit of a general pacification, he had offered to declare the American colonies free and independent states; and added, with evident discomposure of manner, that in admitting the separation of the colonies from the crown of Great Britain, he had sacrificed every consideration of his own to the wishes and opinion of his people.

On the 20th of January, 1783, the preliminaries of peace were signed at Paris, the American signatures being those of John Adams, Benjamin Franklin, John Jay, and Henry Laurens. Before signing the address,

Franklin, it is said, put on triumphantly the dress suit, which he had never worn since the day of Wedderburn's attack in the British privy council.[53]

The British monarch acknowledged by these arrangements the freedom, sovereignty and independence of the United States, relinquishing all claims to the government, proprietary, and territorial rights of the same. The boundaries allowed embraced a larger extent of territory than the States, when colonies, had claimed. At the commencement of the negotiation, the British commissioners had claimed the country north of the Ohio as a part of Canada, to which, indeed, the Quebec act annexed it. They sought also to extend the western limits of Nova Scotia, as far as the Pemaquid, according to the old French claim. These points, however, were compromised; the peninsula of Upper Canada was yielded to the British, the eastern boundary of the United States remaining fixed at the St. Croix. The northern limit of Florida, according to the proclamation of 1763, was agreed to as the southern boundary of the United States, being the river St. Mary's from its mouth to its source, a due west line thence to the Apalachicola, and from that river to the Mississippi, the 31st degree of north latitude. But, by a secret article, it was agreed that if Britain, at the peace with Spain, should still retain West Florida, the northern boundary of that province was to be a due east line from the mouth of the Yazoo to the river Chattahoochee.

Full liberty was secured to the Americans to take fish of every kind on the Grand Bank, and all other banks of Newfoundland, as also in the Gulf of St. Lawrence, and all other places in the sea where they had formerly been accustomed to fish. The navigation of the Mississippi, from its source to the ocean, was for ever to remain free and open to the subjects of Great Britain and the citizens of the United States alike. All the British armies, garrisons and fleets, were to be withdrawn with all convenient speed from the United States, without causing *any destruction, or carrying away of negroes, or any other property of the Americans*; this last clause being inserted at the instance of Henry Laurens, who represented the slaveholding interests of America, and who had arrived at Paris two days previous to the signing of the preliminaries. A great deal was said on the subject of allowing compensation to the American loyalists, an unfortunate class which had strong claims on the British government. The American commissioners, however, resolutely opposed all compensation, Franklin even declaring that they would rather risk a war by themselves alone than consent to any indemnification for the enemies of and the traitors to their country. A clause was, however, inserted, earnestly recommending the legislatures of the respective States to provide for the restitution of all estates, rights, and properties which had been confiscated, belonging to real British subjects.

While these negotiations and events were taking place in Europe, all was not peace and satisfaction in America; and as regarded the case of the loyalists, the prospect of peace with the concession of Great Britain was anything but acceptable. We will take one incident to show the state of feeling between the two parties. After the American successes in the Carolinas and Georgia, and the capitulation of York Town, the loyalists, maddened by the loss of their property and friends, and the hopeless prospects before them for the future, determined to take the law into their own hands, and on the first occasion hang a republican in retaliation. White, a loyalist, had been put to death for some cause on the 30th of March; on the 12th of April, therefore, Joshua Huddy, a captain in Washington's army, was seized and hanged, with the following label on his breast: "We, the refugees, having beheld with grief the murders of our brethren, determine not to suffer without taking vengeance, and thus begin; and have made use of Captain Huddy as the first object to present to your view; and further determine to hang man for man while there is a refugee existing. *Up goes Huddy for Philip White!*"

Savage as was this spirit of vengeance, it was the natural growth of the terrible struggle which for so many years had been going forward in the heart of the country, and which gradually transformed men into fiends. This Philip White, it appears, was murdered by a set of men called the "Monmouth Retaliators," at the head of which was a General Forman, otherwise "Black David." Captain Huddy, it was said, was also himself a retaliator. Sir Henry Clinton immediately ordered the murderers of Huddy to be arrested; and Captain Lippincott, their leader, being tried by court-martial, a verdict of Not Guilty was returned, on the plea that he had merely acted in obedience to the commands of his superiors, the "Directors of the Board of Associated Loyalists." Washington, dissatisfied with this decision, demanded that Lippincott should be given up to him, to be tried by republican law, which being refused, he wrote again, declaring that he, too, in that case, would retaliate. A few days after this second letter, Sir Henry Clinton was superseded by Sir Guy Carleton, who brought with him the first intimation of the willingness of the British government to treat for peace with the United States on the basis of their independence. To him Washington applied on the subject of Lippincott, declaring, as he had already done to Sir Henry Clinton, his intention of retaliation, if Lippincott were not given up. The young officer selected by lot for this melancholy and wicked purpose was Captain Asgill, a prisoner taken at York Town, son of Sir Charles Asgill, and only nineteen years of age. Sir Guy Carleton, in reply to Washington's demand, very properly broke up the Society of Associated Loyalists; but Lippincott was still not given up. In the meantime, the rank and peculiar circumstances of young Asgill had aroused a strong party to intercede in his behalf; but it was not until November that this young man was set at liberty and allowed to return home. Whether in reality he would have suffered innocently under Washington's threat of retaliation, we cannot say; but his liberation appears rather to have been the result of interference than a voluntary concession on the part of the American commander. Lady Asgill wrote, in July, a very affecting letter to the French minister Vergennes, beseeching his interference as a friend of Washington's, with that commander; and this letter being read by Vergennes to the king and queen of France, they commissioned the minister to add their desires to his own, "that the inquietudes of an unfortunate mother might be calmed, and her tenderness reassured." Washington, on this, forwarded the copy of Lady Asgill's letter, which had been sent to him, together with that of the French minister, to congress, and the result was an order from that body, dated 7th of November, to set Captain Asgill at liberty.

CHAPTER XIII.
STATE OF THE COUNTRY AFTER THE WAR.

Another great cause of anxiety at this moment, though by no means a fresh one, was the poverty of the American government, which rendered the situation of the Republic, even after it had achieved its object, extremely critical. In the prospect of peace, and the consequent disbanding of the army, where was the money to be found to pay its long arrears, to say nothing of the gratuities which had been promised to both officers and men on the termination of the war? In May, 1782, Washington wrote of his army on the Hudson, as destitute of provisions and in a state of disorder and almost mutiny; and that if the British knew his real situation, and were to make a sudden attempt, he must be driven from his post. Of the army in the South, also, General Greene wrote in August an account still more melancholy. He said that of his men, one-third were "entirely naked, with nothing but a pair of breeches about them, and never came out of their tents," and that the remainder were "as ragged as wolves." Their food was as bad as it could be, "their beef perfect carrion, and even of that they had often none at all;" and that the spirit of the army was so mutinous that executions were not unfrequent to check it. Washington feared that even this terrible remedy would lose its effect, and that peace with Britain, if it came, might be succeeded by a social war, so difficult would it be to disband an army with weapons in their hands, who had no prospect before them but poverty and starvation. Well might a deep gloom rest at this time upon his mind.

In the month of July, the rate of interest demanded for money was sixty per cent. In September, Morris, on whose credit the national bank in Philadelphia had been established, confessed that he had no money, and as to borrowing more, it would only increase the mischief, as he saw no prospect of payment.

About this same time the French auxiliary army marched from Virginia to Boston, where it embarked. Hildreth says that the conduct of the French troops, during the two years and a half that they had been in the country, had been very exemplary. They had done less mischief on their marches than the same number of American soldiers; and the regularity with which all their supplies were paid for in cash, contrasted most favourably with the means by which the American troops were too often subsisted.

The boundary line of some of the states having, as we have already said, been a fertile subject of dispute for many years, became in some few instances settled during the present year. Hence, the western boundary of Pennsylvania being decided, Pittsburg returned again to the jurisdiction of that state. The quarrel, too, was adjusted between Connecticut and Pennsylvania, relative to the territorial claim to Wyoming, which also was settled in favour of the larger state, not wholly, however, to the satisfaction of the people of Wyoming.

Between Vermont and New York an old dispute existed. New York asserted a claim to the whole territory—Vermont resolutely resisted it; and being peopled by a stout, determined race, the Green Mountain Boys had, as we have already related, declared themselves, in 1778, an independent state, and as such had applied to congress for admission into the Union. The delegates of New York prevented their admission, but nothing daunted by their rejection, they organised their own constitution, and chose the farmer and innkeeper, Thomas Chittenden, as governor. To be an innkeeper in those primitive, sturdy times, was not to be a man of an inferior class: three American generals, Putnam, Wheedon, and Sumner, were innkeepers, as well as the clear-headed and stout-hearted governor of Vermont. Besides the dispute with New York, the Green Mountain Boys had a second with their equally sturdy neighbour, New Hampshire, the ground of which was this: sixteen newly-settled townships, on the eastern side of the Connecticut River, had applied to be received as a part of Vermont, in order to escape from the heavy taxes which the war rendered it necessary to impose. The townships on both sides of the river next endeavoured to constitute themselves into a new state, under the name of New Connecticut. This secession caused New Hampshire, in retaliation, to lay claim to the whole territory of Vermont. New Hampshire and New York both claiming Vermont, Massachusetts next started up as a claimant also, and demanded, on the plea of her old rights, the whole southern portion of this coveted little state. Congress now offered to interfere and settle the question of this disputed territory, which Massachusetts objected to, in the fear that by this means she would not come in for any portion at all. Vermont, in the meantime, had made up her mind to abide no decision of congress, any more than to yield to any of the separate claimant states, and now took a step, in the persons of her bold sons, the farmer Chittenden and the two warlike brothers Ethan and Ira Allen, the true intention of which has never yet been clearly ascertained. Negotiations were entered into with the British authorities in Canada, probably with a twofold view of guarding against invasion from that side in the present critical state of their affairs, and of operating on the fears of congress. The scheme appeared to answer its purpose; congress promised to recognise Vermont as an independent state, providing she would relinquish her encroachments on New York and New Hampshire. Vermont deliberated; and New York and New Hampshire protesting against the interference of congress, declared that they would send in troops to establish their claims to the whole. Civil war seemed at hand, when Washington interfered, like the parent among his quarrelsome children, and recommended that the New Hampshire townships should be restored to the original state, which was agreed to, and Vermont again applied to be received into the Union, when again New York interfered to prevent the accomplishment of her wishes. This was in February, 1782, when peace with Great Britain was looked upon as certain. And now came a time when Vermont triumphed over her more powerful neighbours, and cared very little for admission into the Union. She was thus free from continental debt, and the perpetual calls of congress for money.

The opposition which New York made to the admission of Vermont into the Union was strengthened by the four Southern States, who dreaded lest their own backwoodsmen should follow the example of the bold little northern state. Kentucky, which in 1781 had increased so greatly that it was divided into three counties—Jefferson, Fayette, and Lincoln—had, as we already know, long since petitioned congress on the subject, and similar ideas prevailed among the settlers on the Tennessee.[54]

Though the main armies were lying in a state of inactivity during the present year of pacific negotiation, war still prevailed, and that with unusual severity, on the western frontiers. The Christian Delawares settled on the river Muskinghum, in the present state of Ohio, where they had many flourishing and populous villages, suffered cruelly at this period. Unlike the Indians in general, they had, as followers of Christ, renounced war and the weapons of war, and aimed at preserving throughout these troubled times a perfect neutrality. The hostile Indians, on their way from Detroit and the north-west to the American frontiers, demanded supplies from these Delawares, whose villages lay directly on the war-path, and which they had no means of refusing. Hence they were regarded by the backwoodsmen as "the half-way-house" of the enemy, and compelled, in the autumn of 1781, to abandon their peaceful and prosperous homes, and remove to Sandusky on Lake Erie. The following winter, being reduced to great suffering from the want of provisions, they obtained permission to return to the Muskinghum, to gather in the corn left standing in the fields. Just then some murders being committed, near Pittsburg, by a wandering party of Shawanees, the Delawares, though innocent, were suspected, and about ninety men of the neighbourhood, under the leadership of one Williamson, marched to the Muskinghum to take vengeance. For want of a canoe, they crossed the river in a wooden trough made to hold maple sap, two men at once, and arrived at the centre village, where a party of Christian Indians were gathering in their corn. The Indians of another village were sent for, and a council held to decide on their fate. Williamson referred the matter to his men. Sixteen only voted for mercy, the remainder, holding the faith common on the frontiers, that "an Indian had no more soul than a buffalo," were for the murder of all. They rushed on their prey, knife in hand, and soon ninety unarmed Indians, avowing, like themselves, faith in Christ, lay bleeding on the ground.

Nor did this satisfy them. Flushed with success, continues Hildreth, from whom we take this account, 480 men marched in May, under Colonels Williamson and Crawford, to complete the destruction of the Christian Indians, by assailing Sandusky, which, however, lay in the midst of Indians of a very different character. Waylaid by a hostile party near Sandusky, they were attacked by an overwhelming force, and obliged to retreat with much loss of life. Williamson made his escape, but Crawford and many more fell into the hands of the Indians, who burned him at the stake, together with his son and his son-in-law, in revenge for the murders at the Muskinghum.

1782 was a disastrous year in Kentucky, from the same cause. Several Indian battles occurred, but the one at the Big Blue Lick was the bloodiest ever fought in Kentucky. We will give it somewhat in detail, from Lippincott's Cabinet History of Kentucky, as a specimen of border warfare; and a picture also of the perils of backwoods-life. On the southern banks of the Elkhorn stood Bryant's Station, containing about forty cabins, strongly palisadoed and garrisoned by fifty men. On the 12th of August, news reached them that a Captain Holden, with a party of seventeen, had been defeated by the Indians near the Upper Blue Licks, and that the loyalist, Simon Girty, with other refugees, and an army of 600 Indian warriors, might be almost hourly expected. The garrison, thus warned, were under arms when Girty and his army approached. The enemy, aware that preparation was made for their reception, left a considerable body in ambush near the spring which, at some little distance, supplied the station with water, and only a small portion appeared before the place, hoping to entice the garrison outside their defences, while the remainder were so posted, in case this scheme succeeded, as to storm one of the gates and cut off their return. Fortunately, however, when just about to sally forth, a sudden firing in the opposite direction made them aware of their danger, and closing their gates, they awaited the enemy within their defences. But they had no water. Without water they must perish. In this difficulty the women came to their aid. They would venture to fetch water from the spring, in the hope that the Indians lying in ambush would not unmask themselves merely to women. Accordingly a body of elderly matrons marched down to the spring, where lay about 500 Indian warriors in ambush. Their faith saved them; they supplied the wants of the station, and not a single shot was fired.

Messengers were sent off to all the nearest stations to summon help, which might now soon be expected; accordingly thirteen young men sallied out upon the decoy-party, and at that moment Girty rushed forward at the head of the main body towards the gate intending to force an entrance. But the garrison was ready for him and his party, and they were driven back. In a few minutes they were again out of sight. About two o'clock in the afternoon, sixteen men on horseback, and about double that number on foot, from a neighbouring station, approached in aid of their besieged friends. All was silent, no enemy to be seen. On one side of the road which led to the village, lay a large field of 100 acres full of standing corn; a thick wood was on the other, and amid the corn and within the wood were the Indians crouched, waiting within pistol-shot the approach of this little band. As the horsemen entered the lane a sudden firing commenced. They put spurs to their horses, the lane was deep in dust, amid a cloud of which they escaped and reached the fort unharmed, the gates of which were opened to receive them. The men on foot were less fortunate; passing by a short cut through the corn, they heard the firing and rushed to the succour of their friends. Luckily the Indian guns being then mostly discharged, and the rifles of the Kentuckians loaded, they had some advantage, and by pointing them at the Indians, and dodging and running deeper into the corn, were enabled to keep them at bay for some time.

Some entered the wood and escaped through the cane thickets; some were shot down; others maintained a running fight, stopping to load and fire from behind trees. One stout young fellow, being hard pressed by Girty and several Indians, fired; Girty fell, but the ball struck a thick piece of soling-leather which lined a pouch which he wore, and saved his life. Six white men were killed, not so many Indians.

The Indians now returned to the fort, and knowing that the neighbouring station would soon take the alarm and rush to the aid of their friends, the chiefs proposed to raise the siege, but Girty determined to try the effect of negotiation first. Crawling on his hands and knees, therefore, in Indian fashion, to the close neighbourhood of one of the gates, where stood the stump of a tree, he mounted it, and with a flag of truce in his hand hailed the garrison, commending them for their bravery, but assuring them that resistance was vain, as he had 600 men with him and hourly expected reinforcements and artillery, and advising them, therefore, to surrender, when not a hair of their heads should be hurt—otherwise he would blow the whole place into the air. "Shoot down the villain!" said many voices; but the flag of truce protected him. No answer being returned, he cried, "Do you know who it is that speaks to you?"

"Do we know you?" exclaimed an energetic young man named Reynolds, who undertook to give reply in the name of the garrison; "Yes, we know you, Simon Girty!" and then proceeding in the same strain, he said, that he himself had a good-for-nothing rascally dog, and that for want of a bad name he called him Simon Girty; adding, that if he had artillery coming he might bring it up; that they too expected reinforcements; and that, in short, if Girty and his gang remained four-and-twenty hours longer before the place, their scalps would be soon drying on the roofs of the cabins.

Such was the reply to Girty. It was very offensive, but it was irresistible, and the next morning they retired so precipitately that several pieces of meat upon their roasting-sticks were left and their fires still burning. By noon 160 men had assembled at Bryant's Station, under Colonels Todd, Trigg, Boone, and the celebrated Major M'Gary. The Kentuckians are remarkable for their impetuosity, which amounts almost to rashness. In the afternoon they were all ready and impatient to set off in pursuit; M'Gary objected to this precipitancy, but was overruled. The party was mostly mounted.

At the Lower Blue Licks they came in sight of the enemy, who, having reached the southern bank of the Licking, were then ascending the rocky ridge on the other side. The Indians halted for a moment, turned round and gazed at their pursuers, and then quietly proceeded onward. The Kentuckians halted also, and consulted together what was best to be done. Boone, who understood perfectly the Indian mode of warfare, expressed his belief that an ambush was planted in a ravine about a mile in advance. He advised to wait for Logan, who might be expected soon to join them with reinforcements. Waiting, however, did not suit their ardent temperaments; and M'Gary suddenly raising the war-whoop, spurred his horse into the stream, waving his hat and shouting, "Let all who are not cowards follow me!" and all followed him.

As Boone had expected, no sooner had they reached the ravine than they were attacked; a deadly fire poured in upon them; they staggered and fell in every direction, the enemy in the meantime being completely concealed. They fled back to the river; the Indians pursued, and now the slaughter with the tomahawk commenced. The ford was narrow, and great numbers were killed there. It was a scene of horrible confusion—horses plunging, riders falling, others attempting to mount, and amid all, the bloody Indian tomahawk doing its cruel work.

One man named Netherfield, who had been laughed at as a coward, and who had never dismounted, was the first to reach the opposite shore. Here, soon joined by some of his comrades, he looked round, and seeing the massacre that was going forward, pulled rein as he exclaimed, "Halt! fire on the Indians! Protect the men in the river!" And on this all wheeled round, fired, and rescued several poor fellows in the stream over whom the tomahawk was lifted.

Reynolds, the young man who replied to Girty, had a narrow escape. Finding in the retreat an officer wounded, he dismounted and gave him his horse, when he was immediately seized by three Indians. They were just about to despatch him, when two other white men rushed by. Two of the savages started in pursuit, and the third having stooped to fasten his moccasin, Reynolds sprang away from him and escaped.

More than sixty Kentuckians were slain in this battle; among whom were six officers and the son of Daniel Boone. Such as regained the shore, too weak to rally, started homeward in great dejection. On their way they met Logan. He had reached Bryant's Station with 500 men, soon after their departure. Nothing now remained but to go back and bury the dead. Logan accompanied them. Arrived at the scene of carnage, an awful spectacle presented itself; the dead bodies were strewed over the ground as they had fallen; the heat was intense, and birds of prey were feeding on the carcases. The bodies were so mangled that none could distinguish friend or relative. The dead were buried as rapidly as possible.

Nor was this all the carnage. The Indians after the defeat had scattered, but only to sweep through other settlements, carrying everywhere destruction before them.

Innumerable instances of suffering fortitude and heroism abound in this portion of the American border-history. One passage from the life of a Kentucky pioneer we will give, even at the risk of being thought to dwell too long on this subject.

During this same troubled year of 1782, late in the summer, predatory bands of Indians having committed great ravages in the vicinity of Elizabeth Town, Silas Hart, surnamed by the Indians "Sharp-Eye," assembled a party of settlers and pursued the marauders. In the pursuit Hart shot their chief, and his brother, having vowed vengeance, came secretly with a small band of warriors to Elizabeth Town, and commenced the work of plunder and destruction.

The neighbourhood was roused, and the Indians fled, Hart being again the foremost in pursuit. Finding it impossible to overtake the savages, the people returned to their homes; and the Indians, who kept close watch upon their movements, turned when they turned and followed them back to the settlement.

Hart reached home, some five miles from Elizabeth Town, about dusk, and fearing no enemy, went to bed and slept soundly. The next morning, the Indians, who had secreted themselves round the house in the night, suddenly appeared at the door, and the brother of the fallen chief deliberately shot Hart dead. The son of Hart, a boy of twelve, no sooner saw his father fall than, grasping a rifle, he sent a bullet through the chief before he could enter.

The Indians rushed into the house; again the foremost warrior was killed by a blow from a hunting-knife in the hands of the resolute boy; the family, however, were speedily overpowered and carried into captivity. The daughter, unable to bear the fatigues of a forced march, was despatched by the Indians at a short distance from the settlement. The mother and son were doomed to a lingering and painful death.

When the prisoners reached the Wabash, preparations were made for their execution. Fortunately, the extraordinary heroism of the boy having touched the heart of an influential woman of the tribe, his life was spared at her intercession. Mrs. Hart was also saved from the stake by the intervention of a chief. The mother and son were finally ransomed and returned to their desolate homes.

The back settlements of South Carolina were ravaged also by parties of loyalists and Cherokees, the brother of General Pickens being on one occasion made prisoner. At the head of a body of South Carolina and Georgia militia, General Pickens, in return, invaded and laid waste the Cherokee country.

In February, General Greene being reinforced by the Pennsylvanian troops under Wayne, despatched him into Georgia, when Clarke, who commanded there for the British, drew in his outposts, and having ravaged and destroyed everything in his way, retired to Savannah. The people of Georgia, republicans and loyalists, were so impoverished by mutual plunder, that even seed-corn was hardly to be had. In June, Wayne's camp was attacked by a body of Creek Indians, who, however, were repulsed with loss. In July, the British forces evacuated Savannah, carrying with them not less than 5,000 negroes. In October, a new expedition against the Cherokees, undertaken by Pickens, resulted in a treaty by which Georgia obtained all the Cherokee lands south of the Savannah and east of Chattahoochee, and the Creeks shortly after relinquished all claim to the lands east of the Altamaha and Oconee. Skirmishing continued in the neighbourhood of Charleston till near the end of the year, in which some valuable lives were lost, that of the younger Laurens being one. On December 14th, Charleston was evacuated.[55]

CHAPTER XIV.
FIRST YEARS OF PEACE.

The year 1783 commenced with the old money difficulties. Peace was now certain; but the disbanding of the army without money to pay its arrears, was a difficulty which all the wisdom and the courage of the young republic knew not how to overcome. Many schemes were suggested; among the rest, one had been started the preceding year, which, however, met with no encouragement; but as it presents the noble spectacle of a human being superior to temptation and ambition, we must be allowed to pause upon it for a moment. One Louis Nicola, a colonel of the Pennsylvanian line, regarding the financial difficulties of America as the result of republican principles, became the agent of a party in the army who held similar views. It was proposed, therefore, that a monarchical government should be established, with Washington at his head, the army, of course, coming in for a fair share of offices and emoluments. Nicola was employed to lay the plan before the commander-in-chief, which he did in a plausible and elaborate letter. The government proposed for America was, however, to be no ordinary monarchy; "nevertheless," said the writer, "strong arguments might be adduced for admitting the title of king."

Washington's ambition was not of that vulgar kind. The proposal astonished, displeased and grieved him. He replied that no occurrence during the whole war had caused him so much pain, as now to learn that such ideas existed in the army, ideas which he viewed with abhorrence and reprehended with severity. "I am at a loss," continued he, "to conceive what part of my conduct can have given encouragement to an address which to me seems big with the greatest mischief which could befall my country. If I am not deceived in the knowledge of myself, you could not have found a person to whom your schemes are more disagreeable." "Nevertheless," said Washington, turning to the root of the mischief, "no man possesses a more sincere wish to see ample justice done to the army than I do; and as far as my powers and influence, in a constitutional way, extend, they shall be employed to effect it."

No more was heard of making Washington king. But the causes of the army's discontent remained no less this year than they had done the last, although congress did its utmost for their removal. Discontent and disaffection were growing apace. Even Washington began now to be censured for indifference towards their troubles, because he had not removed them, and because his own private property left him independent of pay, which in fact, he had declined from the first.

Congress was anxiously deliberating on some means of raising money, when an anonymous invitation appeared, calling upon the general and field-officers, with an officer from each company, to attend a meeting on the following day, for the purpose of taking their own affairs into consideration. At the same time an artful and energetic address was circulated, written, as was afterwards discovered, by Captain Armstrong, aide-de-camp to Gates, appealing to the passions of the officers, setting forth their unrequited dangers and sufferings, and advising them no longer to ask for justice from congress, but with arms in their hands to obtain it from that body through their fears.

Washington, who was still in camp at Newburgh, seeing the fearful crisis which was now at hand, issued an order denouncing the anonymous call for the meeting as irregular, and naming a later day, on which the officers were invited by himself to assemble for the purpose of receiving the report of their committee sent to congress; while, in the meantime, he had personal interviews with individual officers, and used all his influence to calm their passions and to infuse a spirit of confidence and patience.

The meeting assembled, and Washington rose to read a short speech which he had prepared. He took off his spectacles to wipe them, remarking that his eyes had grown dim in the service of his country, but that he had never doubted her justice. He then, reading from the paper, appealed to the patriotism and good sense of the officers, and entreated them to rely on the justice of congress, and stigmatised the anonymous addresses as the work of some British emissary, whose object was disgrace to the army and ruin to the country. Then repeating in public the remonstrances he had used in private to different officers, he retired from the meeting. No one rose to counteract the effect of the speech. A series of resolutions was then passed, expressive of unshaken confidence in congress, "and abhorrence and disdain of the infamous proposal" contained in the anonymous addresses.[56]

Washington had pledged himself to the army to use his utmost influence with congress, and he redeemed his pledge. The half-pay for life which had been promised, was soon after commuted into five years' full pay at once, the certificates to be issued for it to bear interest at six per cent.

The insurrection among the officers had been quelled, but the army itself was not satisfied. Three months' pay had been promised, but as it was not forthcoming, the men thought probably that neither could they do better than appeal to the fears of congress, as the officers themselves had just before recommended. Congress was sitting at Philadelphia, when a letter demanding their pay was sent to that body by the Pennsylvanian troops, just returned from the South, and immediately afterwards that part of the troops stationed at Lancaster marched to Philadelphia for the same purpose. Congress desired that the militia might be called out; but the council of Pennsylvania, with President Dickenson at their head, frightened at this threatening aspect, demurred, alleging that the militia would not act unless some outrage were committed. The mutineers, on reaching the city, were joined by the troops in barracks, and under the command of seven sergeants surrounded the State-house, where congress and the state council were sitting, and demanded immediate payment. They were only induced to disperse on being allowed to choose a committee to represent their grievances.

Congress, which felt itself doubly insulted by the mutineers and the pusillanimity of the Philadelphia council, adjourned in disgust to Princetown, where they were received with great respect. Washington, on hearing of the revolt, sent 1,500 men, who instantly dispersed the mutineers, several of whom were tried and condemned by court-martial, but afterwards pardoned.

It now became a warmly-agitated question where congress should permanently hold its sittings, since Philadelphia had proved herself so incapable of protecting that august body. One party advocated a federal city being established on the Delaware, another on the Potomac. Maryland offered Annapolis; New York, Kingston on the Hudson: while the council of Philadelphia apologised and endeavoured to bring back congress to their city, but in vain. It was finally agreed that, as soon as two suitable sites could be found, two federal cities should be created, at which congress should alternately hold its sittings. In the meantime Annapolis and Trenton were to be used for that purpose, the next session to be held at Annapolis. The following year congress sat at Trenton, but adjourned to New York, where it continued to meet till the year 1800, by which time the city of Washington had been prepared for a suitable federal seat of government. Washington stands in a territory ten miles square, called the District of Columbia, which had been ceded to the general government by the States of Maryland and Virginia for that purpose.

On the 19th of April, 1783, exactly eight years after the battle of Lexington, the news of the preliminaries being signed between Great Britain and the United States, with the consequent cessation of hostilities, was published in the camp at Newburgh. The proclamation of peace was celebrated, four days afterwards, in Greene's camp, by fireworks and musketry; and the very army, "ragged as wolves," was at that moment so short of food that for several days they had been without either bread or rice. On June 8th, Washington published a farewell letter addressed to the governors of the States, urging oblivion of local prejudices and politics, indissoluble union, a proper peace establishment, and careful provision for the payment of the public debt. On November 3rd was issued a proclamation from congress for the general disbanding of the army, which took place on the 5th; Washington having the day previous issued his farewell orders. On the 25th, the British troops having all embarked at New York, a detachment of the American army, under General Knox, entered and took possession. And here we may remark, that during the last year, 1782, the desertions from the British army in New York had been very frequent, especially from Arnold's corps, the men going off with their horses and arms, by threes, fives and sixes at a time, as did also many Hessians.

WASHINGTON'S RECEPTION AT NEW YORK.

On the same day that the Americans regained possession of New York, Washington also entered it, preparatory to taking leave of the army. We will give the account of these remarkable events from Dunlap's History of New York, who quotes principally from the narrative of an eye-witness:—"On that memorable day, the 25th of November, General Washington entered the city by the Bowery, the only road at that time, accompanied by his friends and the citizens, mostly on horseback. At an appointed hour the British troops had embarked, and their gallant fleet was standing to sea over the bay.

"The military of the American army were under the command of General Knox, who took immediate possession of the fort, and prepared to hoist the American colours and fire an appropriate salute. The British, after taking down their flag, had 'knocked off the cleats and slushed the flag-staff,' so as to prevent the American colours from being hoisted. But after an hour's hard labour, in which a sailor-boy played a distinguished part, the American standard was hoisted on Fort George by this same sailor-boy, a true type of bold young America; and a salute was fired of thirteen rounds immediately, and three cheers were given.

"At the time the flag was being hoisted, the river was covered with boats filled with soldiers, to embark on board the shipping that lay at anchor in the North River,—the boats at the time lay on their oars, sterns to shore, to observe the hoisting of the American colours, during which time they preserved a profound silence. The boats rowed off to their shipping when the salute of thirteen guns was fired.

"The commander-in-chief took up his head-quarters at the tavern known as 'Black Sam's,' so called from its keeper, Samuel Francis, being a man of a dark complexion, and there he continued until December the 4th. On that day at noon the officers assembled, when their beloved leader entered the room, and after addressing them in a few words, concluded by saying: 'I cannot come to each of you to take leave, but shall be obliged to you if you will come and shake me by the hand.'

"General Knox, who had served with him from the commencement of hostilities, was the first to experience the parting grasp of the hero's hand; and in turn all present, with tears and in silence, pressed that hand which had guided a nation through the storms of war, and was destined afterwards to rule its destinies. Leaving the room, he passed through a line of his brave soldiers to Whitehall, where he entered into a barge waiting for him. He turned to the assembled multitude, waved his hat, and then bade them a silent adieu, as they thought, for ever."

Congress was sitting then at Annapolis, and Washington hastened thither, to deposit in the hands of those from whom he had received it, in the year 1775, his commission of commander-in-chief of the American forces.

On his way, he deposited in the Controller's office at Philadelphia, the account of his expenses during the war, secret-service money included, which amounted to £19,306 11s. 6d. A public audience was appointed by congress to receive him, and briefly addressing it, he offered his congratulations on the termination of the war, and concluded by saying: "Having finished the work assigned me, I now retire from the great theatre of action, and bidding an affectionate farewell to this august body, under whose orders I have so long acted, I here offer my commission and take my leave of all the employments of public life."

From Annapolis Washington hastened to his home at Mount Vernon, which he had visited but once during the eight years of his arduous public service, and where he continued quietly living as "Farmer Washington" until summoned by the public voice to a convention, for the amendment of the government founded by the old confederacy of sovereign States, and of which we shall speak in its place.

We now return to the evacuation of America by the British. Four days after the British troops had left New York, Long Island and Staten Island were given up. The whole sea-coast was thus once more wholly American; but the western frontier-posts of Oswegatchie, Oswego, Niagara, Presque Isle (now Erie), Sandusky, Detroit, and Mackinaw, were still held by British garrisons.

WASHINGTON TAKING LEAVE OF THE ARMY.

Henry Laurens, it will be remembered, had caused the insertion of an article in the treaty of peace, to prohibit the carrying away of slaves under the protection of the British. This referred principally to Virginia and the Carolinas, where great numbers of slaves had joined the British, under promise of protection. Sir Henry Clinton, however, was not disposed to pay attention to this prohibition; and when Washington reminded him of it, he replied that it would be highly dishonourable to the British flag to surrender any who had taken refuge under it. Accordingly he sent off all such negroes in the first embarkation, in order that their safety might be secured. They were taken to Nova Scotia, and thence many of them emigrated to Sierra Leone, where their descendants, as merchants and traders, now constitute the wealthiest and most intelligent population of that African colony.[57]

There had also been an attempt, on the part of Britain, to provide for the safety and indemnification of the loyalists, in the treaty of peace. Little, however, could be done for them by this mere *recommendation* of justice and humanity. The difficulty of finding transports for the removal of the loyalists, who had crowded into New York with their families, delayed the evacuation of that city considerably. The penalty of the American laws compelled them to abandon their country, although at the sacrifice of wealth and property. Many of them, however, spite of the confiscations, possessed considerable wealth, which had been made during the war by privateering and as sutlers to the British army. Those from the Northern States settled principally in Nova Scotia or Canada; 450 sailed to Nova Scotia in the month of October, from New York, under a strong convoy. They were furnished by the British with provisions for a year; rations for a passage of twenty-one days; clothing; tools for husbandry, together with arms and ammunition. They were to receive also grants of land. The greater number of them, however, gradually returned to the United States, when a few years had worn away the inveteracy of the hatred felt against them. Those from the Southern States found refuge in the British West India Islands. The feeling against the loyalists was very strong in the South, where the sufferings of the people had been severe and more recent. In reestablishing the State government of South Carolina, none were allowed to vote who had taken British protection. Among the very earliest proceedings of the assembly, was the passage of a law banishing the most active British partisans, and confiscating their property. The services of General Greene were rewarded by a grant of 10,000 guineas, to purchase him an estate. The Georgia Assembly passed a similar law of banishment and confiscation, and Greene received also from this province the present of a confiscated estate; while North Carolina acknowledged his services by a grant of wild lands.[58]

The loyalists, finding that the mere recommendation of indemnity from Great Britain did not secure it to them from the State government, appointed a committee of their body to lay their grievances and their faithful services before the British parliament. A commission was accordingly appointed to inquire into and report upon their claims and losses; and in 1791, 4,123 claims were admitted, amounting to upwards of £8,000,000. All claims of £10,000 and under were paid in full, the remainder in a three-and-a-half per cent. stock. Claimants whose losses were the deprivation of lucrative offices received equivalent pensions. On the whole they were extremely well provided for and indemnified. The Penn and Calvert families received a considerable portion of this parliamentary allowance; besides which, we must not omit to mention that, in 1779, Pennsylvania, by act of assembly, granted to the heirs of William Penn, on the relinquishment of quit-rents and proprietary claims, the sum of £130,000, to be paid by instalments, commencing the first year after the peace. The State of Maryland was less liberal, as regarded her proprietary claims, on the plea of the illegitimacy of the infant representative of the Calverts.

Whilst the great struggle for independence had been going on, and every state in turn, New Hampshire excepted, had been the scene of a desolating war, the heart of the nation had still been so vigorously alive that the organisation of the local governments and the arrangement of terms for confederation and union had never for one moment been lost sight of. Liberty and enlightenment gradually advanced, although the revolution made no violent change in the political institutions of America, beyond casting off the superintending power of the mother-country, and that power in a great degree was replaced by the authority of congress.

"The most marked peculiarity of the revolution," continues the able historian, Hildreth, to whom we are so largely indebted, "was the public recognition of the theory of the equal rights of man"—a theory set forth in the declaration of colonial rights, made by the first congress at Philadelphia; solemnly reiterated in the Declaration of Independence; and expressly or tacitly recognised as the foundation-principle of all the new governments. This principle however, encountered, in existing prejudices and institutions, many serious and even formidable obstacles to its general application, giving rise to several striking political anomalies. Of these the most startling was domestic slavery, an institution inconsistent with the equal rights of man. That this anomaly was felt at the time, is clearly enough evinced by the fact that no distinct provision on the subject of slavery appears in any State constitution, except that of Delaware, which provided "that no person hereafter imported from Africa ought to be held in slavery under any pretence whatever; and that no negro, Indian, or mulatto slave ought to be brought into this state for sale from any part of the world."

Prior to the revolution the anti-slavery struggle had begun in New England; and in 1777, a number of slaves on board a prize-ship taken by an American privateer and brought into Salem for sale, were at once set at liberty by the interference of the General Court, and yet the provisional congress of Massachusetts at the same time forbade any negro to enlist into the army. Its Bill of Rights declared all men to be born free and equal, and this was considered by the Supreme Court to prohibit slavery.

The assembly of Pennsylvania in 1708 forbade the further introduction of slaves, and gave freedom to all persons thereafter born in the state. The most enlightened and illustrious citizens of Virginia and Maryland responded to the feelings which led New England and Pennsylvania to abolish slavery in their states, and they too forbade the further introduction of slaves and removed the restrictions on emancipation, though slavery as an institution was retained. New York and New Jersey followed the example of Virginia and Maryland, forbidding also the introduction of slaves from other states. The Quaker population of North Carolina strongly advocated the same Christian line of conduct, but were not supported by the legislators of the state. South Carolina and Georgia made no alteration whatever in their laws regarding slavery.

The importation of "indented servants," so numerous in some of the states, and who were slaves in a modified sense, ceased with the war of the revolution. But in Connecticut, even to within the present century, debtors unable to meet the claims against them might be legally sold by their creditors into temporary slavery.

The year 1784 brought with it all the anxieties and difficulties consequent on the termination of a struggle, such as that through which America had just passed. The crisis of a great fever was over, and the sufferer was left with prostrated strength, excited nerves, and irritable temperament. Wisdom and prudence, and the vigour of his youthful constitution would, however, restore him to perfect health. In the meantime many a long depression and many a sally of impatience and petulance must be borne.

This was precisely the case with America. She had suffered from every calamity of war; her towns had been burned, her country ravaged, her frontiers laid waste by Indians; her citizens had been called out to serve in her army, and to suffer even more than the average miseries of camps, hunger, nakedness, and disease, with insufficient hospital resources. Citizen had been armed against citizen, and even brother against brother. Civil war had here assumed its direst aspect. Agriculture, trade and manufactures, had decayed during the war, and thousands of otherwise industrious and prosperous inhabitants were thrown out of employment, and so totally impoverished as to be nearly destitute of clothing. The once imposing navy was now completely annihilated. Almost every vessel, whether home-built or purchased, had been destroyed or had fallen into the hands of the enemy. The only ship of the line built during these disastrous years, and finished in 1782, was presented to the king of France, to supply the loss of one of his in Boston harbour. Add to all this an immense debt, the natural consequence of war, universal distress and discontent.

Congress met; and financial affairs claimed its first attention. Secondly came an important fact. Virginia ceded all her claims to lands lying north-west of the Ohio. New York had already set this example two or three years before, and now prided herself on having been the first to do so. By her act of cession, Virginia stipulated for the security of the French inhabitants already occupying those lands, and that those lands should be erected into republican states, to be admitted into the Union with the same rights as the older states. This led to vast plans for the laying out of states, and the government of the immense territory which the United States expected to acquire by the cession of the claims of the different states. The originators of these plans were Jefferson, who sat in congress as delegate from Virginia; Chase, of Maryland; and Howell, of Rhode Island. Among other proposed conditions for new states was the following: "After the year 1800, there shall be neither slavery nor involuntary servitude, other than in the punishment of crimes whereof the party shall have been duly convicted." But the requisite votes of nine states could not be obtained, and this condition was lost.

Everything was done by congress to reduce the public expenditure. The military force retained at the peace amounted to 700 men, placed under Knox, in garrison at West Point and Pittsburg. These however, being thought too many, all were disbanded, excepting twenty-five men to guard the stores at Pittsburg, and fifty-five for West Point and other magazines, while no officer above the rank of captain was retained. Nor was even a minister-of-war considered necessary.

In March, 1785, Benjamin Franklin, after an absence of nine years, solicited his recall, and Jefferson was appointed to succeed him as the American representative at the French Court, and just about the same time John Adams was appointed to the same office in England. The now aged Colonel Oglethorpe, the founder of Georgia, was the first person who waited on the American minister in London. Great Britain declined as yet to send over a diplomatic agent to the United States.

In October, 1784, a treaty was concluded at Fort Schuyler between the United States and the chiefs and warriors of the Six Nations, by which the Mohawks, Onondagas, Cayugas and Senecas, who during the war had been adherents of the British, consented to peace and the release of prisoners. At the same time they ceded all their claim to the territory west of Pennsylvania. In the following January a similar treaty was entered into with the Wyandots, Delawares, Chippewas and Ottawas, by which the two former nations agreed to limit themselves to a tract on Lake Erie. The Shawanees refusing to form any pacific treaty, congress empowered the enlistment of 700 men for three years, to defend the western frontiers.

Again Kentucky, which now numbered six instead of three counties, and which had a supreme court and court-house, together with a jail, although as yet built only of hewn logs, resolved to form a separate state, and accordingly petitioned Virginia for permission to do so. They had no printing-press or newspaper as yet, but the address on this important occasion was circulated in manuscript.

Tennessee was rapidly increasing likewise, and beginning again, like her neighbour, to think of independence, although as yet a great portion of the present territory remained in the hands of the Indians. Under the name of Franklin, or Frankland, a provisional government was organised, with John Sevier at the head, which, though leading to violence and almost civil war, and put down for the present, yet rose up again in due time, like a growth of the forest, and John Sevier was the first legalised state's governor, with a recognised place in congress. Nor were the Wyoming people yet satisfied, and a John Franklin there, with Ethan Allen of Vermont, and other "wild Yankees," as they were called, agitated for an independent existence, until at length Pennsylvania, who had acted like a step-mother to them, pacified their uneasiness by granting their reasonable requests. The settlers of Maine also were stirred by the same craving for independence, and agitated for it and a remission of taxes.

Massachusetts surrendered to the United States, in April, her claims to the western territory; and in May, congress enacted an ordinance for the survey and sale of the lands north-west of the Ohio. Regular surveys on a systematic and uniform plan were commenced. The plan is described by Hildreth as consisting of a series of lines perpendicular to each other, the one set running north and south, the other east and west, by which means the federal lands were to be lotted out into townships of six miles square, each township to be again subdivided by similar lines into thirty-six sections, each containing a square mile. The survey has since been carried to half and quarter sections, and even to sixteenths. One section in each township was to be reserved as the basis of a school fund, which however, it is to be regretted, has not always been attended to. The public lands, when ready for market, were to be sold by public auction, the minimum price being one dollar per acre, to which the expenses of survey were to be added.

The whole attention of congress was not, however, devoted to such agreeable subjects as the survey and sale of the great western territory. The early instalments of foreign debts were falling due in addition to the old pressure for money. It was no use to impose taxes, for each state had its own local debts, and congress had no legal power to enforce their payment. Nevertheless, in the midst of all these urgent and accumulating cares, congress being possessed of powers to regulate the currency and coinage of the country, turned its attention to this subject. A decimal scale was adopted, and the dollar, as the coin best known and most common in

America, was taken as the money unit. A mint was established in October, 1786, but the poverty of congress allowed no coinage excepting a few tons of copper cents.[59]

We have spoken of the uneasy, restless spirit which was agitating in the newer settlements, the resistance against taxation being in many cases the primal cause, while others were by no means wanting, among which may be reckoned the disorganisation of the social state by the long war, the regular useful and arduous occupations of the male population having been interrupted, and a vast number of discontented, impoverished and unoccupied men thrown upon society. The general court of Massachusetts had found it necessary to impose taxes which, perhaps, in any case would have been ill received, but which now led to general resistance and even rebellion. The discontented had arms in their hands; they had seen the country free itself from the tyranny of Britain by these means, and now they were about to try the same against what they considered the tyranny of their own government. In September of 1786, the number of the malcontents appearing so large and formidable, the militia were called out to protect the sittings of the court, which it was the object of the insurgents to prevent; and so conciliatory and considerate was the spirit of the government, that their grievances were taken under consideration and as much as possible redressed. Bills were passed for diminishing legal costs, law charges being at that time enormous; and for allowing the payment of taxes and private debts in specific articles instead of specie, of which there was scarcely any in the country; as well as for applying certain revenues, formerly devoted to other purposes, to the payment of governmental taxes. So far were concessions made; still the agitation continued, and the Habeas Corpus Act was suspended for eight months. Under the plea of raising troops to act against the north-western Indians, congress enacted the enlistment of 1,300 men, to sustain the government of Massachusetts. Nevertheless full pardon for past offences was promised to all, if they would cease from these illegal agitations.

But the seriousness of the occasion only increased, and at length some few of the agitators were lodged in Boston jail. This was the token for more determined measures, and upwards of 1,000 armed men, under the command of Daniel Shays, a late captain in the continental army, of Luke Day and Eli Parsons, appeared at Worcester, where the supreme court had just adjourned, and placed guards over those houses where the judges lodged, so as to prevent the sitting of the court, while the remainder took up their quarters in an old revolutionary barracks in the neighbourhood. Another still larger body, also under the command of Shays, marched towards Springfield, where was the federal arsenal under the guard of General Shepherd, of which they intended to possess themselves.

This was in the depth of an unusually severe winter, and the insurgents suffered bitterly from the cold and want of provisions; nevertheless their ardour was unabated. Arrived at Springfield, and in reply to the demand that the arsenal should be surrendered, General Shepherd, after warning and entreating them to retire, fired upon them. The first discharge was over their heads; no notice was taken. The second was into the ranks; a cry of "Murder!" arose, and all fled in confusion, leaving three men dead on the field and one wounded.

General Lincoln pursued with 3,000 militia, called out to serve for thirty days; but the insurgents fled to Pelham, where they posted themselves upon two hills, rendered almost inaccessible by a great fall of snow. They offered to disperse on condition of general pardon, which Lincoln, however, was not empowered to grant, and then being sorely pressed for food, made a sudden retreat to Petersham. Lincoln, informed of this retreat, set off at six in the evening, and marching all night forty miles, through intense cold and a driving snow-storm, reached Petersham by daybreak, to the astonishment of the rebels, who had not the least idea of this movement, and accordingly fled in disorder or were taken prisoners.

The energy of Lincoln broke up this formidable confederacy. Straggling parties still were in existence, and occasional collisions took place between them and the authorities, but the public danger was at an end. In May, a pardon was proclaimed to all who, within three months, should take the oath of allegiance, with the exception of nine persons. All insurgents, however, were deprived for three years of the right to vote, to serve as jurymen, or to be employed as schoolmasters, innkeepers, or the retailers of ardent spirits. Of the nine condemned to death, four escaped from prison, four were afterwards liberated, and one was condemned to hard labour.

In September, tranquillity was so generally restored that it was judged safe to disband such troops as still remained in service. The leniency which had been shown towards the insurrectionists was the only safe course. The sentiment of the people was with them, and at the general election the ensuing year, all who had been active against them lost their votes. Hancock was elected governor in the place of Bowdoin.

It had long been felt that the Articles of Confederation were insufficient for the growing national exigencies. As early as 1782 it was recommended to form a convention for their revision and amendment. Great care had been taken in framing the original articles that no power should be delegated which might endanger the liberties of the individual states. Congress had no authority to enforce its own ordinances; and now, when the external danger was removed by peace, they were, as we have seen, disregarded and contemned also. It was evident to all that a more energetic form of government was required. In 1783, John Adams, then in Europe, suggested to congress the expediency of strengthening the general government. On a motion of Madison, in a convention of the delegates from five of the Middle States met at Annapolis in 1786, it was concluded that nothing short of a thorough reform of the existing government would be effectual for the welfare of the country. Congress approved, and passed a resolution recommending a general convention of delegates for that purpose to be held at Philadelphia.

Before, however, we proceed to the important business of this convention, we must notice a few facts which mark the progress of opinion in the States. In 1784, soon after the treaty of peace was signed, Franklin received overtures from the pope's nuncio at Paris, relative to the appointment of a vicar apostolic for the United States. Congress being referred to, replied that the business was of a spiritual nature and did not fall under their cognisance. John Carroll, of Maryland, was soon afterwards consecrated archbishop of the United States. Catholics, though still suffering under political disabilities in some of the states, had freedom of worship everywhere, and very soon a Catholic church was opened even in the puritan city of Boston.

The Church of England in America, which suffered much during the war, reorganised herself after the peace, and became established on a reformed basis. The title of lord bishop, and all other titles descriptive of temporal power and presidency, were dropped, and the clergy and dignitaries of the church declared liable to deposition from office in case of misconduct, by the state and general conventions. The liturgy was purged and modified to suit a republican country. The English bishops demurred at these innovations, but there was no remedy; and in 1787, White of Philadelphia, and Madison of Virginia, together with Seabury, who had been ordained by the episcopal Church of Scotland, were consecrated bishops, and formed the nucleus of episcopal authority in America.[60]

In 1784, Thomas Coke, one of Wesley's ablest coadjutors, and ordained by him bishop, arrived at New York, bringing with him Wesley's plan for the organisation of the Methodist Episcopal Church. Methodism was now wanted in America; it was the element of religious excitement, which the temper of the times required, and it spread rapidly, especially among the poorer classes of the Southern States. It commenced by excluding slaveholders from its communion; but as God suffers his sun to shine on the just and unjust alike, methodism opened its pale to sinners of every description. The zeal of the Methodists aroused the somewhat slumbering energies of the Baptists, and religious revivals commenced, especially in the Middle and the Southern States. They were the safety-valves in many cases for the excited and agitated popular mind. The Presbyterians, as the

Episcopalians had done, reorganised their church on a national basis. In New England, by that necessary law of reaction which never fails, latitudinarianism had followed the sternness of the puritan creed, and made its way with the learned, while universalism was adopted by the less educated.[61]

CHAPTER XV.
FORMATION OF THE FEDERAL CONSTITUTION.

In May, 1787, the convention met for the revision of the Articles of Confederation, twelve states being represented by men distinguished by their talents, character, practical abilities, and public service. Franklin, who had been among the first to propose a Colonial Union in 1754, was there; Dickinson, as delegate from Delaware; Johnson, of Connecticut; and Rutledge, of South Carolina, who had been movers in the Stamp Act Congress of 1765. Besides Benjamin Franklin, there were present seven who had signed the Declaration of Independence, all tried men and true; while the revolutionary army was represented by Washington, Mifflin, Hamilton and Pinckney; eighteen were members at the same time of the Continental Congress. Altogether this important convention numbered about fifty delegates. Rhode Island sent no representative.[62]

On the 29th of May the business of the convention was opened by Randolph of Virginia, this honour being conceded to Virginia as her due, the idea of the convention having originated with her. All the business, however, proceeded with closed doors and an injunction of inviolate secrecy. The members were not even allowed to take copies of the proceedings. They had met to revise and amend the Articles of Confederation, instead of which it was soon deemed advisable to form a new constitution. Long and arduous debates followed; months went on in discussion and deliberation; the soundness and wisdom of purely democratic and republican governments were questioned; committees sat; adjournments took place; causes of dispute occurred; rival parties contended, federalists and anti-federalists; slaveholding and free states, difficulties having arisen even then between the slaveholding and the non-slaveholding states as regarded representation, and every other interest. But if doubt and difficulty and discord arose, they were met and overcome. Nor can any greater argument be advanced in favour of the sound wisdom and the true patriotism of every party, than that all opposing interests and all questions of contention were gradually compromised; and spite of every opposing element, spite of selfish interests, and the jealousies and rivalries of opposing parties, a rough draft of the proposed Constitution was prepared by the beginning of August, and forms, in fact, the present Constitution of the United States. It is simply as follows, and well worthy to be read and considered.

We, the people of the United States, in order to form a more perfect union, establish justice, insure domestic tranquillity, provide for the common defence, promote the general welfare, and secure the blessings of liberty to ourselves and our posterity, do ordain and establish this Constitution for the United States of America.

ARTICLE I.

SECTION I.

All legislative powers herein granted shall be vested in a congress of the United States, which shall consist of a senate and house of representatives.

SECTION II.

I. The house of representatives shall be composed of members, chosen every second year by the people of the several states, and the electors in each state shall have the qualifications requisite for electors of the most numerous branch of the state legislature.

II. No person shall be a representative, who shall not have attained to the age of twenty-five years, and been seven years a citizen of the United States, and who shall not, when elected, be an inhabitant of that state in which he shall be chosen.

III. Representatives and direct taxes shall be apportioned among the several states which may be included within this Union, according to their respective numbers, which shall be determined by adding to the whole number of free persons, including those bound to servitude for a term of years, and excluding Indians not taxed, three-fifths of all other persons.[63] The actual enumeration shall be made within three years after the first meeting of the congress of the United States, and within every subsequent term of ten years, in such manner as they shall by law direct. The number of representatives shall not exceed one for every 30,000, but each state shall have at least one representative: and, until such enumeration shall be made, the state of New Hampshire shall be entitled to choose three, Massachusetts eight, Rhode Island and Providence Plantations one, Connecticut five, New York six, New Jersey four, Pennsylvania eight, Delaware one, Maryland six, Virginia ten, North Carolina five, South Carolina five, and Georgia three.

IV. When vacancies happen in the representation from any state, the executive authority thereof shall issue writs of election to fill such vacancies.

V. The house of representatives shall choose their speaker and other officers; and shall have the sole power of impeachment.

Much was said in the convention on the question of the elective franchise. Franklin's argument is worth remembering. He was opposed to any restriction on the right of suffrage. He said that it was of "great consequence not to depress the virtue and public spirit of the common people, of which they had displayed a great deal during the war, and which contributed principally to the favourable issue of it; and he did not think that the elected had any right, in any case, to narrow the privileges of the electors;" and universal suffrage was established. A member of the house must be twenty-five years of age, and have been for seven years a citizen of the United States, being an inhabitant, at the time he is elected, of the State for which he is chosen. No person, however, holding any civil office under the authority of the United States, can, at the same time, become a member of congress.

By the constitutional rule of appointment, three-fifths of the slaves in the Southern States are computed in establishing the appointment of the representatives of the lower house, which is supposed to be delegated by the *free* citizens of the United States. This is considered as a necessary consequence of the previously existing state of domestic slavery in that portion of the country.

SECTION III.

I. The senate of the United States shall be composed of two senators from each state, chosen by the legislature thereof, for six years: and each senator shall have one vote.

II. Immediately after they shall be assembled, in consequence of the first election, they shall be divided as equally as may be into three classes. The seats of the senators of the first class shall be vacated at the expiration of the second year; of the second class, at the expiration of the fourth year; and of the third class, at the expiration of the sixth year, so that one-third may be chosen every second year; and if vacancies happen by resignation, or otherwise, during the recess of the legislature of any state, the executive thereof may make temporary appointments, until the next meeting of the legislature, which shall then fill such vacancies.

III. No person shall be a senator who shall not have attained to the age of thirty years, and been nine years a citizen of the United States, and who shall not, when elected, be an inhabitant of that state for which he shall be chosen.

IV. The vice-president of the United States shall be president of the senate, but shall have no vote, unless they be equally divided.

V. The senate shall choose their other officers, and also a president *pro tempore*, in the absence of the vice-president, or when he shall exercise the office of president of the United States.

VI. The senate shall have the sole power to try all impeachments. When sitting for that purpose, they shall be on oath, or affirmation. When the president of the United States is tried, the chief-justice shall preside: and no person shall be convicted without the concurrence of two-thirds of the members present.

VII. Judgment in cases of impeachment shall not extend further than to removal from office, and disqualification to hold and enjoy any office of honour, trust, or profit under the United States: but the party convicted shall, nevertheless, be liable and subject to indictment, trial, judgment, and punishment, according to law.

SECTION IV.

I. The times, places, and manner of holding elections for senators and representatives, shall be prescribed in each state by the legislature thereof; but the congress may, at any time, by law make or alter such regulations, except as to the place of choosing senators.

II. The congress shall assemble at least once in every year, and such meeting shall be on the first Monday in December, unless they shall, by law, appoint a different day.

SECTION V.

I. Each house shall be the judge of the elections, returns, and qualifications of its own members, and a majority of each shall constitute a quorum to do business; but a smaller number may adjourn from day to day, and may be authorised to compel the attendance of absent members, in such manner and under such penalties as each house may provide.

II. Each house may determine the rules of its proceedings, punish its members for disorderly behaviour, and, with the concurrence of two-thirds, expel a member.

III. Each house shall keep a journal of its proceedings, and from time to time publish the same, excepting such parts as may, in their judgment, require secrecy; and the yeas and nays of the members of either house, on any question, shall, at the desire of one-fifth of those present, be entered on the journals.

IV. Neither house, during the session of congress, shall, without the consent of the other, adjourn for more than three days, nor to any other place than that in which the two houses shall be sitting.

SECTION VI.

I. The senators and representatives shall receive a compensation for their services, to be ascertained by law, and paid out of the treasury of the United States. They shall, in all cases except treason, felony, and breach of peace, be privileged from arrest during their attendance at the session of their respective houses, and in going to and returning from the same; and for any speech or debate in either house, they shall not be questioned in any other place.

II. No senator or representative shall, during the time for which he was elected, be appointed to any civil office under the authority of the United States, which shall have been created, or the emoluments whereof shall have been increased during such time; and no person, holding any office under the United States, shall be a member of either house during his continuance in office.

SECTION VII.

I. All bills for raising revenue shall originate in the house of representatives; but the senate may propose or concur with amendments, as on other bills.

II. Every bill which shall have passed the house of representatives and the senate shall, before it becomes a law, be presented to the president of the United States; if he approve, he shall sign it, but if not, he shall return it, with his objections, to that house in which it shall have originated, who shall enter the objections at large on their journal, and proceed to reconsider it. If, after such reconsideration, two-thirds of that house shall agree to pass the bill, it shall be sent, together with the objections, to the other house, by which it shall likewise be reconsidered, and if approved by two-thirds of that house, it shall become a law. But in all such cases the votes of both houses shall be determined by yeas and nays, and the names of the persons voting for and against the bill shall be entered on the journal of each house respectively. If any bill shall not be returned by the president within ten days (Sundays excepted) after it shall have been presented to him, the same shall be a law, in like manner as if he had signed it, unless the congress, by their adjournment, prevent its return, in which case it shall not be a law.

III. Every order, resolution, or vote, to which the concurrence of the senate and house of representatives may be necessary (except on a question of adjournment), shall be presented to the president of the United States; and before the same shall take effect shall be approved by him; or, being disapproved by him, shall be repassed by two-thirds of the senate and house of representatives, according to the rules and limitations prescribed in the case of a bill.

SECTION VIII.

The congress shall have power—

I. To lay and collect taxes, duties, imposts and excises; to pay the debts, and provide for the common defence and general welfare of the United

States; but all duties, imposts, and excises shall be uniform throughout the United States.

II. To borrow money on the credit of the United States.

III. To regulate commerce with foreign nations, and among the several states, and with the Indian tribes.

IV. To establish a uniform rule of naturalisation, and uniform laws on the subject of bankruptcies throughout the United States.

V. To coin money, regulate the value thereof, and of foreign coin, and fix the standard of weights and measures.

VI. To provide for the punishment of counterfeiting the securities and current coin of the United States.

VII. To establish post-offices and post-roads.

VIII. To promote the progress of science and useful arts, by securing, for limited times, to authors and inventors, the exclusive right to their respective writings and discoveries.

IX. To constitute tribunals inferior to the supreme court.

X. To define and punish piracies and felonies committed on the high seas, and offences against the law of nations.

XI. To declare war, grant letters of marque and reprisal, and make rules concerning captures on land or water.

XII. To raise and support armies; but no appropriation of money to that use shall be for a longer term than two years.

XIII. To provide and maintain a navy.

XIV. To make rules for the government and regulation of the land and naval forces.

XV. To provide for calling forth the militia to execute the laws of the Union, suppress insurrections, and repel invasions.

XVI. To provide for organising, arming, and disciplining the militia, and for governing such part of them as may be employed in the service of the United States, reserving to the states respectively, the appointment of the officers, and the authority of training the militia, according to the discipline prescribed by congress.

XVII. To exercise exclusive legislation, in all cases whatsoever, over such district (not exceeding ten miles square), as, may by cession of particular states, and the acceptance of congress, become the seat of the United

States, and to exercise like authority over all places purchased by the consent of the legislature of the state in which the same shall be, for the erection of forts, magazines, arsenals, dock-yards, and other needful buildings:—and

XVIII. To make all laws which shall be necessary and proper for carrying into execution the foregoing powers and all other powers vested by this constitution in the government of the United States, or in any department or office thereof.

SECTION IX.

I. The migration or importation of such persons as any of the states now existing shall think proper to admit, shall not be prohibited by the congress, prior to the year one thousand eight hundred and eight, but a tax or duty may be imposed on such importation, not exceeding ten dollars for each person.

As we have already said, this question of slavery was a fertile apple of discord in the convention, and even then it threatened to break up the Union; South Carolina and Georgia insisted on having slavery in the fullest meaning of the accursed thing, or they would not enter the Union. They would not only hold slaves, but they would import them; and hence the Constitution provided for "*the migration of such persons as any of the States now existing shall think proper to admit,*" prior to the year 1808, when the importation of slaves was to cease. Until January, 1808, South Carolina traded to the African coast for the souls and bodies of men, all the other states having before that time entirely discontinued it. While we are on the subject of slavery, we must mention that, when, in the convention, the articles of the proposed Constitution were being drawn up, one for the mutual delivery of fugitives from justice came in due course, on which Pierce Butler proposed, and Charles C. Pinckney, both of South Carolina, seconded, the motion that fugitive slaves and servants should be included. Wilson of Pennsylvania objected, and Butler withdrew his motion; but the next day introduced a clause, substantially the same with that now found in the Constitution, viz.: "that no person held to service or labour in one state, under the laws thereof, escaping into another, shall, in consequence of any law or regulation therein, be discharged from such service or labour, but shall be delivered up on claim of the party to whom such service or labour is due." (See Article IV. Sect. iii.) This being copied from one of the provisions of the old New England Confederation, passed unobserved.

II. The privilege of the writ of habeas corpus shall not be suspended, unless when, in cases of rebellion or invasion, the public safety may require it.

III. No bill of attainder, or ex post facto law, shall be passed.

IV. No capitation or other direct tax shall be laid, unless in proportion to the census, or enumeration, herein before directed to be taken.

V. No tax or duty shall be laid on articles exported from any state. No preference shall be given, by any regulation of commerce or revenue, to the ports of one state over those of another; nor shall vessels, bound to or from one state, be obliged to enter, clear, or pay duties in another.

VI. No money shall be drawn from the treasury, but in consequence of appropriations made by law; and a regular statement and account of the receipts and expenditures of all public money shall be published from time to time.

VII. No title of nobility shall be granted by the United States; and no person holding any office of profit or trust under them, shall, without the consent of congress, accept of any present, emolument, office, or title of any kind whatever, from any king, prince, or foreign state.

SECTION X.

I. No state shall enter into any treaty, alliance, or confederation, grant letters of marque and reprisal; coin money; emit bills of credit; make any thing but gold and silver coin a tender in payment of debts; pass any bill of attainder, ex post facto law, or law impairing the obligation of contracts, or grant any title of nobility.

II. No state shall, without the consent of congress, lay any imposts or duties on imports or exports, except what may be absolutely necessary for executing its inspection laws: and the net produce of all duties and imposts, laid by any state on imports and exports, shall be for the use of the treasury of the United State, and all such laws shall be subject to the revision and control of congress. No state shall, without the consent of congress, lay any duty of tonnage, keep troops, or ships of war, in time of peace, enter into any agreement or compact with another state, or with a foreign power, or engage in war, unless actually invaded, or in such imminent danger as will not admit of delay.

ARTICLE II.

SECTION I.

I. The executive power shall be vested in a president of the United States of America. He shall hold his office during the term of four years, and, together with the vice-president, chosen for the same term, be elected as follows:

II. Each state shall appoint, in such manner as the legislature thereof may direct, a number of electors, equal to the whole number of senators and representatives to which the state may be entitled in the congress; but no senator or representative, or person holding an office of trust or profit under the United States, shall be appointed an elector.

III. The electors shall meet in their respective states, and vote by ballot for two persons, of whom one at least shall not be an inhabitant of the same state with themselves. And they shall make a list of all the persons voted for, and of the number of votes for each; which list they shall sign and certify, and transmit, sealed, to the seat of government of the United States, directed to the president of the senate. The president of the senate shall, in the presence of the senate and house of representatives, open all the certificates, and the votes shall then be counted. The person having the greatest number of votes shall be the president, if such number be a majority of the whole number of electors appointed; and if there be more than one who have such majority, and have an equal number of votes, then the house of representatives shall immediately choose, by ballot, one of them for president: and if no person have a majority, then from the five highest on the list, the said house shall, in like manner, choose the president. But in choosing the president, the votes shall be taken by states, the representation from each state having one vote; a quorum for this purpose shall consist of a member or members from two-thirds of the states, and a majority of all the states shall be necessary to a choice. In every case, after the choice of the president, the person having the greatest number of votes of the electors shall be the vice-president. But if there should remain two or more who have equal votes, the senate shall choose from them, by ballot, the vice-president.

IV. The congress may determine the time for choosing the electors, and the day on which they shall give their votes: which day shall be the same throughout the United States.

V. No person, except a natural born citizen or a citizen of the United States at the time of the adoption of this constitution, shall be eligible to the office of president, neither shall any person be eligible to that office, who shall not have attained to the age of thirty-five years, and been fourteen years a resident within the United States.

VI. In case of the removal of the president from office, or of his death, resignation, or inability to discharge the powers and duties of the said office, the same shall devolve on the vice-president, and the congress may, by law, provide for the case of removal, death, resignation, or inability, both of the president and vice-president, declaring what officer shall then act as president, and such officer shall act accordingly, until the disability be removed, or a president shall be elected.

VII. The president shall, at stated times, receive for his services a compensation, which shall neither be increased nor diminished during the period for which he shall have been elected, and he shall not receive, within that period, any other emolument from the United States, or any of them.

VIII. Before he enters on the execution of his office, he shall take the following oath, or affirmation:

"I do solemnly swear (or affirm) that I will faithfully execute the office of president of the United States, and will, to the best of my ability, preserve, protect, and defend the constitution of the United States."

SECTION II.

I. The president shall be commander-in-chief of the army and navy of the United States, and of the militia of the several states, when called into the actual service of the United States; he may require the opinion, in writing, of the principal officer in each of the executive departments, upon any subject relating to the duties of their respective offices, and he shall have power to grant reprieves and pardons for offences against the United States, except in cases of impeachment.

II. He shall have power, by and with the advice and consent of the senate, to make treaties, provided two-thirds of the senators present concur; and he shall nominate, and, by and with the advice and consent of the senate, shall appoint ambassadors, other public ministers and consuls, judges of the supreme court, and all other officers of the United States whose appointments are not herein otherwise provided for, and which shall be established by law. But the congress may, by law, vest the appointment of such inferior officers as they think proper in the president alone, in the courts of law, or in the heads of departments.

III. The president shall have power to fill up all vacancies that may happen during the recess of the senate, by granting commissions, which shall expire at the end of their next session.

SECTION III.

He shall, from time to time, give to the congress information of the state of the Union, and recommend to their consideration such measures as he shall judge necessary and expedient; he may, on extraordinary occasions, convene both houses, or either of them, and in case of disagreement between them, with respect to the time of adjournment, he may adjourn them to such time as he shall think proper; he shall receive ambassadors and other public ministers; he shall take care that the laws be faithfully executed, and shall commission all the officers of the United States.

SECTION IV.

The president, vice-president, and all civil officers of the United States, shall be removed from office on impeachment for, and conviction of, treason, bribery, or other high crimes and misdemeanors.

ARTICLE III.

SECTION I.

The judicial power of the United States shall be vested in one supreme court, and in such inferior courts as the congress may, from time to time, ordain and establish. The judges, both of the supreme and inferior courts, shall hold their offices during good behaviour, and shall, at stated times, receive for their services a compensation which shall not be diminished during their continuance in office.

SECTION II.

I. The judicial power shall extend to all cases, in law and equity, arising under this constitution, the laws of the United States, and treaties made, or which shall be made, under their authority; to all cases affecting ambassadors, other public ministers and consuls; to all cases of admiralty and maritime jurisdiction; to controversies to which the United States shall be a party; to controversies between two or more states, between a state and citizens of another state, between citizens of different states, between citizens of the same state claiming lands under grants of different states, and between a state, or the citizens thereof, and foreign states, citizens, or subjects.

II. In all cases affecting ambassadors, other public ministers, and consuls, and those in which a state shall be a party, the supreme court shall have original jurisdiction. In all other cases before mentioned, the supreme court shall have appellate jurisdiction, both as to law and fact, with such exceptions, and under such regulations, as the congress shall make.

III. The trial of all crimes, except in cases of impeachment, shall be by jury; and such trials shall be held in the state where the said crime shall have been committed; but when not committed within any state, the trial shall be at such a place or places as the congress may, by law, have directed.

SECTION III.

I. Treason against the United States shall consist only in levying war against them, or in adhering to their enemies, giving them aid and comfort. No person shall be convicted of treason, unless on the testimony of two witnesses to the same overt act, or on confession in open court.

II. The congress shall have power to declare the punishment of treason; but no attainder of treason shall work corruption of blood, or forfeiture except during the life of the person attainted.

ARTICLE IV.

SECTION I.

Full faith and credit shall be given in each state to the public acts, records, and judicial proceedings of every other state. And the congress may, by general laws, prescribe the manner in which such acts, records, and proceedings shall be proved, and the effect thereof.

SECTION II.

I. The citizens of each state shall be entitled to all the privileges and immunities of citizens in the several states.

II. A person charged in any state with treason, felony, or other crime, who shall flee from justice, and be found in another state, shall, on demand of the executive authority of the state from which he fled, be delivered up, to be removed to the state having the jurisdiction of the crime.

III. No person, held to service or labour in one state under the laws thereof, escaping into another, shall, in consequence of any law or regulation therein, be discharged from such service or labour, but shall be delivered up on claim of the party to whom such service or labour may be due.

SECTION III.

I. New states may be admitted by the congress into this Union, but no new state shall be formed or erected within the jurisdiction of any other state; nor any state be formed by the junction of two or more states, or parts of states, without the consent of the legislatures of the states concerned, as well as of the congress.

II. The congress shall have power to dispose of and make all needful rules and regulations respecting the territory, or other property, belonging to the United States; and nothing in this constitution shall be so construed as to prejudice any claims of the United States or of any particular state.

SECTION IV.

The United States shall guarantee to every state in this Union a republican form of government, and shall protect each of them against invasion; and on application of the legislature, or of the executive (when the legislature cannot be convened), against domestic violence.

ARTICLE V.

The congress, whenever two-thirds of both houses shall deem it necessary, shall propose amendments to this constitution, or, on the application of the legislatures of two-thirds of the several states, shall call a convention for proposing amendments, which, in either case, shall be valid, to all intents and purposes, as part of this constitution, when ratified by the legislatures of three-fourths of the several states, or by conventions in three-fourths thereof, as the one or the other mode of ratification may be proposed by the congress: Provided, that no amendment, which may be made prior to the year 1808, shall, in any manner, affect the first and fourth clauses in the ninth section of the first article; and that no state, without its consent, shall be deprived of its equal suffrages in the senate.

ARTICLE VI.

I. All debts contracted, and engagements entered into, before the adoption of this Constitution, shall be as valid against the United States under this Constitution, as under the confederation.

II. This Constitution and the laws of the United States, which shall be made in pursuance thereof; and all treaties made, or which shall be made, under the authority of the United States, shall be the supreme law of the land; and the judges in every state shall be bound thereby, anything in the constitution or laws of any state to the contrary notwithstanding.

III. The senators and representatives before-mentioned, and the members of the several state legislatures, and all executive and judicial officers, both of the United States and of the several states, shall be bound by oath, or affirmation, to support this Constitution: and no religious test shall ever be required, as a qualification to any office or public trust under the United States.

ARTICLE VII.

The ratification of the conventions of nine states shall be sufficient for the establishment of this Constitution, between the states so ratifying the same.

Done in convention by the consent of the states present, the seventeenth day of September, in the year of our Lord, one thousand seven hundred and eighty-seven, and of the Independence of the United States of America, the twelfth. In witness whereof, we have hereunto subscribed our names.

New Hampshire.—John Langdon, Nicholas Gelman.

Massachusetts.—Nathaniel Gorham, Rufus King.

Connecticut.—William Samuel Johnson, Roger Sherman.

New York.—Alexander Hamilton.

New Jersey.—William Livingston, David Brearley, William Patterson, Jonathan Dayton.

Pennsylvania.—Benjamin Franklin, Thomas Mifflin, Robert Morris, George Clymer, Thomas Fitzsimons, Jared Ingersoll, James Wilson, Gouverneur Morris.

Delaware.—George Read, Gunning Bedford, jun., John Dickenson, Richard Bassett, Jacob Broom.

Maryland.—James M'Henry, Daniel of St. Thomas Jenifer, Daniel Carrol.

Virginia.—John Blair, James Madison, jun.

North Carolina.—William Blount, Richard Dobbs Spaight, Hugh Williamson.

South Carolina.—John Rutledge, Charles C. Pinckney, Charles Pinckney, Pierce Butler.

Georgia.—William Few, Abraham Baldwin.

GEORGE WASHINGTON, *President.*

WILLIAM JACKSON, *Secretary.*

Hildreth tells us that, as regards the injunction of secrecy with respect to the proceedings of the convention, it was never removed. At the final adjournment the journal was entrusted to the custody of Washington, by whom it was afterwards deposited in the Department of State. It was first printed by order of Congress in 1818. Yates, one of the members, took short notes, which were printed after his death, in 1821. Still more perfect notes by Madison have been recently published.

The first sitting of congress, after a great deal of discussion respecting the seat of the Federal Government, was settled, on the 13th of September, 1788, to be at New York. The first Wednesday in the following January was appointed for the choice of the presidential electors; the first Wednesday in February for the election of President and Vice-president; and the first Wednesday in that year, being the 4th of March, for the first meeting of congress, for the organisation of the government of the United States under the new constitution.

Washington received the unanimous vote of the electors, and became President-elect; John Adams, having the next highest number, was entitled to the office of Vice-president. To these events we shall, however, return presently; in the meantime other circumstances require our attention. But in order to give a complete view of the constitution of the United States, we will in this place present twelve amendments, which were made at different times; the first ten on the first, the eleventh on the third, and the twelfth on the eighth sitting of congress.

AMENDMENTS.

ARTICLE I.

Congress shall make no law respecting an establishment of religion, or prohibiting the free exercise thereof; or abridging the freedom of speech, or of the press; or the rights of the people peaceably to assemble, and to petition the government for a redress of grievances.

ARTICLE II.

A well regulated militia being necessary to the security of a free state, the right of the people to keep and bear arms shall not be infringed.

ARTICLE III.

No soldier shall, in time of peace, be quartered in any house without the consent of the owner, nor in time of war, but in a manner to be prescribed by law.

ARTICLE IV.

The right of the people to be secure in their persons, houses, papers, and effects, against unreasonable searches and seizures, shall not be violated; and no warrants shall issue, but upon probable cause, supported by oath or affirmation, and particularly describing the place to be searched, and the persons or things to be seized.

ARTICLE V.

No person shall be held to answer for a capital, or otherwise infamous crime, unless on a presentment or indictment of a grand jury, except in cases arising in the land or naval forces, or in the militia when in actual service, in time of war, or public danger; nor shall any person be subject for the same offence to be twice put in jeopardy of life or limb; nor shall be compelled, in any criminal case, to be a witness against himself, nor be deprived of life, liberty, or property, without due process of law; nor shall private property be taken for public use without just compensation.

ARTICLE VI.

In all criminal prosecutions, the accused shall enjoy the right to a speedy and public trial, by an impartial jury of the state and district wherein the crime shall have been committed, which district shall have been previously ascertained by law, and to be informed of the nature and cause of the accusation; to be confronted with the witnesses against him; to have compulsory process for obtaining witnesses in his favour, and to have the assistance of counsel for his defence.

ARTICLE VII.

In suits at common law, where the value in controversy shall exceed twenty dollars, the right of trial by jury shall be preserved, and no fact, tried by jury, shall be otherwise re-examined in any court of the United States, than according to the rules of the common law.

ARTICLE VIII.

Excessive bail shall not be required, nor excessive fines imposed, nor cruel and unusual punishments inflicted.

ARTICLE IX.

The enumeration in the Constitution, of certain rights, shall not be construed to deny or disparage others retained by the people.

ARTICLE X.

The powers not delegated to the United States by the Constitution, nor prohibited by it to the states, are reserved to the states respectively, or to the people.

ARTICLE XI.

The judicial power of the United States shall not be construed to extend to any suit in law or equity, commenced or prosecuted against one of the United States, by citizens of another state, or by citizens or subjects of any foreign state.

ARTICLE XII.

The electors shall meet in their respective states, and vote by ballot, for president and vice-president, one of whom, at least, shall not be an inhabitant of the same state with themselves; they shall name, in their ballots, the person voted for as president, and, in distinct ballots, the person voted for as vice-president; and they shall make distinct lists of all persons voted for as president, and of all persons voted for as vice-president, and of the number of votes for each, which lists they shall sign and certify, and transmit, sealed, to the seat of the government of the United States, directed to the president of the senate. The president of the senate shall, in the presence of the senate and house of representatives, open all the certificates, and the votes shall then be counted. The person having the greatest number of votes for president shall be the president, if such a number be a majority of the whole number of electors appointed; and if no person have such a majority, then from the persons having the highest numbers, not exceeding three on the list of those voted for as president, the house of representatives shall choose immediately, by ballot, the president. But, in choosing the president, the votes shall be taken by states, the representation from each state having one vote; a quorum for this purpose shall consist of a member or members from two-thirds of the states, and a majority of all the states shall be necessary to a choice. And if the house of representatives shall not choose a president, whenever the right of choice shall devolve upon them, before the fourth day of March next following, then the vice-president shall act as president, as in the case of the death or other constitutional disability of the president.

The person having the greatest number of votes as vice-president shall be the vice-president, if such number be a majority of the whole number of electors appointed; and if no person have a majority, then from the two highest numbers on the list, the senate shall choose the vice-president—a quorum for the purpose shall consist of two-thirds of the whole number of senators, and a majority of the whole number shall be necessary to a choice.

But no person, constitutionally ineligible to the office of president, shall be eligible to that of vice-president of the United States.

CHAPTER XVI.
EMIGRATION TO THE WEST—
WASHINGTON, THE FIRST PRESIDENT.

While the convention at Philadelphia occupied themselves with the new constitution, the vast territory north of the Ohio River was formed, by the congress at New York, into a territorial government under the name of the North-Western Territory. Among other provisions of the government of this new territory was the carrying out of an important republican principle which some of the older states had not yet adopted; this was the equal division of all landed as well as personal property between the children of persons dying intestate. The fullest religious freedom was also insured; provision made for schools and for justice and humanity towards the Indians, and a strong protest entered against slavery, inasmuch as it was declared that there should be neither slavery nor involuntary servitude in the said territory, otherwise than as punishment of crimes of which the party shall have been duly convicted.

Seventeen millions of acres on the northern bank of the Ohio were now in possession of the United States, in consequence of the already mentioned treaties with the Six Nations. These formerly powerful and warlike tribes now retained but a small hold upon the lands which had once been their own. They were beginning, like their more feeble eastern brethren, to pass away from before the white man. The entire Mohawk nation emigrated in a body into Canada, and other Indian nations followed their example.

The pressure of war being removed from the eastern states, their restless and adventurous sons now went forth to explore and establish peaceable settlements, with all the amenities of domestic life and civilisation, in the wilderness. The State of New York located her disbanded soldiers on the land-bounties which she had promised them, upon such western lands as she retained after resigning her larger claims to the Union; Pennsylvania followed this example. Occupation was thus given to the unemployed, and a source of vast wealth opened to the impoverished. In July of this same busy year, the Ohio Company was formed, for the settlement of portions of this great territory, with the Rev. Manasseh Cutler, Winthrop Sargeant, and other citizens of New England, at its head.

In September, the Kentuckians, now holding their fourth convention at Danville, once more applied to congress for admission into the Union; but though they had now advanced so far as to have a spokesman in congress, in the person of one of the Virginian delegates, a Kentucky lawyer, and were possessed of a newspaper, the "Kentucky Gazette," printed and published at Lexington, they were again unsuccessful in their application.

General St. Clair was elected governor of the new territory north-west of the Ohio, and thither flowed the great tide of emigration from the New England states, which had hitherto poured into Vermont, New Hampshire and Maine. All New England was now astir with the movement westward, and again we have chronicles of migration and early settlement, as in the days of the Pilgrim Fathers. Quaint and beautiful are the details which exist of these movements. The plans were drawn in Boston, and at Providence in Rhode Island, of great cities to be erected on the banks of rivers flowing as yet through the wilderness; the intending emigrants met to draw lots for their future homes in these cities, each "town-lot to be ninety feet front and 180 feet in depth;" the centre street of the city to be 150 feet wide. As in the old times, "the Mayflower" set sail with the pioneer settlers; and on the 7th of April, 1788, General Rufus Putnam, the leader of this party, landed at the mouth of the Muskinghum, opposite Fort Harmer. Nothing can be pleasanter than the records of these early Ohio settlements. Captain Pipes, the chief of the Delawares, with about seventy of his tribe, came down for the purpose of trading with the garrison of Fort Harmer, shook hands with the new-comers, and welcomed them cordially to the shores of the Muskinghum, on the head waters of which river they themselves resided. The settlers arriving from the stern climate of New England, where they had left frost and snow, were struck by the contrast presented by the vegetation of their new home. The pea-vines, say they, and buffalo-clover, with various other plants, were nearly knee high, and afforded a rich pasture for their hungry horses. The trees had commenced putting forth their foliage, the birds warbled a welcome song from their branches, and all nature smiled at the approach of the strangers.

On these auspicious shores the settlers immediately commenced felling trees for their log-houses, and for the clearing of the land; while General Putnam resided in a tent which they had brought with them. In five days they had cleared and sown several acres of land. A month later one of the settlers wrote—"This country for fertility of soil and pleasantness of situation exceeds all our expectations. The climate is exceedingly healthy; not a man sick since we have been here. We have started twenty buffaloes in a drove. Deer as plenty as sheep in other places. Beaver and other animals abundant. I have known one man to catch twenty or thirty in one or two nights. Turkeys are innumerable; they come within a few rods of us in the fields. We have already planted a field of 150 acres of corn." In July, another writer says—"The corn has grown nine inches in twenty-four hours for two or three days past."

The city, which was laid out according to the great plan already formed, and including within its area the remains of an ancient fortified town, somewhat similar to those since discovered in Central America, and which were here carefully preserved, received the name of Marietta. This name was an abbreviation of Marie Antoinette, the name of the young queen of France, and was intended as a mark of respect to that sovereign, in consequence of the attention and kindness with which she had treated Franklin when at the court of Louis XVI., and of the interest which she had taken in the American struggle. The leaders of this settlement were principally old soldiers, and it was natural in them to remember with gratitude the kind offices which this young and beautiful woman had rendered to their cause; nor is their veneration for the classics less distinguishable. There was the "Capitolium" of the city, and the "Via Sacra," while the garrison, with block-houses at the corners, was called "Campus Martius," "as if," says the historian, "in anticipation of the Indian war, which soon commenced, and continued for five years, during which time it was strictly a military camp." Every feature of the infant colony bore the stamp of sylvan prosperity; the early regulations for the government were written out and posted on the smooth trunk of a large beech-tree. The 4th of July, the anniversary of the Declaration of Independence, was celebrated by "a sumptuous dinner, eaten under a bowery which stretched along the banks of the Muskinghum." The table, we are informed, was supplied with venison, buffalo and roast-pigs, with a variety of fish. Among the latter was a pike weighing 100 pounds, which was caught at the mouth of the Muskinghum, by Judge Gilbert Devoll and his son Gilbert, and the tail of which dragged on the ground when suspended upon a pole between the shoulders of two tall men. On this occasion an oration was made by one of the judges, the first political oration ever made in Ohio.

On the 9th of July, General St. Clair arrived as governor of the colony, and was received in "the bowery" with Arcadian honours, and the firing of fourteen guns. So rapid was the progress of this settlement, that before the end of the summer the city-lots, with their streets and open public spaces, covered an area extending one mile on the Ohio River, and one mile and 120 perches on the Muskinghum. A substantial bridge was built over the creek which falls into the Muskinghum, in the southern part of the city, called, with their love of classical history, "Tiber Creek," and three other bridges were also built over smaller streams. A road was cut through the forest to the Campus Martius, and the clearing and planting of land went on vigorously. Again and again wrote the settlers of the prosperity and plenty which surrounded them; the harvest was cut in the autumn, and in some cases yielded 104 bushels of ears to the acre, some of these ears yielding a pint and a half of shelled corn each. "As for beans, turnips, pumpkins, squashes, cabbages, melons, cucumbers, etc., they are," says the exultant writer, "the very finest in flavour I ever tasted, and the great production is truly surprising." The district of Marietta was called Washington county.

Emigration and colonisation was now the order of the day. It supplied the want of employment and excitement caused by the cessation of the war, and was a healthy outlet for the energies of the people. Among other emigrants who went out to the western settlements of New York was Daniel Shays, who had been included in a bill just passed of general pardon and indemnity for all concerned in the late insurrection. Shays lived to be very old, supported in his latter days by his pension as a revolutionary soldier. In October, John Symmes, one of the judges of Marietta, purchased a large tract of land between the great and little Miami rivers, and in the following month the first settlement within that purchase, and the second within Ohio, was commenced at Columbia at the mouth of the little Miami, five miles above the site of the present Cincinnati. All went on prosperously; towns were laid out, forests cleared, roads opened, mills and bridges built, and population flocked in. Nor was this alone the case on the Ohio. Within twelve months, more than 10,000 emigrants passed through Marietta on their way to Kentucky and other parts of the Ohio and Mississippi rivers. The West, the "great West," the boast of the American, was putting forth its vast attractions and luring tens of thousands even then.

At the close of 1787, it was doubtful what would be the fate of the Federal Constitution in the States. It was received with distrust and jealousy by a great body of the people, who feared that the extensive powers given by the new Constitution to the federal government would place them under oppressions as grievous as those of the mother-country, which they had just shaken off. On the other hand, it was supported by the wealthy portion of the community, by the public creditors and merchants, the former of whom saw in it their only chance of payment, while the latter hoped everything from the extension and regulation of commerce. In the midst of this doubt and uncertainty, an able series of articles appeared in a New York paper, written by Hamilton, Madison and Jay, advocating the new constitution, and these so completely meeting all objections, helped greatly to settle the question.

Delaware was the first state to adopt the Constitution, on December 7th; five days later Pennsylvania followed the example; and soon after New Jersey, Georgia and Connecticut. Massachusetts weighed and deliberated, with able men on either side, the friends of the Union looking anxiously on, well knowing that on the decision of that important state would depend the decision of others; and at length, on February 7th, the new Constitution was ratified by her, the majority in its favour being nineteen. Maryland gave in her adhesion in April, South Carolina in May, and in June New Hampshire. The Constitution was earnestly advocated and opposed by the different parties in the conventions of Virginia and New York, but both ratified it, the one in June, the other in July.

Eleven states had now adopted the Constitution, and though North Carolina still hesitated, and Rhode Island obstinately held no convention, measures were immediately taken for the organisation of the new government. As was to be expected, Washington received at the appointed time the unanimous vote of the electors, and became president-elect; the next highest number of votes was for John Adams, who was in consequence entitled to the office of vice-president; and senators and representatives under the new Constitution were chosen also in the eleven ratifying states.

The 4th of March was the day appointed for the new government to commence operations, but so many impediments occurred that it was not until the 30th of April that this took place. Some of the causes of this delay are curious. By the help of several public-spirited citizens of New York, who advanced the necessary funds, the old City Hall was prepared for the occasion. The important day was ushered in by the firing of cannon and the ringing of bells. But after all, the building was not ready, and more than that, eight senators only and thirteen representatives made their appearance, not enough to form a quorum in either house. The fact was, that most of the members, many of them from great distances, having to travel to New York on horseback, had found, at that early season of the year, the roads in many places impassable by floods, especially where rivers had to be forded. On the last day but one of March, thirty members, sufficient to form a quorum, being present, business commenced. The vice-president Adams arrived in New York, escorted by a troop of horse, on April 21st, and Washington, as president, proceeded from Mount Vernon in Virginia, to New York, in a sort of triumphal progress, the people everywhere eager to testify their affection and esteem, and on the 29th of April landed at New York, having crossed over from New Jersey in a barge fitted up for the occasion, and rowed by thirteen pilots in white uniforms.

But even now the new Federal Hall was not ready, and Washington took the oath of office, after Divine service had been performed in all the churches, in a balcony fronting the street where the assembled populace could witness the ceremony. The oath was administered by Livingston, Chancellor of New York, who, on its conclusion, exclaimed aloud, "Long live George Washington, President of the United States!" and the multitude answered with enthusiastic shouts.

The inaugural address of Washington was short, and remarkable for its deep tone of gratitude to the Divine Ruler, who had permitted the affairs of America to take a favourable issue; for its pure and elevated sentiment of political wisdom, and of devotion to that beloved country in whose service he had already laboured so faithfully. "The foundation of the national policy," he remarked, "should be laid in the pure principles of private morality; no truth being more thoroughly established than that there exists an indissoluble union between virtue and happiness; between duty and advantage; between the genuine maxims of an honest and magnanimous policy and the solid rewards of public prosperity and happiness." He considered "the success of the republican form of government as an experiment entrusted to the American people," and assured them, "that the propitious smiles of Heaven could never be looked for if the eternal rules of order and right, which Heaven itself had ordained, were disregarded."

His disinterested patriotism was proved by the fact that now, as on the former occasion when he held the office of commander-in-chief, he desired no other compensation for his services than the reimbursement of his expenses.

It was early attempted in the senate to introduce styles and titles of office, and to address the president as "His Highness," but this was resolutely opposed; nevertheless a committee was appointed to consider the subject, and in the meantime the question was decided by the house of representatives, the supporters of republican simplicity. They addressed Washington, in their reply to his opening address, merely as "the President of the United States."

Washington on his part, though a strenuous advocate of republican simplicity, found it necessary to sustain the dignity of his office by a form of etiquette which was considerably censured at the time, but which has ever since continued to regulate the presidential household. He laid it down as a rule to return no visits. Certain days were appointed for levees; nor were any invitations to dinner given, excepting to foreign ministers, officers of the government, and strangers of distinction. The arrangement of the ceremonial at levees and other public occasions was entrusted to Humphries, who had formerly been aide-de-camp to Washington, and later, secretary of legation at Paris, and who was supposed to know a good deal on the punctilios of court life. Trifling matters of ceremonial introduced by Humphries, as the placing the president and his wife on elevated seats at public balls, and requiring the dancers to acknowledge their presence by bows and curtseys, led to trouble in after years, as marks of the monarchical tendencies of the federal party.[64] For the rest the greatest simplicity prevailed; there was neither ostentation nor reserve, and the guests of the first man in the Union were entertained with as much ease, and received as kind a welcome, as though he had still been only "Farmer Washington." On the Sundays, however, no visits were received. He regularly attended church in the morning, and in the afternoon retired to his private apartment. The evening was spent with his family, when sometimes an intimate friend might call, but promiscuous company was not permitted.[65]

The first objects of congress were to establish a revenue for the support of government, and the supply of the exhausted treasury; to organise the executive departments; to establish a judiciary; and to amend the constitution. In order to provide a revenue, duties were imposed on the tonnage of vessels, and on foreign goods imported into the states, among which were ardent spirits. As regarded spirituous liquors, the attention of the public was just turned to this subject by a tract on the great evils attending their use, lately published by Dr. Rush. It was the commencement of the temperance movement, and at the great Federal Festival, held at Philadelphia to celebrate the adoption of the new Constitution, ardent spirits had been excluded, American beer and cider being the only liquors used.

Three executive departments were established to aid the president in the affairs of government—the departments of Foreign Affairs, of the Treasury, and of War. Thomas Jefferson was appointed to the first, Alexander Hamilton to the second, and General Knox to the third, which he had long held, the small navy being also placed under his care. These offices were under the control of the president, and the power of removing them was, after much discussion, placed also in his hands.

The national judiciary now established consisted of a Supreme Court, having one chief-justice and several associate judges, as well as circuit and district courts possessing jurisdiction as specified in the Constitution. Washington declared that "the due administration of justice was the firmest pillar of good government, and that the selection of the fittest characters to expound the laws and dispense justice was an invariable object of his anxious concern." He selected, therefore, the fittest men he knew for those important appointments; and John Jay became chief-justice, and Edmund Randolph attorney-general. Several amendments to the Constitution were proposed, ten of which, as given in the preceding chapter, were afterwards adopted.

The salary of the president was fixed at 25,000 dollars a year, that of the vice-president at 5,000, those of the heads of departments at 3,500. Six dollars a day, with six dollars for every twenty miles of travelling, were allowed to the representatives, and seven dollars, with the same sum for travelling expenses, in the same ratio, to the members of the Senate. The chief-justice of the Supreme Court was to receive 4,000 dollars, and the associate judges 500 dollars less, per annum.

On the 29th of September, the first session of congress closed. In November, North Carolina ratified the Constitution.

During the recess of congress, the president made a tour through the New England states, omitting, however, Rhode Island, which had not yet given in its adhesion to the Constitution. Everywhere he was received with demonstrations of love and respect. "Men, women and children," says Jared Sparkes, "people of all ranks, ages, and occupations, assembling from far and near, at the crossings of the roads and other public places where it was known he would pass. Military escorts attended him on the way, and at the principal towns, he was received and entertained by the civil authorities.

"This journey," continues the same writer, "not only furnished proofs of the attachment of the people, but convinced him of the growing prosperity of the country, and of the favour which the Constitution and the administration of government were gaining in the public mind. He saw with pleasure that the effects of the war had almost disappeared; that agriculture was pursued with activity; that the harvests were abundant, manufactures increasing, the towns flourishing, and commerce becoming daily more extended and profitable. The condition of society, the progress of improvements, the success of industrial enterprise, all gave tokens of order, peace and contentment, and a most cheering promise for the future."

Journeys of this kind, the great object of which was the becoming better acquainted with the capabilities, as well as the condition of the country, were not uncommon with Washington. Already, in 1784, at the close of the war, he had made a journey of 600 miles, to visit his lands on the Ohio, when the practicability of a great scheme suggested itself to him, viz. that of uniting the East and West, by means of intercommunication between the head waters of the Atlantic streams and the western rivers. He pressed the subject upon the notice of the government of Virginia, the result of which was the formation of two companies, "the Potomac Company," and "the Kenhawa and James River Company." Washington thus became the first mover in the great series of internal improvements which took place.

The second session of congress opened on the 6th of January, 1790. Hamilton, the secretary of the treasury, brought forward early his report upon the public debt contracted during the war, and which had hung like a mill-stone so long round the neck of government. Taking an able and enlarged view of the advantages of public credit, he recommended that not only the debts of the continental congress, but those of the individual states contracted on behalf of the common cause, should be funded or assumed by the general government, and that provision should be made for paying the interest by taxes imposed on certain articles of luxury, and on spirits distilled in the country. This report led to long discussion; but in conclusion, congress passed an act for the assumption of the states' debts, and for funding the national debt. Provision for the payment of the foreign debt was made without any difficulty. The debt funded amounted to about 75,000,000 dollars; and it was especially enacted that no certificate should be obtained from a state-creditor, which it could not be ascertained had been issued for the express purposes of compensation, services, or supplies, during the late war. The proceeds of the western lands and the surplus revenue, with the addition of 2,000,000 dollars which the president was authorised to borrow at 5 per cent, constituted a sinking fund to be applied to the reduction of the debt. The effect of these measures upon the country in general was of the most satisfactory kind. The sudden increase of monied capital gave a fresh impulse to commerce and consequently to agriculture.

Shortly after the discussion on the debt commenced in Congress, it was interrupted by petitions from the yearly meeting of the Quakers of Pennsylvania, Delaware and New York, advocating the abolition of slavery, and which were followed up by a memorial from the Pennsylvania Abolition Society, signed by Benjamin Franklin as president, one of the last public acts of this remarkable man's life; he died a few weeks afterwards. This subject led to two months' controversy on the subject of slavery and the slave-trade, the end of which was a report, entered on the journal of the debates, that any state thinking proper to import slaves, could not be prohibited by congress prior to the year 1808, although it had power to prevent their supplying foreigners with slaves, and that they had no authority to interfere in the emancipation of slaves, or in the treatment of them in any of the states.

In May of this year, Rhode Island acceded to the New Constitution, and thus completed the union of the Thirteen States. About the same time an act was passed for accepting a cession of land from North Carolina, and erecting it into a territorial government, under the title of "the Territory South of the Ohio," and which was in every respect to stand upon the same basis as the "Territory North West of the Ohio," with this exception, that slavery was not excluded. This new territory, which forms the present Tennessee, included the late aspiring state of Frankland, and another tract of about 2,000 square miles, which had been settled in 1780 by James Robertson, who, with about forty families, had advanced 300 miles into the wilderness, and there established the town of Nashville on the banks of the Cumberland River; whither, also, he had been followed by many of the officers and soldiers of the revolutionary war, to whom land-bounties had been assigned on the same river. The new territory, for which a governor was presently appointed, was for the greater part in the possession of the Indians at that very time.

Indian wars were the certain result of the advance of the white man into the wilderness, and the frontiers of the more southern states still continued to be the scenes of bloodshed. A war had been carried on for some time between the Creek Indians and Georgia, on the subject of lands said to have been ceded by the Indians to that state, but which they denied. The Creek warriors were well supplied with fire-arms and ammunition, and had the advantage of an able and accomplished chief, a half-breed Indian called, after his father, M'Gillivray, and who had received an excellent education in Charleston. Under this chief the Creeks carried on a fierce and terrible war, which spread alarm even as far as Savannah. Washington, anxious to bring about a negotiation with these formidable warriors, invited M'Gillivray to New York; and accompanied by twenty-eight chiefs and warriors, he arrived there, congress being still in session, and was received with every mark of respect and attention. A treaty of peace was entered into; wampum given and tobacco smoked; after which M'Gillivray having made a speech, and "a shake of peace" between Washington and the chiefs being given, "a song of peace" was raised by the Indians, and the ceremony ended. Peace was established on the frontiers of Georgia, and the lands which the Creeks claimed solemnly guaranteed to them, not much to the satisfaction of the whites.

Thus successful with the Creeks, they were much less so with the western Indians, who encouraged, it was said, by the British in Canada, insisted on making the Ohio their boundary, and infested the banks of the river, attacking the emigrant boats, which descended it, and carrying their ravages far into Kentucky. Pacific overtures having been made in vain by the president to these hostile Indians, General Harmar was sent from Fort Washington, now Cincinnati, with a force of 1,400, to reduce them to terms. He succeeded in destroying the Indian villages and their harvests, but in two engagements near the confluence of the St. Mary's and St. Joseph's in Indiana, successive detachments of the army were defeated with considerable loss.

Congress during this present session passed an act "for the encouragement of learning," which secured a copyright to authors for fourteen years, and if living at the end of that term, for fourteen years longer.

During the session of 1791, a National Bank was proposed by Hamilton, which met with the most vigorous opposition from the republican party, who considered that congress had no constitutional power for such a measure. The supporters of the bill maintained it to be constitutional and necessary for the operations of government. The president required the opinions of the cabinet in writing, and after mature deliberation, gave the bill his signature, and the bank was established at Philadelphia, with a capital of 10,000,000 dollars.

The dissentions on the subjects of the funding system and the bank, originating in the heart of the republic, extended themselves to the extremities, and were a signal for the people to range themselves under two parties. Hamilton and Jefferson were the leaders of these factions, and Washington in vain endeavoured, by his practical wisdom and affectionate remonstrances, to reconcile the two parties. But we have not space to enter at large into the struggles and bitternesses of this party strife. We pass, therefore, on to events.

New York having relinquished her claim to Vermont, though not without the purchase of a release for 30,000 dollars, and the Green Mountain Boys, having adopted the Constitution, were in February admitted into the Union.

The Indian war still continuing, and even with increased violence, additional troops were raised and command given to General St. Clair, governor of the North West Territory, to march to the relief of the suffering settlers; and in October he encamped with 1,400 men near the Miami villages. The chief of the Miamis, at this time, was the powerful Michikiniqua, or the Little Turtle, who by the force of native talent, had raised himself to the military leadership of the confederated western tribes. In his forces, which numbered about 1,500, were included many half-breeds and refugees, among whom was the notorious Simon Girty. St. Clair and his officers were asleep in the midst of their camp, when in the early dawn they were roused by a sudden attack. The carnage which followed was terrible; more than one-fourth of the Americans, and the artillery and baggage, fell into the hands of the enemy.[66] This second repulse spread the greatest terror throughout the north-west 264 frontier even into Pennsylvania. On the news of this disaster, congress resolved to prosecute the war with increased vigour, and provision was made for augmenting the army, by enlistment, to the number of 5,000 men. The defeat of Harmar and St. Clair had, however, created such a dread of the Indians, that a sufficient number of recruits could not be obtained. A clamour was raised against the war; Willett and Daniel Morgan, old revolutionary officers, declined to act as brigadier-generals, Willett openly declaring his doubt of the justice of the war. "The intercourse," said he, "which I have had with these people, and the treatment which I and others have received from them, makes me their advocate. The honour of fighting and beating the Indians is not what I aspire after." Colonel Harden and Major Trueman were then sent with a flag of truce, to attempt a negotiation, but they were both murdered. The Six Nations now, at the request of Washington, interfered to persuade the tribes on the Wabash to withdraw from the confederacy, and make peace with the United States. This was in part effected, and the Miamis agreed to a conference the following spring.

The first census of the inhabitants of the United States was taken this year, when the population was found to be 3,921,326, of whom 695,655 were slaves. By this census the representatives were apportioned, allowing one representative for each 33,000 inhabitants, and thus giving the house 105 members. The revenue, according to the report of the secretary, amounted to 4,771,000 dollars.

In this session, the long-agitated question regarding the locality of the permanent seat of government was decided. A district, ten miles square, comprehending lands on both sides the river Potomac, was selected and the city of Washington laid out, the sales which took place producing the necessary funds for its erection.

Kentucky had the satisfaction, after her long efforts at independence, to be admitted into the Union, in June of 1792. The same year the post-office was organised and a mint was established and located in Philadelphia. The coinage, to be called Federal money, were the eagle, half-eagle and quarter-eagle in gold; the dollar, half-dollar, quarter-dollar, dime and half-dime in silver; the cent and half-cent in copper. The device for the coinage led to considerable agitation; the head of Washington, in the first instance, and other presidents for the time being, with the name and order of succession, being considered an alarming step towards monarchy, like the former proposition of the title of Highness and the present levees of the president, and was therefore rejected. An emblematic figure of liberty was finally adopted.

The first Congress had now closed its sessions. Washington was again elected president, and was inaugurated in March of 1793, John Adams also being re-elected to the office of vice-president.

CHAPTER XVII.
WASHINGTON'S ADMINISTRATION
(continued).

The two parties of Federalists and Anti-Federalists enlisted under their banners the friends and enemies of the new National Constitution, the former asserting the necessity of a strong central government, and the latter opposing, with jealous anxiety, any measure which should lessen the popular power by decreasing that of the individual States. The admirable working, however, of the Constitution under Washington and his able ministry; the increase of commerce; the extension of territory, and the general prosperity, would no doubt within a few years have allayed party animosities, had not an element at that moment come into operation which, if no other causes had existed, would have divided the country into two equally violent parties. This was the French Revolution.

Thomas Jefferson had been recalled from France, where he acted as ambassador of the United States, to take part in the administration under the new Constitution, and brought with him a strong prepossession in favour of the French revolutionists. Nothing could be more natural than that the citizens of the United States, who had so lately and so gloriously achieved their own independence, should sympathise warmly in the struggle of that very nation which had aided them in the time of their difficulty to throw off the despotism under which they was suffering, and the early and better impulse to which had been a spark caught from the American flame of liberty. While the anti-federalists, resisting, as they believed, all dangerous aggressions on their own dearly-bought independence, cordially espoused the French cause; the federalists saw in the outrage and ferocity of the French republicans indications which filled them with the utmost jealousy and alarm, lest the same spirit should break forth upon their shores, and sweep away those wise foundations of order which had been so carefully laid.

With these opposite sentiments towards France were united, as a matter of course, equally opposed feelings towards England. The federalists regarding their country as allied to Great Britain by similarity of language, religion, and literature, were ready even to doubt, with the example of France before them, whether a republican form of government could be relied upon, and to draw still more closely the bonds of union between themselves and the mother-country. They charged the anti-federalists with blind devotion to the French cause, and their leaders, with Jefferson at the head, with being deeply tinctured with the sentiments of the French school of philosophy, and with the design of introducing the same infidel and jacobinical notions into America, as had led to the sanguinary and revolting scenes in France.[67]

The revolutionary party in France regarded the Americans as brethren, and expected from them only applause and sympathy. The French minister who had been sent over by the king was recalled, and citizen Genet, as representative of the new republic, arrived in April, 1793, about a month after Washington's second entrance into office, at Charleston, South Carolina, where he was received with distinguished respect and honour, intended to express the approbation with which America regarded the change in the institutions of France. While the minister of the French republic was thus received with peculiar marks of honour by the anti-federal party, they insisted upon the president resuming office with the most republican simplicity. Jefferson was at the head of this movement, and lest he might appear as the only thorough republican in the cabinet, now that republicanism was the fashion, Hamilton, the opponent of Jefferson, fell into the same idea. Knox and Randolph dissented; and Washington took the oath of office in the Senate-chamber in the presence of the members of the cabinet, various public officers and foreign ministers. The Vice-President Adams, too, assumed a republican simplicity of living; gave up his house in Philadelphia and went into lodgings, leaving his wife at home to manage the farm, to whom writing, he said that his style of living made him very popular, and that he himself was well satisfied with his present simplicity. This republican rage was consequently shocked severely on the occasion of Washington's next birth-day, when visits of congratulation, balls, parties, and other festivities, took place, not in Philadelphia only, where congress was now sitting, but in many other cities and towns; all which were regarded by the democrats as alarming steps towards monarchy, and the press teemed with bitter effusions on the subject.[68]

Genet, the new French minister, flattered by the reception given to him, and supposing that the American nation, whatever its government might be, were ready to embark in the cause of France, proceeded to authorise the fitting out and arming privateers in the port of Charleston, and the enlisting men and giving commissions to cruise and commit hostilities on nations with whom the United States were at peace. He assumed also to authorise the French consuls throughout the Union to erect Courts of Admiralty, for trying and condemning such prizes as might be brought into the American ports; and acting on this assumed authority, proceeded accordingly against several prizes which were very soon brought to Charleston.

Five days before the arrival of Genet at Charleston, the news had reached New York of the French declaration of war against England and Holland. Washington, who was then at Mount Vernon, hastened to Philadelphia, summoned his cabinet, and took into serious consideration the important question, as to what part the United States must take in the present crisis of European affairs. Not wishing to involve his country in the contests of Europe, he himself advocated neutrality, and the cabinet finally came to the same opinion. This step, however, was by no means a popular one. Genet, who was an old and able diplomatist, arrived at Philadelphia immediately after the American government had published their decision. His journey, like his reception, called forth the most extravagant enthusiasm. The very men, says Hildreth, who had reprobated any demonstration of respect to Washington, as savouring too much of the old spirit of monarchical adulation, now seemed almost insane in the fervour of their desire to do honour to the Republic of France, in the person of her minister.

Republican feasts were held in sober Philadelphia; the public press took up the cry; democratic societies were formed; the red cap of Liberty was hoisted; the Marseilles hymn was sung, with two additional verses written by Genet, with reference to the navy; and a large faction, more French than American, seemed all going mad together.

Genet was a firebrand in the country. Not alone did he attempt to exercise sovereignty on the coast, but to organise in Georgia and South Carolina a hostile expedition against Florida, and another in Kentucky against New Orleans. The leadership in this latter undertaking was given to George Rogers Clarke, who formerly distinguished himself in the revolutionary war by the conquest of the Illinois country, but who now had sunk very low by a long course of intemperance. America could not rule her own country as long as Genet remained within it. Nothing could be more opposed than the restless, scheming, hot-headed and unprincipled Genet, and the calm, religious, and sagacious Washington. The excesses into which Genet and his party ran, caused complaints from the British minister. The cabinet resolved to enforce the laws; and Genet, believing that the whole management of American affairs was in his hands, threatened to appeal to the people against their government.

A reaction had already begun, and this very attempt to shake the government served but to strengthen it. Washington requested the recall of Genet, and in the following year his place was supplied by Fauchet, who was instructed to inform the American government that France disapproved of the conduct of her late minister. The Reign of Terror had now commenced in that devoted country, and Genet, who had in the meantime married the daughter of Governor Clinton, of New York, not choosing to return to France settled down in America, dropping at once his character of democratic agitator and sinking into the obscure citizen.

We must now take a rapid glance at the state of affairs in the West. After the defeat of St. Clair in 1791, General Wayne, to whom the Indians gave the name of the Black Snake, was appointed to the command of the American forces. Taking post near the country of the enemy, he made assiduous but vain attempts at negotiating peace, while his troops suffered greatly from a kind of epidemic influenza. The winter of 1793 he passed on the ground where the disastrous battles of 1791 had been fought, and here erected Fort Recovery. The Little Turtle would willingly have made peace, for, said he, addressing the confederated tribes, "we shall not now surprise them, for they have a chief who never sleeps;" but the Indian council insisted on war.

Early in the summer of 1794 operations commenced; Fort Recovery was attacked, and the Indians repulsed, although at the loss of 300 pack-mules and fifty men. In August, a reinforcement of 1,100 men having joined him, Wayne reached the confluence of the Au Glaize and the Maumee rivers, about thirty miles from a British post, where the whole force of the enemy, about 2,000 strong, was collected. Here, taken by surprise, they fled precipitately, and were pursued for two hours at the point of the bayonet. The country was finely cultivated and full of abundant crops. The American commander declared that he had never seen anything equal to it. The banks of those beautiful rivers appeared for many miles one complete village. At this point the conqueror built a strong fort called Fort Defiance, and a second called Fort Adams, to connect it with Fort Recovery.

Wayne offered to treat with the Indians, but they asked ten days for deliberation. This he would not grant, and followed them down the Maumee for two days; on the third he found them strongly encamped by the river, and a battle took place in which they were completely routed. The English lost 107 men; the loss of the Indians was never ascertained. The Indian corn-fields were ravaged up to the very walls of the British fort. Two British companies, it was asserted, with their faces painted to represent Indians, were in the fight; nevertheless, when the routed Indians fled to the fort for refuge, they were refused admittance, which treatment they never forgave; and Buckongahelas, the principal chief of the Delawares, immediately afterwards made peace with the Americans. The British influence over the savages was broken, and their confederacy dissolved. This victory insured peace and security to the whole settlements north-west of the Ohio, and even extended to Georgia.

On the 3rd of August, 1795, Wayne concluded a treaty of peace on behalf of the "Thirteen Fires," as the federal states were called, with the

Indians at Greenville. The principal chiefs, Tarhe, Buckongahelas, Black Hoof, Blue Jacket, and the Little Turtle, attended by 1,100 warriors, were parties to it. This treaty stipulated that the Ohio, with a few reservations, should thence become the boundary of the Indian territory. Besides the extent of country thus ceded, were several detached portions of territory, including the present or former sites of forts in the possession of the British, and about to be surrendered under a treaty with Great Britain, of which we shall speak anon, having, as regards these Indian affairs, somewhat advanced beyond the regular course of events. Among these cessions was a tract opposite Louisville, granted by Virginia to George Rogers Clarke and his soldiers for their services in the Illinois country; the ancient post of Vincennes and other French settlements; Fort Massac on the Ohio; and several other forts on different rivers with adjacent territory, Detroit, Mackinaw, and tracts at Sandusky, Chicago, and at the mouth and head of the Illinois river. The Indians received for these cessions 20,000 dollars worth of goods, with an annual allowance of about 10,000 dollars more.

At the exchange of prisoners which took place on this occasion, many affecting incidents occurred. The war, as against Kentucky, had lasted for about twenty years, during which time a great number of white people had been carried into captivity. Wives and husbands, parents and children, who had been separated for years, were now reunited. Many of the younger captives had quite forgotten their native language, and some of them absolutely refused to leave the savage connexions, into whose families they had been received by adoption.[69]

We now return to Congress and the affairs of the administration. On the 1st of January, 1794, Jefferson resigned his office as secretary of state, and was succeeded by Randolph; William Bradford, of Pennsylvania, supplying his place as attorney-general.

This year was rendered remarkable by an insurrection in Pennsylvania. In 1791, congress had enacted laws laying duties upon spirits distilled within the United States, and upon stills. The operation of these laws had from the first created dissatisfaction, and an organised system of resistance was formed in the four western counties, and especially among the anti-federal or democratic party, to resist and defeat them. Indictments were found against such as had neglected to enter their stills, and the marshal of the district, about to serve the thirtieth warrant near Pittsburg, was met by an armed force which put him and his men to flight. This was the signal for further and more determined violence. The next morning, the house of General Neville, the inspector of the revenue, who had been wounded the day before, was attacked by an armed force, under a man called Tom the Tinker, and entered. Several persons were wounded, and Neville compelled to enter into stipulations to desist from the execution of his office. The following day the attack was renewed by a still more formidable party, but Neville had then fled, and the buildings were burned to the ground by the infuriated mob, the garrison which was stationed there being compelled to surrender. The marshal and the inspector fled to Ohio, and embarking, descended to Marietta, and thence by land to Philadelphia. This was a great triumph to the malcontents; a meeting was held at Pittsburg, and corresponding societies established. The mail from Philadelphia was intercepted, and the letters examined to ascertain beforehand how their affairs had been taken up at head-quarters. These multiplied outrages appeared to the president as very alarming signs of the times, especially as the democratic societies of the West were beginning to affiliate with their ferocious brethren of Paris. Several of the cabinet agreed with Washington in the necessity of using very decided and summary measures, and it was proposed to call out the militia. Again the governor of Pennsylvania, this time Mifflin, doubted his authority to call them out, or their obedience if he did so, and Washington immediately issued a proclamation commanding the insurgents to disperse, and warning all persons against aiding, abetting, or comforting the perpetrators of these treasonable acts, and requiring all officers and other citizens, according to their respective duties and the laws of the land, to use their utmost endeavours to suppress these dangerous proceedings.

The insurgents were no way deterred by this proclamation, and meetings of delegates from all the disaffected districts took place under liberty-trees with liberty-banners floating around them. The president's call for the militia was responded to; and quotas were sent in from Virginia under the old revolutionary officer Morgan, as well as from Maryland, while Mifflin, thinking better of his hesitation, made a tour through the lower counties, and using his extraordinary popular eloquence for the occasion, soon filled up the ranks. Again, on the 25th of September, the president issued a second proclamation, admonishing the insurgents, and forcibly stating his determination, after the spirit of defiance with which the former lenient treatment of the government had been received, to obey the duty assigned to him by the Constitution, and "take care that the laws be faithfully executed," and that he would proceed forthwith to reduce the refractory to obedience.

It was time that summary measures were taken, for disaffection and sedition were spreading in all directions; armed mobs were marching everywhere, erecting liberty-poles and committing deeds of violence. Fifteen thousand men were sent into the disaffected districts, under General Lee of Virginia. No sooner was the news abroad that this formidable army was advancing against them, than the tide of democratic violence began to ebb; liberty-poles were pulled down, and the armed insurgents dispersed. Several of the most active leaders were handed over to the civil authorities for trial, but were afterwards pardoned, as were also two others who were found guilty of treason. Morgan, however, remained in the disaffected counties through the winter, with a body of 2,500 men. The government was strengthened even by this outbreak; the decision and promptitude of the president won the respect, and his lenity the hearts of the country.

During this session an act was passed to raise a naval force consisting of six frigates, as a defence for American commerce against the Algerine pirates; no less than eleven merchant vessels and upwards of 100 citizens having been captured by those pests of the ocean. An act also was passed about the same time for fortifying the principal harbours, the more immediate cause for which was the apprehension of war with Great Britain, which at that time prevailed.

Ever since the treaty of peace in 1783, Great Britain and the United States had been mutually reproaching each other for having violated its conditions. The former complained that the royalists were prevented from recovering possession of their estates, and British subjects from recovering their debts. The Americans, on the other hand, complained that the British had carried away negroes at the close of the war, and that they still obstinately retained those military posts in the north-west, of which such frequent mention has been made. The excitement against Great Britain received, however, at this moment a great accession by two orders in council just issued, and by which all British cruisers were directed to stop and seize all ships laden with provisions bound for any French port, and to bring them for adjudication into the British courts of admiralty. These orders, which in fact went to destroy all neutral trade with the French colonies, produced the utmost excitement in Philadelphia, and for the moment nothing but war with Great Britain was talked of. Congress assembled, and a bill was passed laying an embargo for thirty days, which was again extended to a second thirty; and it was further debated whether all commercial intercourse with Great Britain and her subjects, as far as regarded all articles of British growth or manufacture, should not be discontinued, until she had acceded to their reasonable demands.

Washington foresaw in these violent measures no other issue than war with the mother-country, which he desired under every circumstance to avoid; and believing that the existing differences between the two countries might be brought to an amicable adjustment, resolved to make the experiment. Accordingly, Chief-Justice Jay being appointed to this important mission, embarked on May 13th, being attended to the shore by a great concourse of people, whom at parting he assured of his determination to leave no means untried for the security of the blessings of peace.

This measure being taken for pacific arrangements, congress passed acts for putting the country in a state of defence. The principal harbours were to be fortified, as we have before said, and 80,000 militia to be held in readiness for immediate service; the importation of arms was permitted free of duty, and additional taxes were levied.

About this time, the afterwards celebrated John Quincy Adams, son to the vice-president, received his first public appointment as minister at the Hague, he having already distinguished himself by certain articles in a Boston paper on Genet's proceedings, which attracted Washington's attention.

Hamilton, at the commencement of this year, resigned his office of Secretary of the Treasury, and was succeeded by Oliver Wolcot; and at the close of this session, General Knox having resigned, Timothy Pickering of Massachusetts was appointed Secretary of War.

Jay was successful in his mission, and early in the following year a treaty was laid before the Senate for ratification. This treaty provided that the posts which the British had retained should be given up to the Americans, and compensation made for illegal captures of American property; and the United States were to secure to the British creditor the proper means of collecting debts which had been contracted before the peace of 1783. It did not, however, prohibit the right of searching merchant vessels, and thus violated the favourite maxim of the Americans, that "free ships make free goods." The treaty was not all that Washington himself desired; but as no better terms were to be had, he wisely resolved that, if the Senate approved of it, he would not withhold his signature.

The country was in a state of angry excitement, and ready to reject rather than accept it, even before they knew the exact terms of the treaty, while the Senate, with closed doors, were discussing it and coming gradually to the decision that it should be ratified. At this moment an imperfect copy appeared in a newspaper, and Washington then ordered it to be published.

This was like throwing a lighted brand among combustibles. The partisans of France assailed it with the utmost violence; an outcry was raised against it from one end of the Union to the other, as "a pusillanimous surrender of American rights, and a shameful breach of obligations to France." City after city protested against it, and the popular feeling was expressing itself in acts of outrage and violence, when Washington, with the prompt decision of a wise governor, after protesting and remonstrating against such clauses of the treaty as he considered injurious to the American interests, settled the question by attaching his signature to the treaty. "As regards this treaty," says Jared Sparkes in his Life of Washington, "time disappointed its enemies and more than satisfied its friends. It saved the country from a war, improved its commerce, and served in no small degree to lay the foundation of its durable prosperity. The great points which were said to be sacrificed or neglected—the impressment of seamen, neutral rights and colonial trade—have never yet been settled, and are never likely to be settled while England maintains the ascendancy she now holds on the ocean."

Two other treaties were negotiated about the same time; one with Algiers, by which the commerce of the Mediterranean was opened, and the prisoners who had been in bondage for many years released; but for this was paid the large sum of 763,000 dollars, with an annual tribute in stores of 24,000 dollars, a black-mail which was paid likewise by various European nations, to secure them from the piracies of the Dey. The other treaty was with Spain. Spain had long acted towards the United States in an unfriendly manner. She was fearful lest the principles of liberty and independence which they had so successfully asserted should find their way into her contiguous provinces. She had always endeavoured that the western boundary of this so dangerous neighbour should be fixed at 300 miles east of the Mississippi, and she denied to the inhabitants west of the Alleganies access to the ocean by that great river, the mouth of which was in her province of Louisiana. At length, however, when at home she became involved in a war with France, and in America alarmed by the unauthorised preparations making in Kentucky, under the influence of Genet, to invade Louisiana, she intimated her willingness to adjust her differences with the United States by treaty. An envoy extraordinary was therefore immediately despatched to Madrid, and in October a treaty was signed, by which the western boundary of the American republic was fixed according to their own claims, the navigation of the Mississippi made free to both nations, and the American citizens allowed the privilege of landing and depositing cargoes at New Orleans.

During the recess of congress, and while the president was busied with filling up vacancies in his cabinet, the treaty with Great Britain was agitating the country, and petitions got up against it and numerously signed were presented to the House of Representatives when the fourth sitting of congress commenced. By this time, however, the offensive treaty had been ratified by his Britannic Majesty, and no other means of opposition now remained to the democratic or French party in the House of Representatives but to demand from the president the instructions by which Jay had entered into this negotiation. Washington refused to comply with this demand, asserting that the power to make treaties was vested by the Constitution solely in the president, with the advice and consent of the Senate, and that the House of Representatives had hitherto acquiesced in this mode of procedure. The malcontents were not prepared for this refusal, and the debate which it led to was carried on for many days with great eloquence as well as warmth. But even though Washington hazarded much in opposing the popular branch of the legislature, his was not a mind to be swayed by any lesser consideration from that which he knew to be the true line of duty. He believed that to yield in this instance would be to introduce a dangerous principle into the diplomatic transactions of the nation, and he was firm in his refusal.

The resolution moved in the house, to make the necessary appropriations to carry the treaty into effect, again called forth violent opposition. The people themselves now took up the subject also; meetings were held, and the strength of the two parties fully tried, until at length it was evident that the majority were in favour of the treaty. Petitions in its favour were presented to congress; and lastly, Fisher Ames, of Massachusetts, at that time just risen from his sick-bed, appeared in the house, pale, feeble, and scarcely able to stand, and spoke with such irresistible power on behalf of the treaty, that further opposition was vain. The eloquence of the sick man conquered; and the necessary laws were passed for the fulfilment of this agitated treaty.

The number of 60,000 inhabitants being required to constitute a state government, and Tennessee having attained to a still higher population, was admitted into the Union this year; and Sevier, who had distinguished himself in the extinct state of Frankland, was elected governor. This new State was peopled principally from North Carolina. The first newspaper established at Knoxville was in 1793.

The troubles regarding Jay's treaty with Great Britain were not yet at an end. The French government and its partisans in America, who had, spite of the neutral position assumed by the United States, always calculated upon substantial aid and service being rendered to France, were consequently greatly disappointed and annoyed by the line of conduct which Washington had adopted, and which had tended to knit up, rather than to dissever, the old relationships between the two kindred countries. Washington and the federalists were pronounced to be hostile to the cause of France; to be traitors to their own principles, enemies to the rights of man, and meanly subservient to Great Britain.

Morris, the successor of Jefferson as American representative in France, a man of great sagacity and cool judgment, who having taken an active part in the revolution of his own country, could not yet regard with satisfaction the means adopted to establish a republic in France, was looked upon with suspicion by whatever party for the time being held the reins of government. Accordingly, when the Committee of Public Safety, under Robespierre and his associates, sent letters of recall to Genet, they requested also that another ambassador might be sent to supply the place of Morris. Mr. Monroe, an ardent friend of republican liberty and the rights of man, was sent over. The fall of Robespierre had taken place when Monroe arrived in Paris, and the Thermodorians, who were then in power, received him with considerable coolness, as questioning the loyalty of the nation which he represented to their great goddess of liberty.

The new ambassador by his instructions was empowered to contradict the report circulated in France of the unfriendly feelings of the president and his party towards the cause of that country. Monroe made the most of this permission; and Merlin de Douay and he embraced in public, that the French people might be edified by the spectacle which was to "complete the annihilation of an impious coalition of tyrants;" and the convention passed a decree that the "flags of the two republics should be entertwined and suspended in their hall, in testimony of eternal union and friendship." In return, the French colours were sent to America for the same purpose, by M. Adet, who superseded Fauchet, he being removed at the fall of the Robespierre faction. These colours were duly presented on New-year's-day, 1796, with an address, and the president replying, the colours were ordered to be deposited with the archives of the nation.

These theatrical flatteries were, however, but tricks and cajoleries to induce America to take part in the wars of France; and Monroe, caught in the snare that was laid, was not long before he wrote to urge the policy of a loan to France, adding "that the Americans in that case might at once seize the western posts, and the territory on the Lower Mississippi, occupied by the Spaniards, and trust to French aid to see them out of the war—if war should follow, which he did not conceive likely, either on the part of Britain or Spain, considering the success of the French arms."

The schemes of the infatuated Monroe did not meet with that encouragement in America which he had led the French government to expect; and Jay's treaty being about this time ratified, the French cruisers were ordered to capture, in certain cases, the vessels of the United States, and several hundred vessels laden with valuable cargoes were in consequence seized and confiscated.

Monroe, highly unfit for his office, not only displeased the government at home by his attempt to compromise them, but fell into disgrace at Paris, because he had failed to bring about that close alliance between the United States and France which he had promised. He was recalled; and Charles C. Pinckney, of South Carolina, appointed in his stead, he being furnished with instructions to use every effort, compatible with national honour, to restore the amicable relations which had formerly existed between the two countries.

But events were tending more and more to separate them. The British, at this time, were endeavouring to complete the conquest of the French portion of St. Domingo, the defence of which, for the republic, was left almost entirely in the hands of the black general, Touissaint. Provisions and horses, purchased in America, had been forwarded in American vessels chartered for that purpose, for the supply of the British troops. Adet complained of this, and very soon after had to communicate the decree of July 14, which empowered the seizure of American vessels in the West India seas. In November a proclamation was issued by Adet, commanding, in the name of the French Directory, all Frenchmen in America to assume the tri-coloured cockade. And this cockade was at once mounted, not only by Frenchmen, but by the American partisans of the French Republic. Adet was commencing the career of Genet.

With the close of 1796, which was now at hand, the time for the election of a new president was come. Washington, weary of the anxieties and contentions of public life, had already, in September, published a farewell address to his countrymen, which bore strongly upon the present state of public feeling; he emphatically urged the maintenance of Union, as the palladium of political prosperity and safety; of the Federal constitution, and of the public credit; he solemnly adjured them to avoid sectional jealousies and heartburnings, the baleful effect of party-spirit, and of permanent inveterate antipathies against particular nations or passionate attachments for others. He dwelt at length on the policy of an impartial neutrality and of a disconnexion with the nations of Europe, so far as existing treaties would permit, together with the dangers of foreign influence.

The address bore directly upon the present position of America with regard to France, and was, in fact, so important in this respect, that Adet followed it up with a manifesto which, like the address, was circulated through the newspapers and intended to counteract its effect.

Washington, as president, met the national legislature for the last time in December, and his last words in that character were a fervent desire "that the virtue and happiness of the people might be preserved, and that the government which they had instituted for the protection of their liberties might be perpetual."

CHAPTER XVIII.
THE ADMINISTRATION OF ADAMS AND JEFFERSON.

Had Washington been willing to accept the presidentship yet a third time, the wishes of the nation would gladly have retained him in that office; but this not being the case, the two great political parties were each anxious to see its leader at the head of the administration. The federalists claiming to be the sole adherents of the measures adopted by Washington, and dreading the influence of French sentiments and principles, made the most active efforts to elect John Adams; while the republicans, declaring themselves to be the only true friends of liberty, and accusing their opponents of a dangerous tendency to Great Britain and her institutions, were no less strenuous to elect Thomas Jefferson. The result of the election was that Adams was president, and Jefferson vice-president.

The new president was inaugurated on the 4th of March, Washington being present as a spectator, and well pleased to see his place filled by one whom he considered worthy of so high a trust.

Scarcely had the president assumed his authority, when intelligence reached him that the Directory of Paris had refused to receive Pinckney, announcing to him "their determination not to receive another minister-plenipotentiary from the United States, until after the redress of grievances demanded of the American government, and which the French Republic had a right to expect from it;" and immediately afterwards he was compelled, by a written mandate, to quit the territories of the French Republic.

Congress was immediately called, and met on the 15th of June, when this extraordinary aspect of affairs was submitted by the president to their consideration. Wishing still to preserve peace and friendship with all nations, so far as was compatible with the honour and interests of the United States, the president proposed to institute a fresh attempt at negotiation; but earnestly recommended it to congress to provide in the meantime effectual measures of defence.

As a last effort, therefore, to effect a negotiation, three envoys-extraordinary were appointed, at the head of whom was Pinckney, then at Amsterdam. Their instructions were to establish peace and reconciliation by all means compatible with the honour and the faith of the United States; but to impair no national engagements; nor to permit any innovations upon those internal regulations for the preservation of peace which had been deliberately and uprightly established; nor yet to surrender any rights of the government. These ambassadors, also, the Directory refused to receive. Proposals however were made to them, which proceeded verbally from Talleyrand, the French minister for foreign affairs, through inofficial persons. A large sum of money was in the first place demanded, preparatory to any negotiation being entered into. To this insulting proposal no other reply than an indignant negative could be returned; and when the demand was persistently urged, the envoys broke off any further communication; on which two of them, who were federalists, were ordered to leave France, while the third, who was an acknowledged republican, was permitted to remain.

When these events were known in the United States, they excited universal indignation. For the moment party animosity seemed to be at an end, and one universal sentiment prevailed, "millions for defence, not a cent for tribute." The treaty with France was declared by congress to be void, and authority was given for seizing French armed vessels. Provision was made for raising a small standing army, the command of which was offered to General Washington, who accepted it with reluctance, though entirely approving of these measures. General Hamilton was appointed second in command, and a naval armament decided upon.

TOMB OF WASHINGTON.

The French had already commenced depredations on the American commerce, and reprisals soon followed. In February, 1798, the French frigate L'Insurgent, of forty guns, which had captured the American schooner Retaliation and carried her into Guadaloupe, was compelled to strike her colours to the American frigate Constellation, after a close engagement of an hour and a half, her loss being much the greater. This victory on the side of the United States soon produced overtures from the Directory at Paris, on which Adams immediately appointed Oliver Ellsworth, chief-justice of the United States, Patrick Henry, late governor of Virginia, and William Van Murray, minister at the Hague, to conclude an honourable peace. On their arrival in Paris, they found the Directory overthrown, and Napoleon Bonaparte at the head of the government, with whom a treaty of peace was satisfactorily concluded on September the 30th, 1800; after which the provisional army was disbanded by order of Congress.

Washington, though he took the supreme command of the army, never believed that the French would actually invade the United States. He was not, however, permitted to witness the re-establishment of peace. On the 14th of December, 1799, he calmly and peacefully expired, after an illness of twenty-four hours, at Mount Vernon, his beloved residence, in the sixty-seventh year of his age. The whole nation mourned his loss.

Congress was in session at Philadelphia when the news of this melancholy event reached that city, and both houses immediately adjourned for the remainder of the day. On assembling the next morning, the House of Representatives resolved that the chair of the speaker should be shrouded in black; that the members should wear mourning during the remainder of the session; and that a committee of both houses should be appointed "to consider on the most suitable manner of paying honour to the memory of the man, first in war, first in peace, and first in the hearts of his fellow-citizens."

The Senate testified their respect in a similar manner, and the joint committee of the two houses appointed—that a marble monument should be erected to commemorate the great events in the military and political life of Washington; that an oration suitable to the occasion should be pronounced in presence of both houses of congress; and that the people of the United States should wear crape on their left arms for thirty days.

"No formal act of the national legislature was, however, required," says Jared Sparkes, "to stir up the hearts of the people or to remind them of the loss which they had sustained in the death of a man whom they had so long been accustomed to love and revere, and the remembrance of whose deeds and virtues was so closely connected with that of their former perils, and of the causes of their present prosperity and happiness. The mourning was universal. It was manifested by every token which could indicate the public sentiment and feeling. Orators, divines, journalists, and writers of every class, responded to the general voice in all parts of the country, and employed their talents to solemnise the event, and to honour the memory of him who, more than any other man, of ancient or modern renown, may claim to be called THE FATHER OF HIS COUNTRY."

Both in France and England also was a tribute of respect paid to the memory of this truly great man. On the 9th of February, soon after the news of Washington's death reached France, Napoleon Bonaparte, then first consul, issued the following order of the day to his army: "Washington is dead! This great man fought against tyranny; he established the liberty of his country. His memory will always be dear to the French people, as it will be so to all freemen of the two worlds; and especially to French soldiers, who, like him and the American soldiers, have combated for liberty and equality." It was likewise ordered that for ten days black crape should be suspended from all the flags and standards throughout the Republic. A funeral oration in honour of Washington was also pronounced in the Hôtel des Invalides, then called the temple of Mars, the first consul and all the civil and military authorities being present. The news of Washington's death arrived in England at the time when the British fleet, which had chased the French fleet into the harbour of Brest, was lying at Torbay, and consisted of nearly sixty ships of the line. Lord Bridport, who had the command, on hearing the intelligence, ordered his flag half-mast high, which example was followed by the whole fleet.

During the summer of 1800 the seat of government was removed to the city of Washington, in the District of Columbia, of which we have already spoken. During the same year the territory between the western boundary of Georgia and the Mississippi river, and a portion of the north-west territory called Indiana, were erected into a distinct government, called the Mississippi Territory.

As the time approached for the election of a new president, the two parties made again the most strenuous efforts each to acquire the direction of government. Adams had been elected by the predominance of federal principles, but several things had occurred in his administration which had not only weakened his personal influence, but rendered the party to which he was attached unpopular with the majority. The acts by which the army and navy had been strengthened, and which had placed 80,000 militia at his command, were regarded by the democratic as indications of a wish to subvert the spirit of republican government; while the Alien and Sedition Laws, to which he had given his sanction, completed his unpopularity, and fomented party animosity to an extent which had never been equalled, and tended greatly to the overthrow of the federal party.

The federalists supported for the approaching election Adams and General Pinckney, the democratic party Thomas Jefferson and Colonel Aaron Burr. The two latter were found to have a small majority, the whole of the republican party having voted for them, with the intention of Jefferson being president and Burr vice-president. On counting the votes, however, it was discovered that both were equal; the selection, therefore, of the president devolved upon the house of representatives, who, voting by states, according to the constitution, should decide between the two. Again and again and yet again the balloting was repeated in the house, and the result always the same; nor was it until the thirty-sixth balloting that one altered vote turned the scale in Jefferson's favour. He became president, and Aaron Burr vice-president. To guard against the recurrence of such a difficulty, Article XII. was added to the Constitution.

Tucker, in his life of Jefferson, thus describes the scene which the house of representatives presented on this extraordinary occasion: "The business of the house being confined to balloting, and the result always showing an adherence by every member to his first purpose, some of the members conducted themselves in one way and some in another, according to their various characters and tempers; a portion of the republican party, gloomy, suspicious, and resentful, auguring the worst consequences and preparing their minds for the most desperate results; others, more sanguine, looking forward to a happy termination of the conquest, which they laboured to bring about by the arts of blandishment and conciliation. A few, quietly and steadily doing their duty, determined neither to frustrate the wishes of the people, by changing their votes, nor to submit to any unconstitutional expedient which a majority of both houses might venture to resort to. The federal party, conscious of not having the approbation of the people, exhibited less variety of emotion; they justified themselves by the exercise of a constitutional right, and thought it prudent and decent to conceal their secret satisfaction of vexing and embarrassing their adversaries."

On the election of Jefferson, all the principal offices of the government were transferred to the republican party; Madison was appointed to the department of state; the system of internal duties was abolished, together with several unpopular laws which were enacted during the last administration.

A second census of the United States was taken in 1801, giving a population of 5,319,762, presenting an increase of 1,400,000 in ten years. During the same time the exports had increased from nineteen to ninety-four millions of dollars, and the revenue from 4,771,000 to 12,945,000. A wonderful increase, which has scarcely a parallel in the history of the progress of nations, excepting it may be in some extraordinary cases, like those of California and Australia under the gold impulse, but which as regards the United States must be attributed only to sound laws and political institutions, as well as to the enterprising and industrious habits of the people.

In 1802 the State of Ohio was admitted into the Union, and the following year the first states convention met. Within thirty years from the time when its first settlement of forty-seven individuals was made at Marietta the number of its inhabitants exceeded half a million, and from this extensive and important tract slavery was entirely excluded.

The right of depositing merchandise at New Orleans, which had been granted to the citizens of the United States by the Spanish governor of Louisiana, in a late treaty, and which was absolutely necessary to the people of the western states, was withdrawn this year, and caused a general agitation. A proposal was made in congress to take forcible possession of the whole province of Louisiana; but milder measures were adopted, and the right of deposit was restored. In the year 1800, Louisiana had been secretly ceded to France, and Jefferson, in 1802, opened a private correspondence with Livingston, in Paris, on the subject of this cession. The United States had hitherto, he said, considered France as their natural friend, but the moment she became possessed of New Orleans, through which three-eighths of the produce of the Americans must pass, she would become their natural enemy. The case was different with a feeble and pacific power like Spain; but it would be impossible that France and the United States could continue friends when they met in so irritating a position. That the moment France took possession of New Orleans, the United States must ally themselves with Great Britain; and, he asked, was it worth while for such a short-lived possession of New Orleans for France to transfer such a weight into the scale of her enemy? He then artfully suggested the cession of New Orleans and the Floridas; but adds, and even *that* they would consider as no equivalent while she possessed Louisiana.

In January, 1803, agents were sent over to negotiate the purchase of Florida; but instead of the purchase merely of New Orleans and the Floridas, as had been planned, they were able to effect that of all Louisiana, equal in extent to the whole previous territory of the United States. They owed their good fortune to the war which was so suddenly renewed between France and England, when the government of France, convinced that the possession of Louisiana would soon be wrested from her by the superior naval power of England, readily consented to make sale of it to a third power, and the rather, as the money was very acceptable at that time.[70]

For the trifling sum of 15,000,000 dollars the United States became possessed of that vast extent of country embracing the present State of Louisiana, which was called "the Territory of Orleans," as well as of "the District of Louisiana," embracing a large tract of country extending westward to Mexico and the Pacific Ocean. The treaty was concluded at Paris in 1803. The area of the country thus ceded was upwards of 1,000,000 square miles, but all, excepting a small proportion, occupied by the Indians, its natural proprietors. Its inhabitants, chiefly French, or the descendants of the French, with a few Spanish creoles, Americans, English and Germans, amounted to between 80,000 and 90,000, including about 40,000 slaves.

About the same time the United States acquired another considerable extent of territory. The Kaskaskia Indians, occupying the country which extended along the Mississippi, from the mouth of the Illinois to the Ohio, and which is considered the most fertile in the Union, finding themselves so reduced by wars and other causes as to be unable to defend themselves from the neighbouring tribes, transferred their country to the United States, reserving only for agricultural purposes sufficient to sustain the remnant of the nation. For this valuable acquisition the United States engaged to extend to them protection, and give them annual aid in money, implements of agriculture, and other articles of their choice.

In 1803 an appropriation was made by congress for defraying the expenses of an exploring party across the continent to the Pacific. This was a scheme which the president had much at heart, and under his auspices it was carried out; Captain Meriwether Lewis being at the head of the expedition, while second in command was Captain Jonathan Clarke, brother of George Rogers Clarke, and under them twenty-eight well-selected individuals, with an escort of Mandan Indians. The expedition set out on May 14th, 1804.

Since 1801 war had existed between the United States and Tripoli. Without going into minute details of this war, we will follow the abstract given of it by Willson. "In 1803 Commodore Preble was sent into the Mediterranean, and after humbling the emperor of Morocco, he appeared before Tripoli with most of his squadron. The frigate Philadelphia, under Captain Bainbridge, being sent into the harbour to reconnoitre, struck upon a rock, and was obliged to surrender to the Tripolitans. The officers were considered prisoners of war, but the crew were treated as slaves. This capture caused great exultation to the enemy; but the daring exploit of Lieutenant, afterwards Commodore Decatur, humbled the pride which they felt in this accession to their navy.

Early in February of the following year, Lieutenant Decatur, under the cover of evening, entered the harbour of Tripoli, in a small schooner, having on board but seventy-six men, with the design of destroying the Philadelphia, which was then moored near the castle, with a strong Tripolitan crew. By the aid of his pilot, who understood the Tripolitan language, Decatur succeeded in bringing his vessel in contact with the Philadelphia, when he and his followers leapt on board, and in a few minutes killed twenty of the Tripolitans and drove the rest into the sea.

"Under a heavy cannonade from the surrounding vessels and batteries, the Philadelphia was set on fire, and not abandoned until thoroughly wrapt in flames; when Decatur and his gallant crew succeeded in getting out of the harbour without the loss of a single man. During the month of August, Tripoli was repeatedly bombarded by the American squadron, under Commodore Preble, and a severe action occurred with the Tripolitan gunboats, which resulted in the capture of several, with little loss to the Americans.

"At the time of Commodore Preble's expedition to the Mediterranean, Hamet, the legitimate sovereign of Tripoli, was an exile, having been deprived of his government by the usurpation of a younger brother. Mr. Eaton, the American consul at Tunis, concocted with Hamet an expedition against the reigning sovereign, and obtained from the government of the United States permission to undertake it.

"With about seventy men from the American squadron, together with the followers of Hamet and some Egyptian troops, Eaton and Hamet set out from Alexandria towards Tripoli, a distance of 1,000 miles across a desert country. After great fatigue and suffering they reached Derne, a Tripolitan city on the Mediterranean, which was taken by assault. After two successful engagements had occurred with the Tripolitan army, the reigning bashaw offered terms of peace, which being considered much more favourable than had before been offered, were accepted by Mr. Lear, the authorised agent of government."

Sixty thousand dollars were given as a ransom for the unfortunate American prisoners, together with an agreement to withdraw all support from Hamet.

In July, 1804, General Hamilton, the present head of the federalist party, fell in a duel fought with the vice-president, Aaron Burr, who having lost the confidence of the republicans, and despairing of re-election either as president or vice-president, had offered himself as candidate for the office of governor of New York. He was not elected, and attributing his unsuccess to the influence of Hamilton with his party, sent him a challenge, and Hamilton's death was the result.

This autumn closed Jefferson's first presidential term, and the general prosperity which prevailed gained for him the national favour. Summing up in short the events of his administration, we find that, by a steady course of economy, although he had considerably reduced the taxes, the public debt was lessened 12,000,000 of dollars; the area of the United States about doubled, and the danger of war with both France and Spain averted; the Tripolitans chastised, and a large and valuable tract of Indian land acquired.[71]

Jefferson was re-elected president, and George Clinton, late governor of New York, vice-president.

The wars which raged in Europe in consequence of the French revolution began now to be seriously felt even in America. Napoleon was emperor of France, triumphant and powerful, with most of the European nations under his feet, while England, alone remaining untouched and undaunted, carried on the war against him with more determined resolution than ever. America, profiting by the destruction of the commerce of other nations, entered with her neutral ships into every port, thus maintaining her commercial relations with every country, however hostile to each other. English and American ships were at this time almost the only ones on the ocean.

Already, early in the war, American ships conveying the produce of the French colonies to Europe, were seized and condemned by British cruisers; and now still greater difficulties and impediments were thrown in the way of the neutral trader. In May, 1806, England declared every European port under the control of France, from Brest to the Elbe, in a state of blockade, and every American vessel attempting to enter any of them was captured and condemned. In return, Napoleon declared the British Islands in a state of blockade, by which means the neutral American vessels, trading to any of the British ports, were liable to be seized and condemned by the French. These measures so detrimental to the commerce of the United States, caused loud complaints from the merchants, who demanded from the government redress and protection.

But this was only a portion of the grievance to which this great European war gave birth in America. England assumed "the right of search," which had long been offensive to the Americans, and by this means citizens of the United States, on the plea of their being British subjects, that is, born Britons though naturalised Americans, were seized under the barbarous law of impressment, dragged from their friends, and compelled to serve as British marines, and fight against nations at peace with their own. The three presidents had, each in his turn, remonstrated against this iniquitous law, but in vain; every year added to its enormity; and at length, in June 1807, an event occurred which brimmed the cup of popular indignation against Great Britain. The frigate Chesapeake being ordered on a cruise to the Mediterranean, when at only a few leagues' distance from the Virginia coast, was come up with by the Leopard, a British ship of war, commanded by Vice-Admiral Berkeley; and an officer came on board with an order to search her for four deserters from the Melampus, and supposed to be serving among her crew. Commodore Barron, who commanded the Chesapeake, politely replied that he was not aware of such persons being in his crew; that he wished to preserve harmony with the British commander, but that he never allowed the crew of any ship under his command to be mustered by any officers but his own.

The Leopard, on this manly reply, ranged alongside of the Chesapeake, and commenced firing upon her. The Chesapeake was unprepared for action, and lost three of her men, and eighteen more being wounded, Commodore Barron ordered his colours to be struck. The commander of the Leopard sent an officer on board, mustered the crew, found the men whom he wanted, and then abandoned the ship.

The Chesapeake returned immediately to Hampton Roads, whence she had sailed, and carried with her intelligence which set the whole United States in a flame, more especially as it was proved that three of the men thus seized were American citizens, who had been impressed for the British service and afterwards escaped. The president, on this information, interdicted by proclamation the entrance of any armed British vessel within the harbours or waters of the United States; and an envoy was sent to London to demand satisfaction for this outrage, and security against any further aggression. Vice-Admiral Berkeley was in consequence recalled; two of the men who had been taken as deserters were sent back to America, and a proclamation issued forbidding any further search in national ships of neutral nations for deserters. But this did little, as the celebrated orders in council were published by the British government in November, which prohibited neutrals, except on humiliating terms, from trading with France or her allies; which, in fact, was equivalent to excluding them from almost every port in Europe. Napoleon retaliated, of course, by his Milan decree, which rendered every vessel trading with Britain, or submitting to search by her, liable to confiscation if found near his ports or by his cruisers. Thus were the neutral ships of America still endangered by both belligerent powers.

In return for these vexatious measures, congress, in December, passed a bill laying an embargo; "so that all American vessels were prohibited from sailing to foreign ports, all foreign vessels from taking out cargoes, and all coasting vessels were required to give bond to land their cargoes in the United States. This embargo was strongly opposed by the federalist party, and great were the complaints of a total stop being thus put to foreign commerce. All, however, hoped for a favourable result from a measure which, if it were seriously felt by the United States, would, it was believed, be still more seriously felt by their enemies."[72]

This embargo failed to obtain any concession from France and England, and being in itself so injurious to the commercial interests of the United States, was repealed in 1809, at which time, however, congress interdicted all commercial intercourse with France and England.

Such was the situation of the country when Jefferson, having been eight years in office, and following the example of Washington, refused to accept of re-election, prepared to retire from the administration. But before we speak of this event, we must briefly return to a cause of anxiety and agitation, originating in the designs of the late vice-president, Aaron Burr.

Burr, while in office, offended both prevailing parties. The federalists by his fatal encounter with Hamilton, who was the idol of that party; and the republicans by his supposed intrigues against Jefferson. Under these circumstances, finding himself everywhere unpopular, he retired as a private citizen to the newer western states. Here, restless, scheming and ambitious, he engaged in an enterprise the full scope and intention of which seems never to have been completely fathomed. With the ostensible design of forming a large agricultural settlement on the banks of the Washita in Louisiana, he put himself at the head of a great number of people, who were armed and organised, and for whose use boats were purchased and built on the Ohio. The nature of his preparations, which had a warlike rather than a peaceful character, and the disclosures of some of his associates, led to the supposition that his real object was of a very different character—was, in fact, no less than to separate the western states from the Union, to add Mexico to them, and place himself at their head. "Nothing," says the President Jefferson, writing on this subject to La Fayette, "has more strongly proved the innate force of our form of government than this conspiracy. Burr had probably engaged 1,000 men to follow his fortunes, without letting them know his projects, otherwise than by assuring them that the government approved of them. The moment a proclamation was issued, undeceiving them, he found himself left with about thirty desperadoes only. The people rose in a mass wherever he went, and by their own energy the thing was crushed in an instant, without its having been necessary to employ the military excepting to take care of their respective stations. His first enterprise would have been to seize New Orleans, which he supposed would powerfully bridle the upper country, and place him at the door of Mexico."

"Burr was arrested in the Mississippi territory, in January 1807, and brought before the highest court in the territory. Here making a favourable impression on the grand jury, he moved to be discharged, but this being refused, he made his escape with a single companion, and was again taken on his way to Florida. Carried now to Richmond, in Virginia, for trial, the whole United States waited with intense interest for the result. The former character and station of the accused, the novelty and boldness of his enterprise, the air of mystery in which it was involved, all contributed to the excitement. Nor was party-spirit inactive, the federalists, spite of his offences against them, wishing to prove him innocent, for the sake of thwarting the executive and proving the president vindictive and tyrannical."[73]

The trial commenced in May, and on the 23rd of June the grand jury found him and several of his associates guilty of treason. He was then committed to prison, but on the plea of such close confinement being likely to affect his health, he was removed to a publichouse with a guard over him. On the 3rd of August, the court having adjourned so long, he was put on his trial, and on the last day of that month was discharged, on the plea that there was not sufficient evidence to prove his guilt. The republican party attributed this result to the interest of the faction which chose to support him for political purposes, and the case probably might not have ended here, had not the public mind been at that very time diverted by subjects of yet greater interest. These were the British interference with American commerce and shipping, and the affair of the Chesapeake, which electrified the nation to its remotest extremities, and fused all party animosities for the moment into one general indignation; and Burr, taking advantage of this removal of public attention from himself, sailed for England, where he was afterwards suspected of being an agent of mischief to the United States.[74]

CHAPTER XIX.
ADMINISTRATION OF JAMES MADISON—
WAR WITH GREAT BRITAIN.

On March 4th, 1809, James Madison was elected president, and George Clinton re-elected vice-president. The embargo, as we have said, was repealed, though commercial intercourse with France and England was still prohibited. It was, however, provided that if either nation revoked her hostile edicts, the prohibition should cease by proclamation from the president to that effect. Soon after the accession of the new president, therefore, Mr. Erskine, the British minister plenipotentiary to the United States, having informed him that the British orders in council should be repealed by the 10th of June, the renewal of commercial intercourse with Britain was proclaimed for the same day. But the British government disavowed the acts of its representative; the orders in council remained unrepealed, and non-intercourse was again proclaimed.

In March, 1810, Napoleon retaliated the act of congress forbidding the vessels of the United States to enter the ports either of France or her allies, by the decree of Berlin, which ordered all American vessels and cargoes arriving in any of the ports of France, or the countries occupied by French troops, to be seized and condemned. In November, however, of the same year, these hostile decrees were revoked by France, and commercial intercourse was renewed with that country.

But England would revoke nothing, and the feeling between the two countries grew daily more and more hostile, although the ultra-Whigs in England, as the federalists in America, used their utmost to bring about amicable relationships between the two countries. In March, 1811, Pinckney, the American minister, was suddenly recalled from London; and British ships being stationed before the principal harbours of the United States for the purpose of enforcing the British authority, open acts of hostility took place in May of the same year. The British frigate Guerrière, exercising the assumed right of search, carried off three or four natives of the States from some American vessels, whereupon orders came down from Washington to Commodore Rodgers to pursue the British ship and demand their own men. Rodgers sailed from the Chesapeake on the 12th of May, in the President frigate, and not meeting with the offending Guerrière, fell in with a smaller vessel, the Little Belt, towards evening of the 16th of May. The President was a large ship, the Little Belt a small one; the President hailed, and in return, the Americans declared, a shot was fired.

The British, on the other hand, declared that the President fired first; however that might be, a severe engagement took place, the guns of the little Belt were silenced, and thirty-two of her men killed and wounded. Through the night the two ships lay at a little distance from each other to repair their damages, the British ship being almost disabled.

This was the muttering of the thunder before the storm; an earnest of that which was approaching. But before we proceed to the actual breaking out of the war, we must turn for a moment to the West, where a hostile confederacy and formidable preparations were discovered among the Indians, fomented by the British in Canada. At the head of this alarming confederacy was the great Shawanese chief, Tecumseh, and his twin brother, Laulewasikaw, who, in order to give to their undertaking a solemn and mysterious character, had assumed the name of the Prophet, and who, pretending to direct communication with the Great Spirit, acquired a powerful influence over the awestruck Indians, who implicitly obeyed his commands.

Tecumseh, who had been always hostile to the whites, and active in the later efforts against them, was a man of powerful mind, and possessed of all those stoic qualities which give a grandeur even to the most savage nature. He was in the battles of the confederated tribes in the late war, and one of those who, in opposition to the advice of the Little Turtle, rejected peace; and when finally peace was made at Greenville, he retired with the Prophet to the Pottawattamies, Wyandots, and other tribes, over whom the two, and especially the latter, gained a powerful ascendency, even to the extent of causing to be put to death some of the oldest and most powerful chiefs of various tribes. Tecumseh and his brother, as we have said, were enemies of the white intruders, and the object of all their endeavours was to be rid of these troublesome guests. For several years, therefore, the frontier inhabitants in the vicinity of the sources of the Mississippi had suffered grievously. At length, in the autumn of 1811, Indian hostilities having assumed an alarming and frightful character, Governor Harrison, of the Indiana territory, was directed by congress to march towards the residence of the prophet on the Wabash, and put a stop to their barbarities. On the 7th of November, having reached the vicinity of the prophet's town, he was met by a deputation of chiefs, who, in the name of the prophet, offered peace and submission, requesting him to encamp for the night. Suspecting treachery, General Harrison ordered his men to sleep on their arms, and long before dawn the faithless Indians made their attack. A bloody battle ensued, but the Indians were routed; and after totally destroying the prophet's town, and establishing a strong fort, the American general retired to Vincennes. Tecumseh was not in this fight, but at that time engaged in inciting the more distant tribes. This victory produced peace for a season.

Erskine, the British minister, was replaced by Mr. Foster, who was empowered to make restoration for the damage done to the Chesapeake, to restore the men forcibly taken from her, and offer pecuniary compensation to the families of those seamen who had fallen in the action. Admiral Berkeley had been deprived of command in consequence of his majesty's displeasure; and, in fact, every possible concession was made, excepting that which America required, viz. to give up the impressment, and to revoke the orders in council. America had just reason to complain; for these orders, now that a free commerce was restored with France, were enforced with greater rigour than ever, and a great number of richly-laden American ships destined for the ports of France had fallen into the hands of British cruisers.

In November, the president recommended that the United States should be put in an attitude of defence, and congress agreeing thereto, provision was made for the increase of the regular army to 35,000, and also for the enlargement of the navy. The president was empowered to borrow eleven millions of dollars; the duties on imported goods were doubled, and taxes laid on domestic manufactures and nearly all descriptions of property. Early in April, 1812, congress passed an act laying an embargo of ninety days on all ships and vessels of the United States. This was intended to lessen the number of trading vessels that would otherwise be at the mercy of England when war was declared, and which, in fact, were comparatively useless in any case, for commercial intercourse had now been so long suspended or intercepted that grass grew on the deserted wharfs of New York and Philadelphia. By the end of May, most of the fast-sailing ships, brigs, and schooners of their merchant service, were fitted out as privateers or men of war. On the 4th of June a bill passed the house of representatives declaring war against Great Britain, and on the 17th the senate, and two days afterwards the president, issued a proclamation of war. This decisive act did not, however, meet with universal approbation. The federalist party, occupying generally the northern and eastern states, and strongly attached to Britain, put forth their solemn protest against the war; and when the news reached Boston, many citizens appeared in mourning, and the church bells were tolled.

Exertions were immediately made to enlist 25,000 men; to raise 50,000 volunteers, and to call out 100,000 militia for the defence of the sea-coast and frontiers. Henry Dearborn, one of the few surviving officers of the revolutionary war, was appointed major-general and commander-in-chief, and his head-quarters were at Greenbush, near Albany, on the Hudson.

At the time of the declaration of war, General Hull, governor of Michigan, was at the head of 2,500 men, well supplied with artillery and ready to march, but waiting then at Detroit, the capital of Michigan, for orders; the intention being to invade Canada. The English were, however, on the alert; and Major-General Brocke, knowing of the gathering of Hull's forces at Detroit, and believing that war was inevitable, sent discretionary orders to the British officer in charge of Fort St. Joseph to act against the enemy as should appear advisable. Hull, also, had received discretionary orders to invade Canada, "if consistent with the Safety of his own posts." On the 12th of July, therefore, he crossed the river Detroit and encamped at Sandwich, intending to march upon the British post at Maldon, or Amherstburgh, a stronghold of the British and their Indian allies. From Sandwich, Hull issued a bold proclamation inviting the *oppressed* citizens of Canada to throw off their allegiance to the British and become citizens of the Republic. Brocke also began to move, and on the 27th of July surprised the American post at Mackinaw, which Hull had left singularly unaware of present circumstances, and the commandant of which received the first knowledge of the declaration of war by being summoned to surrender to a combined British and Indian force, and who not being prepared to defend the place, having but fifty-seven men, surrendered, thinking himself fortunate to obtain for his little band the honours of war. Thus was one of the strongest positions in the United States placed at once in the hands of the British. Nor was this all; Major van Horne, who had been sent by Hull to convey a party bringing up provisions to his camp, was attacked by a united force of British and Indians, headed by Tecumseh, and defeated.

Hull lay inactive for a month in Canada, Amherstburgh in the meantime being reinforced, and then suddenly re-crossed the Detroit on the night of the 7th of August, to the bitter vexation and disappointment of his troops, and encamped under the walls of Detroit. Colonel Procter was despatched after him by Major-General Brocke, and advanced to Sandwich, where batteries were raised, and where he was presently joined by Brocke with reinforcements. On the very day after Hull reached Detroit, having sent 600 of his best troops again to convey provisions, they were attacked in the woods by a British and Indian force, again under the terrible Tecumseh, and a severe fight took place upon the very ground where Van Horne had before been defeated.

On the 16th of August, Major-General Brocke crossed the river a few miles above Detroit without interruption, and immediately marched against the American works with about 700 British troops and 600 Indians. The American troops, advantageously posted and outnumbering the enemy, anxiously awaited the order to fire, when, to their unspeakable astonishment and indignation, they were suddenly ordered to retire within the fort, on the walls of which they beheld a white flag in token of submission. The indignation of the army was so great, that, crowding into the fort without any orders, many it is said wept; others, in stacking their arms, dashed them violently on the ground.

Not only the army at Detroit, but the whole territory, with all its forts and garrisons, were surrendered to the British. The British were as much astonished at this surrender as the Americans themselves. General Hull, being exchanged for thirty British prisoners, was arraigned before a court-martial. He was acquitted of treason, but convicted of cowardice and unsoldierlike conduct, and sentenced to death, but was afterwards pardoned by the president in consideration of his revolutionary services. His name, however, was struck from the rolls of the army.

Leaving Colonel Proctor to hold possession of the Detroit frontier, Brocke moved off rapidly along the Niagara frontier, from which quarter, also, arrangements had been made, during the summer, for the invasion of Canada, and where a body of troops was collected, under command of Stephen van Rensselaer. Early in the morning of Oct. 13th, a detachment, under Colonel Solomon van Rensselaer, crossed the river and gained possession of the heights of Queenstown, on which was a small battery. At the moment of success the enemy received a reinforcement, under General Brocke, and a long and obstinate engagement ensued, in which the gallant Brocke was killed; and spite of all the exertions General van Rensselaer could make the republicans retired with great loss. A singular circumstance occurred on this disastrous day. General van Rensselaer commanded the militia of New York, in the ranks of which federalist principles were very prevalent; when, therefore, they were needed to support their failing brethren on the other side of the river, they refused to embark, on the plea that they had scruples of conscience against carrying offensive war into the British territories.

Soon after the battle of Queenstown, General van Rensselaer retired from the service, and General Alexander Smyth, of Virginia, assumed the command; and issuing an address, announcing that he would retrieve the honour of his country by another attack on Canada, he invited the young men of the country to share in the glory of the enterprise. Between 4,000 and 5,000 responded to his call; but after storming a battery on Black Rock and thus opening a way for the much-vaunted undertaking, it was suddenly abandoned; the troops, to their great astonishment, were recalled, and sent into winter-quarters.

In the meantime, Ohio and Kentucky had collected forces for the support of Hull, which were on their march to Detroit when the news of the surrender of that post met them. Harrison, governor of the Indiana territory, who possessed the entire confidence of the West, and brigadier-general in the army, was appointed by congress to the command of these forces, amounting to nearly 10,000. With these he marched to the north-western parts of Ohio, to protect the country against the incursions of the Indians, which were becoming more and more terrible every day.

On the 2nd October, 2,000 mounted volunteers from the territories of Indiana and Illinois assembled at Vincennes, under the command of General Hopkins, and on the 10th, set out on an expedition against the Kickapoo and Peoria towns. On the fourth day, alarming masses of smoke and flame, advancing with the wind, were seen in the distance, by which they perceived that the Indians had set fire to the long thick grass of the prairie over which they had to pass. The troops became mutinous, and demanded to return. Hopkins called a council of his officers, and agreed to take the sense of the army. The majority were for returning. The general, mortified at this result, commanded the army to follow him onward; but they turned their horses' heads and rode off almost to a man. Hopkins could do no less than follow. With better success, the same officer, in the month of November, marched from Fort Harrison against the Prophet's town and a Kickapoo village, which were both destroyed.

Nor were the achievements of the republican forces under Dearborn calculated to retrieve the honour of the American arms. A detachment marched from Plattsburgh, on Lake Champlain, a short distance into Canada, where they surprised a small body of combined British and Indians, and destroyed a considerable quantity of stores. That was the extent of their operations. After the misfortunes of Detroit and Niagara, the army in all its branches seemed paralysed.

While defeat and disgrace, however, attended the arms of the republic by land, the most brilliant success crowned their efforts on sea.

On August 19th, Captain Isaac Hull, commanding the Constitution of forty-four guns, engaged the British frigate Guerrière of thirty-eight guns, that very frigate which had been the great cause of quarrel about the English deserters, and after an action of half an hour, nearly every mast and spar being shot away, Captain Dacres, who commanded the Guerrière, struck his flag. One-third of the crew were either killed or wounded, while the American vessel lost only seven, and eight men wounded. The Guerrière was so shattered that it was impossible to get her into port, and she was burned. Again, on the 18th of October, the American sloop Wasp, of eighteen guns, commanded by Captain Jacob Jones, had an encounter with the British frigate Frolic, of twenty-two guns, which after a bloody fight of three-quarters of an hour, was boarded by the Americans, when only three officers and one seaman were found on the forecastle, while the decks, slippery with blood, were covered with the dead and dying. The Frolic lost eighty men, the Wasp only ten. The Wasp, with her prize, was captured the same day by a British seventy-four. A few days after, the frigate United States, commanded by Captain Decatur, engaged the British frigate Macedonian. The action lasted nearly two hours, when the Macedonian struck her colours, being nearly disabled, and her loss amounting to upwards of 100 men, while the Americans lost but five, and eight wounded. This engagement took place near the Canary Islands, and the prize was brought safely into New York harbour. Finally, in December, the Constitution, now commanded by Commodore Bainbridge, achieved a second victory, after a most desperate encounter with the Java, of forty-nine guns and four hundred men. The combat took place off the coast of Brazil; nor did the Java strike her flag until she was a mere wreck, with 161 killed and wounded. Like the Guerrière, she was burned. These naval victories were peculiarly gratifying to the Americans, especially as being gained on an element where the American citizens had suffered so much. Many British merchantmen were also captured by American privateers, which now issued from every port. Above 300 prizes was taken in the first seven months of the war.

As regards this extraordinary series of naval successes, the English naval historian records, that "the Java, for instance, was perhaps the worst-manned ship that we ever had afloat. Our Admiralty, obliged to keep at sea in all parts of the world such an immense number of men of war, straitened in their finances, and finding it difficult to obtain at short notice crews for all their ships, had certainly sent to sea a great many vessels exceedingly ill-manned. The Java had been patched up and commissioned only on the 17th of August of the present year. The greatest difficulty was to provide her with any crew; sixty-nine Irishmen were on board who had never been to sea before. She appears to have had but eight tried and excellent seamen; and including officers, not fifty on board had ever been in action before. The Constitution, on the other hand, had a crew consisting entirely of able-bodied and practised sailors, there being the usual proportion of deserters from English ships, and of other subjects of Great Britain, *whose treason and dread of the gallows disposed them to fight desperately.*" Such was the consolation which England took to herself in this hour of mortification.

Very soon after declaration of war, the United States communicated to Great Britain her willingness to pacificate on condition that the orders in council should be repealed, the impressment of American seamen discontinued, and those already impressed restored. These conditions, however, were rejected by Lord Castlereagh, then Secretary of Foreign Affairs, although negotiation was entered upon and an armistice proposed. The arbitrary conduct of the British government towards America met with strong opposition even in England. On June 16th, Mr. (now Lord) Brougham, who had always strenuously advocated the revocation of these orders in council, moved an address to the Prince Regent, beseeching him to recall or suspend the orders, and to adopt such other measures as might tend to conciliate neutral powers. Lord Castlereagh opposed the motion, but stated that government intended to make a conciliatory proposition to the United States; and accordingly on the 23rd of June the orders in council were revoked as far as regarded America. Great Britain still, however, reserved to herself the right of impressment, and the United States, rejecting negotiation on these terms, prepared to prosecute the war.

As regarded pacification with Great Britain, the Emperor Alexander of Russia offered himself as mediator between the two countries; and the United States sent over three commissioners, one of whom was John Quincy Adams, empowered to negotiate with deputies clothed with similar authority on the part of Great Britain; they were also authorised to conclude a treaty of commerce with Russia, and to strengthen the amicable relationships between the two countries.

On the 4th of March, 1813, James Madison was re-elected president, and Elbridge Gerry was elected vice-president.

In June, bills passed congress authorising the construction of four ships, carrying each seventy-four guns, and six frigates each of forty-four guns. The military service was also to be increased; a loan of 16,000,000 of dollars for the present was also authorised, with the issue of treasury notes to the amount of 5,000,000 more.

The scene of military operations in 1813 comprehended the extensive northern frontier. At the opening of the campaign, the army of the west, under General Harrison, lay near the head of Lake Erie; the army of the centre, under General Dearborn, between lakes Erie and Ontario; and that of the north, under General Hampton, occupied the shores of Lake Champlain. The invasion of Canada was still the object of the American armies.

Sir George Prevost, governor of Canada, and commander-in-chief, could not bring any great force into the field, but his numbers were formidably increased by a vast number of Indian auxiliaries. The defence of Upper Canada was committed to Colonels Proctor and Vincent, and that of Lower Canada to General Sheafe.

The head-quarters of Harrison were Franklinton, in Ohio, and thence Brigadier-General Winchester, an old revolutionary officer, marched in advance to attack a party of the British stationed at Frenchtown, twenty-six miles from Detroit. The British were routed, and Winchester encamped in the open field outside the town; and here on the morning of the 22nd of January, they were suddenly attacked by Colonel Proctor, who, with about

500 British and an equal number of Indians, had marched from Amherstburgh. The surprise was complete; and though the Americans rallied and made a desperate defence, their generals, Lewis and old Winchester, were taken prisoners; the latter by Round-head, a famous Indian chief, who, before surrendering his prisoner to the British colonel, stripped him of his hat and uniform, which he himself assumed. A more disastrous fight, or one characterised by more horrible detail, never occurred. It is said that Proctor assured his prisoner Winchester that if his men would surrender they should be preserved from the savage barbarities of the Indians, on which he ordered his men to give up their arms. Proctor, however, did not keep faith, and the promised protection was not afforded. The town was burned, and the savages held a carnival of blood and horror. Five hundred were killed, and the same number made prisoners. The victory and the account of spoils obtained at Frenchtown brought down the warlike tribes from the Wabash, and even the Mississippi, to join the British arms, whose honour was tarnished by suffering these savage barbarities to be enacted under their banner. In July the Six Nations declared war against the Canadas, and the United States, following the example of the British, accepted the services of the Indians. General Harrison was so dismayed at the fate of Winchester, that leaving Franklinton he erected Fort Meigs, near the rapids of the Miama River, which falls into Lake Erie; and here, on the 1st of May, he was besieged by Colonel Proctor, with a force of 1,000 British and 1,200 Indians. On the 5th of May, General Clay advanced with 1,200 Kentuckians to his relief, and although with considerable loss, attacked and dispersed the besiegers, on which a great number of the British Indian allies, notwithstanding the entreaties of Tecumseh, who was faithful to the cause he espoused, deserted; and the Canadian militia-men, greatly to the disgust of Colonel Proctor, retired to their farms, after which he returned with but few followers to Amherstburgh.

Pursuant to the law passed by congress, efforts were made to build and equip fleets upon the lakes. The preceding year the Americans possessed but one brig of sixteen guns on Lake Ontario; but by April of the present year, Commodore Channing, the naval commander on that station, had built and equipped a squadron sufficiently powerful to contend with that of the British. On the 25th of April, 17,000 troops were conveyed in the new flotilla across the lake, from Sackett's Harbour, for the attack on York, the capital of Upper Canada, the depository of British military stores. On the 27th the troops landed, headed by General Pike, and, though opposed by a strong force of British and Indians, who were soon driven back to the garrison, a mile and a half, carried one battery by assault, and were still advancing, when the powder-magazine blew up, hurling immense quantities of stone and timber upon the advancing troops, and killed many. Pike received a mortal wound; but his troops, after a moment's halt, pressed forward, and soon gained possession of the town. Sir George Prevost, who seems to have been a man of great indecision, if not of cowardice, is blamed severely by the British historians for having ordered a retreat before their own case was hopeless. York being gained, the squadron and troops returned to Sackett's Harbour, after which they attacked Fort George, situated at the head of the lake, which, after a warm engagement, was abandoned by the British, who, headed by General Vincent, retreated to a good position on Burlington Bay.

While the American army was thus employed, Sir George Prevost having learned that General Dearborn had left Sackett's Harbour with but a small garrison, despatched Commodore Yeo, commander of the British fleet on Lake Ontario, to gain possession. On the morning of the 29th, about 1000 British troops landed, but were repulsed by General Brown, and re-embarked so hastily, as to leave their wounded behind.

In the latter part of July, about 4,000 British and Indians, the former under General Proctor, the latter under Tecumseh, again appeared before Fort Meigs, now commanded by General Clay. After waiting a few days, and not succeeding in drawing out the garrison as he hoped, Proctor withdrew his forces and proceeded to Fort Stephenson, at Sandusky, which was garrison by 120 men, under Major Coghan, a young man of one-and-twenty. The defence of this place was one of the bravest on record. The British were repulsed with great loss, and fled so precipitately that they left behind them a quantity of clothes and military stores.

While all this was going forward on land and on the inland seas, the coast was harassed by predatory warfare carried on by large detachments from the British navy. One squadron stationed in Delaware Bay captured and burned every merchant ship they could seize, while another burned the farms and houses along the Chesapeake Bay; several towns also were burned. Various naval actions took place. On the 23rd of February, Captain Lawrence, in the Hornet sloop-of-war, encountered the Peacock sloop-of-war, which was, after an engagement of fifteen minutes, so much damaged that she sank, and spite of every effort of the captors to save the lives of those whom they had just attacked, she went down with thirteen men on board. On his return to shore, Captain Lawrence was appointed to the command of the Chesapeake frigate, then in harbour at Boston. For several weeks the British frigate Shannon, of equal force, commanded by Captain Broke, had been cruising before the port, challenging to combat any American frigate. It had already been triumphantly sung in England,

And as the war they did provoke,

We'll pay them with our cannon

The first to do it will be Broke,

In the gallant ship, the Shannon.

This challenge was accepted by Captain Lawrence, and on the 1st of June, the Chesapeake sailed to meet her rival. Towards evening of the same day they met, and instantly engaged with unexampled fury. In a very few minutes the challenge was decided against the Chesapeake; every officer capable of taking command was killed or wounded; Captain Lawrence received a mortal wound, and the rigging was so cut to pieces, that she fell on board the Shannon. Lawrence received a second wound and was carried below. At the moment when Broke boarded her, Lawrence was asked if her colours should be struck. "No," replied he, "they shall wave while I live!" But her colours were struck already, and the gallant and brave young man, delirious with suffering, cried continually for four days while life lasted, "Don't give up the ship!" an expression which became consecrated to his countrymen. The Shannon carried her prize into Halifax, and there poor Lawrence died, and was buried, his pall being borne by the oldest captains in the British navy, who mourned for him with generous sympathy. War makes such men enemies, and their *duty* it is to kill each other!

The next encounter at sea was disastrous likewise to the Americans, the sloop Argus being taken in St. George's Channel by the British sloop Pelican. The commander of the Argus was mortally wounded, and was buried with honour in England; and soon after the brig Enterprise, commanded by Lieutenant Burrows, captured the British brig Boxer, commanded by Captain Blyth. Both commanders were killed in the action, which took place off the coast of Maine, and were interred side by side with military honours at Portland, their bodies being rowed to land by masters of vessels, with the funeral stroke of the oar, while minute-guns were fired by the vessels in harbour.

From sea-fights we now pass on to an encounter between the British and American squadrons on Lake Erie. The American squadron was commanded by Commodore Perry, a young inexperienced man, that of the British by Captain Barclay, a veteran who had lost, like Nelson, one arm while serving under that commander. On the 10th of September, the British commander not having a single barrel of flour left, and no alternative but attempting to clear the lake or starvation, accepted the offer of battle. The wind changed immediately after he had sailed, giving the Americans the advantage. Perry, forming his line of battle, hoisted his flag, and the words of the dying Lawrence, "Don't give up the ship," met the eyes of all and were hailed with universal acclamations. Since that day they have become the motto of the American navy. The firing commenced about noon, and being directed principally against the Lawrence, the flag-ship, she soon became unmanageable, having all her crew, with the exception of four or five, killed or wounded. Commodore Perry then left her in an open boat, and transferred his flag to the Niagara, which, passing through the British, poured broadsides into five of the vessels at half pistol-shot. Towards four o'clock every vessel had surrendered. The day, however, was not lost to the British until the first or second in every vessel had been killed or dangerously wounded. Poor Barclay's one arm was shattered before he left the deck. Commodore Perry gave intelligence of the victory to General Harrison thus laconically: "We have met the enemy, and they are ours. Two ships, two brigs, one schooner, and one sloop."

This defeat rendered the rapid retreat of General Proctor and the Indian chiefs who were with him inevitable. They therefore began to dismantle the forts, and to abandon all the positions on the Detroit, thus leaving the Michigan territory again in the possession of the Americans. But they could no longer retreat without fighting. General Harrison passed over between 5,000 and 6,000 men, and interposed between Proctor and the country to which he was directing his steps. On the 5th of October, a severe battle was fought at the river Thames, when the British army was taken by the Americans. On this day the famous Tecumseh was slain, bravely fighting in the thick of the battle. Six hundred of the British were made prisoners. Proctor escaped with 200 cavalry. Among the trophies of the victory were six brass field-pieces, which had been given up by Hull, on two of which were inscribed the words, "Surrendered by Burgoyne at Saratoga."

By this victory was broken up the great Indian confederacy, in which, though 3,000 warriors still remained, the bond of union was gone with Tecumseh. The Ottawas, Chippewas, Miamis, and Pottawattamies, now sent deputies to General Harrison and made treaties of alliance with the Americans.

But before this confederacy was broken, in the month of August, the Creeks and Seminoles, who had been visited by Tecumseh, and into whom he had breathed his hatred of the whites, had commenced a cruel war against the frontier inhabitants of Georgia, in which nearly 300 white inhabitants had been fearfully massacred. On this, General Jackson, at the head of 2,500 volunteers of Tennessee, marched into the Creek country, while Georgia and Mississippi sent upwards of 1,000 more. Battles were fought at divers places with their wild sonorous Indian names—Tallushatchea, Talladega, Autosse, Emuefau, and others—in all of which the Indians were defeated. The last stand of the Creeks was at the great bend of the Tallapoosa, called by the Indians Tohopeka, and by the whites Horse-shoe-bend. Here about 1,000 of their warriors had assembled in a strong fort, which was soon compassed by a detachment under General Coffee to prevent escape. The main body advanced under General Jackson; the outworks were carried, and the Indians seeing no chance of escape, and scorning to surrender, fought till nearly all were slain. Only two or three Indian warriors were taken. This was the last effort of the Creeks; their power was broken, and the few remaining chiefs gave in their submission.[75]

CHAPTER XX.
EVENTS OF 1814, AND CONCLUSION OF THE WAR.

During the year 1814 the Americans again prepared for the invasion of Canada, but no ground was gained. Without going into minute details, we will content ourselves with giving the principal warlike events of the year, whether in the North or the South.

Early in the season, General Brown was detached from the army of General Wilkinson at Sackett's Harbour, where he had been assiduously disciplining his army, to the Niagara frontier. At the beginning of July he crossed the Niagara, took Fort Erie, and advanced into Canada. When he reached the British lines of Chippawa, he found General Riall strongly entrenched there. A sanguinary conflict took place, the advantage remaining on the side of the Americans. Riall retreated to a better position at Fort Niagara, where he was reinforced by General Drummond, with part of Wellington's veterans; for the pressure of the war having abated in Europe, the British army in America was reinforced by these able soldiers.

The Americans encamped near the Falls of Niagara, on the morning of the 25th of July, and towards four o'clock in the afternoon the British army appeared in sight. The two armies engaged in what was called Lundy's Lane, at a short distance from the Falls, and here was fought one of the most obstinate battles that took place during the war. They fought till midnight, close to the great cataract, the roar and din of which was silenced by the firing of twenty-four pieces of ordnance and 8,000 muskets, and which was heard distinctly lifting up its eternal voice amid the momentary pauses of the battle. Wonderful bravery was displayed on both sides, and the loss of life was about equal. The Indians fled early in the battle. General Drummond was wounded on the British side; Generals Brown and Scott on the American, the command devolving now on General Ripley, who remained in quiet possession of the field, and who, after collecting his wounded, retired to Fort Erie, whither he was pursued by Drummond, at the head of 5,000 men, and who, having made an assault upon the fort, was repulsed with the loss of 1,000. Two days later, Brown having again resumed command, a successful sortie was made from the fort, and the besiegers were driven back with great loss. There was great loss of life on both sides, and though reinforced from Plattsburgh, Fort Erie was abandoned and destroyed; and the American army, recrossing the Niagara, went into winter-quarters.

No sooner had the detachment left Plattsburgh, than Sir George Prevost, now so well supplied with Wellington's veterans, thought it a good opportunity to destroy the American flotilla on Lake Champlain and advance into New York. On the 6th of September he reached Plattsburgh, which is situated on Lake Champlain, on the northern bank of the little river Saranac. No movement of the British during the war had roused in an equal degree the American patriotism, and volunteers poured in from the northern parts of New York and the Green Mountains of Vermont. For four days the American troops opposed every attempt of the British to force the passage of the stream. About eight o'clock on the morning of the 11th, the British fleet, under Captain Downie, bore down and engaged that of Commodore Mac Donough, which lay at anchor prepared for battle, and the most desperate encounter ensued which had taken place on any of the lakes. During the conflict on water, the British on land began a heavy cannonade upon the American lines, and attempted again and again to cross the Saranac, but only to be driven back by the American militia. The utmost blame attaches to Sir George Prevost for his inefficient command and his many blunders on this occasion; nevertheless, great valour was shown by the British, but to little effect; and in the afternoon the British fleet was captured, Captain Downie having been killed soon after the contest began; and towards evening the British commenced a precipitate retreat, leaving behind them immense quantities of stores, ammunition, and provisions; about 200 were slain, and strange to say, 800 deserted to the American side.

On the 15th of August, the very day on which the British general, Drummond, was repulsed from Fort Erie, ruin was approaching the city of Washington, the federal capital of the United States. The British, on the return of spring, had renewed their predatory inroads on the banks of the Chesapeake, in pursuance of governmental orders to destroy and lay waste such towns and districts of the coast as might be found assailable; and now, about the middle of August, Admiral Sir Alexander Cockburn, having on board the land troops of Major-General Ross, another Peninsula hero, entered the Potomac, on which river Washington stands, and which empties itself into the Chesapeake. The British general landed his forces, 5,000 in number, and commenced his march to Washington, distant twenty-seven miles; Admiral Cockburn proceeding at the same time up the river in a flotilla of launches and armed boats. Washington was not defenceless, although her defenders, neither by land nor water, appear to have been very efficient. On the 22nd, the expedition reached Pig Point, and descried the flag of the American flotilla. It was naturally supposed that it was the intention of Barney, the American commodore, to dispute the passage of the river; but, to the surprise of the British, the shipping was found to be on fire. Sixteen out of seventeen vessels were blown up to prevent their falling into the hands of the British. On the 20th, General Winder, who commanded the land forces, being joined by the marines of Commodore Barney, marched out to meet the advancing enemy, and encamped at Marlborough, where they were inspected by the president, by General Armstrong, secretary of war, and by various heads of other departments, who, appearing to despair at the first glance, at once dispersed. On the 24th, General Ross and his troops reached Bladensberg, a village five miles from the capital, where a stand was made, principally by seamen and marines, the commodore being wounded and taken prisoner. The example of President Madison had been followed; the American army retreated across the Potomac. Nothing was easier than the task which Ross had undertaken. At the head of 1,600 men, after a skirmish which did not last half an hour, he took possession of Washington. The work of destruction began immediately. The capitol, or senate-house, the president's house and public offices, the arsenal, the navy yard, and the bridge over the Potomac, all were destroyed. On the following night a leisurely retreat was commenced, and the British troops, meeting with no resistence on their return, re-embarked on the 30th.

Little as had been the spirit shown in the defence of Washington, the ruthless destruction of its public buildings and records aroused a spirit of indignation which more than anything else during the war united the Republic in one general sentiment of hostility against the invaders.

In the meantime, another portion of the British fleet had ascended the Potomac, and on the 29th appeared before the town of Alexandria, which fearing pillage and destruction, surrendered all its merchandise and shipping. Elated with this success, the British admiral, on the 11th of September, made his appearance at the mouth of the Patapsco, fourteen miles from Baltimore, which was strongly fortified. On the 12th the British landed at North Point, and commenced their march towards the city, when they were met by a large force, who resisted them bravely. Although the Americans were obliged to retreat, this enterprise cost the life of General Ross and a great number of others. The day following, the British abandoned the attempt and retired to their shipping.

On the ocean the fortune of the combatants was about equal. The Essex, commanded by Captain Porter, struck to a British frigate and sloop-of-war. The American sloop Peacock captured the Epervier. The sloop Wasp, commanded by Captain Blakeley, captured the English brig Reindeer in St. George's Channel, and afterwards, in the same cruise, sank the Avon. She made several other prizes, but never returned into port, and was supposed to have foundered at sea.

The last great land action of the American war was at the city of New Orleans. Not contented with ruining the trade of all the towns on the Mississippi, by blockading that river, the British commanders resolved upon attacking New Orleans. The operations of the British in Louisiana commenced by a small expedition, which, being aided by the Spaniards, took possession of Pensacola, in the middle of August. The British commander, Colonel Nicholls, brought with him a great quantity of arms, which were intended for the Indians, who were invited to flock to the British banner. But they refused the invitation, as did also Lafitte, the chief of the pirates of Barataria, though he received liberal offers to enlist in their cause. Lafitte and his followers had been outlawed by the American government; but such was the patriotism of these otherwise lawless men, that while they deluded the British commander with the hope of joining him, it was merely to gain a knowledge of his intended movements, which were communicated to Claiborne, governor of Louisiana, who in return pardoned the whole band, and invited them to come forward in defence of their country. They did so, and rendered essential service.

General Jackson, who after the peace with the Creeks had taken up his quarters at Mobile, the capital of the Alabama territory, as commander in the South, remonstrated with the Spanish governor of Pensacola on affording shelter to the enemies of the United States. But no regard being paid to his remonstrances, he marched against the place, stormed the town, and compelled the British to evacuate Florida. Returning to Mobile, he learnt that preparations were making for the invasion of Louisiana, and accordingly hastened to New Orleans, which he found in great alarm and confusion. By his exertions order and confidence were restored, the militia organised, and fortifications erected. His command was supreme, and his energy unabating. Every man who could carry a musket or wield a spade was set to work on the fortifications or drilled as a soldier.

New Orleans stands upon the eastern bank of the Mississippi, at about 110 miles from the sea. It is built upon a narrow tract of land, confined on one side by the river, and on the other by almost impassable morasses. Even though unfortified, it presented the greatest obstacles to an invader. Below the town, however, were some strong forts which commanded the navigation of the river, so that the approach to the town either by land or water was equally difficult.

The British expedition ascended the river as high as possible, and then landed about eight miles below the city. This was on the 23rd of December, and on the following evening General Jackson made a sudden and furious attack on their camp; but though the loss of life was considerable, this was merely a check. On Christmas-day, Sir Edward Pakenham, the chief in command, took up a strong position about six miles from the city, between which and himself the American army was drawn up. Fighting went on day after day, the utmost bravery being shown by both parties, and the English advanced still nearer to the city, finding it necessary with every advance to assault and take the formidable field-works which the indefatigable republicans had thrown up, as though they had been regular fortifications. "At length," says the writer of "Knight's Pictorial History of England," "on the night of the 31st of December, having procured the material, one-half of the English army was ordered out to throw up a chain of works; the men halted at about 300 yards from the enemy's line, and here, the greater part of them laying down their muskets, applied themselves vigorously to their task, while the rest stood armed in case of an attack. The night was dark; the English maintained a profound silence, and the Americans kept a bad watch, for it was the last night of the year, and conviviality abounded in the republican camp. In this manner six batteries were completed before the dawn of New-year's-day, and thirty pieces of heavy cannon mounted. There had not been much digging and trenching, for every storehouse and barn in the country was filled with hogsheads of sugar and molasses, and these being rolled to the front were placed upright to serve as parapets to the batteries. The morning of New-year's-day, 1815, was very dark and foggy amid those swamps and bogs of New Orleans, and the day was considerably advanced before the Americans discovered how near the British had approached to them, or the novel use they had made of their molasses and sugar-hogsheads."

The Americans made several vigorous but unsuccessful attacks, seeming to produce no other effect than to knock in pieces the hogsheads and scatter their contents. Several days went on, and both parties received strong reinforcements. Sir Edward Pakenham resolved now on a combined attack on both sides of the river, for which purpose he caused a canal to be dug across the entire neck of land, so as to convey his troops to the other side. It was a most arduous undertaking, and for two nights consecutively not a man in the British army closed an eye. On the 8th of January the great attack was to take place. The British forces amounted to upwards of 10,000, the attacking columns being provided with ladders and facines.

Behind their breastworks of cotton-bales, which no balls could penetrate, 6,000 Americans, mostly militia, all good marksmen, and principally from Tennessee and Kentucky, silently waited the attack. As the advancing columns came within reach of the batteries, they were met by an incessant and destructive cannonade; but closing their ranks as fast as they were opened, they continued steadily to advance, until within reach of the American musketry and rifles. The extended American line now presented one vivid stream of fire, throwing the enemy into confusion and covering the plain with the wounded and the dead. In an attempt to rally his troops,

Sir Edward Pakenham was killed; General Gibbs, the second in command, was mortally wounded, and General Keane severely so. The British now fled in dismay from the certain death which seemed to await them; General Lambert, on whom the command had devolved, being unable to check their flight. Seven hundred dead were left on the field, and upwards of 1,000 wounded.[76] The loss of the Americans was seven killed and six wounded.

The Americans on the west side of the river did not, however, behave with much bravery; they fled on the first onset, and were closely pursued by the British, until the latter, receiving intelligence of the total discomfiture of the main army, re-crossed the river and returned to their intrenchments.

No further attempt was made; and on the 18th, Lambert, with his wounded and stores, was on his way to the fleet. Nothing was abandoned but ten pieces of artillery. The success of General Jackson, afterwards president of the United States, caused him to be regarded with great honour by his countrymen, and won for him the appellation of "the conqueror of the conquerors of Napoleon;" whence probably comes the Yankee boast, "the Britishers licked all the world, and we licked the Britishers."

From New Orleans General Lambert sailed to Mobile, and on the 7th of February invested that place, which surrendered to him on the 11th.

On the 17th of February, whilst New Orleans was yet rejoicing over her victory, a special messenger arrived from Europe, bringing a treaty of peace, which had been signed at Ghent, in the month of December, before the terrible battle was fought at New Orleans. This treaty, which was immediately ratified by the president and the Senate, stipulated for the restoration of all places taken during the war, and for the revision of the boundary of the American and British dominions; it engaged that each nation should put an end to all subsisting hostilities between them and the Indian tribes, and both parties likewise covenanted to continue their efforts for the total abolition of the slave-trade. The whole northern and eastern states, to whom the war had been very unsatisfactory, and who were continually and violently opposed to all measures of the administration regarding it, rejoiced extremely in this peace. The Englishman who took out the ratification of the treaty was carried by the citizens and people through the streets of New York in triumph and jubilee.[77]

America, however, had not even yet quite done with war. From the treaty of 1795 peace had been preserved with Algiers by the annual payment of a tribute. In July of 1812, the Dey, believing America, then engaged in war with England, would not be able to defend her shipping, extorted a large sum of money from the American consul at Algiers, to purchase the freedom of himself and other citizens of the United States, and commenced a piratical warfare against every American vessel that came in the way of his cruisers, and many American citizens were in this manner condemned to slavery.

Two squadrons were therefore fitted out, under Commodores Decatur and Bainbridge. The former sailed from New York in May, 1815, and proceeding up the Mediterranean, captured, in June, two Algerine brigs; after which, sailing to Algiers, the Dey was so much alarmed, that he cheerfully signed a treaty very advantageous to the Americans. Proceeding then to Tunis and Tripoli, Decatur also obtained satisfaction for various aggressions, after which he joined Bainbridge at Gibraltar, and resigning to him the command, the latter visited the three piratical cities, whose submission was complete.

In order to secure the tranquillity of the western and north-western frontiers, measures were taken to form treaties of peace with all the various tribes which had lately been in hostility with the United States. A congress of chiefs met for this purpose at Detroit, in the month of September, when alliances of friendship were made, by means of which extensive portions of territory were ceded, and the tribes acknowledged to be under the protection of the republic.

The charter of the former National Bank having expired since 1811, a second National Bank, called the Bank of the United States, was incorporated by charter for twenty-four years, with a capital of 35,000,000 dollars.

In December, the territory of Indiana was admitted into the Union as a state, and the territory of Mississippi divided, and the western portion admitted into the Union as the State of Mississippi, while the eastern portion became the territory of Alabama. During the same month two piratical establishments—the refuge also of runaway negroes, the one on Amelia Island, on the coast of Florida, the other at Galveston, on the coast of Texas—were broken up.

The time for the election of president being now come, James Monroe was chosen, and Daniel D. Tomkins vice-president.

About the year 1790, establishments for the home manufacture of coarse cotton fabrics were commenced in the state of Rhode Island. The embarrassments to which commerce was subjected increased the demand for these goods, and large capitals were invested in manufacturing establishments. At the close of the war, however, when British goods were again imported, it was found that, owing to the great improvements in machinery, merchants were able to afford their goods at a much lower price than the American manufacturer. In order, therefore, to enable the manufacturer to withstand this formidable competition, a new tariff was formed in 1816, by which the double imposts which had been laid during the war were removed, and an increased duty imposed on various manufactured goods. The return of peace, however, though it embarrassed the mercantile interests, gave a stimulus to agriculture, and thousands of citizens who found themselves impoverished, removed westward, where lands were cheaper and more fertile than in the eastern states. Emigration from England also set in like a spring-tide, and so great was the increase of an active and valuable population, that within two years of the establishment of peace, six new states had sprung up in the recent wilderness.[78]

The African Colonisation Society for Free Blacks originated in this year, not under the auspices of government, but that of private individuals. It is questionable, however, whether this scheme is one of pure benevolence, although much is said of Africa being civilised and christianised by this means; and the slave born in America, perhaps of the second or third generation, is expatriated when shipped over to Africa. Is not the true benevolence and the true Christianity rather to gradually, wisely and justly abolish slavery—to prepare the black man to be a good and useful citizen of a great and free country, and more productive to his master as a servant than as a slave?

Madison's second term of office expiring, he declined, as his predecessors had done, a third re-election; and on March 4th, 1817, James Monroe was elected president, and Daniel D. Tomkins re-elected vice-president.

Peace and prosperity go hand-in-hand, and with prosperity a wise nation seeks to promote by every possible means the improvement and comfort of the people. Hence great public works were now undertaken by the American States governments; roads and canals were constructed in every part of the Union, the wealthy and enterprising state of New York, at the head of which was De Witt Clinton, taking the lead. The great western canal, connecting Lake Erie with the Hudson, and the northern canal, connecting that river with the waters of Lake Champlain, were completed. A great road was also constructed by order of congress, which, passing through the seat of government, connected the eastern with the western states. Military posts were established for the security of the frontiers at the mouth of St. Peter's on the Mississippi, and at the mouth of the Yellow Stone River on the Missouri, above 1,800 miles above its junction with the Mississippi. Thus was the influence of civilisation radiating like light into the far wilderness.

Towards the close of 1817, the Seminole Indians and the remnant of the Creeks commenced depredations on the frontiers of Georgia and Alabama. The hostile spirit of the Indians was further incited by another Indian prophet and two English traders, Arbuthnot and Ambrister, who had taken up their residence among the Indians. General Gaines was sent against them, but his force being insufficient for the purpose, General Jackson was ordered to take the field and to demand aid from the governors of the adjacent states. Jackson knew where he was most likely to find the aid he needed; and inviting volunteers from Western Tennessee, soon saw himself at the head of 1,000 men. With these he marched into the Indian territory, which he presently overran, meeting with no opposition from the Seminoles, who had fled into Florida. Once in Florida, Jackson seemed to think it as well, in the words of a homely proverb, to kill two birds with one stone; accordingly he attacked and took possession of St. Mark's, a feeble Spanish post, and removed, in a very summary manner, the Spanish authorities to Pensacola; where meeting with Arbuthnot and Ambrister, had them tried by court-martial and executed, after which he took possession of Pensacola and shipped off the authorities to Havanna.

There was a bold energy in this unprincipled proceeding which won for it public approbation, although it called down much animadversion, and congress discussed it for two years, endeavouring to pass a vote of censure, which the majority would not allow. In February, 1819, however, a treaty was negotiated at Washington, by which Spain ceded to the United States Florida and the adjacent islands. The king of Spain was dissatisfied with the treaty, and endeavoured to set it aside, but the United States, like General Jackson, had their way, and in 1820 the treaty was ratified.

In 1819 the southern portion of Missouri territory was formed into a territorial government, under the name of Arkansas, and in December of the same year, Alabama was admitted as a state into the Union. Early in 1820 also the province of Maine, which since 1652 had been attached to Massachusetts, was separated from it and became an independent state.

A violent controversy arose in congress on the subject of slavery, when Missouri first applied for authority to form a State government, which arrayed the South against the North, the slaveholding against the non-slaveholding states. Missouri, having been considered a portion of Louisiana, had derived from her connexion with the French and the Spaniards the custom of holding slaves, which she considered as her right. It was proposed, however, that in "admitting the territory to the privileges of a state, slavery, or involuntary servitude, should be prohibited, except for the punishment of crimes of which the party should have been duly convicted; and that all children born within the said state after its admission into the Union should be free at the age of twenty-five." This clause divided congress into two parties: the non-slaveholding states demanded the restriction; the southern and slave states rejected it. The contest of opinion was violent in the extreme. Two principles seemed involved in this question; not only resistance to slavery, but resistance to the interference of congress in the internal government of individual states; and hence many advocates of sound liberty and friends to the emancipation and elevation of the slave opposed the restrictive clause.

After much violent discussion, the Missouri question was settled by a compromise, which, while it allowed slavery in Missouri, prohibited it in all the territory of the United States north and west of the northern limits of Arkansas; and in August, 1821, Missouri became the twenty-fourth state in the Union.

In 1821 Monroe entered upon his second presidential term, having been re-elected, as was also Daniel Tomkins as vice-president.

The fourth census, taken in the year 1820, showed the population of the United States to be 9,625,734; about a million and a half of whom were slaves.

On the 7th of March in this year, General Jackson was appointed governor of Florida and Elijeus Fromentin chief-justice. The Spanish officers, very unwilling to give up their posts, threw many impediments in the way of the new government, and refused to give up the archives which had been stipulated for; and even when they were obtained, certain documents were kept back by Don Cavalla, the Spanish governor. But Jackson, who very well understood how to exercise authority, sent an armed force to bring Cavalla before him; and as he still refused, had him carried from his bed to prison, when he took possession of the papers, after which he was discharged. Again these summary measures were severely commented upon; but they were only according to Jackson's mode of action—prompt, overbearing, and successful. Florida was divided into two counties, St. John's, on the east of the Suwaney river, and Escambia on the west. Jackson's term of office expired with the rising of congress, and he declined a re-appointment.

In 1822 a convention of navigation and commerce was concluded on terms of reciprocal and equal advantage between France and the United States. In the same year the ports of the West India Islands were opened to the American Republic by act of the British parliament.

The American commerce having for many years suffered greatly from the depredations of pirates in the West Indies, a small naval force was sent against them, which recaptured five American vessels in the vicinity of Matanzas in Cuba, and destroyed upwards of twenty piratical vessels. But depredations still continuing, a larger force was sent out the following year, under Commodore Porter, which broke up their retreats in these seas, and sent them to other hiding-places, whence they reappeared after a time.

In 1823 congress recognised the independence of the South American republics, and ministers were sent to Mexico, Buenos Ayres, and Chili. The same year, articles of convention for the suppression of the African slave-trade were signed in London by agents sent for that purpose from the United States, and officers were commissioned by each nation to capture and condemn such ships as should be concerned in this illicit traffic.

During the summer of 1824 the venerable La Fayette, now seventy years of age, visited America, by express invitation from congress, after the lapse of nearly half a century. He was received at New York with every demonstration of respect, and made a tour through all the states of the Union, upwards of 5,000 miles, which was in fact a triumphal progress, state vying with state as to which should show him most affection and honour. Finally he sailed from Washington, in September, in an American frigate prepared for his accommodation, and called the Brandywine, from the battle in which he was wounded.

In the year 1825, John Quincy Adams was inaugurated as president, and J. C. Calhoun, of South Carolina, vice-president. The administration of the ex-president had been marked by singular prosperity. Sixty millions of dollars of the national debt had been paid off, and party-feeling had so much abated that this period is signalised as "the era of good-feeling." The new president, taking a review of the past in his inaugural speech, remarked: "The year of jubilee since the first formation of our Union is past, that of our Declaration of Independence is at hand. Since that period a population of 4,000,000 has multiplied to 12,000,000. A territory bounded by the Mississippi had been extended from sea to sea. New states have been admitted to the Union in numbers almost equal to those of the first confederation. Treaties of peace, amity, and commerce have been concluded with the principal dominions of the earth. The people of other nations, inhabitants of regions acquired not by conquest but by compact, have been united to us in the participation of our rights and duties, our burdens and our blessings."

On the 4th of July, 1825—that jubilee of the Declaration of Independence of which the president had just spoken, and which was celebrated throughout the Union as a great national festival—died two venerable ex-presidents, John Adams and Thomas Jefferson, both members of the early colonial congresses; the former of whom nominated Washington as commander-in-chief of the army, the latter drew up the celebrated Declaration of Independence.

CHAPTER XXI.
EVENTS OF TWENTY YEARS.

We must now rapidly pass over the remaining quarter of a century, and in so doing merely pause upon such events as give a marked character to the progress of the years.

The first which we shall notice is of a moral rather than a political character; one calculated to produce infinite results for the happiness of humanity. It was in the year 1826 when temperance societies took their first organised form. At that time one of the besetting sins of the Americans was the use of ardent spirits; and so widely-spread was this pernicious habit of dram-drinking, that the statistics of that period present a calculation that, out of a white population of 10,000,000, between 3,000,000 and 4,000,000 were habitual spirit-drinkers, of whom 375,000 drank daily on an average three gills of ardent spirits, while an equal number consumed more than twice the quantity, and of course were drunkards—a disgrace to themselves and their country, and a perpetual source of discomfort to their relatives and friends. In this situation of things, continues Hinton, in his History, from which we have taken the above calculations, a few individuals in the state of Massachusetts undertook the gigantic and seemingly impracticable task of bringing about a reformation. The means which they proposed was the establishment of temperance societies, the members of which bound themselves to total abstinence from spirituous liquors. The scheme was considered as ridiculous; and even many who beheld drunkenness with disgust smiled at the inadequate weapon with which it seemed to them this monster vice was about to be attacked. But God crowned their grain-of-mustard-seed-effort with gigantic success. Societies on the plan of the parent-institution, and zealously co-operating with it, sprang up in all parts of the Union. In September, 1832, there were in the state of New York alone, about 4,000 temperance societies, of which one-thirtieth of the whole population were members. And since that time the cause has progressed immensely. In 1841 there were 2,000,000 pledged teetotallers, 15,000 whom were reformed drunkards; and in 1846 about 5,000,000. In Maine, Massachusetts, New York, Vermont, Maryland, Wisconsin and Michigan, legislative enactments have first restrained, then prohibited, under pains and penalties, the traffic in intoxicating liquors.

One other event, which occurred during the presidentship of John Quincy Adams, and in which he took a very lively interest, must be mentioned—the formation of the anti-masonic societies. The cause was this: One William Morgan, a quiet, inoffensive man, a citizen of Batavia, in

Genesee County, New York, was about to publish a book, disclosing, as was said, the secrets of Freemasonry. On the 11th of September, 1826, it being then Sunday, this man was taken from his home, his wife, and children, under colour of a criminal process, into Ontario County, examined and discharged. The very same day, however, instead of being allowed to return home, he was again arrested and thrown into jail by the persons who brought the first charge against him. Again these same people paid his debt, and immediately upon his issuing from prison, which was then in the darkness of night, he was again seized, gagged, and forced into a carriage, which was rapidly driven 150 miles, relays of horses and carriages being prepared along the whole line of road, and in this manner conveyed, as after inquiry showed, to the Canadian frontier, lodged in solitary confinement within the walls of an old fortress, and after five days was supposed to be transported, at the dead of night, "to the wide channel of the Niagara river, by four royal archcompanions and sunk to the bottom. Nine days were occupied in the execution of this masonic sentence; and at least 300 worthy brethren and companions of the order were engaged as principals or accessories in the guilt of this cluster of crimes."[79]

It was in vain that the legislature of New York passed an act ordering a strict investigation of the subject. Although numerous persons were proved to be implicated in the abduction, it was impossible to procure any evidence of the manner in which the unfortunate man had been destroyed. All that could be learnt was, that a body, said to be that of Morgan, was found below Fort Niagara. It being impossible, therefore, to bring forward testimony which would warrant a charge of murder, it was resolved to prosecute on that of abduction. But here again insuperable difficulties were thrown in the way by the masonic fraternity. Many witnesses were removed out of reach, grand juries were packed, intimidation exercised, and every art put in practice to insure impunity to the criminals. And although in some instances convictions were obtained, and the conspirators punished, all the chief actors managed to set the law at defiance.

Morgan's abduction, and the formidable influence which the masonic fraternity was found to possess, in the attempt to convict for that crime, excited extreme indignation and disgust against these secret and powerful societies in the minds of the citizens of New York, who argued that secret societies were not only dangerous, but incompatible with the institutions of a republican government, that their oaths and mysteries were illegal and immoral, and that the use of them must disqualify for offices of public trust. A political party, called Anti-Masonic, soon rose in the western part of the state, which acquired such great influence that its leaders became members of the legislative body. The example of New York was followed by the states of Vermont, Massachusetts, Pennsylvania, Rhode Island,

Connecticut, New Jersey, Maryland, Delaware, Ohio, and the territory of Michigan. But freemasonry existed through it all.

About the time that the anti-masonic party began to decline, the anti-slavery party arose. It still has its work to do; to battle with oppression and crime a thousand times greater than that of freemasonry. May God help the right!

The presidential election of 1828 was decided in favour of General Jackson of Tennessee, with whose arbitrary and decisive military movements we are already acquainted; and John Calhoun, of South Carolina, was chosen vice-president. When, on the 4th of March, 1829, Jackson assumed the reins of government, he found the country rich and prosperous, at perfect peace with all nations, and having in the national treasury a surplus of more than 5,000,000 dollars.

During the year 1828, congress enacted a tariff law, laying protective duties on such imported articles as competed with certain manufactured goods and agricultural products of the United States, by means of which additional duties were laid on wool and woollen goods, iron, hemp and its fabrics, distilled spirits, silk-stuffs, window-glass and cottons. The manufacturing states were well pleased with this law, which, however, was highly unsatisfactory to cotton-planters of the southern states. This tariff law was the fertile source of agitation, and almost revolution, during the presidentship of General Jackson.

In April of 1832, the Winnebagoes, Sacs, and Foxes, Indian tribes inhabiting the upper Mississippi, commenced hostilities under their celebrated chief, Black Hawk, re-entering the lands which had been sold to the United States, and which were now occupied by the citizens of Illinois. The so-called sale of Indian lands was frequently anything but with the free-will of the red man, and, as in this very instance, the Sac Indians were extremely unwilling to vacate their lands; but American generals, of the same character as the president, unscrupulous and resolute, not troubled either with too much conscience or too much sensibility, were ever at hand ready to pledge themselves "within fifteen days to remove the Indians, dead or alive, over to the west side of the Mississippi." The conduct of Black Hawk on this occasion is worthy to be related. Gaines, the American general, rose in the council of the chiefs, and said that the president was displeased with the refusal of the Sacs to go to the west of the great river. Black Hawk replied that the Sacs, of which he was the chief, had never sold their lands, and were determined to hold them.

"Who is this Black Hawk? Is he a chief?" inquired the general. "What right has he in the council?"

Black Hawk rose, and gathering his blanket round him, walked out of the assembly. The next morning he was again in the council, and rising slowly, said, addressing the American general: "My father, you inquired yesterday, 'Who is this Black Hawk? Why does he sit among the chiefs?' I will tell you who I am. I am a Sac; my father was a Sac; I am a warrior, and so was my father. Ask those young men who have followed me to battle, and they will tell you who Black Hawk is; provoke our people to war, and you will learn who Black Hawk is."

The people *were* provoked to war, and the Americans learned to know Black Hawk. He and his warriors came mounted and armed into the country which they still claimed as their own, and broke up the settlements of the white intruders, killing whole families and destroying their dwellings. Generals Scott and Atkinson were sent out against them. But an enemy more formidable than the red man went with them, and thinned their ranks more remorselessly than the hatchet of the savage. This was the cholera. The troops embarked in steamboats at Buffalo, and the disease made its first appearance on board. Great numbers died; great numbers also deserted on landing, and fled to the woods, where they perished either from the disease or starvation. Scott was not able to reach the scene of action. Atkinson, by forced marches, came up with Black Hawk's party on the 2nd of August, near the mouth of the Upper Iowa. The Indians were routed and dispersed, and Black Hawk and his two sons and several great warriors made prisoners. Nothing in the history of humanity is much sadder than the putting down and destroying the last remnants of these once powerful tribes. Driven out from their fertile lands, thousands literally died of starvation; and if, as in the case of the Sacs, they were headed by a chief of superior intellect, who could not patiently submit to be uprooted like a weed from the soil of his fathers, and who clung to it with a love as intense as that of the Swiss for his mountains, then fire and sword swept him and his followers from the land, and they were killed as traitors. God sees these things, and permits them; nevertheless they are great iniquities. Black Hawk and his sons were sent to Fort Jefferson, and put in irons; they were taken to Washington, and had an interview with President Jackson, when a treaty was concluded, and the captives relinquished all claim to their territory, and consented to remove west of the Mississippi. After this they were taken through several of the eastern cities, that they might see the power and greatness of the whites, and how hopeless it was to contend against them. Black Hawk ended his days on the Des Moines river, where his people had settled. He had a bark cabin, which he furnished, in imitation of the whites, with chairs, a table, a mirror, and mattresses. He was no longer the great warrior; in the summer he is said to have cultivated a few acres of land, on which he grew corn, melons, and other vegetables. His last speech was at Fort Madison, on the 4th of July, a festival to which he had been invited, and thus he spoke: "It has pleased the Great Spirit that I am here to-day. I have eaten with my white friends. The earth is our mother; we are now on it, with the Great Spirit above us. It is good. I hope we are all friends here. A few winters ago I was fighting against you. Perhaps I did wrong—but that is past; it is buried—let it be forgotten. Rock River was a beautiful country; I loved my towns, my corn-fields, and the home of my people. I fought for it. It is now yours; keep it as we did; it will produce you beautiful crops."

Such was the spirit of the old, exiled Indian chief; he was a Christian in practice, though not in name.

As the last chief of a once great and powerful people, we must be allowed to say a few more words respecting Black Hawk, which we give from the pen of one who knew him personally. "A deep-seated melancholy," says he, "was apparent in his countenance and conversation, and he spoke occasionally of his former greatness with an inexpressible sadness, representing himself as at one time master of the country north-east and south of us. In the autumn of 1838 he set out for the frontier, where payment was to be made to the tribe of a portion of their annuity. The weather was both hot and wet, and he appears to have imbibed on his journey the seeds of the disease which terminated his life. In October the commission was to meet the tribes at Rock Island, but Black Hawk was then too ill to accompany them. On the 3rd of October he died, after an illness of seven days. His only medical attendant was one of the tribe who knew something of vegetable antidotes. His wife, who was devotedly attached to him, mourned deeply for him during his illness. She seemed to have a presentiment of his approaching death, and said, 'He is getting old—he must die; Monotah is calling him home!'

"After his death, he was dressed in the uniform presented to him at Washington, and placed upon a rude bier with bark laid across, on which he was carried by four of his braves to the place of interment, followed by his family and about fifty of the tribe, the chiefs being all absent. They seemed deeply affected and mourned in their usual way, shaking hands and muttering in gutteral tones prayers to Monotah for his safe passage to the land prepared for the reception of all Indians. The grave was six feet deep and of the usual length, situated upon a little eminence about fifty yards from his wigwam. The body was placed in the middle of the grave in a sitting posture, upon a seat constructed for that purpose. On his left, the cane given him by Henry Clay was placed upright, with his right hand resting upon it. Many of his old trophies, his favourite weapons and some Indian garments were placed in the grave. The whole was then covered with plank, and a mound of several feet in height thrown over, and the whole enclosed with pickets twelve feet in height. At the head of the grave was placed the American flag, and a post was raised at the foot, on which, in Indian characters was inscribed his age, which was about seventy-two."

As an instance of the rapid growth of civilization in the wilderness of the West, we will give a few sentences from the graphic pen of Judge Hall, when speaking of this very region in the year of Black Hawk's death. "The country," says he, "over which Black Hawk, with a handful of followers, badly mounted and destitute of stores or munitions of war, roamed for hundreds of miles, driving off the scattered inhabitants, is now covered with flourishing settlements, with substantial houses and large farms—not with the cabins and clearings of border-men, but with the comfortable dwellings and the well-tilled fields of independent farmers. Organised counties and all the subordination of social life are there; and there are the noisy school-house, the decent church, the mill, the country store, the fat ox and the sleek plough-horse. The Yankee is there with his notions and his patent-rights, and the travelling agent with his subscription book; there are merchandise from India and from England, and in short all the luxuries of life. And all this within six years. Six years ago the Indian warrior ranged over that fertile region which is now covered with an industrious population, while the territories of Wisconsin and Iowa and vast settlements in Missouri have since grown up, beyond the regions which was then the frontier and the seat of war."

Such was the state of the West in 1832. Now in twenty years from that time the white population has advanced still farther and farther westward, removing at every step the Indian frontier. Iowa, Missouri and Wisconsin have now taken their position as states of the Union, and religion and education are establishing true civilization in the former wilderness, and may atone to heaven for the wrongs done to the Indian on this very soil.

But we must now return to the events of our general history.

The tariff bill, which passed into operation at the close of the session of 1832, caused, as we have said, great excitement in the southern states. South Carolina was the head-quarters of the opposition; and the party adverse to the bill called themselves the State-rights party, afterwards "nullifiers," because having in November held a convention at Columbia, they issued an ordinance in the name of the people, declaring that congress had exceeded its powers in laying on protective duties, and that all such acts should from that time be utterly *null* and *void*. And finally they declared, that should congress attempt by force to bring their act into operation, the people would not submit; and that any act of congress authorising the employment of a naval or military force against the state, should be *null* and *void*; and that in such case the people would hold themselves absolved from any political connexion with the other states, and would forthwith proceed to organise a separate government, and do all other acts and deeds which a sovereign and independent state has a right to do.

Further still; the legislature of South Carolina met on the 27th of November, when Governor Hamilton gave in his concurrence to the ordinance, and recommended that the authorities of the state and of the city of Charleston should request the withdrawal of the United States troops, which had been stationed there to guard against a slave insurrection; that the militia should be called out, and provision made for obtaining heavy ordnance and other munitions of war.

This novel doctrine, says Willson, of the right of a state to declare a law of congress unconstitutional and void, and to withdraw from the Union, was promptly met by a proclamation of the president, in which he seriously warned the ultra-advocates of "States-rights" of the consequences that must ensue if they persisted in their course of treason to the government. He declared that, as chief-magistrate of the Union, he could not, if he would, avoid the performance of his duty; that the laws must be executed, and that any opposition to their execution must be repelled if necessary by force.

This proclamation was extremely popular, and was supported even in South Carolina, where there existed a strong party called "Friends of the Union." Party animosities were for the moment forgotten throughout the States, and all united in agreeing to support the president in asserting the supremacy of the laws. Nor did the president talk only; with his usual prompt decision he caused Castle Pinckney, a fortress which commands the inner harbour of Charleston, as well as the town, to be put in complete order of defence; strongly garrisoned Fort Moultrie, and ordered several ships of war to be stationed in the bay. Every one saw that he was in earnest, and even the most violent nullifiers shrunk back from a contest against the whole nation with a man like General Jackson at its head.

Fortunately for the peace of the nation, the cause of discord and discontent was in great measure removed by a compromise bill, introduced into congress by Henry Clay. This bill was for modifying the tariff, and ultimately reducing the duties to a proper standard. It was strongly opposed by the supporters of the manufacturing interests, but nevertheless, having passed both the House of Representatives and the Senate, received the president's signature early in March, 1833. It was, however, accompanied by an act which provided for the collection of duties on imports, and was called the Enforcing Bill, which was strongly objected to as giving the president an almost unlimited power over commerce. On the 4th of March, 1833, General Jackson entered his second presidential term, Martin Van Buren, of New York, being elected vice-president. Very soon after the re-election of President Jackson, a great excitement was occasioned on account of the removal from the Bank of the United States of the government funds deposited there, and their transfer to certain state banks. The opponents of the administration censured this measure as an unauthorised and dangerous assumption of power by the executive; and the public confidence in the moneyed institutions of the country being shaken, the pecuniary distresses of 1836 and 1837 were charged upon the hostility of the president to the Bank of the United States; while, on the other hand, these very distresses were ascribed to the management of the bank, which the president declared to have become "the scourge of the country."[80]

Again the pent-up and out-driven Indian tribes making, as it were, a dying effort to save themselves, rose into rebellion, and the story again is very sad. The Chickasaws and the Choctaws had, during the last few years, quietly emigrated west of the Mississippi, into the territory bordering on Arkansas, which had been allotted to them instead of their own lands, and as an inducement to remove voluntarily, the United States had paid the expenses of their journey, and supplied them with a year's provisions. Other tribes there were, however, who were not so easily managed, and it is of their struggles to maintain a footing on their own lands that we have now to speak. The Cherokees were the most civilised of the Indian tribes; they had an established government, a national legislature, and written laws. Their rights had been protected during the administration of John Quincy Adams, against the claims of Georgia. Under the administration, however, of the unscrupulous and aggressive General Jackson, the legislature of Georgia, which acted very much in the spirit of the president, extended its laws over the Indian territory comprised within their boundaries, and among other severe enactments it was declared, that "no Indian nor the descendants of an Indian, residing within the Creek or Cherokee nation of Indians, should be deemed a competent witness or party to any suit, in any court where a white man is a defendant." It was in vain that the Supreme Court of the United States protested against these acts as unconstitutional. Georgia persisted in its hard enactments, and President Jackson informed the alarmed and anxious Cherokees that "he had no power to oppose the sovereignty of any state over all who may be within its limits." Their case was precisely as if a fly, caught in a spider's web, had appealed for deliverance to another spider, when the advice would have been that of President Jackson to the Cherokees—"they must abide the issue, without any hope that he would interfere."

They did abide the issue, until, worn out by oppressions and vexations, some of their chiefs were induced to sign a treaty of evacuation. In vain the Cherokees as a nation protested against it; lived quietly and inoffensively; availed themselves of the civilisation of the whites, and wished to profit by it; they were still the red men, the aborigines of the forest, and they must become once more dwellers in the wilderness. There was no help for them. Their general emigration was decided upon in 1835, but it was not effected until three years later.

The same year in which the removal of the Cherokees was decided, the Seminole Indians of Florida began to resist the settlement of the whites in their vicinity, the immediate cause of their hostility being again an attempt to remove them west of the Mississippi. In September, 1823, soon after the purchase of Florida by the United States, a treaty had been made with the Seminoles, by which they relinquished their claims to large tracts, reserving certain portions to themselves for residence. The terms of this treaty being disputed, a second was made at Payne's Landing, in Florida, in 1832, when it was stipulated that the Seminoles should relinquish their reservation, and remove west of the Mississippi, a delegation of their chiefs being sent out at the expense of the United States to examine the country assigned to them, whither the Creeks were already gone; and, according to the treaty, if it were found that they, the Creeks, would live amicably with them, and that the country was agreeable to them, then the treaty should be binding. The report of the delegates was not satisfactory. The country which was assigned to them was of a stern character, unlike that of their native Florida; it produced no light-wood for fuel, which was easy to fell, and to which the Seminoles were accustomed. The savage wilderness of Nebraska did not allure them; and the Indians, they reported, were bad; they preferred to remain in Florida, and they accordingly maintained that the treaty was not binding. Macanopy, their king, opposed their removal, and Osceola, their most celebrated chief, said that he "wished to rest in the land of his fathers, and for his children to sleep by his side."

But the wishes of Macanopy and Osceola were as nothing beside the will of President Jackson; and General Wiley Thompson was sent as the government agent to Florida, to arrange the removal of the Seminoles. Thompson reported that the Seminoles were unwilling to emigrate, and received for reply that they must go; that his military force should be increased, and that the annuities which the Seminoles received under the treaty of 1823 should not be paid until they consented to leave the country. The Seminoles took council together and promised to go the following spring; and Thomson, writing to the president, said, "I believe that the whole nation will come into this measure, but it is impossible not to feel a deep interest and much sympathy for this people."

But when the spring came, and government measures began to be put in operation for their removal, the heart of the whole people was roused as one man, and they declared that they "could not leave their homes and the graves of their fathers." This persistance in opposition was attributed to

Osceola, whose bearing was proud and gloomy, and by order of General Thompson he was put in irons. Dissembling his wrath, Osceola obtained his liberty, and not only gave his consent to the removal of the whole nation, but so completely won the confidence of the government agent as to be entrusted with various commissions in different parts of the country, which he executed faithfully. In the meantime, however, he was concerting with the Indians a plan of deep revenge, which in the month of December began to take effect.

The remainder of this mournful history we will briefly relate from Marcius Willson. "At this time General Clinch was stationed at Fort Orange in Florida. Being supposed to be in danger from the Indians, and also in want of supplies, Major Dade was despatched from Fort Brooke, at the head of Tampa Bay, with upwards of 100 men, to his assistance. He had proceeded about half that distance, when he was suddenly attacked by the enemy, and he and all but four of his men were killed; and those four, horribly mangled, afterwards died of their wounds. At the time of Dade's massacre, Osceola with a small band of warriors was prowling in the vicinity of Fort King. While General Thompson and a few friends were dining at a store only 250 yards from the fort, they were surprised by a sudden discharge of musketry, and five out of nine were killed. The body of General Thompson was found pierced with fifteen bullets. Osceola and his party rushed in, scalped the dead, and retreated before they could be fired upon by the garrison.

"Two days later, General Clinch engaged the Indians on the banks of the Withlacoochee, and in February of the following year, General Gaines, the commander of the north-western division, was attacked near the same place. In May, several of the Creek towns and tribes joined the Seminoles in the war. Murders and devastations were frequent; the Indians obtained possession of many of the southern mail-routes in Georgia and Alabama, attacked steamboats, destroyed stages, burned several towns, and compelled thousands of the whites, who had settled in their territory, to flee for their lives. A strong force, however, joined by many friendly Indians, being sent against them, and several of the hostile chiefs having being taken, the Creeks submitted; though such was their desperation, that many Indian mothers killed their children rather than that they should become prisoners to the pale-faces. During this summer great numbers were transported west of the Mississippi.

"In October, Governor Call took command of the forces in Florida, and with nearly 2,000 men marched into the interior, when several engagements took place."

The time for the election of president being now come, Martin Van Buren was chosen, and Richard M. Johnson, of Kentucky, vice-president. The war in Florida, though it still raged, was for the time disregarded, owing to the monetary and mercantile distresses of the country, which reached their crises almost immediately after the accession of Van Buren. And yet so prosperous had the country been, only in the preceding June, that a large amount of surplus revenue had accumulated, which was given up to the people, and distributed in three instalments among the several states in proportion to their respective representations in congress. While this extraordinary prosperity lasted, there was a perfect frenzy of speculation; hundreds made immense fortunes, and tens of thousands were reduced to want. During the months of March and April of 1837, the failures in the city of New York alone amounted to nearly 100,000,000 dollars. The great extent of the business operations of the country, and their intimate connexion with each other, caused the evil to extend into all channels of trade. It was felt from the highest to the lowest. The third instalment of the surplus revenue, which we have already mentioned, having not yet been paid to the different states, was now applied to the necessities of government; but no means of relief were attempted for the people, it being contended that the case did not call for governmental interference, but a reformation in individual extravagance and a return to the old neglected ways of industry. A destructive fire in New York, which occurred at the close of 1835, and the loss by which was estimated at 17,000,000 dollars, added to the present distress.

Nevertheless *growth*, which is the principle of American life, went on. In September, 1835, Wisconsin was erected into a territory, and Arkansas into a state; and now, in the midst of the general distress, Michigan was admitted into the Union, making the twenty-sixth state; the original number of thirteen being doubled.

We must now resume and conclude our account of the Seminole war, which at this critical moment added to the expenses of the nation; while the climate of a country abounding in swamps and marshes, amid which the war was carried on, proved more fatal to the whites than even the Indians themselves. After several encounters early in the season, a number of chiefs came to the camp of General Jessup, and signed a treaty, by which hostilities were to cease, and the Seminoles engaged to remove beyond the Mississippi. But again the war broke out, and Osceola being suspected as the cause, was seized in the month of October, when, with several other chiefs and about seventy warriors, he arrived under the protection of a flag of truce at the American camp. This was the finishing stroke to the misfortunes of the Seminoles. It was a base action; but the treachery of Osceola was pleaded in its palliation. The Indian chief was now in the safe custody of the pale-faces, but the strength of the Seminoles was not yet broken. He was confined in Fort Moultrie, on Sullivan's Island, opposite Charleston. Though a captive, he was not treated with unkindness. He was visited by the principal people of Charleston, and all was done for him which could render him comfortable, but his spirit was broken. It is related by one gentleman who visited him frequently, that the expression of his countenance was the most melancholy that could be conceived. He, however, is said never to have uttered any lamentation, although he often spoke with bitterness of the manner in which he had been taken prisoner, and of the injustice which had been done to his people. His person was handsome, his voice melodious, and his eyes filled with a gloomy fire.

Although his bearing and his fate awoke, as we have said, a universal interest for him, and Mr. Edin in particular, who felt an enthusiasm for the handsome and unhappy Seminole chief, brought him presents, he was indifferent to all; he grew more and more silent, and from the moment when he was put in prison his health declined, though he did not appear to be ill. He ate very little and refused all medicine. The captive eagle could not live when deprived of the free life and air of his forest.[81]

Osceola was a captive, but his people were not quelled. They, however, after they lost his leadership, strove not so much to maintain a hold on their country as to fight out the quarrel with their enemies. Accordingly, for three years more the war went on. In 1839, General Macomb, who had assumed the chief command of the army, induced a number of chiefs in the southern part of the peninsula again to sign a treaty of peace. By this treaty they were permitted to remain in the country until they could be assured of the prosperity of their friends, who had already emigrated. Again the treaty was broken, and in June of that year the territorial government offered 200 dollars for every Indian, dead or alive; and thus a war of extermination having begun, was continued till the year 1842.

In 1837, a patent was granted to S. F. B. Morse, for the Electric Telegraph.

The census of 1840 gave the population of the United States as 17,068,666.

The Democratic or Whig party succeeded, in the following election, in returning William Henry Harrison, "the hero of the Thames and the Tippacanoe," as president, in opposition to Van Buren, and John Tyler, of Virginia, as vice-president. On March 4th, 1841, Harrison was inaugurated, and exactly one month afterwards, his health being feeble, he expired; when the vice-president, according to the Constitution, became president.

Monetary affairs were at this time engrossing public attention, and so great were the present pecuniary difficulties, involving many mercantile houses in ruin, that congress adopted the extraordinary expedient of passing a bankrupt law, which operated throughout all the states. And not only did this law become available for individuals, but was taken advantage of by various states themselves, and a great obloquy for the time was cast on the nation—this was called *repudiation*. With returning prosperity, however, most of the states resumed payment, and little, if any state repudiation of debt has remained.

In 1842, a long existing dispute between the United States and England, regarding the north-eastern boundary, was adjusted. Lord Ashburton was sent from England as a special envoy, and Daniel Webster and he arranged the terms of a treaty by which this important question of north-eastern boundary, which had even threatened war, was amicably and finally settled.

In 1844, serious disturbances occurred in the state of New York, called the Anti-Rent Disturbances, of which a few words must be permitted us, and which we will give principally from Mrs. Willard.

"In the early history of the state, we have seen, that under the Dutch government certain settlers received patents of considerable portions of land, that of Van Rensselaer being the most extensive, comprehending the greater part of Albany and Rensselaer counties. These lands were divided into farms, containing from one hundred to one hundred and sixty acres, and leased in perpetuity on the following conditions. The tenant must each year pay to the landlord or 'patron,' a quantity of wheat, from twenty-two-and-a-half bushels to ten, with four fat fowls, and a day's service with wagon and horses. If the tenant sold his lease, the landlord was entitled to one-quarter of the purchase money. The landlord was also entitled to certain privileges on all water power, and a right to all mines. In process of time the tenants began to consider these legal conditions as anti-republican, as a relic of feudal tyranny. Stephen Van Rensselaer, who came into possession of his patent in 1780, had in the kindness of his nature omitted to exact his legal right until 200,000 dollars of back rent was owing, which, on his death in 1840, was found appropriated by will. The enforcement of these long-neglected demands gave rise to much dissatisfaction, and finally they were forcibly resisted, when the States' government called out the military, but still to no purpose.

"In the summer of 1844, the anti-rent disturbances broke out with great violence in the eastern towns of Rensselaer, and in the Livingston Manor in Columbia County. The anti-renters formed themselves into associations to resist the law, and armed and trained bands, disguised as Indians, scoured the country, compelling every person whom they met to give in their allegiance to this revolt, by saying 'Down with the Rent!' Not contented with this, they proceeded to violence, and tarring and feathering, and other outrages of the most fearful kind took place. Sometimes a thousand of these pretended Indians, more fearful even than the real ones, assembled in a body. Similar disturbances occurred at the same time in Delaware, where Steele, the deputy sheriff, was murdered in the execution of his official duties.

"In 1846, Silas Wright was chosen governor of the state, and by his wisdom and firmness the public order was restored. On the 27th of August, he proclaimed the county of Delaware in a state of insurrection; resolute men were made sheriffs, military aid was given, and the leading anti-renters taken and brought to trial. The murderers of Steele were condemned to death, but their punishment commuted to perpetual imprisonment."

March 3rd, 1845, the two former territories of Iowa and Florida were admitted as states into the Union.

CHAPTER XXII.
WAR WITH MEXICO.—ANNEXATION OF TEXAS.—VAST INCREASE OF TERRITORY.—THE MORMONS.

We have already related how the adventurous La Salle, when endeavouring to establish a colony at the mouth of the Mississippi, mistook his reckoning, and entered the bay of Matagorda instead. This gave the French nation a claim to Texas. The fort built by the unfortunate La Salle was soon demolished by the Indians, and the Spaniards from their neighbouring Mexico disputed also the French right of possession, they claiming the whole of this coast as a portion of their own territory.

The first permanent settlement of the whites in Texas was by the Spaniards, in 1684, when, under San Antonio de Bexar, the fort of that name was established. In 1719 also a colony settled there from the Canary Isles. Various missionary stations and military posts were also established at different places, so that the Spaniards became the assured possessors of the country, with an increasing population. The missionary stations, unlike the simple log-huts and chapels of the early French jesuits, were massive fortresses of stone, the churches decorated with images of saints and paintings, and surmounted by enormous towers. The ruins of several of these vast erections still remain in various parts of Texas, and produce a very striking effect, especially in a country where the traces of civilised life are so scanty. The Spanish population of Texas was, however, inconsiderable at the time of the Mexican revolution in 1810, owing to the incursions of the savage Comanches and other Indian tribes, and to the police regulations of the Spanish government. As regards the relative positions and feelings of the Mexican government and that of the United States, we will give a few remarks from an American writer.[82] "The Mexican authorities were not so desirous of occupying Texas as of keeping her a desolate waste; that she might present an impassable barrier between themselves and their Anglo-American neighbours. The cause of this is not of difficult solution, and is derived from the old mother-country. At the time when Mexico was first colonised, Spain was at the head of the Roman Catholic countries, and all heretics were held in abhorrence by her, and exterminated by the inquisition and the sword. The changes which knowledge and general enlightenment have produced in the Protestant world universally, and even in the Catholic when it has been forced into closer contact with progressive opinion, have not reached Mexico, which has been shut up as it were, and which has jealously retained all her native aversions, prejudices and jealousies. Besides which, Mexico as a colony belonged less to the Spanish nation than to the Spanish kings, and was governed by their viceroys, regardless of the well-being of the people, merely as an estate to produce a revenue. No possible rivalry with the mother-country was permitted; meanwhile the mines were industriously worked, no commerce was permitted to the Mexicans, nor might they rear the silkworm or plant the olive or the vine.

"When, however, the English colonies asserted and established their own independence, Spain, fearing a similar revolt in her own colony, somewhat relaxed her laws regarding their trade with foreign nations, but only under severe restrictions and enormous duties, so that the freedom on the one hand might be nullified by the restrictions on the other. Very little change took place in Mexico.

"At length, in 1810, when the Spanish nation fell under the arm of Napoleon, the Mexicans revolted. But the people were not united, and after a war of eight years the Royalist party prevailed. A second revolution took place in 1821, under Iturbide, when the Mexicans succeeded in throwing off the Spanish yoke. Iturbide proclaimed himself king, and the people, wishing for a republic, deposed him; he was banished, and returning was executed. A new leader arose in the person of Santa Anna, under whose auspices Mexico was divided into States, with each a legislature, and over the whole a general government with a federal constitution similar to that of the United States. But Santa Anna was not a second Washington; the constitution became subverted, and he the military tyrant of the country."

Having given this brief sketch of the condition and government of Mexico, we now return to Texas. When, in 1803, the United States purchased Louisiana from France, the disputed claim to Texas became transferred to them, and in 1819, when Florida was granted to them by Spain, they ceded to that country their claims to Texas as a portion of Mexico. But although they had resigned their claim to Texas, the United States could not resist their natural impulse at extension and colonisation, and, in 1821, favoured by the Mexican authorities, who hoped that the bold and determined Anglo-American settler would be a good defence against the hostile Comanches, the first attempt at the colonisation of Texas was successfully made. The intended leader of this movement was Moses Austen, of Durham, in Connecticut, who obtained a grant of land from the Mexican authorities for the settlement of a colony between the rivers Brazas and Colorado. Death prevented Moses Austen from carrying out his plans, which, however, were fully and most successfully executed by his son, Steven F. Austen. The success of Austen's colony soon alarmed the Mexican authorities; and well it might, for these sturdy republicans once planted there would soon take such firm root as to displace any other possessor. Nor was it long before evidences of their intentions were apparent. In 1827, a movement was attempted by the settlers of Nacogdoches to throw off the Mexican yoke and to establish a republic under the name of Fredonia. The attempt was unsuccessful, but the Mexican authorities were alarmed, more especially as soon after some overtures were made on the part of the United States government to purchase Texas.

In 1833, there were about 10,000 American settlers in Texas; and at that time dissatisfaction and discontent were prevailing largely among them. The Spanish Mexicans of the province carried against them every measure in the government, and when Steven Austen was sent to the city of Mexico to petition for redress, he was first neglected, and then thrown into a dungeon. In 1835 Austen was once more in Texas. The usurpations of Santa Anna had in the meantime increased the public discontent, and the Texians generally prepared to throw off the yoke of his despotism. Adventurers from the American states hastened to take part in the approaching contest, which sooner or later was sure to be advantageous to their nation. A provisional government was appointed, and Samuel Houston placed at the head of the army in Texas.

In December the Texian forces, under General Burleton, besieged the strong fortress of Alamo and the city of Bexar, which was garrisoned by General Cos and 1,300 Spaniards and Mexicans. In a few days the fortress was taken, and the Mexicans obtained permission to retire; so that within a very short time not a single Mexican soldier remained east of the Rio Grande.

Santa Anna, who understood too well the spirit of the people, no sooner saw the stronghold of Bezar taken by a party whose purposes were so adverse to his own, than he entered Texas in person, and with 4,000 men invested Goliad and Bezar, which had unfortunately been left in the hands of a very inadequate force. The attack commenced and continued for several days, the fortress of the Alamo in Bezar being defended by its little band with a courage, says Samuel Goodrich, worthy of Leonidas and his Spartans. After having held out for a considerable time they sustained a general assault on the night of the 6th of May. They fought until Travis, their commander, fell, and seven only of the garrison were left when the place was taken, and the little remnant was torn to pieces. Two human beings only were left, a woman and a negro servant. Among those who fell on this terrible occasion was the celebrated David Crockett of Tennessee, a man well known from the eccentricity of his mind and the independence of his character; he was found surrounded by a heap of dead whom he had slain.

Colonel Fanning, who commanded at Goliad, by direction of the Texian authorities evacuated this place on the 17th of March, but had scarcely reached the open country when they were surrounded by the Mexicans with a troop of Indian allies. They defended themselves all day, and killed a great number of the enemy; during the night, however, the Mexicans being reinforced, they were obliged to surrender, on condition of being treated as prisoners of war: good faith, however, was unknown to Santa Anna, and no sooner were they in his power than he ordered them to be drawn out and shot. Four hundred men were thus murdered in cold blood; one of the soldiers saying to his fellows, when the inhuman order was given, "They are going to shoot us; let us face about and not be shot in the back." This bloody tragedy, which stamped the name of Santa Anna with infamy, took place on the 27th of March, 1836.

These direful tidings aroused, at the same time, the American hatred and sympathy. After this they would not permit Texas to remain in the hands of so cruel and false an enemy.

Santa Anna, encouraged by his victory and confident of success, pursued the Texian army, now under the command of General Houston, as far as San Jacinto, where Houston resolved to risk a battle, although his force was less than 1,000 and the enemy double his number. This was on the 21st of April. The Texians commenced the attack, rushing furiously forward to within half-rifle distance, with the ominous battle-cry of "Remember the Alamo!" The fury with which they assailed the enemy was irresistible, and in less than half an hour they were masters of the camp, the whole Mexican army being killed, wounded, or prisoners. The following day Santa Anna himself was taken, without arms and in disguise.

The plausibility of this artful leader induced his captors to believe him favourable to the independence of Texas. At his request he was sent to the United States, and had an interview with President Jackson, whom he succeeded also in winning, and by whom he was permitted to return to Mexico. No sooner in Mexico than he disclaimed his late proceedings and again commenced war on Texas. In the meantime the United States, England and France recognised the independence of that country. But her struggle was not at an end; and gaining strength by the contest, the Texians, in 1841, assisted by a body of American adventurers, proceeded to take possession of Santa Fe, the capital of New Mexico, lying on the eastern side of the Rio Grande. This attempt was unsuccessful, but it opened, as it were, a door into New Mexico, and the American foot being once planted there, as elsewhere, was but the forerunner of possession.

In 1844 Texas made application to be received into the American Union. Great discussion followed; both President Jackson and his successor, Van

Buren, opposed it, on the ground of the existing peaceful relations with Mexico, but the great body of the American people were favourable to it. The question of annexation was made the great test question of the following election, and James Polk and George M. Dallas owed their elections to its support. Accordingly, on the 4th of March, 1844, they were inaugurated, and Texas already in February had been admitted into the Union. The annexation of Texas was of course resented by Mexico, her minister at Washington declaring it to be "the most unfair act ever recorded in history."

The conditions of annexation required from the authorities and people of Texas were as follows: 1st. That all questions of boundary should be settled by the United States; 2nd. That Texas should give up her harbours, magazines, etc., but retain her funds and her debts, and, until their discharge, her unappropriated lands; 3rd. That additional new states, not exceeding four, might be formed *with slavery* if south of lat. 36½°, but if north, *without*.

The annexation of Texas led to war with Mexico. In July an armed force under Colonel Zachery Taylor, was sent out to protect the new territory against the threatened invasion of Mexico, besides which negotiations were opened for the adjustment of the quarrel, the United States being desirous of purchasing a peaceful boundary on the Rio Grande and the cession of California.

Whilst these negotiations were pending with but little hope of a successful termination, a difficulty arose between the United States and England respecting the northern boundary of Oregon. The brief history of this north-western state is as follows. In the spring of 1792, Captain Robert Gray, of Boston, discovered a river to which he gave the name of his vessel, the Columbia. This was the first knowledge which the Americans had of this river. In 1804–5, Messrs. Lewis and Clarke, under the commission of the American government, explored this river from its mouth to its source. After the year 1808, the country was occupied by various fur companies. These are the circumstances upon which the United States based her claims to the territory as far as 54° 40'. But English merchants being settled in the country, England also asserted her claim, and a discussion of rights and claims ensued, which became so hot on both sides as even to threaten war between the two countries. Fortunately, however, the question was amicably adjusted by the treaty of 1846, by which the 49th degree became the frontier of the United States to the north, Vancouver's Island was wholly relinquished to the British, to whom also the right of navigation in the Columbia was conceded.

War with Mexico continued through the whole of 1846–47, and in May of the following year, left the Americans in quiet possession of the northern provinces of Mexico proper, a vast and important territory including New Mexico, Utah, and California. The incidents of the war were of an adventurous and romantic character. The wonderfully varied and tropical character of the country, and the wild and guerilla kind of warfare amid scenes rendered memorable in the old chivalrous days of Spanish glory and enterprise, gave an extraordinary charm to a war which perhaps cannot be justified on strict principles of Christian morality. Young adventurers flocked to the armies of Generals Wool, Kearney, and Taylor, impatient to take part in a enterprise which was dangerous and exciting in the highest degree. It is said that when the news of the imminent danger of the army on the Rio Grande reached the United States, that everywhere young men hastened westward to defend their brethren, fight the Mexicans, and push forward for the Halls of the Montezumas; and that Prescott's work, the "History of the Conquest of Mexico," being just then published and universally read, greatly increased the enthusiasm.

In April, 1847, Peubla, the second city in Mexico, was taken by the Americans under General Scott, and in the following September, the grand city of Mexico itself. "Three hours before noon," says Mrs. Willard, who seems to have the strongest sympathy with this war, "General Scott made his entrance, with escort of cavalry and flourish of trumpets, into the conquered city of the Aztecs. The troops for four-and-twenty hours now suffered from the anarchy of Mexico more than her prowess had been able to inflict. Two thousand convicts let loose from the prisons attacked them from the house-tops, at the same time entering houses and committing robberies. The Mexicans assisting, these fellows were quelled by the morning of the 15th.

"General Scott gave to his army, on the day of their entrance into Mexico, memorable orders concerning their discipline and behaviour. After directing that companies and regiments be kept together, he says, 'Let there be no disorders, no straggling, no drunkenness. Marauders shall be punished by court-martial. All the rules so honourably observed by the glorious army in Peubla must be observed here. The honour of our country, the honour of our army, call for the best behaviour from all. The valiant must, to win the approbation of God and their country, be sober, orderly, and merciful. His noble brethren in arms will not be deaf to this hasty appeal from their commander and friend.'

"On the 16th, he called the army to return public and private thanks to God for victory; and on the 19th, for the better preservation of order and suppression of crime, he proclaimed martial law. Thus protected by the American army, the citizens of Mexico were more secure from violence, and from the fear of robbery and murder, than they had ever been under their own flag."

Nor does this statement appear to be overdrawn. An English writer[83] on Mexico, who was in the country the two years following the war, dates the commencement of an improvement in this degraded people from the American invasion. "Nothing," says he, "could exceed the jealous suspicions with which the Mexicans formerly regarded other nations, more particularly perhaps the people of the United States. The hatred and rancour with which the very name of American was mentioned while hostilities were in progress, were immeasurable. But at the present time kindly feelings are being fostered with a large proportion which will lead to happy results for both countries.

"In respect of the broad principles of commerce, productions and restrictions, the intercourse of Mexico with other nations has at present led to but few salutary results. Exclusiveness and shortsighted suspicion still remain the governing features of their commercial policy; liberality, innovation, and improvement, being carefully guarded against. Foreign productions of importance are excluded as ruinous, and the country is effectually protected against honourable traffic, though left open to the lawless proceedings of swindlers and smugglers of every grade.

"When the Americans marched upon the interior of the country," after gaining every battle on the outskirts, said an intelligent Mexican, who had been seized upon by the American army and compelled to serve as a guide, "the most horrible ideas of their cruelty and rapacity were set afloat. As they drew near the capital, we were given to understand that there was no torture nor disgrace to which they would not subject the inhabitants, if they conquered us. The priests made themselves particularly busy in influencing the minds of the people in every part of the city against them, and members of the secular clergy went from house to house of the wealthier classes, to arouse their zeal against the invaders, and to procure sums of money for the benefit of the cause. It was generally believed that our enemies were neither more nor less than a kind of monsters, permitted by heaven to visit us as a judgment upon our crimes and neglect of the holy church.

"'For my own part such a dreadful idea of our enemies had taken possession of me, that I could neither eat nor sleep; I was like one bereft of his senses; every avenue of my mind seemed closed but that of fear. Sleeping or waking, I was haunted by the image of our invaders, and I was in the act of making a precipitate retreat at the moment I was surrounded by several hostile soldiers. But, above all, was a popular horror associated with the American generals. The people were taught to believe them the most atrocious impersonations of cruelty and rapacity which it was possible to imagine. It was reported that they had sworn to hang every Mexican who should fall into their hands, and that they had approached the capital with the most malicious determination to wreak their vengeance upon it.' The Mexican prisoner related, therefore, that when he found himself in the hands of such dreaded foes he was in momentary expectation of being shot or hanged, and could not at first understand why his execution was delayed. Still more was he astonished when he beheld the American generals themselves. Instead of fierce tyrants with bloodthirsty visages, as he had been taught to regard them, he beheld, he said, two agreeable-looking, fair men, with paternal countenances and amiable manners. General Scott made a good impression; but General Taylor attracted by his unassuming dignity and awed by his firmness.

"'I am sure,' continued this narrator, 'that many of my countrymen have a great respect for the people of the United States; they have reason for it. Their officers were kind instead of cruel to us; they spared our houses and our property; they were just to our storekeepers. Indeed, in many respects, our city has had cause to regret the period when they went away.' The cruelties of the Mexicans in this struggle were of the most unsparing character; every American or Texian who was captured was killed in some ruthless manner, their dead and mangled bodies being left to be recognised by their friends. It was their practice," says Mr. Mason, "to extort by the most brutal threats and unlicensed conduct, the money and property of individuals unfortunate enough to be in their vicinity, or failing this to outrage their families, or sacrifice them to their mean revenge. They exhibited the utmost baseness and duplicity in all attempts at compromise and interchange of prisoners; and they stripped and plundered the bodies of the American dead left on the field of battle, burning and disfiguring them in the most brutal manner.

"The generosity of the American general shines in happy contrast with these deeds of their enemies. A large party of wounded Mexicans were left in the hospital totally unprovided for on the retreat of Santa Anna's army from Buena Vista, where the Americans gained a signal victory in February, 1847, and which in fact made them masters of the northern provinces of Mexico Proper. In the disastrous flight which followed this defeat, hundreds of the wounded were left by the wayside to be drowned by the waters, even before death, and numbers who had escaped unscathed in the battle, perished on the march in the agonies of thirst and hunger. On General Taylor becoming acquainted with the fact, he despatched such medical assistance as he could spare, together with between thirty and forty mules laden with provisions, to their assistance. This, it is said, being only one instance out of many that might be recorded to the credit of the Americans." And no more than what is right; for the Americans, though chargeable with an aggressive spirit in many cases, with a greed of territory and a lust of colonisation, like their old Anglo-Norman ancestors, were yet Christians, and it is by this Christianity alone, which the conqueror must never forego, that the citizens of the United States will in process of time extend themselves over the whole of the western hemisphere.

We have heard above the testimony of a Mexican to the character of the American invaders. And as regards the moral state of Mexico, we will give an average statement of the amount of crime for one year in the city of Mexico, the population of which is but little above 130,000:

	MALES	FEMALES.	TOTAL.
Robbery	1,800	590	2,390
Quarrelling and Wounding	2,937	1,805	4,742
Bigamy, etc.	421	203	624
Homicide	180	42	222
Incontinence, etc.	75	37	112
Forgery	11	3	14
Throwing Vitriol	41	17	58

9,237

Besides which, about 900 dead bodies are found in the streets and suburbs annually, the cause of which is never known and rarely inquired into. In the above list of crimes is found vitriol throwing, which probably is new to some of our readers, but is so common in Mexico, as the above author assures us, that its appalling evidences are frequently visible in the streets; and not only among the lower classes, but among the wealthy, who have fallen victims to the demoniac vengeance of these ignorant and brutal people.

The taking of Mexico was the crisis of the war. But though the enemy's capital was in the hands of the Americans, they made use of their conquest for no other purpose than to establish peace. In vain Santa Anna endeavoured to carry on the war; his power was gone for the present, and in October, being abandoned by his troops, he once more became a fugitive. In the following February a treaty was laid before congress, and on the 29th of May, the treaty being signed between the two nations, peace was declared to the American army in Mexico.

The stipulations of the treaty were, that Mexico should be evacuated within three months, prisoners on each side released, and Mexican captures made by the Indians within the limits of the United States were to be restored. These limits, as they affect Mexico, begin at the mouth of the Rio Grande, and proceed thence along the deepest channel of that river to the southern boundary of New Mexico. From thence to the Pacific they follow the river Gela and the southern boundary of Upper California. The United States might, however, navigate the Colorado below the entrance of its affluent the Gela. If it were found practicable and judged expedient to construct a canal, road, or railway along the Gela, both nations were to unite in its construction and afterwards to participate in its advantages. The navigation of the river to be obstructed by neither nation. Mexican citizens within the limits of the relinquished territories of New Mexico and Upper California to be allowed a year to make their selection whether they would continue Mexican citizens and remove their property, for which every facility was to be furnished, or whether they would remain and become citizens of the United States. The United States stipulated to restrain the incursions of all the Indian tribes within its limits against the Mexicans, and to return all Mexican captives hereafter made by the Indians. In consideration of territory gained, the United States government agreed to pay to Mexico 15,000,000 dollars, and also to assume her debts to American citizens to the amount of 3,500,000 more. Three millions were paid down to Mexico at once, congress having the preceding winter placed that sum in the hands of the president in anticipation of this arrangement.

Thus was the contest ended, to the incalculable advantage of America, and of Mexico likewise, though her benefit will lie in the nearer proximity of a more enlightened government, free institutions, and an advancing people.

The territory of Wisconsin was admitted into the American Union as a state, in May, 1850.

A vast extent of country, as we have already said, fell into the hands of the United States government, in consequence of its Mexican conquests. An important portion of this was Utah, so called from the tribe of Indians inhabiting it, and which was formed into a territorial government as early as 1850. But this remarkable country, with its vast mountain chains, its deserts, its affluent valleys, and its great Salt Lake, together with its extraordinary people, the Mormons, deserve more than a mere summary mention. The Rocky Mountains on the east and the Sierra Nevada on the west, form the boundaries of Utah; besides these, two lofty chains intersect the country from north-east to south-west. The Great Basin, a considerable portion of which is sandy desert, is an elevated valley, composing the western portion of Utah; it is in circuit about 12,000 miles, and lies about 5,000 feet above the level of the sea. The great valley of the Colorado, on the east, although not fully explored, is said to be wonderfully fertile, abounding in wood, and admirably fitted for the purposes of agriculture. Its northern portion, and the whole district of the Great Salt Lake, are full of natural beauties, and abundantly repay cultivation.

The Great Salt Lake is perhaps the most singular feature of Utah. Its form is irregular, in extent it is about seventy miles, and contains many islands. It is extremely salty, and so shallow as not to be available for the purposes of navigation. Its western banks, intersected by rivulets impregnated with salt and sulphur, are totally devoid of vegetation, excepting such small shrubs as spring up among the glittering saline particles, and here the mirage frequently displays its fantastic show, as in the deserts of the East. Fresh water and green turf are unknown through an extent of one hundred miles, while a coating of solid salt incrusts the earth, upon which the mules pass as upon ice. This lake never freezes. The river Utah, or the Jordan as it is called by the Mormons, is a small river of fresh water which unites Lake Utah to the Great Salt Lake. Lake Utah, thirty-five miles long, receives the waters of a great number of fresh-water streams which descend from the mountains, and keep the waters of this lesser lake fresh, although on its southern limits a considerable vein of salt has been found imbedded in the clay.

These lakes are about 4,000 feet above the level of the sea.

Lake Utah, as well as the rivers which flow into it, abounds with excellent fish, which with the chase furnish a subsistence to the Indians of this district.[84]

Into this singular region, with its snow-capped mountains, its elevated valleys, its sandy deserts, and salt and sulphurous waters, came, in the year 1848, a people whose social and religious system forms as singular an anomaly in the midst of modern civilisation as the country itself which they chose amid the more ordinary aspects of nature. These, as is well known, are the Mormons.

The commencement of this sect was only eighteen years previous to the great emigration westward, and has become an historical event. Joseph Smith, the Mormon prophet, a man of low origin, a native of Palmyra in the state of New York, pretended to have found written plates of gold, which he also pretended to translate by miraculous inspiration, and gave forth as the book of Mormon, representing himself to be a great prophet of the latter day, a new Moses or Mahomet. The character of Smith appears from his youth upwards to have been that of a religious enthusiast, if not impostor. When only fourteen, during one of those periods of religious excitement called revivals, he declared that he had been favoured with a heavenly vision, in which two angelic personages freed him from the power of the Enemy and forbade him to join himself to any Christian sect. As he approached manhood he pretended to a knowledge of the occult sciences, and used the divining rod in the discovery of gold, at which period he was known as "Joe the Money-Digger." The greatest treasure, however, which came into his hand, whether by occult knowledge or by angelic revelation, was, he said, the Book of Mormon, though no one ever saw the golden plates on which he asserted that it was written. As regards this so-called Book of Mormon, it is now generally supposed to have been the production of one Solomon Spalding, a Presbyterian minister, who, after various unsuccesses, wrote a tedious work of fiction on the History of the North American Indians, as the descendants of the patriarch Joseph, from the reign of Zedekiah to the fifth century of the Christian era, and which purported to have been buried by Mormon, its original compiler. This work, which never found a publisher, some years after its author's death fell by some means into the hands of Sidney Higdon, an associate of Smith's. The Book of Mormon was published, and Joe Smith was impudently announced by it to be a second Prophet and Saviour of mankind, who should establish a great Zion in America. Ill-founded and absurd as his pretensions were, he soon obtained an immense influence over the ignorant, not only in America but in England, and his sect increased not by hundreds but thousands. The principles of this sect are as yet but imperfectly understood. If, however, they are to be inferred from their bible, they will be found based on Christianity, whatever extravagances and impurities they may have engrafted upon it. This book is said to contain, in the first place, the whole of the Christian Bible, to which are added the writings of later prophets, of whom Meroni and Mormon are asserted to be the last. These give a more definite prophecy of Christ, but still adhere to the details of his life as related by the Evangelists, but in no instances propound any new religious doctrines or theory. The sect asserts, however, that Joe Smith, being directly descended from these later prophets, not only inherited their divine gifts, but was endowed with the spiritual privilege of divine communication, which he had the power of imparting to others; and that by means of these divine and miraculous gifts he and his followers are brought into closer communication with Christ than any other body of Christians.

While we must believe that these high pretensions of Joe Smith's are delusions if not imposture of the most daring kind, it is still an interesting question what was the secret of the wonderful influence which he possessed over such thousands in the present age, and by which he was able not only to form them into a vast organised society, but even after his death to leave them so firmly knit together that no sign of dissolution appears amongst them. No doubt, however, but that Joe Smith was an extraordinary man, however unprincipled, gifted with a measure of that far-seeing power which assumes to be prophetic, and possessed of that subtle influence which subdues to its dominion the minds of all who are brought within its sphere, besides which he had great knowledge of human nature, and framed his government upon a hierarchical basis so as to enslave the multitude to a powerful priesthood. As regards the prophetic gifts of their first leader, the Mormons declare that Joe Smith distinctly foretold the time and manner of his own death, so that when it occurred the sect, instead of being disheartened and broken up, only regarded it as the accomplishment of a divine ordination, as a testimony to the truth of their faith, and other men of a like spirit with Smith took his place.

The Mormons, in the year 1838, established themselves and built a temple at Kirtland in Ohio; they then removed into Michigan, afterwards into Missouri, whence they were expelled on the charge of an attempt to assassinate the governor. From Missouri they removed into Illinois, whence they were again driven out by the inhabitants. In this last state, however, they remained long enough to found a city called Nauvoo, in which they built, upon the fine slope of a hill, a vast and magnificent temple in a barbaric style of architecture, according as they asserted, to directions laid down in the book of Mormon, the effect, however, of which was extremely imposing. Mormonism was now flourishing. The wealth and population of the community increased greatly. Smith was not only Prophet and High Priest but Mayor of Nauvoo, and even, it is said, offered himself as candidate for the Presidentship of the Union. At Nauvoo also it was that the grossest feature of Mormonism first revealed itself—Smith pretended that he had received a revelation allowing him to have many wives. This and other things roused the public indignation, and Joe Smith and his brother, on the charge of having been concerned in robbery and murder, were lodged in prison at the town of Carthage; and while in prison were themselves murdered by a band of a hundred men who forcibly entered in disguise for that purpose. Although this outrage was as great as that for which the Mormon leader was incarcerated, the public indignation continued to be so unabating against them, that the following year they sold all their possessions in Illinois, deserted their city and temple, and again, like the children of Israel of old, commenced their wanderings in the wilderness, their chosen head and prophet on the death of Smith being Brigham Young, the son of an Eastern States' farmer. After a long and arduous march of 3,000 miles, amid difficulties and dangers and the endurance of many sufferings, and having crossed the Rocky Mountains they reached the Great Salt Lake, on the fertile shores of which they settled down as in a land of Goshen. Here a great prosperity has again commenced for them; their numbers increase annually, and even so early as 1846 they were able to furnish 500 volunteers for the Mexican war.

At the present time the Mormons number about 30,000. They are building a vast city, twelve miles in circumference, the houses of which are of brick, and their new temple, on a scale still more magnificent than the former, is of stone, the plan it is said having been revealed to Brigham Young in a miraculous vision. About 13,000 inhabitants reside in the city, the remainder having established themselves on the banks of the Jordan, which river, as we have said, connects Lake Utah with the Great Salt Lake. They have already commenced the cultivation of the soil, which is found to produce seventy-five bushels of wheat per acre, and which is favourable to the growth of the potato, though the climate is too severe for the Indian corn. Rain is rare in the country, and irrigation is therefore indispensable. They have erected corn and saw-mills on the streams of water which descend from the mountains, wood being abundant for this purpose, besides which they have iron-works and coal-mines, and various factories. They have dug canals and built bridges. They have established regular mails with San Francisco on the Pacific and New York on the Atlantic. Public baths, supplied from the hot springs of that volcanic region are erected in the city, and they have founded also a university, where lectures on the sciences, conformable to Mormon views, are delivered. The climate is extremely salubrious.

The Mormon government is a hierarchy; and the one great doctrine which is impressed upon the people is submission in all things to the priesthood; but all sects and opinions are tolerated amongst them. If all is true which is said of their social life, morality amongst them is at a very low ebb. Nevertheless, accounts are so contrary, that Miss Bremer, for instance, states on what she considered good authority, "that the habits and organisation of the community were according to the Christian moral code, and extremely severe." Whatever it may be however, whether it ministers to the evil or the good in human nature, there seems to be a very popular element in Mormonism, for it reckons about 100,000 members within its pale, both in Europe and America, and those in Europe seem to be rapidly removing themselves to this New Jerusalem on the banks of the Great Salt Lake. One cause of their success, doubtless, is the wonderful system of organisation which prevails amongst them. They do not undertake the task of establishing their settlements according to the usually independent mode of individual and ordinary squatters, but all is the result of organised industry, and the result astonishes all. Captain Stansbury, in his Survey of Utah, thus describes the mode which they adopt for the founding of a new town. "An expedition is sent out to explore the country, with a view to the selection of the best site. An elder of the church is then appointed to preside over the band designated to make the first improvement. This company is composed partly of volunteers and partly of such as are selected by the Presidency, due regard being had to a proper intermixture of mechanical artizans, to render the expedition independent of all without." And still further to illustrate this system, we will extract a letter given by the author of a very comprehensive article on Mormonism in the "Edinburgh Review," and to which we are already indebted. "In company of upwards of 100 wagons I was sent on a mission with G. A. Smith, one of the Twelve, to Iron County, 270 miles south of Salt Lake, in the depth of winter, to form a settlement in the valley of Little Salt Lake, now Parowan, as a preparatory step to the manufacturing of iron. After some difficulty in getting through the snow, we arrived safe and sound in the valley. After looking out a location, we formed our wagons into two parallel lines, some seventy paces apart; we then took the boxes from the wheels and planted them about a couple of paces from each other, so securing ourselves that we could not easily be taken advantage of by any unknown foe. This done, we next ran a road up the ravine, opening it to a distance of some eight miles, bridging the creek in some five or six places, making the timber and poles, of which there is an immense quantity, of easy access. We next built a large meeting-house, two stories high, of large pine-trees, all neatly joined together. We next built a square fort with a commodious cattle-yard inside the enclosure. The houses were some of hewn logs, others of dried bricks, all neat and comfortable. We next inclosed a field, five by three miles square, with a good ditch and pole-fence. We dug canals and water-ditches to the distance of thirty or forty miles. One canal to turn the water of another creek upon the field for irrigating purposes, was seven miles long. We built a saw-mill and grist-mill the same season. I have not time to tell you half the labours we performed in one season. Suffice it to say, that when the governor came along in the spring, he pronounced it the greatest work done in the mountains by the same amount of men."

This system of judicious organisation, by which his proper place is appointed to every man, has been carried throughout the Mormon movements, and much of their success may be attributed to this cause. The march from Missouri to the Great Salt Lake was conducted on this system. Captain Kane, who was an eye-witness, describes 3,000 persons, among whom were many women and children, journeying across an unknown and wilderness country with all the discipline of a veteran army. "Every ten of their wagons was under the care of a captain; this captain of ten obeyed a captain of fifty; who in his turn obeyed a member of the High Council of the Church."

The great route to the western states of Oregon and California by the South Pass, runs about sixty miles north of this city of the Mormons, and one still nearer may be taken. The inhabitants supply the travellers with fresh mules, oxen, and provisions for the journey. The road of Independence west of the Rocky Mountains is good, and the number of travellers which frequent it immense. The Mormons have established ferry-boats on the Platte and Green Rivers.[85]

Such is the history and the present position of the Mormon settlement of Utah. Already in 1850 they petitioned congress for admission into the Union, under the designation of the State of Deseret, a name taken from their Book of Mormon, but as yet they rank only as a territorial government.

CHAPTER XXIII.
CALIFORNIA—STATISTICAL REVIEW OF
THE UNITED STATES.

The American state of California, a portion of the Mexican Upper California, came, as we have already said, into the possession of the United States through their Mexican conquests, and, as the event has proved, has supplied an important epoch not only in the history of the United States, but of the world itself.

The first discoverer of Upper California was Sir Francis Drake, in the year 1579, when, having doubled Cape Horn, he coasted the Pacific shore in the vain hope of discovering a passage to the Atlantic Ocean, and took possession of the country, to which he gave the name of New Albion, in the name of his sovereign, Queen Elizabeth. This discovery, however, not being followed up by colonisation, the English lost the right of possession, which was claimed by the Spaniards as a portion of the conquests of Cortez, which were prior to the discovery of Sir Francis Drake.

In 1603, Philip III. of Spain sent out Sebastian Viscaino to examine the coast of Upper California in search of suitable harbours for the Spanish East India ships. He discovered and took possession of San Diego and Monterey, giving on his return glowing descriptions of the beauty and fertility of the country. The Spaniards, however, made but little progress in colonisation, owing in part to the hostility of the natives. Their principal, and in fact first permanent settlement was at San Diego, but the coast, nevertheless, was frequented by their ships on account of its valuable pearl-fisheries. Although the Spanish government did not consider the colonisation of Upper California worth the expense, priests of the Franciscan order established several missionary stations, in the hope of converting the natives. Twenty-one stations were thus formed on the most fertile lands, each occupying about fifteen square miles. The buildings of those stations were contained in an enclosure of adobe or sun-dried brick. To the principal missions was attached a presidio, where was a quadrangular fort, in which was placed a company of soldiers for the protection of the missionaries, and to assist them also in bringing the refractory natives under their influence. The result was, that about half the Indians in the missionary district became nominal Christians and menial labourers at the same time. The very constitution of these missions, however, was calculated to prevent any effectual colonisation of the country by the whites, inasmuch as, while the missionaries themselves were monks and nuns, the soldiers at the presidios were not permitted to bring their wives with them; so that *homes* did not immediately spring up there as among the wiser colonists, who understood by this means how to attach the settler at once to the soil. Neither was money allowed to be in circulation, and the *Padre* of the mission held everything under his control. As might be expected, therefore, these missions never took deep root in the country, and only the few places where families were allowed to settle, are those in which towns sprung up, of which Ciudad de Los Angeles, San Diego and San Francisco were the principal, no one of which, in the year 1840, contained 1,000 inhabitants. Of the general population of Upper California, Humboldt states, that in 1802 it consisted of 15,562 converted Indians and 1,300 of other classes; in 1840 it is estimated that the number of whites was 5,000, of mistigoes or mixed 2,000, and of natives about 18,000. From this time, when the American exploring parties, of which we shall speak presently, had opened as it were a door into these hitherto unknown regions, and the advancing tide of western emigration reached its threshold, population began rapidly to increase; so that the Hon. Butler King states, in his official report, that "in 1846 Colonel Fremont had little difficulty in calling to his standard some 500 fighting men, and that, at the close of the war with Mexico, from 10,000 to 15,000 Americans and Californians, exclusive of converted Indians, were then in the territory. The immigration of American citizens in 1849, the year following the cession of California to the United States, was estimated at 80,000, that of foreigners at 20,000."

We are indebted to Mrs. Willard for the greater portion of the following rapid sketch:—

"This country during the Spanish rule constituted a part of the viceroyalty of Mexico or New Spain. When Mexico became a federal republic, not finding California sufficiently populous to form a state, she established over it a territorial government. The Californians, like the Mexicans, sometimes had their revolutions, and declared themselves independent; but they always returned again to their allegiance, and till the opening of the war between the republics of America and Mexico, they were governed as a territory of the latter. Los Angeles was the seat of the territorial government; a member of the eminent family of Pico was at its head, and General Castro, the military chief, made Monterey his residence.

"A few years since the country between the Rocky Mountains and the Pacific was as little known as the centre of Africa. In the years 1803 and 1804, Messrs. Lewis and Clarke, sent out by President Jackson, explored the Missouri to its sources, crossed the Rocky Mountains in latitude 47°, then struck upon the head waters of the Columbia, and followed its source to the Pacific Ocean. Settlements succeeded these discoveries and those subsequently of Captain Grey. The purchase of Louisiana from France, in 1803, carried the American dominion from the Mississippi to the heights of the Rocky Mountains. All the country beyond those mountains and south of Oregon was, previous to the late war with Mexico, in the possession of that country, and in 1840 its place on the map of the world was a blank.

"The American government in 1838, sent out, chiefly for the benefit of trade and commerce, a naval exploring expedition under Captain Charles Wilkes, to coast the American continent to the south and west, and to explore the islands of the Pacific. Captain Wilkes was directed to make surveys and examinations of the coast of Oregon and the Columbia River, and afterwards along the coast of California, with especial reference to the Bay of San Francisco. After executing this order in August and September, 1841, he pronounced the harbour of San Francisco to be 'one of the finest, if not the very best in the world.' The town, then called *Yerba Buono*, he said, consisted of one large frame building, occupied by the Hudson Bay Company; the store of an American merchant, a billiard-room and a bar; the cabin of a ship occupied as a dwelling; besides out-houses, few and far between. The most prominent man in the region was Captain Sutter, a Swiss by birth, and once a lieutenant in the Swiss guards of Charles X. of France, but who had immigrated from Missouri to California. Having obtained from Mexico a grant of land thirty leagues square, he located his residence within it and near the confluence of the American river with the Sacremento; here he built a fort at the junction of the rivers and laid out a town, to which he gave the name of New Helvetia, but which has since been called Sacremento City. Captain Wilkes reported favourably of the soil and productions of the country.

"In 1842, John C. Fremont, at that time a lieutenant of topographical engineers, being ordered on an exploring tour, left the mouth of the Kansas in the month of June with a party of about twenty. He travelled along the fertile valley of this river; struck off upon the sterile banks of the Platte River, followed its South Fork to St. Vrain's Fort, and thence northerly to Fort Laramie, on the North Fork of the same stream. Following up, from this point, the North Fork and then its affluent the Sweet Water River, he was conducted by a gentle ascent to that wonderful gateway in the Rocky Mountains called the South Pass. He had found on his lonely way a few straggling emigrants bound to Oregon, but not one to California. Having explored the vicinity of the South Pass, his orders were executed, and he returned.

"The next year, again under the auspices of government, and with a party of thirty-nine, he set out earlier in the season, with special orders to examine and report upon the country between the Rocky Mountains and the line of Captain Wilkes's explorations on the Pacific coast. He now crossed the Rocky Mountains further south, and where they were 8,000 feet in height. He then examined and laid open, by his report, the region of the Salt Lake, having reached that extraordinary expanse of salt water by following its beautiful affluent, the Bear River.

"Fremont, now brevet captain, was, on September 19th, at Fort Hall, on his way to Oregon. Here he met a Mr. Chiles, the only emigrant he had yet seen to California. Having, in the manner dictated by his orders, explored Oregon, he turned south and commenced his route to California, by traversing in winter the terrible and dangerous snows of the Sierra Nevada. From this seemingly interminable way, the lost and famished wanderers emerged upon the waters of the Sacremento, and they followed its affluent, the American Fork, to Sutter's Fort, ignorant of the golden treasures beneath their feet, soon to set in motion a rapidly concentrating population from every corner of the world. After their wants had been kindly supplied by Captain Sutter, the party travelled south and beheld and enjoyed the vernal beauties of the flowery valley of the San Joaquin. Turning then to the southern extremity of the Sierra Nevada, they next passed the arid waste of the Great Desert Basin.

"They had discovered and named on their way new rivers and mountain passes; and had laid open regions which had heretofore, except to the hunter and the savage, been but the hidden recesses of nature. They had explored California and made known an overland route."

Mr. Polk entered upon the presidential office resolved to carry out the Mexican war, as well as to make its results advantageous to his country by putting her in possession not only of New Mexico but of California also, the importance of which he fully estimated as opening up a great commercial state on the Pacific, even before its almost fabulous wealth of gold had become known.

The Mexican war went on, the American interests being advanced at every step, and finally the treaty of Guadaloupe Hidalgo established peace between the two republics, and gave the United States government possession of that vast territory which she coveted with a prescient wisdom, and which it assuredly was the will of God that she should people with her industrious and enterprising sons.

This treaty, which put the Americans in possession of California, was signed in February, 1848, and by a coincidence so extraordinary, that had it been imagined by a writer of fiction, it would have been considered improbable, if not impossible, the discovery of the gold was made within one month from that time. The first gold was found in the lands of that Captain Sutter whom we have already mentioned, on the American Fork of the Sacremento, and almost immediately afterwards in various other localities. The possession of the vast extent of what was so lately Mexican territory, with its framework of society so different to that of the United States, had caused considerable anxiety in the minds of many thoughtful men as to the result. It was feared that many years must pass before a sufficient number of American citizens had settled in these new lands to fuse the old elements into a congruous mass, and that before this should take place bloodshed and disruption might have made the acquired territory a dear purchase. But Providence, who overrules human events for the wisest and best purposes, signally set at rest all these doubts, by permitting the discovery of the gold, which would act as the most tempting lure to call away, not only from the older states, but from the very ends of the earth, a population which would at once sweep away the old influences and begin all anew. Gold, which in so many instances had been a dire curse, was here converted into a blessing.

The tide of emigration set in. In the following year, 1849, 30,000 souls from the United States alone emigrated to California. No outpouring of people in the Middle Ages ever equalled this. We will give a little sketch of this great movement from the graphic and elegant pen of Bayard Taylor, who saw with his own eyes what he describes:—

"Sacremento city was the goal of the emigration by the northern routes. From the beginning of August to the last of December, scarcely a day passed without the arrival of some man or company of men and families, from the mountains, to pitch their tents for a few days on the banks of the river, and rest from their months of hardship. The vicissitudes through which these people had passed, the perils which they had encountered, and the toils they had endured, seem to me without precedent in history. The story of 30,000 souls accomplishing a journey of more than 2,000 miles through a savage and but partially explored wilderness, crossing on their way two mountains equal to the Alps in height and asperity, besides broad tracts of burning desert and plains of nearly equal desolation, where a few patches of stunted shrubs and springs of brackish water was their only stay, has in it so much heroism, daring and sublime endurance, that we may vainly question the records of any age for its equal. Standing as I was at the closing stage of that grand pilgrimage, the sight of those adventurers, as they came in day by day, and the hearing of their stories, had a more fascinating, because more real interest, than the tales of the old travellers which so impress us in childhood.

"It would be impossible to give, in a general description of the emigration, viewed as one great movement, a complete idea of its wonderful phases. The experience of any single man, which a few years ago would have made him a hero for life, becomes mere common-place when it is but one of thousands; yet the spectacle of a great continent, through a region of 1,000 miles from north to south, being overrun with these adventurous bands, cannot be pictured without the relation of many episodes of individual bravery and suffering. Without giving an account of the emigration generally, I will content myself with a sketch of what was encountered by those who took the northern route, the great overland highway of the continent, that very route which we have described Captain Fremont as having opened.

"The great starting-point for this route was Independence, where thousands were encamped through the month of April, waiting until the grass should be sufficiently high for their cattle, before they ventured on the broad ocean of the plains. From the 1st of May to the 1st of June, company after company took its departure from the frontier of civilisation, till the emigrant trail from Fort Leavensworth on the Missouri, to Fort Laramie at the foot of the Rocky Mountains, was one long line of mule-trains and wagons. The rich meadows of the Nebraske, or Platte, were settled for the time, and a single traveller could have journeyed for the space of 1,000 miles, as certain of his lodgings and regular meals as if he were riding through the agricultural districts of the middle states. The wandering tribes of Indians on the plains, the Pawnees, Sioux, and Arapahoes, were alarmed and bewildered by this strange apparition. They believed that they were about to be swept away for ever from their hunting-grounds and graves. As the season advanced, and the great body of the emigrants got under way, they gradually withdrew from the vicinity of the trail, and betook themselves to grounds which the former did not reach. All conflicts with them were thus avoided.

"Another and more terrible scourge, however, was doomed to fall upon them. The cholera, ascending the Mississippi from New Orleans, reached St. Louis about the time of their departure from Independence, and overtook them before they were fairly embarked on the wilderness. The frequent rains of the early spring, added to the hardships and exposure of their travel, prepared the way for its ravages, and the first 300 or 400 miles of the trail were marked by graves. It is estimated that about 4,000 persons perished from this cause.

"By the time the companies reached Fort Laramie the epidemic had expended its violence, and in the pure air of the elevated region they were safe from further attack. But then the real hardships of their journey began. Up and down the mountains that arise in the Sweet Water Valley; over the spurs of the Wind River chain; through the Devil's Gate, and past the stupendous mass of Rock Independence, they toiled slowly up to the South Pass, descended to the tributaries of the Colorado, and plunged into the rugged defiles of the Tampanozu Mountains. Here the pasturage became scarce, and the companies were obliged to take separate trails in order to find sufficient grass for their teams. Great numbers also suffered immensely for want of food, and were compelled to kill their horses and mules to keep themselves from starvation. Nor was it unusual for a mess, by way of variety to the tough mule-steaks, to kill a quantity of rattlesnakes, with which the mountains abounded, and have a dish of them fried for supper."

We have already spoken of the assistance rendered to these vast trains of adventurers by the Mormons, then lately settled at their new city on the Great Salt Lake. "Remarkable," says Bayard Taylor, "must have been the scene which was presented during the summer. There a community of religious enthusiasts, having established themselves beside an inland sea, in a grand valley shut in by snow-capped mountains, 1,000 miles from any other civilised spot, and dreaming only of rebuilding the Temple and creating a new Jerusalem, were aroused by the advance of these vast pilgrim-bands. And indeed, without this resting-place in mid-journey, the sufferings of the emigrants must have been much aggravated. The Mormons, however, whose rich grain lands in the valley of the Utah River had produced them abundance of supplies, were able to spare sufficient for those whose supplies were exhausted. Two or three thousand who arrived late in the season remained in the valley all winter.

"Those who set out for California had the worst yet in store for them. Crossing the alternate sandy wastes and rugged mountain chains of the Great Basin to the Valley of Humboldt's River, they were obliged to trust entirely to their worn and weary animals for reaching the Sierra Nevada before the winter snows. The grass was scarce and now fast drying up in the scorching heat of midsummer. The progress of the emigrants along the valley of Humboldt's River was slow and toilsome in the extreme. This river, which lies entirely within the Great Basin, and has no connexion with the sea, shrinks away towards the end of summer and finally loses itself in the sand at a place called the Sink. Here the single trail across the desert divided into three branches, many companies stopping at this place to recruit their exhausted animals, though exposed to the danger of being detained there the whole winter by the snows of the Sierra Nevada. Another large body took the upper route through Lawson's Pass, which leads to the head of the Sacramento Valley; while the greater number fortunately chose the old and travelled trails leading to Bear Creek and the Yuba, by way of Truckee River, and to the head waters of the Rio Americano.

"After leaving the Sink of Humboldt's River, and crossing a desert of about fifty miles in breadth, the emigrants reached the streams which are fed from the Sierra Nevada, where they found good grass and plenty of game. The passes, however, were terribly rugged and precipitous, leading directly up the face of the great snowy ridge. As, however, these mountains are not quite 8,000 feet above the level of the sea, and are reached from a plateau of more than 4,000 feet, the ascent is comparatively short, while on the western side more than 100 miles of mountain country must be passed before reaching the level of the Sacremento Valley. Many passes in the Sierra Nevada were never crossed before the summer of 1849. All the emigrants concurred in representing this western slope of the mountains as an abrupt and broken region, the higher peaks of barren granite, the valleys deep and narrow, yet in many places timbered with pine and cedar of immense growth."

The advance parties arriving at San Francisco, brought the news of the thousands who remained behind, and who, but for help, would probably perish either among the terrible passes of the mountains or in the great desert of the Sink. Relief companies were, therefore, despatched into the Great Basin to succour the emigrants remaining there, and who for want of provisions could not proceed. Not only did the authorities of San Francisco exert themselves for this purpose, but private individuals also. Major Rucker despatched a party with supplies and fresh animals by way of the Truckee River to the Sink of Humboldt's River, while he himself took the command of the expedition to Pitt River and Lawson's Pass. The first party, after furnishing provisions on the road to all whom they found in need, reached the Sink, and started the families who were still encamped there, returning with them, and bringing in the last of the emigration only a day or two before the heavy snows came on, which entirely blocked up the passes. Major Rucker also brought in his company of emigrants after immense labour, and Mr. Peoples, an auxiliary whom he had found it necessary to send out in another direction, accomplished also his work of mercy. A violent storm, relates this gentleman, came on as they were passing the mountains of Deer Creek, and the mules, unaccustomed to the severe cold, sank down and died one after another. The people, whose spirit of enterprise and power of endurance seemed in many deadened by their sufferings, were forcibly compelled to hurry forward with the remaining animals. The women, who seemed to have much more energy and endurance than the men, were mounted on mules, and the whole party pushed on through the bleak passes of the mountains in the face of the storm. By extraordinary exertions, they were all finally brought into the Sacremento Valley, with the loss of many wagons and animals.

"The greater part of those who came in by the lower routes," continues Bayard Taylor, "started after a season of rest for the mining region, where many of them arrived in time to build themselves log-huts for the winter. Some pitched their tents along the river, to wait for the genial spring season, while others took their axes and commenced the business of wood-cutting in the timber on its banks, and which wood, when shipped to San Francisco, paid them well."

"By the end of December, the last man of the overland companies was safe on the western side of the Sierra Nevada, and the great interior wilderness resumed its ancient silence and solitude until the next spring; when again it would become populous with these modern crusaders."

Nor was the emigration to California confined alone to those who reached it by land. Ships thronged the beautiful harbour of San Francisco, bringing in their thousands likewise. So great was the concourse, that between the 7th of December, 1848, and the 20th of January, 1849, ninety-nine vessels left the ports of the United States alone for California, and from Oct. 1849, to Oct. 1850, nearly 49,000 emigrants arrived by sea at San Francisco, and about 20,000 by land.

At the presidential election of 1848, General Zachary Taylor, the hero of the Mexican war, was chosen president, and Millard Fillmore, of New York, vice-president. The following year, Minnesota, adjacent to the head waters of the Mississippi, was admitted into the Union.

The vast growth of the national territory, and the consequent increase of states governments which would sooner or later take place, gave rise to the most violent contests between the slavery and the non-slavery parties which as yet had been known. The north and the south were again arrayed against each other, and the secession from the Union was the threat to which South Carolina again resorted. Whilst this great political battle was being fought in congress during the sessions of 1849–50, California, which had so suddenly acquired a population far exceeding that required by the Constitution for the establishment of a territorial government, could obtain no guidance or aid from congress, excepting merely a law regarding the revenue. Amid this perplexing and difficult state of affairs, however, the sagacity and prudence of the Californians themselves saved them from anarchy and ruin, and proved how true is the assertion that the American citizen is gifted with the innate power of self-government. The wisest senate that ever sat could not have reduced a social and political chaos into a state of more perfect harmony and order, than did these legislators of the far west by their simple and constitutional laws.

Again we turn to Bayard Taylor, whose work on California possesses all the merits and intrinsic value of the early annalists of the Puritan states. We will briefly follow him in his account of the state organisation of California.

"In the neglect of congress," says he, "to provide for the establishment of a territorial, it was suggested that a convention should be called for the framing of a state constitution, and that California should be admitted at once into the Union, without passing through the territorial stage, leaping with one bound, as it were, from a state of semi-civilisation to be the thirty-first sovereign state of the American Confederacy.

"On the 4th of September, the convention met at Monterey, when Dr. Robert Semple, of the Sonoma district, was chosen president, and conducted to his seat by Captain Sutter and General Vallijo. Captain William G. Marey, of the New York volunteer regiment, was elected secretary, after which the various posts of clerks, assistant secretaries, translators, doorkeepers, sergeant-at-arms, etc., were filled. The day after their complete organisation they were sworn to support the Constitution of the United States.

"The building in which the convention met was probably the only one in California suited for the purpose. It is a handsome two-story edifice of yellow sandstone, situated on a gentle slope above the town. It is called Colton Hall, on account of its having been built by Don Walter Colton, former Alcade of Monterey, from the proceeds of a sale of city lots. The stone of which it is built is found near Monterey; it is of a fine mellow colour, easily cut, and will last for centuries in that mild climate. The upper story, in which the convention sat, formed a single hall about sixty feet in length by twenty-five in breadth. A railing running across the middle divided the members from the spectators. The former were seated at four long tables, the president occupying a rostrum at the further end, over which were suspended two American flags and an extraordinary picture of Washington, evidently the work of a native artist. The appearance of the whole body was exceedingly dignified and intellectual, and parliamentary decorum was strictly observed.

"The Declaration of Rights, which was the first subject before the convention, occasioned little discussion. Its sections being general in their character, and of a liberal republican cast, were nearly all adopted by a nearly unanimous vote. The clause prohibiting slavery was met by no word of dissent; it was the universal sentiment of the convention. Without capitulating the various provisions of the constitution, it is enough to say that they combined with few exceptions the most enlightened features of the constitutions of the older states. The election of judges by the people; the rights of married women to property; the establishment of a liberal system of education, and other reforms of late introduced into the States Governments east of the Rocky Mountains, were all transplanted to the new soil of the Pacific coast.

"The adoption of a system of pay for the officers and members of the convention occasioned some discussion. The Californian members, and a few of the Americans, demanded that the convention should work for nothing, the glory being sufficient. The majority overruled this, and it was finally decided that all should be paid, the members receiving sixteen dollars per day, and the different officers on a higher scale, in proportion to their duties. The expenses of the convention were paid out of the civil fund, an accumulation of the duties received at the ports. The funds were principally silver, and at the close of their labours, it was amusing to see the various members carrying away their pay tied up in handkerchiefs or slung in bags over their shoulders. The little Irish boy who acted as page was nearly pressed down by the weight of his wages.

"One of the most exciting questions was a clause which had been crammed through the convention on its first reading, prohibiting the entrance of free people of colour into the state. On the second reading it was rejected by a large majority; several attempts to introduce it in a modified form also signally failed.

"The boundary too, which came up towards the close of the convention, assumed a character of real interest and importance. The great point in dispute was the eastern boundary, the Pacific being the natural boundary on the west, the meridian of 42° on the north, and the Mexican line on the south. After many attempts to extend this eastern boundary, variously from the Sierra Nevada Chain, to the banks of the Colorado River, it was settled by following the old Mexican boundary, which after all appeared to satisfy every body. The state had thus 800 miles of sea coast, and an average of 250 miles in breadth, including both sides of the Sierra Nevada, and some of the best rivers of the Great Basin. As to the question of slavery, the character of the country will settle that. The whole central region, extending to the Sierra Madre of New Mexico, can never sustain a slave population. The greater part of it resembles in climate and general features the mountain Steppes of Tartary, and is better adapted for grazing than agriculture."

Among other creditable facts of this convention, it is worthy of mention that various native Californians, with their chivalric Spanish names, sat among the members, and were even elected to offices under the new government.

On October the 12th, the convention brought its labours to an end, and a ball was given by the members of the convention to the citizens of Monterey, in the hall where they had sat, on the following evening.

Of the ball we need say nothing, but merely close our account with the signing of the convention, which might not unworthily take its place, as an historical picture, near that of the scene in the cabin of the Mayflower, when the Puritan Fathers solemnly put their names to the compact of good government before landing in the New World. Again we turn to our agreeable eye-witness.

"The morning after the ball, the members met at the usual hour to perform the last duty that remained to them, that of signing the constitution. They were all in the happiest humour, and the morning was so bright and balmy that no one seemed disposed to call an organisation. At length, Mr. Semple being sick, Captain Sutter, the old California pioneer, was appointed to his place. The chair was taken, and the members seated themselves round the sides of the hall, which still retained the pine-trees and banners left from last night's decorations. The doors and windows were open, and a delightful breeze came in from the bay whose blue waters sparkled in the distance. The view of the balcony in front was bright and inspiring. The town below, the shipping in the harbour, the pine-covered hills behind, were mellowed by the blue October haze, but there was no cloud in the sky, and the mountains of Santa Cruz and the Sierra de Gavilan might be clearly seen on the northern horizon.

"An address to the people of California, which had been drawn up by committee, was first read and adopted without a dissenting voice. A resolution was then passed to pay Lieutenant Hamilton the sum of 500 dollars for engrossing the constitution on parchment, a higher amount than was ever paid before for similar services, but on a par with payment in California. Before the convention for the signature of their names, an adjournment of half an hour took place, during which I amused myself by walking through the town. Everybody knew that the convention was about closing, and it was generally understood that Captain Benton had loaded the guns at the fort, and would fire at the proper moment a salute of thirty-one guns, such, including California, being the number of the United States. The citizens therefore, as well as the members, were in an excited mood. Monterey never before looked so bright, so happy, so full of pleasant expectation.

"About one o'clock the convention met again. Mr. Semple was now present. First, salaries were voted; 10,000 dollars annually, and General Riley as governor of California, and 5,000 to Mr. Halleck as secretary of state, after which they affixed their names to the completed constitution. At this moment a signal was given; the American colours run up the flag-staff in front of the government buildings and streamed out on the air. The next moment the first gun boomed from the fort, and its stirring echoes came back from one hill after another till they were lost in the distance.

"All the native enthusiasm of Captain Sutter's Swiss blood was aroused; he was the old soldier again. He sprang from his seat, and waving his hand round his head, as if swinging his sword, exclaimed, 'Gentlemen, this the happiest day of my life. It makes me glad to hear those cannon; they remind me of the time when I was a soldier. Yes, I am glad to hear them! This is a great day for California!' Then recollecting himself, he sat down, the tears streaming from his eyes. The members, with one accord, gave three tumultuous cheers, which were heard from one end of the town to the other. As the signing went on, gun followed gun from the fort, the echoes reverberating grandly around the bay, till finally, as the loud peal of the *thirty-first* was heard, there was a shout, 'That's for California!' And everyone joined in giving three times three for the new star added to our Constitution."

Thus was California, as was represented on her great seal of state, born full-grown, like Minerva, into the national confederacy.

The first Californian senators to congress were John C. Fremont and William M. Gwin. On February 13th, 1850, the constitution of California, together with her petition to be admitted into the Union, were sent to congress by the president.

The clause excluding slavery from the new state awoke all the old animosity of the slavery question, especially as the southern boundary of California lay south of the line of the Missouri compromise. Nor was this the only subject which agitated congress at this time. Texas claimed the whole country as far as the Rio Grande, thus embracing a portion of New Mexico, which the New Mexicans, of Santa Fe violently resisted, being determined not to come under the rule of Texas. Colonel Monroe was at this time American commandant of Santa Fe, and having received private instructions from Washington, a convention was called and a state constitution was framed, and while Texas was preparing to seize the disputed territory by force, New Mexico petitioned to be admitted into the Union. Again, on this very subject of disputed territory, the north and south came to issue, the southern states advocating the claim of Texas, which if established would extend the area of slavery, and the north opposing it for the very same cause.

At length, after the two hostile parties had waged war for some time without either gaining ground, Henry Clay brought in his Compromise Bill, the object of which he stated to be, "to settle and adjust amicably all existing questions of controversy between them, arising out of the institution of slavery, upon a fair, equitable and just basis." The Compromise Bill was, in May, referred to a committee of thirteen, and in September its measures passed as mutual concessions and compromises for the sake of union, viz.: 1. California was admitted into the Union as a state, with her constitution excluding slavery, and her boundaries extending from Oregon to the Mexican possessions. 2. The Great Basin, east of California, containing the Mormon settlement near the Great Salt Lake, was erected, without mention of slavery, into a territory, by the Indian name of Utah. 3. New Mexico, with a boundary which satisfied her inhabitants, was also erected into a state without mention of slavery; congress giving to Texas, in relinquishment of her claims, ten millions of dollars, with which Texas was to pay former debts for which the United States had been in honour bound. 4. A law was passed abolishing the slave-trade, but not slavery, in the district of Columbia; and 5. The Fugitive Slave Law was passed, a law so cruel in its operations as to call forth, as it were, a universal groan from the non-slavery states, and to fan up afresh the otherwise cooling embers of hostility.

The census of 1850 reported the population of the United States to be 23,267,498, of which 3,197,589 were slaves. In the same year the amount of emigration from Europe to America exceeded 300,000.

We have thus brought down the history of the United States to the middle of the present century, and the reader cannot fail of having been impressed with a sense of the vitality which has ever marked the progress and development of the Anglo-American States, and which, from the smallest beginnings on the Atlantic shore, have now extended with an irresistible force to the far Pacific.

Politically and morally the Republic of the United States has been a grand, successful experiment. While the nation has grown with an unexampled rapidity, it has not overlooked the essential foundations of national greatness—the religious and social advancement of the people. The school-house and the place of worship have sprung up simultaneously with human dwellings in the wilderness. And though anomalies exist in the characters of her institutions, though the blot of slavery darkens the page of her history, and her abundant harvest fields have been watered by the blood of the Indian, still, even for the slave is there hope of the amelioration of his condition, and it may be of his redemption, through the growing enlightenment of the South. And as regards the Indian, missionary-labour is increasing among his people, and where they are capable of receiving the instruction and civilisation of the whites, it is given. In 1850, there were 570 missionaries, more than half of whom were women, labouring earnestly in the wilderness, together with 2,000 preachers and helpers among the natives themselves. A thousand churches, of various Christian denominations, have been erected, and the number of professing Christian Indians amounts at this time to 40,537. A great number of schools have been established, and are increasing daily, where the Indian children, to the number of 30,000, receive instruction in reading, writing, and arithmetic, as well as in handicraft trades. The women easily acquire these latter. Printing presses have been introduced among them, and works in thirty different languages produced.[86]

While these facilities are given for education among the Indians, those which are afforded for society at large are on the most ample and liberal scale. Education is indispensable to the man and woman of the New World, and a system of school education is being universally established there, which shall make the enlightenment of the moral and intellectual being common to all, irrespective of creeds and parties, open alike to man and woman.

We will conclude with a few facts drawn from the report of Messrs. Whitworth and Wallis on the Industry of the United States in 1850. "The energetic character of the American people," say these gentlemen, "is nowhere more strikingly displayed than in the young manufacturing settlements that are so rapidly springing up in the northern states. A retired valley and its stream of water become in a few months the seat of manufactures; and the dam and water-wheel are the means of giving employment to busy thousands, where before nothing more than a solitary farm-house was found.

"Great facilities are afforded in many of these states for the formation of manufacturing companies. The liabilities of partners not actively engaged in the management are limited to the proportion of the capital subscribed by each, and its amount is published in the official statement of the company. In the case of the introduction of a new invention, or a new manufacture, the principle of limited liability produces most beneficial results.

"The cost of obtaining an act of incorporation is very trifling. In one case, where the capital of the company amounted to 600,000 dollars (£120,000), the total cost of obtaining an incorporation was fifty cents— two shillings and one penny!

"In America, where labour is more expensive than with us, great ingenuity has been used in the making of labour-saving machines. Timber is sawn up for all kinds of purposes in building, laths are cut, boards for flooring prepared and planed, doors, window-frames, or staircases made, planed, tenoned, mortised and joined by machinery, at a much cheaper rate than by hand-labour. Wood is sawn up at railroad stations, and other places where a great consumption of fuel is required, by sawing-machines, driven by horse-power. Boxes are made by the same means, being tongued and grooved properly and put together by machinery. These labour-saving machines are applied also to the making of furniture and agricultural implements, mowing and reaping machines, and self-acting churns, in the making of all of which labour-saving tools are again used. Among machines of this class must not be omitted the sewing-machine, the use of which is carried to great extent in the New England states. One large manufactory at Waterbury is occupied exclusively in the manufacture of under-vests and drawers, the cloth waistbands of the latter being stitched by the sewing-machine at the rate of 430 stitches per minute. In a shirt manufactory of New Haven, entire shirts, excepting only the gussets, are made by sewing-machines. By the aid of these machines one woman can do as much work as from twelve to twenty hand-sewers. The workwomen work by the piece, and are frequently able to finish their estimated day's work by two o'clock, and when busy work overtime. When will the older countries be able to give sufficient remunerative employment to their women, so as, like these happier New England states, to dispense with the starvation-drudgery of the poor needlewoman, and make the "Song of the Shirt" applicable no longer?

"The railroads of America are constructed on a much less expensive scale than with us. Economy and speedy completion are the points which are especially considered in that country. A single line of rails nailed down to transverse logs, and a train at rare intervals, are deemed to be sufficient as a commencement, and as traffic increases additional improvements are made.

"As regards either a railroad or a telegraphic line, if a company or a private individual should propose or construct them, or could show that they would be beneficial to the public, an act may be obtained authorising him to proceed, as a matter of course; no private interests can oppose the passage of the line through any property; there are no committees, no counsel, no long array of witnesses and expensive hearings; compensation is made simply for damage done, the amount being assessed by a jury, and generally on a most moderate estimate. With a celerity that is surprising a company is incorporated, the line is built, and operations are commenced.

"As may be well conceived, the advantages derivable from the Electric Telegraph were at once appreciated by the United States, and that wonderful discovery, which opened a system of communication annihilating distance, received immediate encouragement both from the federal government in Washington and the governments of the different states. In 1844 congress made a liberal grant to put in operation the first telegraphic line that was erected in the states—that between Washington and Baltimore; and before seven years had elapsed, the committee on Post-offices and Post-roads presented to the senate their report on the route which they had selected for a gigantic telegraph line, nearly 2,500 miles in length, connecting San Francisco with Natchez on the Mississippi, and thence with the vast network of lines that by that time had covered the Atlantic states. Such was the rapid development of this system of communication, supported by the federal government and fostered by that of the states, which passed general laws authorising the immediate construction of telegraph lines whenever they could be conducive to the public interest, and affording every facility for companies for that purpose.

"The aggregate length of the telegraphic lines in the United States exceeded, in 1852, 15,000 miles, and this number is continually increasing. The average cost of constructing a line is estimated at £37 per mile. So moderate is the scale of charges by the telegraphic wires, that the electric telegraph is used by all classes of society as an ordinary means of transmitting intelligence; government dispatches and communications taking the precedence. Newspapers make great use of it, as well as commercial houses.

"The most distant points connected by electric telegraph are Quebec and New Orleans, which are 3,000 miles apart; while a network of lines extends to the west as far as Missouri, about 500 towns and villages in those remote wildernesses being provided with stations.

"The cotton manufactures of the United States are principally centralized in New England and Pennsylvania, but out of the thirty-one states of the Union there are seven only in which the spinning or manufacture of cotton is not carried on, viz., Louisiana, Texas, Michigan, Illinois, Iowa, Wisconsin, and California. The census of 1850 returns 1,054 establishments for the manufacture of cotton goods, consuming 641,240 bales of cotton, and manufacturing goods to the value of £1,000,000 sterling. The number of persons employed in these mills are 33,150 males and 59,136 females. In Alabama slave labour is said to be largely employed, with whites as overseers and instructors. The mills at Lowell, in Massachusetts, on the falls of Powtucket on the Merrimack river, are the most celebrated in the United States, as having been the first where advantage was taken of great natural advantages, with a large and well directed capital, resulting in extensive and systematic operations for the realisation of a legitimate profit; whilst the social position of the operative classes was sedulously cared for, and their moral and intellectual elevation promoted and secured. These works at Lowell were commenced about thirty years ago, and the town now contains 35,000 inhabitants. The example of the Lowell manufacturers has been followed throughout the Union, and in every case with the same favourable results. The number of operatives in the Lowell mills is 6,920 females and 2,378 males.

"By the census returns of 1850, twenty-four of the thirty-one states of the Union, and the district of Columbia, had establishments engaged in some department of the woollen manufacture. The seven states in which this branch of industry had not been commenced, were South Carolina, Florida, Alabama, Mississippi, Louisiana, Arkansas, and California. The

New England States had not so many establishments in operation as the two states of Pennsylvania and Virginia, and only five more than those of New York and Ohio. Thus it will be seen that, whilst the cotton manufacture is located more exclusively in the Eastern States, the woollen manufacture is extended in almost equal proportions over the whole of the Middle States, and extends itself into the western regions and towards the south. The extent of the woollen manufactures of Massachusetts, however, is seen in the fact, that whilst in the 380 mills of Pennsylvania the consumption of wool is 7,560,379 lbs., employing 3,490 males and 2,236 females, producing 10,099,234 yards of cloth and 1,941,621 lbs. of yarn, of the annual value of 5,321,866 dollars, about £1,300,000 sterling; 119 establishments in the first-named state consume 22,229,952 lbs. of wool, employ 6,167 males and 4,963 females, and produce 25,865,658 yards of cloth and 749,550 lbs. of yarn, of the annual value of 12,770,565 dollars, about £3,000,000 sterling. The difference of the modes of manufacture in the two states above-named, as illustrated by the cotton trade, is here shown again in the fact, that a very large proportion of the woollen mills of Pennsylvania is yarn only, a large amount of this being consumed in home manufacture for domestic use, or in the weaving of mixed goods and carpets by hand, and this, too, in addition to the home-spun woollen yarns mentioned as being worked up with the cotton yarns produced for that purpose. The 130 establishments in Ohio, as well as 121 in Virginia, 25 in Kentucky, and 33 in Indiana, would appear to manufacture the greater portion of the yarns spun therein; it is probable, therefore, that the yarns of Pennsylvania are largely used for the supply of the west in the materials for home weaving. After all, however, this department of industry is becoming daily more and more exceptional; but it is interesting as illustrating the early condition of a new country in its efforts to supply its own wants, in the absence of that larger development of manufacturing means and appliances which capital, skill, and a large and ever-increasing demand can alone establish on a firm and enduring basis.

"The total number of persons employed in the various establishments for the manufacture of woollen goods in the United States in 1850 was 22,678 males and 16,574 females.

"The state of Massachusetts is largely engaged in the manufacture of paper. At Lee, Berkshire County, there are 19 paper mills employing a capital of about 200,000 dollars (about £50,000 sterling). In Norfolk County, Massachusetts, there are 17 mills, and in Worcester County 15 mills, employing a capital of £100,000 sterling in this manufacture. In 1845, up to which date the last general statistical information on the state of Massachusetts is published, there were 89 paper mills consuming 12,886 tons of materials, and making 4,763 tons, giving 607,175 reams of paper per annum, the value of which was 1,750,373 dollars (about £430,000 sterling), and employing 1,369 operatives; and this certainly gives no exaggerated view of the general position of the paper trade in nearly all the New England states,—New York, New Jersey, and Pennsylvania,—at the present date.

"The materials used are chiefly raw cotton and mill waste. Linen rags are imported from Europe, but the principal consumption appears to be cotton, either as above-named or in rags. The general character of the printing paper is of a low quality, with a very small amount of dressing or size. In writing papers the make is quite equal to the general run of European papers, but the finish is not always so perfect. It is stated, however, that whilst the Americans try to imitate the English finish, the latter are trying to imitate that of makers of the United States.

"The printing operations are extensive and well conducted, particularly in book-work. The printing of newspapers alone forms a large item in the industry of the country. In the New England states, according to the Abstract of the Census of 1850, there were 424 newspapers; in the Middle states, 876; in the Southern states, 716, and in the Western states, 784; and the following table shows the daily, weekly, and monthly issues, and aggregate circulation, as given by the above authority:—

	Number.	Circulation.	Number of copies printed annually.
Dailies	350	750,000	235,000,000
Tri-weeklies	150	75,000	11,700,000
Semi-weeklies	125	80,000	8,320,000

Weeklies	2,000	2,875,000	149,500,000
Semi-monthlies	50	300,000	7,200,000
Monthlies	100	900,000	10,800,000
Quarterlies	25	29,000	80,000
	2,800	5,000,000	422,600,000

"With an educated people, taking a vital interest in all public questions, the newspaper press is likely to increase even in a greater ratio than it has done during the past decade. The number of German emigrants has caused the establishment of newspapers for their use; and at Cincinnati alone there are four daily newspapers published in the German language.

"Typefounding is carried on to a great extent at Boston, New York, and Philadelphia, and there are single establishments in several other of the large cities. The whole of the type used in the United States, besides a large quantity exported to the British provinces and the various states of South America, is produced in these foundries.

"The boot and shoe trade of the United States is of a very extensive character, and the systematic manner in which it is carried on worthy of being understood and adopted elsewhere. A scale or series of sizes is adopted, say in women's and children's shoes from one to six, and even higher numbers, the half constituting a size between each. The various portions of the boots and shoes are cut out to these sizes and half-sizes. These are put up with all the requisite trimmings necessary to complete the articles, in sets of 60 pairs for the common kinds, and 24 pairs for the finer qualities.

"Being cut out and made up into sets, they are sent to be 'fitted' for the maker—that is, the various parts of the upper leathers are stitched together.

Much of this is now done by one of the various kinds of sewing machines. The neatness, accuracy and strength of stitch is superior to hand work. The upper leathers thus 'fitted' are then sent to the 'binder,' who finally prepares them for the 'maker,' by whom they are soled and heeled. Being complete in make they then go to the 'trimmer,' whose work consists in punching the string-holes, stringing and putting on buttons, and in ladies' shoes, bows and rosettes.

"Soles are cut out by machinery. A knife with a curvilinear edge is set in a frame and worked with a treadle, after the manner of a lathe. By a lateral motion in the machine, it can be adapted to the cutting of any requisite width of sole, and being once fixed to a given width, the process of cutting is very rapid, and material is saved by the leather being cut at right angles to the surface, instead of diagonally, as by the ordinary knife.

"When finished, the goods are made up in boxes containing one dozen of assorted sizes. They are then sent in cases to the wholesale dealer, who supplies the retailer. A case contains five boxes making up the 60 pairs of assorted sizes of which a set of the commoner kind consists as manufactured. These manufactures are found in all parts of the New England states, but chiefly in the states of Massachusetts, Maine, Vermont, and New Hampshire. The finer quality of hoots for gentlemen are chiefly made at Randolph and Abington, Massachusetts; the heavier kind of shoes, and the coarsest kind, usually called 'brogans,' at Danvers in the same state. These 'brogans' are chiefly manufactured for the Southern markets, for the use of slaves, and are similar to the shoes worn by the miners of South Staffordshire.

"The following table, compiled from the 'Statistics of the Condition and Products of certain branches of industry in Massachusetts for the year ending April 1st, 1845,' will show the extent of the boot and shoe trade in the six above-named towns at that date:—

Towns.	Kinds.	Number of Pairs made.	Males employed.	Females employed.
Randolph	{Boots	227,131 }		

	{Shoes	332,281 }	815	649
Danvers	Both	1,150,300	1,586	980
Lynn	{Boots	2,000 }		
	{Shoes	2,404,722 }	2,719	3,209
Reading	Shoes	274,000	358	385
Woburn	{Boots	909 }		
	{Shoes	350,920 }	425	484
Haverhill	Shoes	1,860,915	2,042	1,680

"Pennsylvania is the largest iron-producing state in the Union, although by the census of 1850, twenty-one states are returned as producing pig iron, and only two, Florida and Arkansas, as not having establishments for the manufacture of iron castings; whilst in nineteen states wrought iron is made.

"In the production of pig iron 377 establishments were in operation in 1850; and of these 180 were in Pennsylvania, 35 in Ohio, and 29 in Virginia.

"The capital invested amounted to 17,346,425 dollars (about £4,500,000 sterling), the produce being 564,755 tons per annum, employing 20,291 males and 150 females.

"In the manufacture of iron castings, 1,391 establishments were engaged. Of these 643 were in the states of New York and Pennsylvania,—323 in the former and 330 in the latter; 183 others being in the state of Ohio. The capital invested amounted to 17,416,361 dollars, being about the same as in pig iron. 322,745 tons of castings are produced per annum, giving employment to 23,541 males and 48 females; the value of the castings, and other products, being estimated at about £6,250,000 sterling.

"Wrought iron is manufactured at 422 establishments in 19 states. Pennsylvania has 131, New York 60, New Jersey 53, Tennessee 42, and Virginia 39; the remaining 97 being situated in 14 other states. The capital invested was 14,495,220 dollars, or about £3,500,000 sterling; 13,178 males and 79 females being employed. The quantity manufactured amounted to 278,044 tons, the value of which, with other products, was 16,747,074 dollars, or about £4,100,000 sterling.

"In nearly all the large cities, iron foundries are to be found, cast-iron being largely employed in the construction of buildings both of wood and brick; and in Philadelphia, as also to some extent in other cities, whole elevations of houses, used as retail shops in the principal streets, are of cast-iron. In these cases, the construction of the building is usually modified to suit the material of the front, and, in some instances, an approximation is made towards adapting the decorative part of the elevation to the material and the construction. In general, however, the ordinary forms, as used in stone and wood, are followed, and the whole painted and sanded in imitation of Connecticut red sandstone. The construction of some of these elevations is at once simple and effective, alike for strength as architectural effect, and there appears to be very little difficulty in taking out an old front and substituting a new one, as the whole is well braced together by ties and screws—the side walls sustaining the structure in all essential points. This use of cast-iron may eventually produce a style of street architecture of a different character to that which now prevails, and which is in imitation of European modes of construction and decoration."

We have merely given above the slightest idea of the vast industrial operations of the United States, which embrace every branch of arts and manufactures; but that little is enough to show how great are their resources, and what an immense field is opened to their enterprise, to their skill and inventive genius.

As we have already said, education is one feature of the American national character, and art-education, as applied to manufactures, is now beginning necessarily to attract serious attention in the United States. Hence schools of design have been established in Philadelphia, New York,

Boston, Baltimore and other cities; most of these being, however, intended for the art-education of women.

From art-education, which can only be available for a portion of the public, we pass to that which is made indispensable by the wise legislation of the United States.

"The compulsory educational clauses adopted in the laws of most of the states, and especially those of New England, by which some three months of every year must be spent at school by the young factory operative under fourteen or fifteen years of age, secure every child from the cupidity of the parent, or the neglect of the manufacturer; since to profit by the child's labour during *three-fourths* of the year, he or she must be regularly in attendance in some public or private school conducted by some authorised teacher during the other fourth.

"This lays the foundation for that wide-spread intelligence which prevails amongst the factory operatives of the United States; and though at first sight the manufacturer may appear to be restricted in the free use of the labour offered to him, the system re-acts to the permanent advantage of both employer and employed.

"The skill of hand which comes of experience is, notwithstanding present defects, rapidly following the perceptive power so keenly awakened by early intellectual training. Quickly learning from the skilful European artizans thrown amongst them by emigration, or imported as instructors, with minds, as already stated, prepared by sound practical education, the Americans have laid the foundation of a wide-spread system of manufacturing operations, the influence of which cannot be calculated upon, and are daily improving upon the lessons obtained from their older and more experienced compeers of Europe.

"Commercially, advantages of no ordinary kind are presented to the manufacturing states of the American Union. The immense development of its resources in the west, the demands of a population increasing daily by emigration from Europe, as also by the results of a healthy natural process of inter-emigration, which tends to spread over an enlarged surface the population of the Atlantic States; the facilities of communication by lakes, rivers, and railways; and the cultivation of European tastes and consequently of European wants; all tend to the encouragement of those arts and manufactures which it is the interest of the citizens of the older states to cultivate, and in which they have so far succeeded that their markets may be said to be secured to them as much as manufacturers, as they have hitherto been, and will doubtless continue to be, as merchants. For whether the supply is derived from the home or foreign manufacturer, the demand cannot fail to be greater than the industry of both can supply.

This once fairly recognised, those jealousies which have ever tended to retard the progress of nations in the peaceful arts, will be no longer suffered to interfere, by taking the form of restrictions on commerce and the free intercourse of peoples."

THE END.

·